Financial Planning for the Individual

(8th Edition)

A guide to investment and personal finance

SIMON PHILIP FIFP, CFP
Partner, Deloitte & Touche

Published by
GEE Publishing Ltd

Previous editions published in 1986, 1987, 1989, 1994, 1996, 1998 and 2000.

8th edition published by GEE Publishing Ltd 2002.

ISBN 1 86089 959 5

GEE Publishing Ltd
100 Avenue Road
Swiss Cottage
London NW3 3PG
tel: 020 7393 7400
www.gee.co.uk

Typeset by
Multiplex Medway Ltd, Walderslade, Kent.

Printed in Great Britain by Creative Print and Design, (Wales) Ebbw Vale.

Contents

Biography of Simon Philip

Simon Philip is a partner in Deloitte & Touche and CEO of Deloitte & Touche Wealth Management Limited. He is a Fellow of the Institute of Financial Planning and Chairman of its Technical Committee, and is a Certified Financial Planner. He is Consultant Editor of *The Financial Adviser's Factbook* and is regularly quoted in the financial press on personal finance issues. He advises a large number of personal and corporate clients.

Preface

Regular readers of *Financial Planning for the Individual* will be aware that its main purpose is to state, in concise and easily readable terms, the main aspects involved in financial planning for individuals. This edition is no different. It is primarily aimed at professional advisers and individuals wishing to make maximum use of their money.

Since the seventh edition was published in 2000, there have been substantial changes in legislation and the investment product marketplace and these have been incorporated in the text. Significant new content has also been added, particularly in rewritten chapters on pension matters.

Tax allowances, savings rates and life assurance rates have also been updated. Thought was given to removing interest rates, given their volatility. It was, however, felt that they are useful for relative comparison with the other savings products described, rather than being particularly informative in an absolute sense. For information, the rates were stated at a time when Base Rate was 4%.

As always, there are a number of people to whom I owe great thanks for their contribution to the preparation of this edition. David Wells shouldered his usual significant part of the burden. His deep knowledge of all investment matters adds considerably to the text. His organisational skills have also been much appreciated. John Pengelly made an enormous contribution to the rewriting of the chapters on pension matters and his knowledge and enthusiasm have brought about some long overdue format changes. Ann Whitfield of Macfarlanes has brought her deep experience of private client legal matters to bear on the chapters on Wills and Trusts. I would also like to thank Michael Voller of the Michael Voller Tax Consultancy for his usual highly informed thoughts on Lloyd's and Paul Parker of Professional Mortgage Services for his contribution to the chapter on mortgages.

I would also like to thank my colleagues. They are a fantastic team to work with and their friendship and support in the last nine months, when our professional situation has been far from ideal, has meant a huge amount. Many of the issues that this book seeks to capture have arisen from work done for our clients and without them it would be far less practical. Particularly, Orlando Harvey Wood, Patricia Mock, Georgia Chacholiades and Ashley Wilkinson have had specific input.

Finally, I would like to thank the Kelly family whose support ensures that the book continues and my family – Alison, Annabel and Georgina – who always provide the utmost encouragement and sanctuary at the end of the working day.

Simon Philip
London
July 2002

1 Introduction to financial planning

A definition of financial planning for the individual could be: 'finding the best ways of utilising the financial facilities that exist in order to maximise personal wealth and minimise personal taxation'. This book is concerned with achieving that optimum state.

The range of knowledge required to manage one's own financial affairs successfully can be very wide, covering the whole field of savings, investments, pension arrangements, life assurance policies, mortgages, provision for education fees and tax planning. Under the heading 'investments' alone, the opportunities extend from the traditional areas of unit trusts, single premium life assurance investment bonds and stocks and shares to specialist investments such as works of art, stamps, forestry and even bloodstock. However, while many individuals will have little cause to venture into the less traditional fields, they will still be faced with a myriad of options in every aspect of financial planning.

The key to successful planning lies not just in making the right selection, but making the decision that best suits one's personal requirements. This involves striking the correct balance between savings and investments, ensuring one has sufficient liquidity, and establishing that investments are tax efficient and provide the return at the right time, at an acceptable level of risk.

The benefits of thorough forward planning of financial matters, both in the long and the short term, cannot be over emphasised. To this end, this first chapter includes a comprehensive examination of how to recognise indicators which signal the need for financial action and how to establish the requirements of any individual.

For the purpose of convenience, the male gender has been generally used throughout the book. However, unless otherwise stated, the information applies equally to females.

1:1 Signposts for action

There are a number of circumstances that should signal that appropriate action may be necessary, including:

(a) substantial unearned income by way of interest received from cash deposits;

(b) no life assurance premiums paid, indicating that life cover may be required;

(c) the payment of income tax at the higher rate;

(d) an investment portfolio of very small holdings in many individual companies, with the resultant copious paperwork;

(e) a substantial proportion of an estate in a marriage being in one spouse's name;

(f) a higher rate taxpayer with large holdings in loan stocks or high yielding gilts;

(g) substantial cash deposits being held, whilst a mortgage is outstanding;

(h) income-producing assets being held by a higher rate taxpayer, when a spouse is taxed at lower rates;

(i) credit balances on directors' current accounts in private companies while the companies have substantial cash balances at the bank;

(j) no pension scheme contributions in the accounts of companies;

(k) no pension contributions paid where the individual is self-employed or in non-pensionable employment;

(l) the imminent acquisition of a capital sum, for example, from the sale of a business or property or other asset or an inheritance;

(m) no capital funding arrangements for share purchase or partnership purchase on death or retirement;

(n) an income which just exceeds the maximum for age allowance purposes;

(o) no will;

(p) no provision for income in the event of ill-health;

(q) an elderly person with grandchildren or nieces and nephews;

(r) the prospect of retirement within the next five to ten years.

The types of action which may be taken in all of these circumstances are dealt with in depth in the subsequent chapters.

1:2 Financial services legislation

A particular problem for both the individual and the professional adviser is the constantly changing financial environment resulting from new legislation and changes in economic and market conditions. The last 16 years have seen substantial financial services legislation implemented, and this has had a considerable impact on investment providers and intermediaries and on their dealings with clients.

Regrettably, financial scandals have also been a feature of recent years and investors are now more aware of the need to obtain advice from competent and honest independent advisers and to examine that advice critically before investing.

1:2.1 The legislation

The Financial Services Act 1986 replaced the Prevention of Fraud (Investments) Act 1958 in order to provide more effective protection for investors. The Financial Services and Markets Act 2000 (the Act) has a wider scope and brings all regulation under the control of the Financial Services Authority (the FSA). It came into full effect on 1 December 2001 (a date known officially as 'N2').

1:2.2 The Financial Services Authority

The FSA was formally constituted by the Act, but began operating before N2 as the successor of the Securities and Investments Board, overseeing the regulatory organisations and professional bodies responsible for different sectors of financial services. It is an independent, non-governmental body, financed by the financial services industry and reporting to Treasury ministers, with four statutory objectives:

(a) to maintain confidence in the UK financial system;

(b) to promote public understanding of the financial system;

(c) to secure an appropriate degree of protection for consumers, while recognising their own responsibilities; and

(d) to reduce the scope for financial crime.

It regulates about 10,000 institutions: over 7,500 investment firms, over 660 banks, 70 building societies, almost 1,000 insurance companies and friendly societies, 700 credit unions and the Lloyd's insurance market. These institutions employ about 180,000 approved persons.

The FSA:

(a) authorises firms and individuals to carry on investment business;

(b) sets standards for firms – both prudential (governing the way they are run) and for the conduct of investment business;

(c) supervises financial businesses and markets, including the admission of companies to a London Stock Exchange listing;

(d) enforces its rules, through investigations and penalties;

(e) acts to reduce financial crime;

(f) liaises with similar authorities overseas; and

(g) deals with consumer complaints and compensation, through the Financial Ombudsman Service and the Financial Services Compensation Scheme (see **Appendix 1**).

1:2.3 Authorisation

In order to carry on investment business, it is necessary for a person to be authorised to do so, unless specifically exempted. Conducting investment business without authorisation is a criminal offence. Previously, a professional adviser could obtain authorisation from any of a number of organisations, but now all advisers are authorised and regulated (as 'approved persons') by the FSA. Professional firms whose investment business is not 'mainstream' but merely incidental to their normal business activities (for example, solicitors and accountants) continue to be regulated by their professional organisations. These organisations have been given 'designated professional body' status by the FSA for this purpose. A list of them is given in **Appendix 1**.

Since 1988 one of the principles underpinning the regime for financial advisers has been 'polarisation' – the clear division between:

(a) independent intermediaries, who act as the agent of their clients and, on their behalf, use their knowledge of the investment market and the products available to recommend and arrange those best suited to the investor's profile and requirements; and

(b) employees and appointed representatives of investment product providers (for example, insurance companies, unit trust managers, etc), who can represent only those companies and sell only their products.

A high proportion of independent intermediaries have chosen to join 'networks' – organisations which regulate them as appointed representatives and provide research and support to their members. All advisers are obliged to make their status clear to members of the public.

A further choice is available to those involved in arranging investment business and that is to be merely an introducer. Introducers must decide whether they will refer clients to one appointed representative or to independent intermediaries. Introducing investment business to independent intermediaries is not 'investment business' under the Act.

Polarisation has recently come under threat, initially in an Office of Fair Trading report in August 1999, which concluded that it restricted or distorted competition. Following further studies and deliberations, in January 2002 the FSA issued for consultation proposals:

(a) to end polarisation;

(b) to strengthen the standing of independent advice, by removing commission bias;

(c) to maintain a robust independent sector by removing the rules limiting investment in firms of independent advisers; and

(d) to improve consumer awareness of the advice service offered by different types of firms.

Its consultation document also sought views on:

(a) the scope for a tailored advice regime to deliver financial advice more widely; and

(b) the separation of product charges from the cost of advice.

The consultation period ended in April 2002 and the FSA expected to reach decisions in the summer on the future structure of the investment advice industry. It will have been assisted in this by the review of the retail savings industry chaired by Ron Sandler, the former chief executive of the Corporation of Lloyds. He is expected to be critical in particular of charging structures and with-profits contracts.

1:2.4 Investment business

The eight broad categories of investment business defined in the Act as 'regulated activities' are as follows:

(a) dealing in investments;

(b) arranging deals in investments through others;

(c) deposit taking;

(d) safeguarding and administering investment assets;

(e) managing investments belonging to others;

(f) advising others on their investments (both general advice and in relation to specific investments);

(g) establishing, operating or winding up a collective investment scheme, such as a unit trust; and

(h) giving instructions relating to investments through a computer-based system (designed to cover 'fund supermarkets' – Internet-based facilities for the purchase and sale of unit trusts and OEICs, both directly and through ISAs).

The adviser has to comply with strict rules as regards investment work. The following requirements are of particular relevance.

1:2.4.1 Client agreement

An adviser may not enter into a transaction with a client unless it is in accordance with the terms of a written agreement. Although the format for the agreement is not laid down, the FSA lists a substantial number of items to which it must refer. These include a statement of the services to be provided, the basis on which the adviser is to be paid, a statement of the client's objectives and risk profile and any restrictions on the type of investments which he or she wishes to make and details of termination and complaints procedures and of the client's cancellation rights, if any.

1:2.4.2 Know your client

This requirement includes a general provision that an adviser must take reasonable steps to ascertain details of the client's financial and personal situation which are relevant to the investment services to be provided. The adviser should also have reasonable grounds to assume that the client can meet the financial liabilities of the transaction and, most importantly, that he understands the risks involved.

1:2.4.3 Prevention of money laundering

As part of the effort to prevent illegally acquired funds (especially those connected with terrorism) from entering the financial system, all financial businesses are now required to verify the identity of new clients and to ascertain the source of the funds which they are asked to invest or on which they are to advise. The 1993 regulations have now been reinforced by the FSA's own rules and further legislation will come into force during 2002.

1:2.4.4 Best advice

The best advice requirement follows on from the need to know the client. An adviser must not make a specific recommendation to the client unless he knows it is suitable for him. Where a client requests a specific investment which the adviser believes is unsuitable, he must make his view known (preferably in writing) to the client and only proceed if the client still insists; alternatively, the adviser may decline to act. Independent advisers are required to consider all the different types of investments available which meet the client's particular requirements.

Having chosen the most suitable type of contract, the adviser must then select the one which he believes to be the best of that type. He has therefore to keep himself informed as to the current terms in the market for each particular product; there are electronic networks and regular publications which enable him to do this. In some cases, for example annuities and term assurance, cost will be the principal factor.

For others, advisers should take into account such factors as underwriting requirements, likely future investment performance, standards of service, policy charges and the financial strength or stability of each product provider. In assessing the products available, they must include those of non-commission-paying providers.

1:2.4.5 Best execution

This requirement involves the adviser in ensuring that the transaction is carried out on the best terms available. This will include price, charges and any other advantages to the client.

1:2.4.6 Cancellation rules

The cancellation rules of the FSA apply to investment agreements in respect of regular premium life assurance policies and personal pension contracts. Subject to certain exceptions, where the rights of investors are already adequately safeguarded, these rules also apply to single premium life assurance policies and unit trusts and OEICs (whether bought directly or through ISAs).

1:2.4.7 Record keeping

In order for the best advice and best execution rules to be adequately policed, there are strict requirements for the adviser's records to show the reasons for any particular recommendation. Accordingly, all instructions received from a client should be fully recorded. After the instructions have been carried out, the adviser must see that the client is sent a statement giving full details of the transaction.

1:2.4.8 Clients' money

This must be held on trust for the client and held in a separate bank account from the adviser's own monies.

1:2.4.9 Financial resources

These rules lay down the financial resources that must be maintained at all times and vary according to the size, nature and type of investment business and the associated risks involved.

1:3 Professional advice

For some individuals, impartial professional advice will be essential at the outset, often because they do not have the time to devote to assessing their best course of action. However, those who undertake their own financial planning should have an approach as thorough as a professional adviser's. Despite this, it is almost inevitable that at some stage specialist advice will be required.

Obtaining professional advice involves its own selection process. Apart from the requirements of the legislation, it is useful to examine the main criteria which should indicate that the professional adviser is providing a thorough and competent service:

(a) the adviser must be authorised and regulated by the FSA;

(b) the adviser should consider all aspects of the client's affairs without restricting himself to particular areas;

(c) a positive service should be provided, with the adviser approaching the client where appropriate;

(d) regular reviews of the client's affairs should be carried out;

(e) the adviser should recommend non-commission paying contracts and investments if they are most suitable for the client;

(f) where a fee basis operates, any commissions received should be declared and taken into account against the fee or used to obtain better terms for the client;

(g) the adviser should have a good technical knowledge and appropriate professional qualifications;

(h) the adviser should carry an appropriate level of professional indemnity insurance.

An investor intending to appoint a financial adviser should question potential candidates on these points. If the adviser has been recommended by a person who has already used his or her services, this is clearly advantageous.

1:4 Ascertaining client requirements

In order to meet the 'know your client' requirements, it is essential for the adviser to ascertain the circumstances of the client, together with their personal and financial requirements and objectives. To do this, the adviser should normally meet the client at least once and perhaps several times before final advice is given. At the first meeting, the adviser will need to obtain the necessary information. **Appendix 2** is an in-depth questionnaire of a type which a professional adviser might employ and will additionally provide a guide as to where action needs to be taken.

Whilst determining the client's circumstances, it is of paramount importance that the adviser makes detailed enquiries to establish an accurate assessment of the client's risk appetite. These will include questions on the client's understanding of investment products and markets and his attitude to the possibility of financial loss. Any subsequent advice should clearly highlight any recommended investment's downside risks and be appropriate in the context of the risk profile agreed upon.

1:5 Reports

Once the client's requirements are established, the adviser will usually write a report summarising the present position and making proposals for a course of action to be taken. It will be up to the client to decide whether to proceed with them or not. It is preferable that the proposals are made in writing to avoid any misunderstandings that could subsequently arise.

There is no set form of report, as this will mainly depend upon the particular case as well as personal style. Where investment planning is being undertaken, it is often useful for supporting statements to be prepared showing the capital and net spendable income position both in the present situation and that immediately afterwards if the proposed course of action is taken.

1:6 Reviews

Even after a client has acted upon the adviser's proposals, he or she will still need an ongoing service through regular reviews. In most cases, an annual review should be sufficient but this will depend on whether the client's own circumstances have changed, for example, as the result of the inheritance of a capital sum or a change of job, or because of external factors, such as new products or major changes in legislation or economic and market conditions. The management of personal finances can only benefit from regular dialogue between adviser and client. Without this dialogue, opportunities will be missed and the benefits of past advice will be dissipated.

2 Investment planning

Once the individual's personal circumstances and financial requirements have been established as outlined in the previous chapter, consideration can be given to appropriate investment planning.

2:1 Investment considerations

The following specific information should be settled at the outset before a decision is taken on particular investments:

(a) the amount of capital available for investment;

(b) precise details of existing investments;

(c) the ages of the individual and his or her dependants;

(d) the degree of risk the individual is prepared to take, bearing in mind there is often a close correlation between risk and reward;

(e) the period of time for which the investments can be made before access to the capital is required;

(f) whether or not some investments can be subject to a period of notice;

(g) the current and likely future tax position of the individual;

(h) the income required from the investments;

(i) whether the main requirement is capital growth, income, or a combination of the two;

(j) whether the investments are to be made within any particular constraints, such as trustee investments or ethical considerations;

(k) the degree of involvement which the individual may wish to have in arranging and managing the investments;

(l) details of any anticipated capital receivable in the short term, such as proceeds from a life policy or an inheritance;

(m) details of any significant liabilities or personal expenses likely to arise in the near future, for example, tax liabilities or the purchase of a new car;

(n) whether there are any personal priorities or objectives, such as the provision of education fees;

(o) whether adequate arrangements have already been made in respect of the following:

- (i) pension provision;
- (ii) life assurance cover to protect the family in the event of early death;
- (iii) house purchase (consideration should be given to repaying any mortgage or loan);
- (iv) wills and inheritance tax planning;
- (v) permanent health insurance.

Having ascertained the above information, it should be possible to prepare a broad investment structure. For this purpose, capital should normally be invested in three categories in the following order, with the exact proportion in each category based on the individual circumstances.

(a) The first part of the capital should be in an emergency fund for complete security and immediate access, for example a bank or building society deposit account.

(b) The second part of the capital should be in low-risk investments with security of capital, like short-dated gilt-edged securities, money market accounts and cash deposit bonds. Such investments can usually be realised at short notice. A higher net investment return can often be provided from this part of the capital than from the emergency fund. This part of the capital can also be used for the funding of imminent house purchase or annual tax liabilities.

(c) The third part of the capital should be in higher risk/higher reward investments with the aim of providing a higher net return than both the rate of inflation and the rate obtainable from fixed interest investments. The usual assets are carefully selected shares, investment trusts, unit trusts or OEICs. The investments in this category should normally be considered as longer-term investments, with a view to being held for a minimum period of four to five years.

Notes

1. For people who have retired or who will retire shortly, a greater proportion of capital should normally be invested in the first and second parts since they would usually be less able to make good any capital loss out of their future income.

2. In considering the proportion of capital to be invested in the third part, the effect of inflation and normal life expectancy should be borne in mind. These are illustrated in the following tables.

3. The effect of inflation is such that £1,000 in today's money will be worth the amount stated at the end of the period shown if the annual rate of inflation over the period is as indicated.

End of Year	*2½% inflation*	*5% inflation*	*7½% inflation*
1	976	952	930
2	952	907	865
3	929	864	805
4	906	823	749
5	884	784	697
10	781	614	485
15	690	481	338
20	610	377	235
25	539	295	164
30	477	231	114
35	421	181	80
40	372	142	55
45	329	111	39
50	291	87	27

4. Normal life expectancy in the UK is increasing as a result of advances in medical science. The projected figures vary according to the population sampled, but the following table gives an indication of the current expectations

Present age	*Male – years*	*Female – years*
50	33	36
55	28	31
60	24	27
65	19	22
70	15	18
75	11	14
80	8	11
85	6	8
90	4	6
95	3	5

When the general structure for the capital has been decided, various types of investments can then be considered. These may be divided into the two main categories of:

- fixed investments; and
- variable investments.

2:2 Fixed investments

The principal feature of fixed investments is that either the capital or the income arising (and sometimes both) is determined from the outset and is guaranteed (or at least relatively certain) as long as the investment is held. These investments will form the first and second parts of capital (in some cases, they may also be included within the third part).

The specific choice of investment will depend on the exact circumstances of the individual and on the returns available at the particular time together with the current and prospective levels of interest rates in general. The investment yields mentioned in this chapter are those available in May 2002 and are shown gross unless otherwise stated.

The more usual types of fixed investments are as follows:

(a) cash accounts;

(b) money market funds;

(c) cash unit trusts;

(d) Tax Exempt Special Savings Accounts (TESSAs) (no longer available, but existing plans continue);

(e) National Savings investments;

(f) 'instant access' insurance bonds;

(g) guaranteed income and guaranteed growth bonds;

(h) high income insurance bonds;

(i) gilt-edged securities;

(j) eurobonds;

(k) local authority loans;

(l) company debentures and unsecured loan stocks;

(m) permanent interest-bearing shares;

(n) preference shares;

(o) zero dividend preference shares of investment trusts; and

(p) purchased life annuities.

2:2.1 Cash accounts

The range of interest-bearing cash accounts has developed significantly in recent years. There is no longer either a concentration on branch-based accounts (of both banks and building societies) or a clear distinction between current and deposit accounts. New banks have come into being, owned by supermarkets and life assurance companies, and building societies have shed their mutual status and become banks with a Stock Exchange listing.

The main types of cash account available and the rates of interest being paid at May 2002 were:

(a) branch current (cheque) accounts paying no interest;

(b) branch current (cheque) accounts paying a low rate of interest (0.1%–0.5% p.a.);

(c) telephone-operated current accounts paying tiered rates of interest; payments may be made by cheque or by telephoned instructions (1.65%–4.2% p.a.);

(d) high interest cheque accounts paying 0.25%–3.75% p.a.; the rates on some of these are directly linked to the bank's base rate;

(e) branch-based deposit accounts (0.2%–4.0% p.a.);

(f) postal deposit accounts, paying higher rates than branch-based accounts and operated by post from a central office (1.75%–3.8% p.a.);

(g) telephone-operated deposit accounts, with transfers made between the account and the investor's current account (1.0%–3.8% p.a.); and

(h) Internet accounts (paying 0.65%–4.5% p.a.).

Accounts operated electronically by telephone or post require one to four days for money to be available, and so are not strictly 'instant access'. Some deposit accounts require a period of notice for withdrawals or restrict the number of withdrawals which may be made in a specified period. Deposits may sometimes be placed for a fixed period and/or at a fixed rate of interest.

In selecting a deposit account the investor will take into account:

(a) the interest rate offered, in relation to those of other accounts;

(b) the financial strength of the deposit-taker;

(c) convenience; and

(d) any conditions imposed and their impact on his likely use of the account.

Interest is paid under deduction of income tax at the savings rate. This can be reclaimed by non-taxpayers, who can also apply on form R85 to have their interest paid without deduction of tax. This form is obtainable from banks and building societies.

In the unlikely event of a bank or building society becoming insolvent, investors may claim compensation under the Financial Services Compensation Scheme. The maximum compensation is £31,700 – 100% of the first £2,000 plus 90% of the next £33,000. This applies to each depositor and to the total of all deposits held by him with the failed business.

2:2.2 Money market deposit accounts

Money market deposits are usually for a fixed term and usually subject to a minimum investment of £10,000.

'Fixed term' means investments are for a fixed period, during which time investors cannot have access to the money invested. This term can vary from overnight to five years.

The interest paid is calculated on a daily basis and credited at regular intervals, or at the end of the investment period. The rate payable reflects current money market interest rates and varies according to the amount invested and either the investment period or notice required on withdrawal. Like traditional bank deposit accounts, interest is normally paid net of savings rate tax (the main exception to this is for investments of £50,000 or more for a fixed period of at least seven days where the interest is paid gross; these are known as time deposits).

For fixed terms, the following rates were payable at the time of writing (May 2002) by one of the major banks for amounts exceeding £50,000:

- one month – 3.90%
- three months – 3.85%
- six months – 4.00%
- one year – 4.65%.

These rates indicate that the bank believes that interest rates are currently on an upward trend.

Money market deposit accounts may be suitable for individuals with very large amounts as a short-term home until they commit their money on a longer-term basis. An example of this could be where someone intends to invest in the stock market when they consider the time is opportune. For smaller amounts, it is likely that an ordinary deposit account would be more suitable.

2:2.3 Cash unit trusts

Cash unit trusts are managed money funds, investing in a variety of instruments, which are commensurate with a proper degree of security. These investments can include bank deposits, short-dated gilt-edged securities, Treasury Bills and local authority bonds. Some cash unit trusts offer a cheque book facility, making them a very useful way of holding funds needed for occasional substantial payments.

2:2.4 Tax Exempt Special Savings Accounts (TESSAs)

New TESSAs are no longer available, having been replaced by ISAs (see **4:2**) from 6 April 1999. As they were five-year contracts, many are still in existence and the last will not mature until 5 April 2004.

The object of TESSAs was to encourage savers by enabling the accumulation of up to £9,000 of capital over five years in a tax-exempt deposit account. They were available only from banks, building societies and similar European institutions.

Investments into a TESSA could not exceed £9,000 and could either be made by lump sums, not exceeding £3,000 in the first year and £1,800 in each of the next four years, or by regular savings up to £150 per month. If less than the maximum was invested in any year, the shortfall could not be carried forward to be used in subsequent years.

Providing the TESSA is kept open for five years, the interest credited is exempt from income tax.

Interest was fixed at the outset or variable, and credited without deduction of income tax. It can be withdrawn, subject to retention within the TESSA of an amount equal to tax at the savings rate. The net interest is tax free at the time of withdrawal, and the retention is paid out tax free at maturity. At May 2002, TESSAs generally paid rates of up to 4.7% p.a.

If the investor withdraws more than the net interest, that is, some or all of the retained interest or the capital, the TESSA is automatically closed. Savings rate tax on all the interest earned will be deducted. Even if the interest has accrued over more than one year, it will all be taxable in the year of closure. It will also be subject to higher rate tax, if applicable.

The capital of TESSAs maturing after 5 April 1999 may be reinvested either in the cash component of a maxi-ISA, or in a cash mini-ISA (see **4:2**), or in a 'TESSA-only' ISA or 'TOISA'. The amount transferred does not count towards the ISA subscription limits.

The ISA must be opened within six months of the maturity of the TESSA. It does not have to be with the same bank or building society. If it is not, the provider of the TESSA must give the investor a certificate confirming the entitlement to the ISA, to be submitted with the application.

2:2.5 National Savings investments

There are various types of National Savings investments available with the purpose of appealing to investors with different requirements and tax rates. National Savings changed its name to National Savings & Investments in March 2002. The following National Savings investments were available in May 2002:

(a) Fixed Interest Savings Certificates;

(b) Index-Linked Savings Certificates;

(c) Ordinary Account;

(d) Investment Account;

(e) Income Bonds;

(f) Pensioners' Guaranteed Income Bonds;

(g) Fixed Rate Savings Bonds;

(h) Capital Bonds;

(i) Children's Bonus Bonds;

(j) Premium Bonds; and

(k) Individual Savings Account.

In March 2002 National Savings & Investments launched its first equity-based product – the Guaranteed Equity Bond. This was available for only a limited period and offered a gross return, capped at 65%, equal to the performance of the FTSE-100 Index over five years, with the initial capital protected.

2:2.5.1 Fixed Interest Savings Certificates

Fixed interest certificates offer a guaranteed tax-free return if held to maturity. The minimum holding per individual is £100 and the normal maximum holding is £10,000, but husbands and wives can effectively double their maximum holdings by each holding certificates on trust for the other, in addition to their personal holdings. Holders of maturing issues of certificates may use the proceeds to purchase 'reinvestment certificates', for which there is no limit. If the certificates are encashed before maturity, the return provided is lower and depends on the length of time that they have been held.

At May 2002, National Savings offered two fixed-interest certificates:

- 63rd issue five-year certificates – interest: 3.45% per annum compound;
- 12th issue two-year certificates – interest: 3.25% per annum compound.

As these returns were tax free, the interest on the five-year certificates was equivalent to 4.31% per annum gross to a basic rate taxpayer and 5.75% per annum gross to a higher rate taxpayer. For the two-year certificates, the equivalent gross returns were 4.06% and 5.42% per annum, respectively.

National Savings & Investments writes to holders of maturing certificates about ten days before the maturity date. If the investor does not respond in order to encash or reinvest the maturity value, that value is automatically reinvested into a new certificate for the same term (two or five years) as the old one. If the certificate matured before 8 October 2001, it continued to earn interest, but at a very low rate (1.5% per annum at May 2002 – the 'General Extension Rate').

2:2.5.2 Index-Linked Savings Certificates

The return offered by these certificates is tax free and based on the change in the Retail Price Index (RPI) over the investment period together with extra interest at a fixed rate. Index-linking and interest are capitalised on each anniversary so that subsequent growth is based on the value at the beginning of the year. Early encashment, after the first year, will provide index-linking and interest additions (at varying rates) up to the month of withdrawal. The minimum individual holding is £100 and the maximum £10,000, but husbands and wives can effectively double their maximum holdings by each holding certificates on trust for the other, in addition to their personal holdings. As with fixed interest certificates, the proceeds of matured certificates can be invested (without limit) in reinvestment certificates. Certificates held beyond the maturity date continue to be index-linked and to earn interest (at the rate in force at the maturity date).

Whether Index-Linked Certificates prove to be a worthwhile investment will mainly depend on the future level of inflation. In general, for investors who require a guaranteed real return and are unlikely to require access to their capital during the investment period, National Savings Index-Linked Certificates have definite attractions. The choice between Index-Linked Certificates and Index-Linked Gilts will depend on whether an income is required, the amount to be invested and the investment timescale.

At May 2002, National Savings offered two index-linked certificates:

- 23rd issue five-year certificates – interest: 1.6% per annum, plus RPI, compound;
- 12th issue two-year certificates – interest: 1.3% per annum, plus RPI, compound.

As these returns were tax free, the interest on the five-year certificates (assuming inflation at 2.5% per annum) was equivalent to 5.12% per annum gross to a basic rate taxpayer and 6.83% per annum gross to a higher rate taxpayer. For the two-year certificates the equivalent gross returns were 4.75% and 6.33% per annum, respectively.

2:2.5.3 Ordinary Account

The rate of interest offered on this account at May 2002 was 0.6% per annum for each complete calendar month where the balance is £500 or more, provided the account is open for the whole of a calendar year. The rate received on other balances was 0.5% per annum. The minimum deposit per individual is £10 and the maximum deposit £10,000. Interest of up to £70 per annum (£140 per annum if the account is held jointly by two individuals) can be received tax free. Even for higher rate taxpayers, the Ordinary Account is unlikely to be attractive compared to other investments available.

2:2.5.4 Investment Account

This account credited interest at the following rates at May 2002:

Under £500	2.6%
£500 – £4,999	2.7%
£5,000 – £9,999	2.8%
£10,000 – £24,999	3.0%
£25,000 – £49,999	3.2%
£50,000+	3.6%

The interest is taxable, but is credited without any deduction being made at source. Although the maximum deposit per account is £100,000, a higher balance is permitted if it results from interest credited to the account.

Withdrawals are subject to one month's notice or, if the money is required immediately, a 30-day interest penalty.

A deposit in the Investment Account can be a worthwhile investment for an individual not liable to tax, particularly as there is no need for a tax repayment claim or a form R85 to be completed.

2:2.5.5 Income Bonds

The interest rate on Income Bonds at May 2002 was 3.55% per annum payable on the fifth day of each month for investments below £25,000. The rate increased to 3.8% per annum for investments of £25,000 and over. The minimum holding per individual is £500 and the maximum holding £1 million. Although the interest is paid gross, it is subject to tax.

The main disadvantage with Income Bonds is that if the interest is to be paid in full, three months' notice of withdrawal is required and the bonds must be held for a minimum period of one year (if the bonds are encashed earlier, half the normal rate of interest is payable). Instant encashments can be made, but are subject to a 90-day interest penalty. Consequently, this investment is likely to be more attractive to non-taxpayers who require a monthly income and are in a position to give the required period of notice for withdrawals.

2:2.5.6 Pensioners' Guaranteed Income Bonds

These bonds provide a fixed rate of interest for a fixed period. They are only available to those aged 60 and over. Interest is paid monthly without deduction of income tax, making the investment particularly attractive to non-taxpayers.

The minimum investment is £500 and the maximum (to include all Pensioners' Income Bonds held) is £1 million. Withdrawals, in whole or part, can be made at the end of the fixed period without penalty. If the bonds are encashed at any other time, 60 days' notice has to be given and no interest will be paid during the notice period. Alternatively, encashments can be made immediately, but subject to a 90-day interest penalty. The interest rate needs to be assessed in the light of likely changes in rates generally.

At May 2002, three issues of Pensioners' Guaranteed Income Bonds were available:

- Series 25 five-year bonds – interest: 4.90% per annum;
- Series 16 two-year bonds – interest: 4.55% per annum;
- Series 10 one-year bonds – interest: 4.35% per annum.

2.2.5.7 *Fixed Rate Savings Bonds*

These bonds are issued for fixed periods at fixed rates of interest. Interest is paid after deduction of income tax at the savings rate and may be credited monthly, annually or at maturity or paid out monthly. The investment periods and annual interest rates at May 2002 were:

	£500– £19,999	£20,000– £49,999	£50,000– £1 million
1 year	4.1%	4.3%	4.5%
3 years	4.5%	4.7%	4.9%
5 years	4.65%	4.85%	5.05%

The minimum investment is £500 and the maximum (for all bonds held) is £1 million. Applications may be made by post, by telephone (with payment by debit card) or in person at a post office. The bonds can be encashed fully or partially before maturity, but there is a penalty of 90 days' interest. The bonds are suitable for investors who like the security of fixed interest rates and government backing, but more attractive rates may be available from banks and building societies.

2:2.5.8 *Capital Bonds*

At May 2002, Series 6 of these bonds offered a return which averaged 5.0% per annum compound if held for the full five-year period. The interest rose from 4.4% per annum in the first year to 5.61% per annum in the fifth and is paid out at maturity. Although the interest is earned gross and added to the bonds, it is subject to tax (see below). If the bonds are encashed within five years, the return is lower and depends on the length of time the bonds are held. The minimum investment is £100 and the maximum is £250,000. There is no provision for the bonds to earn interest after the maturity date. The bondholder is liable to income tax on the interest added each year even though it is not actually paid to him. The real net return to a taxpayer at maturity is difficult to determine, due to the payment of tax in advance of receiving the proceeds and the uncertainty of future income tax rates. Capital bonds are most attractive to individuals not liable to income tax who require guaranteed capital growth over a five-year period.

2:2.5.9 *Children's Bonus Bonds*

These bonds can be purchased for children under the age of 16 by anyone aged over 16. The guaranteed rate of return at May 2002 was 4.65% per annum for the first five years that the investment is held. This consisted of a basic rate of interest of 3% per annum plus a bonus on the fifth anniversary of 9.6% of the purchase cost. The return is free from tax and no liability arises on parents who gift bonds to their children. The bonds will only provide a return until the holder's 21st birthday and are automatically encashed then. The minimum investment is £25, whilst the maximum for each issue is currently £1,000. Bonds are repayable on one month's notice, but the rate of return is only 2.5% per annum if they are held for less than five years. No interest is paid on bonds held for less than 12 months.

2:2.5.10 Premium Bonds

A Premium Bond is effectively a lottery ticket which can be encashed for its face value (£1 per bond) at any time. Instead of being paid to bondholders, the interest is used to provide prizes for a limited number of investors. Monthly prize draws take place with the maximum prize being £1 million. At May 2002 the prize fund represented approximately 2.4% per annum of the total value of eligible bonds and all prizes (currently over 580,000 each month worth over £33 million) are received free of tax. Bonds are not eligible for inclusion in the prize draw until they have been held for one clear calendar month. The minimum initial holding of Premium Bonds is £100 per individual and the maximum holding £20,000.

Premium Bonds cannot strictly be classified as investments as the only return provided depends on the luck of the draw. The odds against winning any prize are 28,500 to 1. However, it is only the interest which is at stake, as the return of the capital is guaranteed. Consequently, this will be satisfactory for those who are prepared to forgo the interest on their Premium Bonds in order to obtain the chance of receiving a large, tax-free windfall without risk to the value of their capital, other than by inflation. Public interest in Premium Bonds has increased since the introduction of the National Lottery, whose odds (for larger prizes) are considerably longer.

2.2.5.11 National Savings Individual Savings Accounts

National Savings offers a cash mini-ISA (see **Chapter 4**) and a TESSA-only ISA (see **2:2.4**), both of which meet the CAT standards. The minimum deposit for both is £10. At May 2002, the rate on these accounts was 4.15% per annum, and interest is credited annually.

2:2.6 'Instant access' insurance bonds

Insurance bonds offering immediate withdrawals have been developed from guaranteed income bonds (see **2:2.7** below). They offer variable rates of interest which are often attractive in relation to those on bank or building society deposits.

Sample rates at May 2002 were:

Investment	*Interest p.a. net of savings rate tax*	*Gross equivalent*	
		Savings rate taxpayer	*Higher rate taxpayer*
£5,000	2.23%	2.78%	3.04%
£100,000	2.83%	3.53%	3.86%
£500,000	2.93%	3.66%	4.00%
£1,000,000	2.98%	3.72%	4.07%

Higher rate taxpayers benefit from the fact that, although the insurance company has paid corporation tax on its income at 20% (or, possibly, effectively less), the tax credit attaching to the net interest is deemed to be at 22%, leaving only tax at 18% payable.

2:2.7 Guaranteed income and guaranteed growth bonds

The purpose of guaranteed bonds is to provide a fixed rate of income or growth over a preselected term (usually one to five years) in addition to the return of the original capital sum at the end of that period. There are four main types of guaranteed bonds, all issued by life assurance companies. Each has a different structure and accordingly is taxed in a different way, as follows:

(a) a combination of temporary and deferred annuities;

(b) a single premium endowment policy (this is the most common);

(c) a series of single premium endowment policies;

(d) a series of single premium endowment policies plus term assurance.

The following are the principal considerations relating to guaranteed income and guaranteed growth bonds.

(a) The rate of income or growth quoted is net of basic rate tax, but is subject to higher rate tax at the time of payment of the income or at maturity. On income bonds, there may also be a potential higher rate tax charge on the return of capital (where deferred annuities are included as part of the income bonds, a charge to savings rate tax will also arise).

(b) Income payments are generally made annually, although sometimes half-yearly, quarterly or monthly.

(c) If the individual should die during the term of the bond, the amount of the investment is returned (accrued income to the date of death will be paid).

(d) Surrender values, where allowed, are not normally guaranteed and will generally depend on financial conditions at the time. An investor who wishes to dispose of his bond before its maturity may, as an alternative to surrendering it, be able to sell it to a dealer in traded endowment policies (see **10:5**).

(e) The returns are fixed. Therefore, before an investor becomes locked in at a fixed rate of interest, he should be of the view that interest rates are unlikely to rise. However, if he considers that higher rates are likely, it may be appropriate for him to invest in a variable interest investment, such as a building society account, on a temporary basis and then invest in guaranteed bonds at a later date if he proves to be correct.

(f) Since guaranteed bonds are frequently offered by less well-known insurance companies, potential investors should ensure as far as possible that the financial position of the company concerned is sound.

(g) If a person normally qualifies for age allowance, it should be remembered that their position could be affected by the taxation treatment of the guaranteed bonds.

(h) The rates of interest provided by guaranteed income and guaranteed growth bonds tend to lag behind general market interest rates. Therefore, potential investors should be prepared to act quickly when market rates have fallen, but before this is reflected in the rates offered by the guaranteed bonds.

At May 2002, the rates on amounts of £15,000 to £25,000 ranged from 3.25% for one year to 4.5% per annum for five years, equivalent to 4.44% per annum and 6.21% per annum gross respectively for higher rate taxpayers. Slightly higher rates were paid for larger amounts.

For amounts of £50,000 or more invested for at least three months, two insurance companies will arrange a guaranteed bond to mature on a date specified by the investor, for which it will quote a 'bespoke' rate. This is particularly useful for investors who have a known liability (e.g. a tax payment) on a specific date.

2:2.8 High income insurance bonds

From time to time, insurance companies offer bonds which will pay an 'income' of 8% to 10% per annum (monthly, quarterly or annually) for a period of three to six years. Such offers are available for a limited period of four to six weeks.

The counterbalance to these exceptionally high rates is the risk to the capital invested. Repayment of the initial capital in full is dependent on the performance of one or more equity indices – typically, the FTSE-100 in the UK, the Standard & Poor's 500 in the US and/or the Dow Jones Eurostoxx 50 index in Europe. If all the indices are higher at the end of the investment period or have not fallen by more than a specified amount (often the closing index readings are averaged over six or 12 months), all the capital is repaid; if not, only the initial capital less the 'income' payments is returned. These contracts are based on derivative contracts constructed by leading investment banks. Investors need to appreciate the equity risk which underlies these superficially attractive arrangements.

2:2.9 Gilt-edged securities

Gilt-edged securities (gilts) are issued by the British government in the form of loans in order to finance its expenditure. Since the loans are government backed, their repayment on the relevant maturity dates is assured, although in the interim prices will fluctuate according to market forces. The following are some of the more important characteristics of the gilt-edged market for the private investor (the tax treatment of income and capital gains is discussed in **Chapter 12**).

(a) Due to the very wide choice of gilt-edged securities offered, it is usually possible to select a particular issue to fit the investor's circumstances. The various types available are as follows:

- (i) short-dated (with maturity dates within five years);
- (ii) medium-dated (with maturity dates after five years but within 15 years);
- (iii) long-dated (with maturity dates after 15 years);
- (iv) undated (with no maturity dates);
- (v) convertible (gilts with an option for the holder to switch into a longer-dated gilt at a series of fixed dates, typically six months apart, during the life of the convertible stock);
- (vi) index-linked (where both capital growth and income are based on changes in the RPI. See **(f)** below).

Dated gilts (other than index-linked gilts) can be further divided into low-, medium- and high-coupon stocks. Coupons range from 2.5% to 9.5%. Normally, high-coupon stocks will be more suitable for pension funds, charities and individuals not liable to tax, while low coupon issues will be more appropriate for individuals paying tax at the higher rate due to the greater potential for tax-free capital growth. At May 2002, most fixed interest gilts were standing at prices above their repayment values, because of the fall in interest rates in recent years. Prospective investors must, therefore, take the certainty of a capital loss at redemption into account before buying stock.

(b) At maturity, £100 nominal of stock will be redeemed for £100 except in the case of index-linked stocks.

(c) The volatility of the price of a gilt will mainly depend on the nominal rate of the coupon and the length of the period until the redemption date. Low-coupon and long-dated stocks will generally be more volatile than high-coupon and short-dated stocks.

(d) The shape of the yield curve, which plots the current redemption yields of different gilts against their periods to maturity, will normally indicate general expectations for movements in interest rates and the outlook for inflation. Short-dated gilts are more affected by interest rates while longer issues also reflect views on inflation. The redemption yields on very short-dated gilts reflect current interest rates, whereas those on long-dated gilts are slightly lower, reflecting the expectation of lower interest rates and inflation as European economies converge.

(e) Price anomalies can arise in the gilt-edged market, and, by being alert, it is possible for an investor to benefit from them. These anomalies usually occur due to there being a shortage or excess of a particular stock at a particular time. They are, however, usually so small that, after taking dealing expenses into account, the benefit of switching is, for a private investor, minimal.

(f) Index-linked gilts, whereby both the capital and interest exactly reflect the change in the RPI, were first issued in March 1981 and subsequently became available to private investors in March 1982. As a result, an individual was able for the first time to obtain a guaranteed real rate of return on his investments. (The change in the RPI is measured over the period from eight months before the issue date of a gilt to eight months before its redemption date.)

However, in order for this return to be guaranteed, the gilt must be held until redemption, since its price in the interim will be mainly determined by the following factors:

(i) the supply and demand in the market;

(ii) the current level and outlook for interest rates;

(iii) the yields offered by conventional gilts;

(iv) the rate of inflation which has occurred for the period from eight months before the issue date to the present time;

(v) the outlook for inflation from the present time until eight months before the redemption date.

At May 2002, investors could obtain a real rate of return to redemption (capital plus income) of around 1.7% to 2.45% per annum before tax, assuming inflation at 3% per annum.

Index-linked gilts are a worthwhile investment for those investors wishing to obtain a guaranteed real return from part of their capital. This particularly applies to individuals paying tax at the higher rate. Where a gilt is unlikely to be held until its redemption date, it should be remembered that, as in the case of conventional gilts, the stocks with the earlier maturity dates will carry less risk.

(g) Where gilt-edged securities are purchased directly from the Bank of England rather than through a stockbroker, dealing costs are lower, especially for smaller bargains. This route does, however, have the following disadvantages:

(i) a maximum investment is permitted in any one stock of only £25,000 per day (this does not apply to sales); and

(ii) it is not possible to specify either the date of the transaction or the price at which a stock should be purchased or sold.

(h) Interest payments are made without deduction of tax. The investor may, however, request that income tax at the savings rate is deducted before payment of the net amount. All gilt interest is free of tax to non-UK residents.

2:2.10 Eurobonds

Eurobonds are bonds, usually issued in a foreign currency, which are traded internationally. Interest is normally paid gross on an annual basis. Although marketability is usually good in high-quality bonds (Triple A bonds), an investment of less than £20,000 is not practical. Due to the complexity of settlement and the variety of bonds available, professional advice is generally necessary when making an investment.

2:2.11 Local authority loans

Local authorities raise loans in order to assist in financing their expenditure. Although the security provided is generally of a high order, these loans do not have the same backing as gilt-edged securities, or the same marketability. As a result, the yields from local authority loans are usually greater than those available from comparable gilts.

There are two main types of local authority loan.

(a) *Fixed-term unquoted corporation bonds.* These bonds are issued and repaid at par for a fixed period (up to seven years) and at a fixed interest rate. Consequently, the return provided will be in the form of interest only and this will be based on general market rates at the time the loans are raised. Since fixed-term unquoted corporation loans are not marketable, an individual is unable to obtain the repayment of his investment until maturity (or death if earlier).

(b) *Quoted corporation loans.* These loans have many of the features of gilt-edged securities, including a wide range of coupons and maturity dates. However, the market is often small and consequently it is not always possible to buy in reasonable amounts.

The tax treatment of an individual investing in local authority bonds is discussed in **Chapter 12**.

2:2.12 Company debentures and unsecured loan stocks

These loans, which are normally raised by companies to provide, for example, working capital, are often traded on the Stock Exchange. In the case of company debentures, the loans are secured on particular company assets, or a floating charge is made on the assets generally. However, no specific security is provided for unsecured loan stocks.

Company debentures and unsecured loan stocks can be issued in convertible or non-convertible form. When issued in convertible form, stockholders are provided with the option to convert their investments into the ordinary shares of the company at fixed dates on stated terms. The market value of these 'convertibles' would then reflect the value of the company's ordinary shares in addition to the general level of interest rates and the status of the company concerned. A major disadvantage of some company debentures and loan stocks is that there is often a narrow market, with the result that deals cannot always be transacted. Even where they can be arranged, it is not unusual for there to be a wide margin between the bid and offer prices.

Mainly due to the greater risks involved and their inferior marketability, higher yields are available from non-convertible company debentures and loan stocks than from comparable gilt-edged securities. However, from the point of view of security, gilts would still generally be more suitable for most investors.

The tax treatment of an individual investing in company debentures and unsecured loan stocks is discussed in **Chapter 12**.

2:2.13 Permanent interest bearing shares (PIBS)

PIBS form part of the permanent capital of a building society. They have no repayment date and rank after the society's liabilities on its borrowed capital and balances due to depositors. They are more in the nature of an irredeemable loan than 'ordinary' shares.

PIBS are listed on the Stock Exchange and must be purchased through a stockbroker in units of £1,000 (£10,000 for some issues). Their prices are broadly subject to the same factors as affect gilt-edged securities, but, to reflect the lower degree of security, the interest coupons and yields of PIBS are higher (yields were around 7.4% per annum at May 2002). Interest is paid half-yearly, net of savings rate tax.

When building societies are converted into banks, PIBS become perpetual subordinated bonds.

2:2.14 Preference shares

Preference shares issued by companies rank after debentures and unsecured loan stocks in order of security. In the event of the company being wound up, the holders of preference shares would not receive payment until after the loans had first been repaid. Therefore, higher yields would normally be expected from preference shares due to the greater risk involved.

However, there are additional factors which may affect yields on preference shares including, for example, the dividends paid being treated as franked income in a company's hands, whereas interest from debentures and unsecured loan stocks is treated as unfranked income. Since this makes preference shares more attractive to companies, reduced yields are generally offered. Other factors would be the particular terms offered by the preference shares, such as whether they are cumulative or non-cumulative (cumulative means that, if a dividend is missed, it accumulates for later payment), participating rights, voting rights and redemption dates, which could result in lower yields being available.

Like debentures and loan stocks, the higher yields usually offered by preference shares would not generally provide sufficient compensation for most private investors for the greater security and marketability of gilt-edged securities. Furthermore, capital gains arising from preference shares are subject to capital gains tax (this is not the case with gilt-edged securities).

It is now also possible to purchase convertible preference shares, which are treated as wider range investments for trust investment purposes. These are convertible into the company's ordinary shares at fixed dates on stated terms in a similar way to convertible debentures and unsecured loan stocks.

2:2.15 Zero dividend preference shares of investment trusts

Investment trusts invest in portfolios of listed (and sometimes unlisted) investments. As they are companies, investment trusts are able to raise capital not only through ordinary shares, but also through other types of share as well as loans and debentures.

Zero dividend preference shares ('zeros') pay no income (hence their name). However, they have three additional features:

(a) they have first claim on the assets when the trust is wound up;

(b) the date and value of their repayment are fixed in advance; and

(c) their entitlement to part of the trust's assets grows each month.

The repayment of the promised amount on zero dividend preference shares when a trust is wound-up depends entirely on adequate growth in the trust's underlying investments. The decline in equity markets in 2000 and 2001, accentuated by borrowings and investments in the shares of other split capital trusts, led to a crisis in the sector in the autumn of 2001. The fall in the prices of both equities and investment trust shares resulted in a severe decline in the prices of zeros. This affected trusts with sound portfolios as well as those in danger of failing to pay the promised amount on winding up. Zeros are consequently no longer regarded as 'low risk'.

The repayment value of a zero is set at a level which compensates for the lack of income.

Example 1

Issue price 100p on 31 October 1997

Redemption price 160.58p on 31 October 2004

Appreciation 60.58% over 7 years – 7.0% per annum

The annualised rate of appreciation is called the 'gross redemption yield'. This tends to reflect prevailing interest rates but with a margin over the yields on comparable gilts. Potential investors will compare the yields on different trusts' shares and will also have regard for the amount of 'cover' – the extent to which the current value of the trusts' assets exceeds the amount required to repay the zeros in full. This is also expressed as the 'hurdle rate' – the amount by which the assets must grow each year in order to meet the repayment value. When the value of the assets exceeds this value, the hurdle rate is negative. Close attention should also be paid to the nature of the underlying portfolio and the amounts of any borrowings.

Zero dividend preference shares are listed on the Stock Exchange and their prices fluctuate in line with investors' views on the certainty (or otherwise) of their achieving their repayment value. A sale or redemption of zero dividend preference shares may give rise to a chargeable disposal for capital gains tax. If the holding is significant, a liability to tax may be avoided by spreading sales over more than one tax year, using the annual exemption.

2:2.16 Purchased life annuities

Although there are several different types of purchased life annuities (including immediate annuities which commence immediately and deferred annuities which commence at a future date), the following are common features.

(a) In return for a lump sum payment, annuity instalments will be received at regular intervals by the investor either for the remainder of his life or for a preselected term. The annuity can be arranged on a joint life and last survivor basis so that, if required, a guaranteed income can be provided for the annuitant and his wife during their lifetimes. The annuity can also be arranged to increase each year on a preselected fixed basis or in line with a preselected index (see **(b)** below).

(b) The annuity payments may be fixed or variable on one of the following bases:

(i) without-profits level annuity, where the gross payment is determined at the outset and will not change;

(ii) without-profits increasing annuity, where the gross payment increases by a fixed percentage each year (usually between 3% and 10%);

(iii) without-profits index-linked annuity, where the gross payment is fixed for the first year and thereafter varies in line with an index (usually the RPI);

(iv) with-profits annuities, where part of the gross payment is guaranteed, and annual bonuses are declared which increase it and, once declared, become part of the guaranteed payment;

(v) unit-linked annuities, where the gross payment is linked to the investment performance of a selected fund.

The gross annuity is the sum of the capital and income elements before deduction of tax (see **(c)** below);

(c) The annuity paid consists of a capital element and an income element. The capital element represents a partial return of the original investment and accordingly is tax free. The income element is subject to taxation in the normal way. (Where an annuity is subject to guaranteed escalations, the capital content rises pro rata with the gross payments. This is unlike the other forms of annuity described above where the capital content remains the same as at the outset so that any increase in the annuity is subject to income tax.)

(d) The returns provided by annuities will be mainly determined by the following factors:

(i) the type of annuity;

(ii) the yields on long-dated gilts;

(iii) the age and sex of the individual (or individuals in the case of a joint life and last survivor annuity – with this type of annuity, it is the age and sex of the younger person which will have considerably more importance);

(iv) the guarantee period (if any) for which the annuity is to be paid;

(v) whether or not the contract is 'capital protected' (see below);

(vi) the basis of the annuity (see **(b)** above);

(vii) the frequency of payment; and

(viii) the rates offered by individual insurance companies at the particular time. For tax reasons or a company's desire to be competitive (or not) in this market, there are often significant differences between them. It is therefore essential for several quotations to be obtained. A few companies will pay higher rates to those who smoke or are in poor health.

(e) Since annuity rates are constantly changing, individuals should take immediate action if they wish to purchase an annuity at a time of falling interest rates. Annuities should not be purchased when interest rates are towards the bottom of their cycle. The main disadvantage of purchased life annuities is that there is no access to the capital sum paid. In addition, in the event of an individual's death soon after arranging the annuity, there would be no return to his estate unless the annuity was effected with a guaranteed minimum period of payment or on a capital protected basis. Under a capital protected annuity, the insurance company guarantees in the event of death to return any excess of the purchase consideration over the total of the gross instalments paid. Also, unless the annuity is arranged on an increasing or an indexed basis, there is no hedge against the effects of inflation.

A purchased life annuity will be mainly suitable in the circumstances outlined below.

(a) For individuals normally with a minimum age of, say, 75 who wish to increase their net spendable income, but who will not require the return of their capital. This situation could arise when the annuity is included as part of a package. An example of this would be in a home income plan where an annuity is combined with a loan to provide additional income for an elderly home owner (see **13:8.1**).

(b) For funding purposes at any age, for example, a nine-year temporary annuity to provide the premiums for a qualifying life policy (the first premium being paid directly out of capital);

(c) For inheritance tax purposes, when an annuity may be effected to reduce an individual's estate, whilst at the same time securing a high income for life. This action may also make it possible for him to give away other assets during his lifetime, which would otherwise have been retained to produce income or to fund the premiums to a whole of life policy written on trust to fund his potential inheritance tax liability (see **12:5**).

With the fall in interest rates in recent years, coupled with improvements in mortality experience, annuity rates have declined, to the point where in many cases they are unattractive in relation to other income-producing investments.

2:3 Variable investments

Unlike fixed investments where either the capital and/or the income remains fixed once the investment has been made, in the case of variable investments both the capital and income can vary. Therefore, they should only be considered for the third part of the capital, namely higher risk/higher reward investments (this was considered earlier, see **2:1**).

Shown below are the main characteristics and some timing indicators with regard to variable investments. Also discussed are some particular types of investment (unit trusts, OEICs, investment bonds, investment trusts, venture capital trusts, investments under the Enterprise Investment Scheme, personal equity plans and Individual Savings Accounts are dealt with in later chapters).

2:3.1 Main characteristics

Although there are many different types of variable investments, they are all governed by the following common rules:

(a) since an individual can obtain a guaranteed real return over the rate of inflation by investing in index-linked gilts, he should normally only invest in variable investments if he considers it likely that they will provide a higher return;

(b) due to their particular nature, an individual should only invest in variable investments the proportion of his capital which he is prepared to put at risk with the objective of obtaining an above average return;

(c) variable investments should be made on a medium- to long-term basis, with the actual period depending on the particular type of investment and the investor's circumstances.

2:3.2 Timing indicators

Timing is of the utmost importance with many investments, especially where those of a higher risk/higher reward nature are concerned. It is often more likely that an investor will make a profit from a poor investment in a rising market than he will from a quality investment in a falling market.

Although timing is often the most difficult aspect of investment – there is no automatic way of knowing when is the right time to buy or to sell – the indicators shown below, which particularly relate to equity investments, frequently apply.

(a) It is often best to take a contrary view to the general consensus, especially where a longer-term approach can be taken.

(b) An opportune time to make an investment is often when both the relevant market and the investment under consideration have shown major falls. Although it may be worthwhile to wait until the market has steadied, if investment is delayed too long until the outlook has clearly improved, the market is likely to have taken this improvement into account and risen.

(c) When bad news is out and widely known, this is frequently a favourable time to invest. When eventually the news does improve, the stock market is likely to rise.

(d) After a period of general gloom, the institutions, who generally have a large positive cash flow, will normally have a substantial amount of money waiting for investment. When they do invest (and no advance notice is given of this) the weight of money will often cause the stock market to show a sharp rise over a very short period.

(e) A suitable time to sell an investment is often when both the investment concerned and the underlying market have shown considerable rises but have since started to decline.

(f) An indication that a stock market rise may be coming to an end is when there are a large number of rights issues from companies and new unit trust launches.

(g) The trend of the movement in interest rates can indicate the direction of the stock market. If the trend appears to be upwards, this is likely to have a depressing effect on the market, whereas if the trend is downwards, the reverse would generally apply. A rise in interest rates may, however, be welcomed by the stock market as a move to forestall rising inflation.

(h) The stockmarket anticipates events 12 to 18 months ahead. Investors need to do the same.

2:3.3 Ordinary stocks and shares (equities)

The shares of quoted companies provide a popular method of participating in the growth of individual companies and of the economy in general. In addition, most shares provide an income by way of quarterly, half-yearly or annual dividends. While the number of shareholders has grown in the last 20 years as the result of the privatisation of national and regional utilities and the conversion of building societies and mutual insurance companies into public companies, investors must always be aware that share prices are subject to a wide range of factors which may cause them to fall. Equity shareholders must accept the volatility associated with the potential for growth and take an appropriately long-term view.

As a part-owner of a company, the investor in ordinary shares is entitled to vote at general meetings and needs to deal with corporate events, which may include:

(a) a bonus issue of shares (also called a scrip or capitalisation issue). This involves the capitalisation of the company's retained profits or other reserves through the allotment of additional shares pro rata to all ordinary shareholders;

(b) a rights issue. This is an offer to all shareholders of the opportunity to subscribe for new shares at a price below the current market price. It is a way for the company to raise new long-term capital; or

(c) a takeover offer, either made by the company or received by it.

In all these cases, the investor is likely to receive a quantity of correspondence from the company, particularly when there is more than one company seeking to take over the company whose shares he holds. Whilst companies endeavour to make this correspondence as user-friendly as possible, it is often complex and needs professional advice before action is taken.

Unless an individual has the time, the knowledge and the inclination to manage his own investments, he will usually benefit if his investments are handled instead by a stockbroker or investment manager specialising in private portfolio management. However, if the investor does satisfy these requirements, he may sometimes produce superior results to a stockbroker or other discretionary portfolio management service due to the personal attention he is able to provide. It should also be remembered that, in addition to any financial benefit (and the saving in charges), an individual may also obtain considerable satisfaction from choosing his own investments. Where an individual does decide to manage his own investments, these should be spread sufficiently in order to avoid undue concentration of risk. It is mainly for this reason that direct investment in stocks and shares is more appropriate for larger investors.

With the introduction of taper relief for capital gains tax from 6 April 1998 (see **12:2**), individual holdings of stocks and shares may be at a tax disadvantage to collective equity investments, such as unit trusts. This is because every time a share is sold and a replacement purchased, there is potentially a charge to capital gains tax and the taper relief clock will be restarted for the new holding. Unit trusts, OEICs and investment trusts are, however, exempt from capital gains tax on gains realised within the fund; the investor is only liable to tax if he sells his interest in the fund.

2:3.4 Offshore funds

Although offshore funds are usually more suitable for expatriate investors due to their special tax position, they are also generally available to UK residents, to whom they can be attractive in appropriate circumstances.

Offshore funds operate in a similar way to unit trusts with many of the same characteristics, such as full-time professional management, a wide investment spread and the price of their shares being directly related to the value of the underlying assets. However, as offshore funds are not registered in the UK, the following special considerations apply.

(a) To be marketed in the UK, an offshore fund must be either:

(i) recognised by the Financial Services Authority. This means that the managers have obtained specific approval of the fund and its proposed method of operation; or

(ii) regulated in the territory where it is based under legislation which in the opinion of the Department of Trade and Industry provides protection to investors at least equivalent to that in the UK.

In the Financial Times Managed Funds Service, recognised and regulated funds are listed separately under each manager's name, so that the status of a fund can easily be seen.

The territories which have been designated as providing adequate investor protection are Bermuda, Guernsey, Jersey and the Isle of Man.

(b) The taxation position of UK investors in respect of offshore funds was the subject of a consultation paper issued by the Inland Revenue in April 2002. The rules in force at that time were:

(i) the offshore fund itself is generally exempt from taxation apart from perhaps a small amount of local corporation tax and in some cases withholding tax on dividends and interest;

(ii) UK residents are liable to income tax, rather than capital gains tax, on any realised gains, unless a particular fund has obtained 'distributor' status;

(iii) the main condition for distributor status is that at least 85% of the net income arising in the fund must be distributed and not accumulated (since distributor status is not granted by the Inland Revenue until after the end of each accounting period, this cannot be guaranteed at the time the investment is made);

(iv) where a fund does not obtain distributor status it is called an 'accumulator' or 'roll-up' fund. Its income is accumulated within the fund and no tax liability will arise until the investment (or part of it) is sold, when the whole of the gain (capital gain plus undistributed income) will be taxed as income in the year of disposal. This can be very advantageous where the investment is sold in a tax year when the individual's income is low, for example, after retirement or during a period of employment overseas;

(v) the income distributed to investors is payable gross. Investors will then be personally subject to income tax thereon if they are UK residents. Consequently, this produces a cash flow advantage until the tax due is paid. In the case of a non-taxpayer, the need to make a repayment claim may be avoided.

(c) Offshore funds are permitted to invest in a wider range of assets than UK authorised unit trusts. Accordingly, if an individual wishes to invest, say, in currency or commodity funds, only offshore funds would be available.

(d) Several offshore funds (generally known as 'umbrella' funds) are available which effectively allow an investor to switch between a wide range of currency, equity and fixed-interest sub-funds. The basis for umbrella funds is that they are investment companies with a range of separate classes of shares but having a single embracing structure – hence the term 'umbrella'. Investors can buy shares in one or more of these classes of shares, or sub-funds, and can then switch (or convert) from one class to another. Usually, a limited number of switches is permitted each year without charge.

One of the main reasons for forming umbrella funds was to postpone the payment of capital gains tax, as conversions within the fund were not deemed to constitute a sale and purchase. However, such conversions are now regarded as disposals and are therefore chargeable to income tax or capital gains tax as described in paragraph **(b)** above. Consequently, umbrella funds now appear to offer little attraction apart from ease of administration, the low costs of switching between different asset classes and the ability to receive interest or dividends gross.

The following matters should also be borne in mind.

(i) A larger commitment may need to be made to one particular management group than would usually be the case on normal investment grounds. Only a small minority of groups have been able to produce a good past performance record across the whole range of their funds.

(ii) The timing of the switches between the sub-funds is vital. Therefore, unless this is likely to be done regularly to advantage, a well managed general fund is likely to produce superior results.

(iii) If the Inland Revenue considers that there has been an unacceptably high level of investment change within the fund, it may not grant distributor status. This is particularly relevant when actively managed sub-funds are included, such as managed currency funds or bond funds.

(e) Unlike UK unit trusts, few offshore funds at the present time are authorised to advertise for direct subscription in the UK, except during the initial offer of shares through a filed prospectus.

Mainly due to the greater protection provided, onshore funds are usually more suitable for UK investors than offshore funds, except in the following circumstances:

(a) where the investor is a non-taxpayer (this applies particularly to a high yielding fund such as a sterling deposit fund or a fixed-interest income fund);

(b) where the type of investment fund required is not available onshore, for example currency funds;

(c) where there is no intention for the fund selected to seek distributor status and the investor plans to sell his investment in a tax year when his or her income is low.

2:3.5 Currency funds

Currency funds are a particular type of offshore fund and consequently the considerations discussed above will also apply to them. They may form part of an umbrella fund. The two main types of currency funds which are considered below are:

- deposit funds denominated in a single currency; and
- managed currency funds.

2:3.5.1 Deposit funds

For an investment in a currency other than sterling, it will be necessary for a view to be taken of the likely movement of that currency relative to sterling. The result of the investment will then depend on the amount of the currency gain (or loss) and the interest received on the chosen fund.

2:3.5.2 Managed currency funds

The main considerations with regard to managed currency funds are as follows:

(a) as in the case of all managed investments, the expertise of the investment managers is of paramount importance;

(b) movements in currencies are often more difficult to predict than movements in stock markets;

(c) since the rules of most managed currency funds require the managers to invest in a minimum number of different currencies, the relative strength of sterling will have a major influence on the result of the investment. Accordingly, if it is considered that sterling will be generally weak against most foreign currencies, an investment in a managed currency fund should appreciate. However, if sterling should be relatively strong against other currencies, the reverse is likely to apply;

(d) in choosing a specific fund, it is important to compare 'like with like' as far as possible.

A direct equity investment or one made via a fund in an overseas stock market will be affected by both stock market and currency movements (unless, in the case of a fund, the managers have taken action to reduce exposure to movements in the particular currency). Accordingly, if the investment being considered is to be made on a long-term basis, a carefully chosen equity fund investing overseas may be a more suitable alternative to the currency fund alone, unless the investor does not wish to take a position in the stock market concerned.

2.3.6 Foreign currency bank accounts

A bank account in a foreign currency can be opened at a UK bank (subject to the normal rules) as either a current or a deposit account. Accounts may also be opened with banks overseas or with foreign banks in the UK or, if the funds are required for investment in overseas securities, with a stockbroker or investment manager.

Investors will normally open such accounts for reasons of convenience (for example, to pay personal expenses while abroad) or to meet a particular need, rather than as an investment. Exchange rate movements are notoriously difficult to predict and any gains are likely to be the result of chance rather than foresight. Gains arising on the conversion of withdrawals into sterling are subject to capital gains tax (and losses are allowable), if the account is held by an individual resident or ordinarily resident in the UK, unless:

(a) the currency was acquired to meet personal expenses outside the UK; or

(b) the exchange gain is made by a non-UK domiciled individual on an account held overseas. In this case, the gain is taxed only if it is remitted to the UK and no relief is available for losses.

Interest rates will be different from those on sterling accounts and the charges may be higher than in the UK. If the account is in the UK, income tax at the savings rate will be deducted from interest credited (under Schedule D, Case V) on the gross amount arising in the current year.

2:4 Construction of an investment portfolio

The following examples illustrate broad investment portfolios for two individuals aged 30 and 50 respectively, based on their respective circumstances.

Example 2

A man aged 30 has a Lottery win of £400,000. His main personal particulars and requirements are as below:

(a) he is married with two young children but does not wish to educate them privately;

(b) he is employed by a company and is a member of their non-contributory pension scheme. His wife has earnings of £4,500 per annum from a part-time employment;

(c) he pays tax at the basic rate and is not liable to higher rate tax;

(d) he is buying a house for £100,000 ;

(e) he has already effected the permanent health and life assurance protection policies which he considers necessary;

(f) his principal requirements for the investment capital are as follows:

 (i) a combination of income and growth;

 (ii) part of the capital should be easily accessible;

 (iii) £160,000 can be invested on a long-term basis. He is prepared to take some risk with this part of the capital;

 (iv) some of the capital can be invested in his wife's name.

Since the permanent health, life assurance cover and pension requirements have all been dealt with, £300,000 can be used solely for investment purposes. A suitable arrangement could be as follows:

	£	£
First part of capital		
Deposit account with immediate access without loss of interest (see **Note 1**)		50,000
Second part of capital		
A short-dated, medium coupon British Government Stock	20,000	
A medium-dated, index-linked British Government Stock	20,000	
'Instant access' insurance bond	50,000	
		90,000
Third part of capital		
Two individual savings accounts of £7,000 invested in UK equity income unit trusts, OEICs or investment trusts in the names of each of the husband and wife	14,000	
Two UK equity income unit trusts, OEICs or investment trusts with the objective of providing an increasing income and potential for capital growth	48,000	
Two UK growth unit trusts, OEICs or investment trusts with the objective of providing capital growth	50,000	
Two international growth unit trusts, OEICs or investment trusts holding UK and overseas equities with the objective of providing capital growth	48,000	
		160,000
		£300,000

Notes

1. For the purpose of this example, it is assumed that there is no existing investment in a deposit account.

2. Part of the capital should be invested in the wife's name:

   (a) because her 10% income tax band can be used against the income from the gilts; and

(b) because her annual exemption may be needed for the saving of capital gains tax.

Otherwise the income from the gilts will be taxed at 20% and that from the investments at 10% (or 40% if it takes the investor's total income above the higher rate threshold).

3. If the investments are made near the end of a tax year, £14,000 of the funds earmarked for direct investment in unit trusts, OEICs or investment trusts could be reserved for a further investment in the selected ISAs early in the new tax year.

Example 3

A man aged 50 inherits £350,000 from his mother and asks for investment advice. His main personal particulars and requirements are:

(a) he is married with three children who have all left home and are in paid employment;

(b) he is self-employed and is providing for his retirement mainly through personal pension policies. He would like to retire at age 60. His wife does not have any earnings;

(c) he is already subject to a marginal rate of income tax of 40% before his inheritance is taken into account;

(d) his house is jointly owned with his wife and the mortgage has been repaid;

(e) he has effected appropriate life assurance policies to fund for inheritance tax;

(f) his assets already include a portfolio of equities managed by his stockbroker. His wife has relatively few investments;

(g) his principal requirements for the £350,000 inherited are:

  (i) to have access to £75,000 of the capital at short notice;

  (ii) to supplement his existing pension benefits;

  (iii) to achieve capital growth during the next ten years but with risk being kept to a medium level;

  (iv) to purchase a country cottage;

  (v) to use a relatively small amount of the inheritance to acquire some antique furniture for his house.

The above requirements could be met by the following arrangement of his capital:

	£	£
First part of capital		
Deposit account with immediate access without loss of interest (see **Note 1**)		25,000
Second part of capital		
'Instant access' insurance bond	25,000	
A medium-dated, index-linked British Government Stock	25,000	
		50,000
Third part of capital		
Additional personal pension contributions paid under the unused relief provisions (this is discussed in **Chapter 9**)	20,000	
Two individual savings accounts of £7,000 invested in UK equity income unit trusts, OEICs or investment trusts in the names of each of the husband and wife	14,000	
Three managed (UK and internationally invested) unit trusts, OEICs or investment trusts with the objective of providing capital growth	106,000	
Country cottage	120,000	
Antique furniture	15,000	
		275,000
		£350,000

Notes

1. For the purpose of this example, it is assumed that there is no existing investment in a deposit account.

2. Part of the capital should be invested in the wife's name, as this results in the utilisation of her personal allowance and in income being taxed at the 10% and savings rates. Also her annual exemption may be needed for the saving of capital gains tax, for example on the sale of the cottage.

3. The £106,000 proposed for investment in managed unit trusts could instead be added to the existing portfolio with the stockbroker.

4. If the investments are made near the end of a tax year, £14,000 of the funds earmarked for direct investment in unit trusts, OEICs or investment trusts (or in the stockbroker's portfolio) could be reserved for a further investment in the selected ISAs early in the new tax year.

3 Unit trusts, OEICs, investment bonds and investment trusts

The purpose of this chapter is to consider the main characteristics of and principal differences between unit trusts, open-ended investment companies (OEICs), investment bonds and investment trusts. In order to achieve this, unit trusts and investment bonds are first considered together. OEICs and unit trusts are very similar vehicles, both from the perspective of taxation and the underlying investments they hold. Indeed, unit trusts and OEICs are listed together in many performance tables and most OEICs which are available in the UK have been formed by conversion of unit trusts. For this reason, when comparisons are being made between the different collective investment vehicles it may be assumed that OEICs will have the same characteristics as unit trusts, unless specifically stated.

Nevertheless, there are significant differences between unit trusts and OEICs in terms of structure and administration. These areas are dealt with under the section on OEICs (see **3:3**).

At the end of the chapter, a comparison is made between unit trusts and investment trusts. Throughout the book, unless otherwise stated, unit trusts should be taken to mean UK authorised unit trusts.

3:1 Advantages of unit trusts and investment bonds

Unit trusts and investment bonds both enable individual investors to pool their resources, providing the following advantages when compared to investing directly in stock exchange securities.

(a) Full-time professional management is available on a day-to-day basis. However, the investment expertise of fund managers varies considerably and this is likely to be reflected in the results of their portfolios.

(b) As a result of the wide investment spread, the impact of disappointing results from individual investments is reduced. In addition, a spread of management can be obtained by investing in a number of different unit trusts or bonds, thereby further reducing risk. However, the likelihood of making exceptional gains is also reduced.

(c) Due to the large number of different types of unit trusts available, both by country and sector, the exact equity investment requirements of most individuals can usually be met by a careful selection of trusts.

(d) There is a considerable saving in paperwork for the investor, as dealing with scrip issues, rights issues and take-over bids is avoided. In addition, the preparation of tax returns is simplified.

(e) Both unit trusts and investment bonds are tax efficient when properly used. Unit trusts are exempt from capital gains tax on their realised gains, with the result that a fund manager is not inhibited in his investment decisions by tax considerations. Holders of investment bonds are permitted to withdraw 5% of their initial investment each year with the income tax liability deferred until disposal. As far as the unit trust investor is concerned, no capital gains tax liability can arise until the units are sold. This provides an important cash flow advantage in comparison to a direct investment in equities which are actively managed. Furthermore, under the capital gains tax taper relief rules, the taper relief 'clock' will run from the date of purchase of units in a unit trust regardless of any dealings within the trust. This may produce a tax advantage for unit trusts over individually held share portfolios.

(f) Investment bonds provide a convenient method of investing in assets such as property, particularly for relatively small amounts (a few property unit trusts are now also available).

(g) Unit trusts and investment bonds provide an easy and convenient way of investing in overseas equities and fixed-interest securities. This method is often adopted by stockbrokers to obtain the required overseas exposure for their private clients.

(h) Investment bonds generally provide a switching facility between funds at very low cost with no tax being payable by the bondholder on the exercise of this facility.

(i) Since the size of the bargains carried out by unit trusts and investment bonds is usually relatively large, an active investment policy can be undertaken less expensively than by the individual investor himself.

(j) The annual management charge of a unit trust is not subject to VAT and in most cases is deducted in calculating the amount of trust income to be paid out. Effectively, therefore, tax relief is given on the charge. The fees of the manager of a directly invested portfolio, however, are subject to VAT and are not tax deductible.

3:2 Advantages of management by stockbrokers

The main advantages of investing directly in stock exchange securities using the management services of stockbrokers compared to indirect investment through unit trusts and investment bonds are listed below.

(a) A more personal service is offered with the investor normally receiving a half-yearly valuation and report on his own portfolio. An annual list of dividends and capital gains tax calculations are also usually provided.

(b) An investor may derive more interest (and, possibly, shareholder benefits) from investing directly in companies and following their fortunes.

(c) For very large investors, an investment management service may be more advantageous because the size of their portfolios enables them to have a sufficiently broad spread of holdings at a lower cost than through a unit trust or investment bond.

Direct stock exchange investment may also be appropriate where an individual has the time and inclination to make his own investment decisions. Many investors gain considerable personal satisfaction from choosing their own investments, with or without the assistance of a stockbroker, and following their progress in the press on a regular basis.

3:3 Basic constitution

Unit trusts, OEICs and investment bonds are all collective investment schemes, where the unit price is dependent upon the net asset value of the underlying investments. This contrasts with investment trusts where the share price is dependent upon the supply of and demand for shares.

3:3.1 Unit trusts

A unit trust is constituted by a trust deed which is an agreement between the trustees and the managers of the fund. The trust deed covers the main aspects of the running of the trust and is subject to approval by the Financial Services Authority (FSA). The essential characteristics of the deed are that it lays down:

(a) the rights and responsibilities of all concerned;

(b) provisions enabling new investors to join;

(c) the maximum charges that can be made by the managers for administering the fund;

(d) provision for calculating the buying (offer) and selling (bid) prices of units;

(e) the objectives of the trust; and

(f) types of investment permitted.

The role of the trustee, whose appointment is subject to approval by the FSA, is that of a watchdog. A trustee's main duties are to ensure that the terms of the trust deed are strictly observed and to hold the cash and securities belonging to the fund. The responsibility for the choice of investments lies with the managers, although the trustee retains the right of veto.

If a unit trust or OEIC manager:

(a) goes out of business and cannot return investors' money; or

(b) manages a fund negligently, so that investors lose money,

investors can lodge a claim with the Financial Services Compensation Scheme (see **Appendix 1**). The maximum compensation the Scheme will pay is £48,000 – 100% of the first £30,000 plus 90% of the next £20,000.

3:3.2 Open ended investment companies (OEICs)

Open ended investment companies (OEICs) became available in the UK in January 1997. They are, effectively, unit trusts established as companies incorporated under UK and European legislation and so comply with the rules for UCITS (see **3:5**). Instead of trustees, they have a board of directors, one of whom will be the 'authorised corporate director' who will be the fund manager. They also have a single price for their shares, based, as with unit trusts, on the value of their underlying investments. They are, in this respect, simpler than unit trusts (which have separate prices for purchases and sales), although they may impose separate buying or selling charges to prevent dilution of the fund. This 'dilution levy' is designed to protect investors in the fund from the costs incurred on the acquisition or disposal of investments as the result of significant additions to or withdrawals from the fund. OEICs may be constituted as umbrella funds, with different classes of share for different sector or regional funds; they may also issue different types of share.

A number of unit trust groups have converted their funds to OEICs and this trend is likely to continue.

3:3.3 Investment bonds

An investment bond is a non-qualifying single premium life assurance policy. The investments of the bond fund form part of the main assets of the life assurance company and the bondholder has no prior charge on the fund. Consequently, if the life assurance company should find itself in financial trouble, the bondholder could suffer loss on his investment. The compensation payable by the Financial Services Compensation Scheme is 100% of the first £2,000 plus 90% of the value of the policy over £2,000. It is mainly for this reason that great care should be taken before business is placed with new or small life companies. In the case of unit trusts, there is not the same risk in dealing with newly established or small trusts due to the security provided by the trust deed and the fact that only the unitholders have a claim on the fund. With most life companies, the investments are in a separate bond fund which operates similarly to a unit trust. The performance is a function of the underlying value of the investments in the fund, irrespective of the performance of the life company's other investments. Many bond funds themselves invest in unit trusts as well as directly in equities and other assets.

3:4 Underlying investments

3:4.1 Unit trusts

Unit trusts are authorised by the FSA to invest only in quoted securities (subject to 10% of the fund being allowed in unquoted securities).

The main types of unit trusts may be classified under the following broad headings; these are the classifications used by performance measurement organisations.

(a) UK:

- (i) All Companies;
- (ii) Smaller Companies;
- (iii) Equity Income;
- (iv) Equity and Bond Income;
- (v) Gilts;
- (vi) Corporate Bonds;
- (vii) Other Bonds;

(b) International/global:

- (i) Growth;
- (ii) Equity Income;

(iii) Equity and Bond;

(iv) Bonds;

(v) Emerging Markets;

(c) Japan:

(i) General;

(ii) Smaller Companies;

(d) Far East:

(i) including Japan;

(ii) excluding Japan;

(e) North America:

(i) General;

(ii) Smaller Companies;

(f) Latin America

(g) Europe:

(i) excluding UK;

(ii) including UK;

(iii) Smaller Companies;

(h) Managed:

(i) Active;

(ii) Balanced;

(iii) Cautious;

(i) Specialist;

(j) Technology and Telecoms;

(k) Property;

(l) Index Bear;

(m) Money Market;

(n) Guaranteed/Protected.

3:4.2 Investment bonds

Investment bonds are permitted to invest in an even wider range of assets than unit trusts, including investing in unit trusts themselves. The following are the main investment sectors used by performance measurement organisations:

(a) Balanced Managed;

(b) Stockmarket Managed;

(c) Cautious Managed;

(d) Defensive Managed;

(e) Guaranteed Funds;

(f) Distribution Bonds;

(g) UK Equity Income;

(h) UK All Companies;

(i) UK Smaller Companies;

(j) Global Fixed Interest;

(k) Global Equities;

(l) Europe ex UK;

(m) Australasia;

(n) Emerging Markets;

(o) Far East, including Japan;

(p) Far East, excluding Japan;

(q) North America;

(r) Japan;

(s) UK Gilt and Fixed Interest;

(t) Index Linked Gilts;

(u) Money Market;

(v) Currency;

(w) Commodity and Natural Resources;

(x) Property;

(y) Friendly Society – Tax Exempt.

3:4.3 Switching

A switching facility, which is available with most bonds, enables the bondholder to switch from one fund to another within the same policy at very low cost (typically, one free switch in a policy year, with subsequent switches being subject to a minimum charge of £10 and a maximum charge of £25). Since the switch is not considered to be a disposal by the bondholder, no tax is payable on the exercise of this facility.

Despite the apparent attraction of the switching facility, timing and choice of funds are all important. Unless market movements are anticipated correctly, it is possible that switching will not add to the value of the bond.

In the case of unit trusts, switching funds within the same management group can usually be done on preferential terms by reducing (discounting) the initial charge on the units purchased, although the sale is a disposal by the investor for capital gains tax. This also applies to OEICs, even though they are under an umbrella structure. The exception to this is the fund of funds which invests in other unit trusts within the same management group. In these circumstances, a switch between the underlying unit trusts by the fund manager would not be treated as a disposal for capital gains tax purposes by the investor, as he holds units in the 'top' fund.

3:5 Undertakings for Collective Investment in Transferable Securities (UCITS)

Since October 1989, unit trust groups throughout the European Union (EU) have been able to market their schemes in any other EU country. A European agreement on collective investments, UCITS, removed the barriers between individual countries by requiring minimum standards, with the effect that all the schemes became comparable. Under the Financial Services and Markets Act 2000, other countries can become 'designated territories' if their financial regulations are at least as stringent as those in the UK. Consequently, collective investment schemes in these territories can be marketed in the UK in a similar manner to unit trusts, provided that they receive recognition from the FSA.

UK unit trusts can now be sold elsewhere in the EU and European funds can be marketed in the UK. However, each unit trust will operate under the regulations of its own country although it must abide by the marketing regulations of the country in which it is sold. A UK fund bought in Germany, while authorised by the FSA, will be marketed under German regulations. A French unit trust bought in Britain does not offer investors the same protection as an authorised UK fund.

3:6 Life assurance cover

3:6.1 Unit trusts

Since a unit trust is not a life policy, there is no life cover attached. Consequently, the realisation value on the death of the unitholder is the bid value of the units. However, units do not necessarily have to be encashed by the executors, but can instead be passed to beneficiaries or held within a trust created by a will.

3:6.2 Investment bonds

As mentioned above, a bond is a non-qualifying single premium life assurance policy and, consequently, on death (or the death of the last survivor if applicable), the contract terminates and a lump sum is provided which is normally a percentage of the bid value of the units at the date of death (often 101%).

A small number of companies base the life cover on the age of the individual at the time they invest in the bond and on the amount of the original investment. On death, the amount receivable will be the greater of the life cover or the bid value of the units in the bond fund.

3:7 Personal requirements and investment objectives

Before anybody invests in a unit trust or investment bond, they should first consider their personal requirements and investment objectives. These would include the following salient points.

(a) Whether they require capital growth, income, or a combination of the two, from the investment. Having decided on this, it is important to ensure that the purpose of the fund selected meets this objective.

(b) The degree of risk they are prepared to accept, remembering there is often a close correlation between risk and reward.

(c) The period of time for which it is intended to hold the investment. If the investment is being made on a long-term basis, a general or managed fund providing the investment managers with the greatest flexibility is often the most suitable.

(d) If they wish to invest in a specialised fund or geographical area, such as a fund investing in technology shares or Hong Kong, investment fashions can change and therefore it is important to be alert to dispose of the investment at short notice when market conditions are right.

(e) Whether they require the fund to be fully or substantially invested at all times, or whether it is desirable for the investment managers to take a view by going partially liquid if they think it appropriate. Most managers believe it is their responsibility to remain fully invested and for investors to decide on their own level of liquidity.

(f) Whether they require exposure to a particular currency when making overseas investments.

(g) The particular purpose for which the investment is being made; for example, an equity income unit trust can be very useful in a settlement where the interests of the life tenant and remaindermen have to be met by providing a balance of income and capital growth.

An investment bond is often ideal for a trust where income is to be accumulated until, for example, infant beneficiaries reach majority. However, it is unsuitable where income is required for a life tenant, as any withdrawals are regarded as capital repayments from which generally he is not permitted to benefit. However, it is essential that the trust contains a power to purchase investment bonds.

3:8 Past performance

Investors have traditionally used past performance as their principal yardstick for selecting suitable collective funds. They have been encouraged in this by the managers' advertisements, which have used the figures to demonstrate their funds' superiority.

But there has recently been considerable debate as to the relevance of past performance to the selection of a fund. A research paper issued by the FSA in August 2000, 'Past Imperfect?', clearly showed that past performance is not an indicator of future performance. While the paper focused on UK equity funds, it is likely that the same would apply in other investment sectors. When screening funds, therefore, it is important not to expect 'winning' funds to emerge from an analysis of past performance figures.

Such analysis can, however, indicate funds which have outperformed their benchmarks consistently through the skill of their managers, rather than luck. It is important to review the results over a reasonable period – ideally five years – and to look at discrete periods (for example, three months or a year) rather than cumulative figures. These results should be compared with an appropriate index and with those of similar funds. The figures may indicate a trend, and particular attention should be paid to the figures for the last 12 months.

The funds shortlisted as the result of this process should then be examined for other factors, such as:

(a) whether or not there has been a change of manager and/or of strategy during the period reviewed; and

(b) whether there have been wide variations in the performance of the fund. It is preferable to invest in a fund with a consistently above-average performance than one which has produced a mixture of outstandingly good or poor returns.

A new manager may wish to change the structure of the investment portfolio in accordance with his own ideas and this could initially have an adverse effect on the performance. However, this could be less of a disadvantage than it initially appears, since the new manager will normally follow the overall investment policy of the group concerned and, accordingly, any changes are likely to be limited.

3:9 Assessing management expertise

Although it is not possible to know which investment managers will produce the best results in the future, a considered opinion can be formed as to which managers offer above average expertise. However, to do this, a certain amount of research must take place. The following are indicators of management expertise which should help in the selection of a particular fund. The analysis of performance figures outlined in the previous section should produce a shortlist of funds for which further, qualitative, research can be carried out. It is important that the investor reaches an independent view of the merits of the funds he selects and is not swayed by a manager's reputation or its marketing material.

Until quite recently, intermediaries and other professional investors had either to carry out their own research, through written questionnaires and meetings, or to rely on the management company's own material and the output of a single rating agency. An investor may wish to consult a professional financial adviser, but the Internet has helped to make much more information and advice readily available. There are now five ratings agencies with websites (see **Appendix 1**), which highlight not only past performance, but also volatility, style and risk.

At the end of his research, an investor may still have questions and a management company's marketing department will provide information by telephone or in writing. They should, for example, be able to explain:

(a) the general philosophy of the group for the selection of investments and the degree of authority allowed to the individual fund managers;

(b) the general philosophy of the group as far as currencies are concerned when making overseas investments (this applies particularly to the exposure to any movements in currencies relative to sterling);

(c) the practical way the group operates and how fund managers obtain their information, for example through stockbrokers, company visits or internal research;

(d) the length of time for which the individual fund managers have managed a particular fund, together with their other responsibilities and previous experience;

(e) whether the fund manager has other responsibilities which may leave him with insufficient time to give proper attention to the fund and whether he is only nominally responsible for the fund, with the day-to-day management delegated to another person.

They will also provide a copy of the most recent manager's report and of the current asset allocation of the fund.

In practice, it is unlikely that an investor would have sufficient time to be able to obtain all this information. Nevertheless, with the judicious use of the ratings agencies' websites and publications such as Money Management or Planned Savings, sufficient knowledge to make a reasonable assessment of a particular investment can still be gained.

3:10 Unit trusts – general guidelines

The following general guidelines apply in the selection of a unit trust.

3:10.1 General trusts v. specialised trusts

The principal advantage of a general trust is that the fund manager has more scope in his choice of investments with fewer restrictions applying to the type of investments which can be made. General trusts are usually less volatile because of their wider investment spread. In particular, 'portfolio' trusts, whose asset allocation reflects that adopted by the manager for individual private clients, offer a simple way for investors to acquire a broadly spread balanced portfolio through a single holding. With the introduction of taper relief for capital gains tax, this approach to investment will be more tax efficient than a directly invested portfolio.

The main advantage of a specialised trust is that it enables investors to back their own views if they favour a particular sector. In addition, a fund manager can concentrate expertise on the sector concerned. However, if that sector performs poorly, it is difficult for the fund manager to avoid a loss. Unit trust portfolios generally remain fully invested; the managers regard it as the investor's responsibility, not theirs, to increase liquidity if a market fall is anticipated.

Consequently, investors must be prepared to buy and sell unit holdings actively as their views of the investment prospects of different sectors change, although the capital gains tax position and the dealing charges involved should be borne in mind.

3:10.2 Large funds v. small funds

While there is no clear evidence to show that the overall performance of small funds is superior to large funds, experience indicates that funds with very few assets tend to receive little attention from the management company compared with the effort and expertise applied to larger funds. If problems arise with a more substantial fund, the company is more likely to take prompt corrective action. Small funds do, however, often have an advantage due to their greater investment flexibility. If a unit trust investing in small companies becomes too large, for example, the size of each of its holdings can cause difficulties when buying or selling.

A steadily expanding fund has a definite advantage regardless of its size, as the fund managers are able to build up liquidity if required without the need to sell underlying investments. They can also change the 'slant' of the fund by applying new money differently from the existing investments and thereby avoid selling expenses in order to achieve this.

3:10.3 New trusts

The main advantage for an investor of purchasing units in a completely new trust is that the fund manager and the investment house will be especially keen for the trust to perform well. In addition, the only investments in the trust are those selected by the fund manager in the light of current conditions, rather than having been inherited from a previous manager or bought in a different investment climate. The principal disadvantage of subscribing to a new trust is that it is frequently launched after the sector in which the trust will invest has had a substantial rise. Consequently, it may be over valued and due for a fall. It should also be established whether the new manager has a track record of producing above average returns whilst managing a similar fund.

3:10.4 Index tracking trusts

Some management groups run index tracking unit trusts. These are run in a manner designed to follow the movements of a share index, typically the FTSE 100 Index or FTSE Actuaries All Share Index. They do this by holding either all the constituent shares in the index, in the same weightings, or a representative number of them whose price movements are likely to reflect this index as a whole. Index tracking funds are likely to underperform their chosen indices slightly because they bear expenses and there is the likelihood of tracking error. Nevertheless, over the longer term some of them have demonstrated a consistency which puts them well up the performance tables.

Recent international mergers have, however, created a few very large companies which dominate the FTSE 100 index in particular. This, and the increased volatility of share prices, has increased the risk profile of index tracking funds.

3:10.4.1 Exchange traded funds

In April 2000, a new type of index-tracking fund was introduced to the UK – exchange traded funds (ETFs). These have existed in the US since 1993, where they now represent assets of over $36 billion.

ETFs offer the best features of unit trusts and investment trusts, in that:

(a) they are a hybrid of open-ended and closed-ended funds, whose shares are listed and dealt in on the Stock Exchange;

(b) their price movements reflect the 'real time' movements in the relevant index;

(c) they can be bought or sold through a broker at any time during market hours (whereas unit trusts have a single dealing time each day);

(d) there is no significant difference between the price and the net asset value of the shares. Although the initial issue is of a fixed number of shares, institutional investors can at any time exchange a basket of the underlying securities for shares in the ETF and vice versa. This eliminates the opportunity to arbitrage any premium or discount between the price and the net asset value;

(e) the holdings in the portfolio are disclosed daily;

(f) ETF shares are exempt from stamp duty on purchase and have an annual management charge of 0.5% or less.

ETF shares are therefore a cheaper and more flexible vehicle than index-tracking unit trusts, since they have advantages for both professional fund managers and private investors. ETFs are available which track both the main stockmarket indices in the UK, US and Europe and certain specific sector indices.

3:11 With-profits bonds

The substantial market falls that occurred in the late 1980s prompted a number of investors to lose confidence in equity investment. This caused them to seek a means of achieving long-term capital growth, without short-term fluctuations.

Investment bonds investing in insurance companies' with-profits funds provided a solution. The key features of these bonds are as follows:

(a) the with-profits fund invests in a mixture of equities, fixed interest securities and property;

(b) the returns from the fund are in the form of annual bonuses and possibly a terminal bonus at encashment or on the death of the life assured;

(c) once allocated, the annual bonuses cannot be removed, but the rate of bonus is not guaranteed from year to year, depending as it does on the returns earned on the fund's investments. The irrevocable declaration of bonuses is subject to point **(f)** below;

(d) an income withdrawal facility is normally available, although higher rate taxpayers may suffer a tax liability if the withdrawal exceeds 5% of the initial investment;

(e) most bonds have no fixed maturity date so all or part of them can be surrendered at any time. In the early years, surrender penalties may apply;

(f) if at the time of surrender, investment returns have not been sufficient to support the bonuses credited, the company will apply a 'market value adjustment factor' which further reduces the surrender proceeds;

(g) on death, as with conventional investment bonds, a lump sum is provided, which is a percentage of the bid value of the units at the date of death (often 101%). To this amount a terminal bonus is often added.

Whilst a with-profits bond offers the investor a lower-risk alternative to conventional equity investment, the following disadvantages should be borne in mind:

(a) investors for whom equity investment is appropriate should not be concerned about short-term volatility. Most with-profits bonds should be held for a minimum five-year term and over that period, equity investment (either directly or through unitised funds) should produce better returns. With-profits bonds should principally be taken out by those whose resources are not sufficient to sustain the investment risk attaching to equities;

(b) the insurance companies' right to apply the market value adjustment factor means that investors are not protected, if they wish to encash during adverse market conditions;

(c) following the decline in equity markets in 2000 and 2001, both annual and terminal bonuses have been reduced. In some cases bonuses added to the bond are insufficient to support withdrawals of 5% per annum.

3:12 Distribution bonds

As an alternative to with-profits bonds, many companies are now offering distribution bonds. These bonds invest in funds that have a 'safety first' approach to equity investment. This approach manifests itself in the asset allocation, which has a much lower exposure to equities than a managed fund, with a correspondingly higher exposure to gilts, overseas bonds, cash and property.

A further feature of distribution funds is that their portfolios have higher yields than managed funds, making them particularly appropriate for investors who require income. Investors do not need to take all of the income generated by the fund. Any excess can normally be left to build up further. Particular care must be exercised when selecting a distribution fund as the equity exposure can vary. This will affect both the income generated by the fund and the investment risk.

3:13 Taxation

3:13.1 Investment bonds – final encashment

The taxation position on final encashment of an investment bond is as follows.

(a) Final encashment is considered to arise on complete surrender, death (or death of the last survivor of a jointly owned policy), or assignment for money or money's worth.

(b) The gain on the bond is calculated by taking the proceeds on final encashment plus all previous withdrawals and deducting the original cost of the bond and any chargeable amounts already established (known as chargeable excesses – see **3:13.3**).

(c) The gain is taxable as if it were an addition to the investor's income, but credited with basic rate income tax having already been paid. Thus only a higher rate taxpayer or a basic rate taxpayer close to the higher rate threshold would be personally liable to pay tax on the gain. The credit given cannot be reclaimed.

(d) If the investor's total taxable income is close to the threshold for higher rate tax (£29,900 plus allowances in 2002/03), the tax payable is calculated by 'top-slicing'. This method was introduced at a time when there were more bands of higher rate income tax than at present, to prevent a large chargeable excess in one year being taxed unduly heavily. The gain on the bond at **(b)** above is divided by the number of complete policy years that the bond has been held, to arrive at the top slice of the gain. This slice is added to the investor's other taxable income for the tax year of encashment and the tax payable with and without the slice is then calculated. The difference less basic rate tax on the slice is multiplied by the complete number of years that the bond has been held to arrive at the tax liability.

(e) If a loss should arise on final encashment, this will only be allowed to the extent of the amount of the chargeable excesses which have already arisen on partial surrenders in policy years commencing after 13 March 1975. This loss will then be permitted as a deduction in calculating the bondholder's higher rate tax liability in the year of final encashment. It should be noted that each policy is considered in isolation. Therefore, it is not permitted to use the loss on one policy to offset the gain on another.

The following example illustrates the calculation of tax on the encashment of a bond.

Example 4

A married man aged 50 bought a single premium bond for £10,000 on 1 June 1992 and encashes it on 31 August 2002 for £13,000 having used the 5% per annum withdrawal facility throughout. During 2002/03 his earned income was £34,300.

Under the top-slicing process, the gain of £8,000 (£3,000 on encashment plus previous withdrawals of £5,000) is divided by 10 (the number of complete years the bond has been in force) to arrive at the top slice of the gain, namely £800.

		Tax position without top slice of the gain		*Tax position including top slice of the gain*
		£		£
Income		34,300		34,300
Top slice of gain		–		800
		34,300		35,100
Less: personal allowance		4,615		4,615
		£29,685		£30,485
Tax payable thereon	£1,920 @ 10%	192	£1,920 @ 10%	192
	£27,765 @ 22%	6,108	£27,980 @ 22%	6,156
			£585 @ 40%	234
		£6,300		£6,582

	£
Total tax payable including tax on slice	6,582
Total tax payable without tax on slice	6,300
Tax payable including basic rate tax on slice	282
Less: basic rate tax on slice – £800 at 22%	176
Higher rate tax on slice	£106
Total tax on gain – £106 x 10	£1,060

3:13.2 Planning hints

The maximum higher rate tax liability on a gain made on an investment bond is currently 18% (40% less 22%) – even though the income of the life assurance fund has been taxed at the lower (or savings) rate of 20%. Nevertheless, it is still worthwhile to keep any liability to a practical minimum. The following are some planning hints to enable an investor to do this.

(a) Encash the bond in a tax year when the bondholder's marginal tax rate is low. This could be due to retirement, a period of employment overseas or unemployment.

(b) Rearrange the bondholder's affairs to make their income low in the tax year of encashment, perhaps by reinvestment of assets in low or non-income producing securities.

(c) Hold the bond until death, as the bondholder's income in that year is likely to be less than normal since it would be based on that received from the preceding 6 April to the date of death.

(d) Take out a series of smaller bonds, as already mentioned. Many insurance companies issue bonds in ten or more 'segments'. The bondholder will then be in a position to encash separate bonds or segments completely over a number of years and thereby reduce the amount of the top slice to be added to his other income each year. This is likely to have the effect of the gain being taxed at lower rates, if at all.

(e) Take out bonds on a joint life and last survivor basis. Where a bond is taken out by a husband and wife on a joint life and last survivor basis and the bond is not encashed until the second death, the tax charge will be postponed until that time.

If the husband is the first to die, it is likely that the widow's income would be lower following his death. This would then present a suitable opportunity for her to encash the bond if she required the capital sum.

(f) Arrange for a bond to be taken out by the spouse paying tax at the lower rate. Alternatively, a bond should be assigned from one spouse to another if that results in a tax saving on encashment. This assignment must not be for money or money's worth and must be absolute with no control being retained by the transferring spouse.

(g) At some time before encashment, make an additional investment into an existing bond. This is treated for top-slicing purposes as if made at the date of the original investment. Consequently, any gain arising on final encashment on both the original and subsequent investments will be top sliced over the whole period of the original investment, with the result that the overall tax liability can be considerably reduced. This does not, however, reduce the tax liability on the original investment.

Particular care should be taken by a person who would normally qualify for age allowance, since chargeable excesses or gains on a bond are counted as income for the purpose of determining whether the age allowance should be reduced. Top-slicing relief has no effect in these circumstances. However, the 5% per annum withdrawals can be taken without affecting the age allowance.

3:13.3 Investment bonds – partial withdrawals

The taxation position of partial withdrawals from an investment bond is as follows.

(a) Any tax liability is based on the realisation proceeds and not the actual profit thereon. This can produce very harsh results where withdrawals are substantial (see planning hint **(a)**, section **3:13.4**).

(b) Annual withdrawals of 5% per annum of the original investment can be made with no immediate liability to tax but these will be taken into account on final encashment.

(c) The 5% allowances operate on a cumulative basis so, for example, if withdrawals are not taken in the first four years, a tax deferred withdrawal of 25% of the original investment can be taken in the fifth year.

(d) Tax deferred withdrawals are limited to 100% of the original investment (20 years at 5%).

(e) When a withdrawal is made in excess of the above allowances, a chargeable event is deemed to occur. If the bondholder is subject to higher rate tax, the excess may then be liable to income tax at the difference between the higher and basic rate. All withdrawals in a policy year are added together for the purposes of the calculation.

(f) The tax payable is calculated with reference to top-slicing relief which is explained in section **3:13.1(d)**. However, the period over which the gain is top sliced for partial encashments is limited to the number of years which have expired since the most recent chargeable event, or the start of the contract if there has not been a previous chargeable event. However, the year of the partial encashment counts as a further year for top-slicing. For example, a partial encashment after two-and-a-half years, with no previous chargeable gains, would be top sliced over three years.

This is illustrated in the following example.

Example 5

An investment bond is purchased for £10,000 and partial withdrawals are made as follows:

during year 1 – £ 500
during year 4 – £1,400
during year 5 – £2,500
during year 7 – £2,000

End of year	*Cumulative allowance (5% p.a.)*	*Withdrawals in year*	*Total withdrawals*	*Chargeable excess*
	£	*£*	*£*	*£*
1	500	500	500	Nil
2	1,000	Nil	500	Nil
3	1,500	Nil	500	Nil
4	2,000	1,400	1,900	Nil
5	2,500	2,500	4,400	1,900
6	500	Nil	Nil	Nil
7	1,000	2,000	2,000	1,000

For the purposes of top-slicing relief, the chargeable excess of £1,900 in year 5 is divided by 5 and the chargeable excess of £1,000 in year 7 is divided by 2.

(g) Chargeable excesses are calculated on a policy year (not a tax year) basis. For example:

(i) if the bond in Example 5 was purchased for £10,000 on 2 January 1998; and

(ii) if the partial withdrawal of £2,500 in year 5 was on 10 January 2002 (bringing cumulative withdrawals to £4,400 after five complete policy years ending on 1 January 2003); then

(iii) the tax charge would be based on the policy year ending 1 January 2003, in fiscal year 2002/03;

(iv) cumulative allowances to 1 January 2003 are £2,500, resulting in a chargeable excess of £1,900; and

(v) tax due on the chargeable excess would be payable in January 2004.

3:13.4 Planning hints

The following courses are suggested.

(a) Take out a series of smaller bonds in lieu of one larger bond to provide greater flexibility (as mentioned above, this is often achieved by dividing a bond into a number of identical cluster policies or segments). In this way, the bondholder can totally encash a smaller bond if required, rather than resort to a partial encashment of a larger bond with the possible penal tax consequences.

(b) Postpone taking withdrawals when markets are low to avoid the encashment of an undue number of units in the bond fund. This also applies to any automatic withdrawal facility where the bondholder does not need to rely on the withdrawals for income; it is best to defer the first payment for at least six months to allow the price time to recover part of the bid/offer spread.

3:14 Position on death

3:14.1 Unit trusts

At present, there is no capital gains tax payable on gains at death. Consequently, if a unit trust is held until death, capital gains tax will be avoided.

3:14.2 Investment bonds

As already mentioned, death is one of the 'chargeable events', when the bid value of the units of the bond is used in calculating the amount of the gain. If the life cover exceeds the bid value of the units, the excess will not be taken into account in calculating the income tax charge. This charge will be an allowable deduction from the estate in calculating the inheritance tax liability.

3:15 Trusts and settlements

A bond can, in certain cases, be advantageous for some trusts and settlements in that it is a non-income producing asset and there is no tax liability on the settlor, trustee or beneficiary until it is encashed. However, before an investment is made in a bond, it is necessary to ensure that the trustees have the power to invest in non-income producing assets and also the power to invest in life assurance policies. A bond can be particularly suitable in the following circumstances:

- in accumulation and maintenance settlements for the benefit of children;
- as gifts to children either absolutely or contingent upon their attainment of a certain age.

As previously mentioned, an equity income unit trust can be very useful in a trust situation where the requirement is to provide a balance of income for the life tenant and capital growth for the remaindermen. Bonds are not suitable for this purpose because they produce no income. All withdrawals are regarded as coming out of capital.

3:16 Personalised bond funds

Some insurance companies permit individuals with a large investment portfolio to have their own private bond fund for these investments. This enables investors to retain some influence over the management of their investments while receiving the same tax treatment as that applying to investment bonds. The introduction in the Finance Act 1998 of an additional tax charge on personalised bonds issued by offshore life assurance companies in respect of any policy year ending after 5 April 2000 has meant that these bonds are now unattractive to all but a minority of investors. Most bonds of this type now only offer a choice of investments restricted to assets which do not bring the bond within this legislation (for example, unit trusts, OEICs, investment trusts, the insurance company's internal funds or cash. Stocks and shares are not permitted).

The tax charge is based on a deemed 'gain' equal to 15% of the premiums paid each year, and the total of deemed 'gains' from previous years. A deemed gain will also arise on termination of the policy and be taxed in addition to the normal tax charge. A policy year ends on the day before each anniversary of the creation of the policy.

3:17 Share exchange schemes

If an individual already owns stocks and shares, it will often be possible to exchange these investments for unit trusts or investment bonds on favourable terms such as the following.

- Where the individual has stocks and shares with a minimum value of typically £1,000 and these investments are accepted into the portfolios of the unit trust or insurance company, the offer or middle prices are normally allowed on the stocks and shares exchanged, with no deduction being made for selling expenses.

- Where the stocks and shares have a ready market but the unit trust or insurance company does not wish to take them into its portfolios, they will usually be sold on the individual's behalf, often with a waiver of the selling expenses. Accordingly, the gross proceeds are applied to the purchase of the unit trust holding or investment bond.

In all other cases, the individual would be required to dispose of his own investments and bear the charges. Where a person exchanges an investment in this way, it will be treated as a disposal for capital gains tax purposes. Although the terms offered by some share exchange schemes are more advantageous than others, it should be remembered that it is the future performance of the unit trust or investment bond selected that will generally be of far greater importance.

3:18 Unit trusts or investment bonds?

Before a decision is taken as to which of these is the more suitable investment medium, an investor may wish to take one or more of the following factors into account.

(a) Whether the particular fund being considered is available in the form of both a unit trust and an investment bond. In many cases, the fund is only one or the other.

(b) The current and future tax position of the individual. This is of particular importance in the case of investment bonds where the marginal rate of tax payable by the individual in the year of final encashment will be a major factor in determining the amount of any tax liability. Although the maximum personal tax liability is restricted to 18% in 2002/03, this is likely to change if there is an alteration in income tax rates in subsequent years.

(c) The age of the individual. A bond is not normally so suitable for a younger person (say, under age 50) since it is more difficult to postpone final encashment until the time when the investor's income is low, such as following retirement. A bond may also not be suitable for a very elderly person, since death may cause tax to become payable.

(d) The investor's potential capital gains tax position. If the investment objective is capital growth, a unit trust will usually be more suitable if the investor rarely makes use of the annual capital gains tax exemption. Realised gains made within an investment bond are currently subject to capital gains tax at 20% and this cannot be recovered by the bondholder.

(e) Whether a regular 'income' is required. Investment bonds normally provide greater flexibility in this respect, although a number of unit trust managers offer regular income facilities (which may involve selling some units to make the payments up to the required level).

(f) Whether the investment is to be used for a particular purpose, such as in an accumulation and maintenance settlement, or as a gift to children.

(g) Whether the individual is likely to make use of the fund switching facility available within most investment bonds, which, unlike a unit trust switch, does not crystallise a capital gain.

(h) A comparison of the charges, and any discounts available.

3:19 Investment trusts and unit trusts compared

Investment trusts, although companies quoted on the stock market, have many features similar to unit trusts, including full-time professional management, a wide investment spread and the same tax treatment for investors. However, investment trusts have several characteristics which distinguish them from unit trusts.

(a) Investment trust shares may be bought and sold through a stockbroker, but many management groups now offer a cheap dealing service for private investors. By using their own stockbrokers and dealing in large quantities, they are able to offer very low commission rates. The disadvantage is that smaller transactions may only take place weekly, so that the share price may well have changed since the investor made the decision to buy or sell.

Unit trusts are open-ended funds which create or redeem units according to demand. Units are always bought from and sold to their managers. An initial charge of 5% to 6% is usually made when units are sold to an investor.

(b) The share capital of an investment trust is fixed. Consequently, its shares are not redeemed when a large number of investors wish to sell, for example in plummeting markets. With a unit trust, the number of units in issue can be increased or reduced, and if a lot of unitholders sell, the fund manager has to realise investments to provide the cash with which to pay them. A fund which is gradually expanding is normally easier to manage from an investment viewpoint than a fund which is static or contracting.

(c) The share price of an investment trust fluctuates in accordance with the supply and demand for its shares, which can usually be purchased at a discount to the value of its underlying assets. The price at which a unit trust is bought and sold is based directly on the value of its underlying assets (subject to the provisions regarding the calculation of the bid/offer spread). Fluctuations in an investment trust's discount (or premium) will enhance or damage its share price performance.

(d) An investment trust may be converted into a unit trust, or subjected to a takeover (the buyer's object being to acquire an investment portfolio cheaply). In both cases, the investment trust shareholder is likely to make a windfall profit as the discount is eliminated. Unit trusts can only be merged at their net asset value.

(e) The mood of the UK stock market normally has a greater effect on the share price of an investment trust than on the price of a unit trust (the price of an investment trust can be affected even when its underlying assets are wholly invested outside the UK). Accordingly, investment trust prices will often show greater movements than their underlying assets, even before taking into account the effect of any gearing (see **(g)** below). This could, therefore, have an adverse result for shareholders wishing to dispose of their shares in a falling market when the discount on assets often widens, with the reverse applying in a rising market when the discount frequently narrows.

(f) An investment trust has the freedom to invest entirely in unquoted securities, while no more than 10% of a unit trust portfolio may be invested in this way.

(g) An investment trust is able to effect 'gearing' by issuing prior capital in the form of preference shares, debentures or loan stocks and by utilising short-term borrowing facilities. The effect of gearing on an investment trust is that an increase or decrease in the value of its total assets will have an exaggerated effect on the change in the value of the net assets per ordinary share. This arises because the holders of prior capital are entitled to a fixed return of capital if the investment trust is wound up, with the value of the remaining assets being divided between the ordinary shareholders. Gearing also has a similar effect on income. A unit trust is only permitted to borrow within very strict limits and therefore gearing can only be introduced to a minor extent.

(h) A particular type of investment trust which could be suitable to investors seeking specifically either income or capital growth is a split capital trust. These trusts, which were first introduced in the mid-1960s, have a fixed winding-up date and can have several different classes of share capital, with clearly defined rights; in each case the payment of the promised amount on a winding up is dependent on the adequacy of the trust's assets.

(i) *Zero dividend preference shares* (zeros) have a fixed entitlement on winding up, in priority to other classes of share. As their name implies, they pay no dividends; their return is entirely in the form of a predetermined rate of capital appreciation. They are therefore suitable for higher rate income taxpayers who can use their annual capital gains tax exemption and/or taper relief to minimise the impact of tax on their gains.

(ii) *Stepped preference shares* are also prior capital. They offer a fixed and increasing (hence 'stepped') rate of income and a fixed capital entitlement at the end of the trust's life. They are therefore suitable for cautious investors who require predictable returns.

(iii) *Income shares* are entitled to the whole of the trust's income (after prior charges). Since, as a class, they represent only part of the capital but receive all its income, they are 'geared' and are able to pay dividends at a much higher rate than conventional ordinary shares. Their capital entitlement varies: a 'traditional' income share will be repaid at its par value or its original subscription price when the trust is wound up, whereas the repayment price of an 'annuity' income share may be 1p or less. 'Traditional' shares are usually issued with capital shares; 'annuity' shares with zeros and capital shares.

(iv) *Ordinary income shares* are sometimes (more accurately) called highly geared income shares; the latter term highlights the risks of buying them. They are issued in conjunction with zeros and are entitled to the whole of the trust's income and, on winding up, all the assets remaining after the zeros have been repaid. Their price is therefore very sensitive to changes in the value of the underlying portfolio. All types of income share are useful for those seeking a high income, although this will often be at the expense of capital appreciation.

(v) *Capital shares* have no rights to income, but on winding up are entitled to the whole of the assets remaining after all other classes of capital have been repaid. They therefore suit investors who can accept above average risk in pursuit of high capital gains.

There are two other types of investment trust security, both of which entitle their holders to acquire ordinary or income shares.

(i) *Convertible loan stock*, which may be exchanged into shares at the holder's option on fixed dates and in a predetermined proportion.

(ii) *Warrants*, which are no more than a right to subscribe for new shares in the trust at a predetermined price. They are frequently offered 'free' to those who subscribe for shares when a trust is launched. They can, however, be traded independently of the shares – but are for speculators only.

A unit trust is only able to offer one type of unit, since all investors have a *pro rata* share of the fund. Investors do, however, sometimes have a choice between income units and accumulation units. Holders of income units are paid the income to which they are entitled or have it applied to secure additional units, whereas holders of accumulation units have the income accumulated within the fund to enhance the value of their existing units. The reinvested income is nevertheless treated as taxable income of the unitholder.

(i) An investment trust may retain some of its income and use the revenue resources created to supplement its dividend payments when its portfolio income drops. Unit trusts have to pay out all of their income.

(j) An investment trust is effectively prohibited from advertising its shares in the way a unit trust can advertise its units.

(k) The annual management charges of the older and larger investment trusts tend to be lower than those of unit trusts.

3:19.1 Conclusion

Although the choice between an investment trust and a unit trust or OEIC will depend on individual circumstances, the factors which are likely to be of particular importance in determining which will prove to be a better investment are:

(a) the expertise of the investment managers;

(b) the investment scope of the fund (the desired combination of investments may only be available in one form or the other);

(c) the size of the discount on assets at which an investment trust may be bought.

3:20 Unit trust and investment trust regular savings plans

Unit trust and investment trust regular savings plans are investment schemes whereby a fixed amount is invested on a regular basis (usually monthly). These plans are particularly useful to an individual who wishes to spread his investment over a period, rather than commit a lump sum at a particular time. However, although a decision on timing is largely removed, it should be remembered that the investor will only benefit from rising values to the extent that he has already invested in the savings plan.

One of the benefits of regular savings plans is that of 'pound cost averaging', whereby more units are automatically acquired from the regular investment when prices are low than when they are high. Consequently, the average cost per unit purchased over a period is lower than the average of the market prices during that period. Although pound cost averaging is likely to produce greater benefits with a volatile fund than with a more stable fund, it is even more important if a volatile fund is selected that the investor should have the flexibility to be able to postpone encashment until the market is considered high.

The same care should be taken in choosing a regular savings plan as with a lump sum investment. If large regular investments are to be made, it is normally worthwhile to divide the contributions into a number of different plans.

One particular problem which can arise with regular savings plans is the calculation of capital gains tax. Since each contribution to a plan counts as a separate investment, a large number of capital gains tax calculations may be necessary to calculate the indexation allowance when the plans are encashed. However, for disposals made after 5 April 1988, it is possible for an investor to apply for a simplified method to operate, whereby fixed monthly savings are aggregated each year and treated as a single sum invested in the seventh month of the trust's accounting year. Additional payments can also be included, provided they do not exceed twice the regular monthly investment. Otherwise, lump sums will be treated separately.

This problem does not arise for investments since 6 April 1998, as taper relief operates by reference to the number of complete years after that date an asset has been held at the date of its disposal. Each 'batch' of monthly investments in a 12-month period will, therefore, qualify for the same rate of relief. Investments paid before 5 April 1998 constitute a single asset, and those paid before 17 March 1998 benefit from an extra year's taper relief. Investments made within three years before a disposal do not qualify for any taper relief.

3:21 Guaranteed equity bonds

Guaranteed equity bonds are technically insurance bonds issued for a fixed period which offer a combination of:

(a) a minimum guaranteed return, which may be:

(i) the return of the initial investment, either as a capital payment or (in the case of high income bonds) as a combination of income during the period and capital at maturity; or

(ii) the return of a multiple (say 1.25 times) of the initial investment; and

(b) an additional return based on the performance of a share index, which may either be in line with the movement of the index or an enhanced multiple (say 120%) of it.

They are thus, at first glance, attractive to investors who wish to obtain an equity-based return but without the risk of losing money.

The guarantees do, however, have a price. Among the disadvantages are:

(a) the investor may not receive a return in line with that from the index. Often only a percentage (say 95%) of the initial investment moves with the index and there is sometimes a limit on the extent of the gains;

(b) to avoid the effect of a sudden drop in the index near the end of the fixed period, the final index figure is averaged, say over the last six months;

(c) the investor receives no income;

(d) capital is tied up for the fixed period. Encashment is either not permitted or is subject to a severe penalty;

(e) higher rate taxpayers will have an additional liability on the maturity of the bond;

(f) if only the initial capital is returned, it will have been eroded by inflation.

3:22 Protected unit trusts

With the recent falls in share prices, there has been an increased interest in products which offer a degree of protection to the capital invested. The protection comes in a variety of forms: one is a promise that the bid price of the fund will not fall by more than, say, 2% over a three-month period. The upside return is usually linked to the FTSE-100 Index.

The investment managers generally provide the guarantees by investing the majority of the fund in cash and then using the remaining small proportion of the fund to buy an exposure to the FTSE-100 Index through call options. There are, however, a variety of other techniques.

The potential investor in this type of fund needs to be aware of the following disadvantages, which counterbalance the greater security in the event of a stock market fall:

(a) the degree of protection is often related to the bid (selling) price. Since the units are acquired at the offer price, the investor will suffer the full bid/offer spread in spite of having the impact of the market fall limited;

(b) some of the funds pay no income; and

(c) the need to commit some of the fund to assets providing the protection may result in growth lower than on the underlying portfolio.

4 Personal equity plans and individual savings accounts

In order to promote individual share ownership and to give investors a personal interest and a direct stake in UK companies, personal equity plans (PEPs) were introduced with effect from 1 January 1987. Substantial improvements to PEPs were made in subsequent Finance Acts, and from 1 January 1992, investors could take out a 'single company' PEP, in addition to a general PEP, in each tax year. The last subscriptions to PEPs were paid on 5 April 1999; they were succeeded by Individual Savings Accounts (ISAs), but plans in existence on that date continue.

4:1 Main features of PEPs

The main features of PEPs are as follows.

(a) Any UK resident aged 18 or over was able to invest up to £6,000 per annum in a general PEP and £3,000 in a single company PEP. Subscriptions had to be paid by cheque; shares could be transferred into a PEP only in the following circumstances, and subject to time limits:

   (i) shares newly issued in a public offer;

   (ii) shares allotted under a savings-related share option scheme or an approved profit-sharing scheme into a single company PEP; and

   (iii) shares issued to members on the demutualisation of a building society or life assurance company.

   In the first two cases, the cost or value of the shares counted towards the annual subscription limit. In the third case, the shares were treated as having a 'nil' value, and so did not count towards the limit.

(b) Authorised PEP managers included members of the stock exchange, licensed security dealers, banks, building societies and unit and investment trust managers. Some companies offered plans invested only in their own shares (corporate PEPs); these could have been either general or single company plans.

(c) No tax is payable either on capital gains or income, whether paid out or reinvested, in respect of investments held within a PEP or on withdrawals of capital. However, interest arising from cash holdings is subject to savings rate tax in the same way as bank or building society deposits if the amount paid to the investor exceeds £180 in any tax year.

(d) Investments which may be held in a PEP are now (following a change effective from 6 April 2001) the same as for ISAs – see **4:2**.

Single company PEPs (which can now be merged with general PEPs) could only hold:

(i) ordinary shares of UK companies which had a full stock exchange listing; and

(ii) unquoted shares transferred under **(a)(ii)** above.

(e) There is no need for an investor to report details of his plans to the Inland Revenue as the plan manager is responsible for reclaiming the tax on income and for all the paperwork.

(f) A PEP can be transferred from one plan manager to another.

(g) Planholders must be sent regular statements, at least annually, showing details of all plan investments and cash held, the value of the investments, the prices at which purchases and sales have been made and details of all dividends and interest.

(h) There is no limit to the plan manager's charges, but they must be clearly disclosed. Charges can include an initial fee, annual charges for both first and subsequent years, dealing costs, charges on the number of assets held, withdrawal from the plan (including switching to another plan manager), receiving the annual report and accounts and attendance at annual general meetings of companies whose shares are held, and other sundry expenses mainly covering portfolio valuations additional to the first in a year.

4:2 Main features of individual savings accounts

Like PEPs, ISAs are governed by their own regulations. The main features are as follows.

(a) Any UK resident aged 18 or over is able to invest up to £7,000 in each tax year. Those aged 16 and 17 may open cash mini-ISAs. Accounts may not be opened in joint names but, in the case of married couples, both husband and wife may have independent accounts. Subscriptions may be paid by cheque or electronically and applications can have effect for successive years. The only shares which may be transferred into an ISA are those allotted under a savings-related share option scheme or an approved profit sharing scheme. The transfer must take place within 90 days of their transfer to the investor.

(b) An ISA may consist of up to three components:

   (i) a cash component, with a subscription limit of £3,000 each year;

   (ii) an insurance component, with a subscription limit of £1,000 each year; and

   (iii) a stocks and shares component, with a subscription limit of £7,000, less amounts paid to the other components in that year.

   An account which contains all three components or consists only of a stocks and shares component is known as a 'maxi-ISA'. An investor may open only one maxi-ISA each year. Each component may, however, exist separately and an investor may use the products of different providers for each one in each year. In this event, each product is classed as a 'mini-ISA'.

(c) Additionally, an investor may hold a 'TESSA-only' ISA or TOISA, that is, one which has had paid into it the capital element of a matured TESSA (i.e. a maximum of £9,000). The transfer from the TESSA must take place within six months of the maturity date. Alternatively, the investor may transfer the capital element of his matured TESSA to the cash component of a maxi-ISA or to a mini-ISA consisting of a cash component; in both cases, the amount transferred does not count towards the subscription limit.

(d) ISAs will continue to be available at least until 5 April 2009, although the government intends to review them in 2006.

(e) Accounts must be offered by an ISA manager approved by the Inland Revenue. Managers must be:

   (i) authorised under the Financial Services and Markets Act 2000;

   (ii) a European institution permitted to operate in the UK;

   (iii) a bank, building society or permitted European institution (for a cash component only); or

   (iv) an insurance company or friendly society (for the life assurance component only).

(f) No tax is payable either on capital gains or income, whether paid out or reinvested, in respect of investments within an ISA, or on withdrawals of capital, with one exception. Interest on cash held within the stocks and shares or insurance component of a maxi-ISA is paid, subject to the deduction of income tax at 20%, but the interest is otherwise tax exempt and does not have to be reported on the investor's tax return. Tax credits on dividends will be recoverable by the account manager for the benefit of investors in the stocks and shares and insurance components only for the first five years (i.e. until 5 April 2004). Tax deducted from interest will be repayable throughout.

(g) There is no minimum period of ownership required to retain the tax reliefs. Capital and income can be withdrawn at any time, but the account provider may impose charges on withdrawals or on transfers to other managers.

(h) No tax relief is given on subscriptions to an ISA.

(i) Investments which may be held in a stocks and shares component are:

(i) shares issued by a company wherever incorporated and officially listed on a recognised stock exchange. Unlisted shares and those dealt in on the Alternative Investment Market are not permitted;

(ii) securities issued by a company (not an investment trust) wherever incorporated, whose shares or securities are listed on a recognised stock exchange. The securities must not be repayable within five years;

(iii) gilt-edged securities and securities issued by the government of any EEA state which are not repayable within five years;

(iv) shares in or securities of an investment trust, provided its rental income is less than 50% of its total investment income;

(v) units in an authorised unit trust or an authorised UK OEIC, including umbrella funds and funds of funds;

(vi) a UCITS (see **3:5**), provided that not more than 50% of its investments are securities which are not qualifying securities;

(vii) shares acquired under a savings related share option scheme or approved profit sharing scheme; and

(viii) cash (subject to the limitation at **(f)** above).

(j) Investments which may be held in the insurance component are:

(i) single premium life assurance policies on the life of the investor, which cannot be assigned (annuities, pension contracts and personal portfolio bonds are specifically excluded); and

(ii) cash (subject to the limitation at **(f)** above).

(k) Investments which may be held in a cash component are:

(i) cash deposited in a bank, building society or permitted European institution;

(ii) units in a money market fund; and

(iii) deposits or accounts with National Savings & Investments.

These accounts must not be linked to another account in an arrangement giving particularly favourable terms.

(l) There is no need for an investor to report details of his accounts to the Inland Revenue as the account manager is responsible for reclaiming the tax on income and for all the paperwork.

(m) ISAs may be transferred to a different manager at any time after the year of subscription.

(n) If requested by investors, the account manager must arrange for them to receive the annual report and accounts of all companies in which they hold shares. Similarly, investors can request to attend shareholders' meetings, exercise voting rights and obtain other shareholder information. A charge can be (and usually is) made by the manager for these facilities.

(o) Investors must be sent regular statements, at least annually, showing details of all investments and cash held, the value of the investments, the prices at which purchases and sales have been made and details of all dividends and interest.

(p) There is no limit to the account manager's charges, but the government has set benchmarks for ISAs which meet strict criteria for low charges, easy access and fair terms (the 'CAT standards'). Charges must be clearly disclosed and may include one or more of an initial fee, annual charges for both first and subsequent years, dealing costs, charges on the number of assets held, withdrawal from the plan (including switching to another plan manager), receiving the annual report and accounts and attendance at annual general meetings of companies whose shares are held, and other sundry expenses mainly covering portfolio valuations additional to the first in a year.

4:3 Principal advantages and disadvantages

The following are the principal advantages and disadvantages of PEPs and ISAs compared to other main savings media.

4:3.1 Advantages

(a) No tax is payable, either on capital gains or on dividend income, in respect of investments held within a PEP or an ISA (this can be particularly advantageous where the main purpose of the investments is to produce a high income).

(b) Non-taxpayers can avoid the need to reclaim tax by investing in ISAs. Until 5 April 2004, they can also benefit from the recovery of the 10% dividend tax credit, which is not repayable if the holding is owned directly.

(c) There is no additional charge for buying a unit trust through a PEP or ISA; indeed some managers charge less for these plans than for direct investments.

(d) PEPs and ISAs can be discontinued at any time without loss of the tax benefits.

(e) All returns to the Inland Revenue are dealt with by the plan manager. An individual need not disclose the investments or income on his tax return.

4:3.2 Disadvantages

(a) Any specific PEP or ISA administration charge could outweigh the amount of tax relief on dividends, now that the rate of tax credit has fallen to 10%. When the repayment of tax credits to PEPs and ISAs ends on 5 April 2004, the balance between costs and benefits will need to be reviewed even more carefully. Plans which do not levy a separate charge are, therefore, to be preferred.

(b) The maximum investment in ISAs is restricted to £7,000 per tax year per person.

4:4 Other considerations

Other considerations which should be borne in mind are as follows.

(a) The quality of investment management, whether in a discretionary plan or a collective fund, is of paramount importance. This is likely to have a greater bearing on the final investment return than the level of charges.

(b) PEPs and ISAs should normally be regarded as medium- to long-term investments, in the same way as the underlying securities. Any additional initial charges are diluted over a period and the tax benefits increase as the capital and income grow.

(c) The ISA regulations allow investors to invest their own funds and subscriptions may also be paid as a gift.

(d) ISA managers must allow a 14-day 'cooling-off' period, within which an investor must be allowed to change his mind and withdraw his application. If he does so, he will not receive a refund of his full subscription if the value of his investment has fallen.

4:5 Conclusion

The tax reliefs provided are relatively small in view of the fact that:

(a) dividend tax credits are now at only 10%, and, if attached to taxable dividends, satisfy a basic rate taxpayer's liability on that income;

(b) the majority of investors do not pay capital gains tax, as their gains are normally within their annual exemption; and

(c) long-term capital gains are subject to taper relief, which for a higher rate taxpayer reduces the effective tax rate to 24% after ten years.

Accordingly, PEPs and ISAs are most advantageous for higher rate taxpayers who regularly make use of their annual capital gains tax exemption. However, for those investors who wish to start unit trust or investment trust portfolios, an investment within an ISA will be more advantageous because of the tax-exempt environment. For this reason, ISAs are useful vehicles for funding the repayment of mortgages, long-term saving for education fees and as a supplement to approved pension arrangements when saving for retirement.

It should be noted that the favourable tax and charging structure and the lack of penalties on ceasing payments make monthly ISA savings plans a considerably more attractive proposition than ten-year life assurance savings plans, for even the smallest investor.

5 Land and property investments

As an asset class, land and property investments provide a useful complement to stockmarket investments in a portfolio. This has the benefit of reducing the overall risk, as the prices of different types of property move in different (and usually, longer) cycles to those of shares and fixed interest securities.

Property (particularly commercial property) has the following characteristics, some of which it shares with equities and gilts:

(a) it is a 'real' asset, being tangible and, over many periods, a useful hedge against inflation;

(b) it has the potential to appreciate in value, reflecting an expanding economy and/or the benefit of refurbishment or other improvements;

(c) price movements are less volatile than those of equities – and, in the last ten years, gilts as well; and

(d) it provides a stable and growing income, with yields on commercial property (in May 2002) above those of both equities and gilts. Rent increases are reflected in higher capital values. The security of rental income does, however, depend on the quality of the tenant.

There are, however, a number of disadvantages of which potential investors should be aware:

(a) although the property market is well established and efficient, it can be illiquid. It may take some time to arrange a purchase or sale at the right price;

(b) there are significant acquisition costs in the form of legal fees and associated costs and stamp duty;

(c) there are essential running costs, such as insurance and maintenance; and

(d) there will be no income from a let property if a tenant cannot be found or the occupant defaults.

5:1 Main residence

Most investors will already have an investment in property through the ownership of their own home. Given the substantial value which this may represent, it may not be appropriate for them to make any further investment in property.

An individual should, however, regard his main residence primarily as a home for himself and his family and not an investment or a financial planning tool. In most cases it will produce no income and, if sold, the proceeds are likely to be needed to purchase another home.

Home ownership has been encouraged by:

(a) the granting of income tax relief on interest on the first £30,000 of loans for house purchase (although this was ended on 5 April 2000 except for home income plans purchased by the elderly before that date – see **13:8.1**); and

(b) the exemption of the sale proceeds from capital gains tax. The rules for this include a deemed extension of the period of residence for periods of absence for:

   (i) any reason totalling up to three years;

   (ii) employment elsewhere in the UK totalling up to four years; or

   (iii) employment abroad with no limit.

The exemption normally applies to the house and grounds of up to half a hectare, but a larger area is allowed if it is appropriate to the size and character of the house.

Further income tax relief for owner-occupiers covers income from letting a furnished room in their main residence. This 'rent-a-room' relief was introduced as an incentive to those with spare rooms to let them out. Gross rents from such lettings (including the provision of certain services, for example, meals) are exempt from tax if they do not exceed an annual amount of £4,250. If the gross rents do exceed this, taxpayers can elect to pay tax on the excess over £4,250 (without relief for expenses) or to compute the taxable amount in the normal way (i.e. rent less expenses).

5:2 Second homes

Some families buy a second home (e.g. a cottage in the country or at the seaside) for use at weekends and for holidays. Having been acquired for their personal use and enjoyment, the property will not, in many cases, be let and so will produce no income. There may be a return in the form of a capital gain when the property is sold, but in the meantime the owner will have to bear the cost of insurance, maintenance, etc. If the second home is only used occasionally, security will also be a concern.

Where an individual owns two homes, he may, within two years of the purchase of the second, elect (by giving notice to the Inland Revenue) for one of them to be regarded as his principal private residence for capital gains tax purposes. This need not be the property which is occupied for most of the time and the election can be varied subsequently. Any gain on the home which is not so designated will, on disposal, be subject to capital gains tax and so should be the one which is likely to show the smaller gain. If the owner will, in time, use the property as his home in retirement, then it should be borne in mind that any gain on death is exempt. If it is possible that a loss may arise on the sale of either property, the election should be made for that property not to be the principal private residence, so that the loss is allowable.

If an election is not made, the property which is to benefit from the principal private residence relief will be determined by the facts of the case (for example, by the amount of time spent in each one).

There is no tax relief on interest on a loan for the purchase of a second home.

5:3 Let residential property

Any type of residential accommodation which is suitable for occupation, from flats for students to luxury apartments and country mansions, can be purchased for letting to occupational tenants. Because of their own experience in the residential property market, many investors favour this type of asset and, as interest rates fell, the late 1990s saw the emergence of a number of 'buy to let' schemes for new properties promoted by developers. For a time, the level of rents which could be achieved provided a significant margin over the cost of finance, but investors need to exercise great care to ensure that their investment is likely to be profitable. An over-supply of properties, a decline in the level of rents, periods without a tenant and any rise in interest rates could result in the investment becoming uneconomic.

The key to successful letting is to find a satisfactory tenant who will not only pay the rent promptly but also look after the property. Some investors rely on an agent to find a tenant, prepare a proper tenancy agreement, collect the rent and deal with all other aspects of management. The agent's fees for this will be deducted from the rent collected. Others prefer to take care of the property management themselves.

For income tax, the management expenses, an allowance for wear and tear of furniture and any mortgage interest paid may be deducted from the rental income to arrive at the net income subject to tax. If more than one let property is owned, the income and expenses for all of them, both furnished and unfurnished, are combined. In general, any gain on sale is subject to capital gains tax; if the property has been occupied by the owner, however, the gain is time apportioned to exclude the period of owner-occupation. There is, however, an additional exemption, being the lower of an absolute limit of £40,000 and the amount of the gain exempted by virtue of the principal private residence provisions.

5:3.1 Furnished holiday accommodation

A special set of tax rules applies to property which qualifies as furnished holiday accommodation. Briefly, the rental income is deemed to be trading income and so is classified as earned income. It can, therefore, form the basis for contributions to a personal pension plan and losses can be offset under the usual rules for trading losses. For capital gains tax:

(a) the property is treated as business property for taper relief (see **12:2**);

(b) relief for the replacement of business assets (roll-over relief) is available if the whole of the proceeds of the sale are reinvested in further assets to be used for a trade. The purchase of the property may also serve to defer a chargeable gain on a business asset previously sold; and

(c) retirement relief is available until 5 April 2003 (see **12:2**).

The legislation provides a detailed definition of what qualifies as a holiday letting. It is worth noting that the property does not have to be located in a holiday resort. The principal requirement is that it must be available to be let for at least 140 days in a 12-month period, and must actually be let for at least 70 days in that period, of which no more than 31 consecutive days are to the same person.

5:4 Residential property overseas

Many of the principles discussed in previous sections of this chapter also apply to residential property overseas – with the added problems of distance, local laws and taxes and fluctuating exchange rates. In investment terms the principal financial return is likely to be from capital appreciation, although property may also be let at least for part of the time. Expert local advice on both the property market and aspects of property ownership in the overseas location must be taken before purchasing.

UK-resident and domiciled individuals are taxable on rental income, less expenses and mortgage interest, from letting property overseas. Only a proportion of the expenses will be deductible if the property is partly occupied by the owner and travel expenses will not be allowable at all if there is an element of private purpose to a visit. Foreign tax can normally be offset against the UK liability. If the owner is either not domiciled in the UK or a British subject not ordinarily resident in the UK, he or she will be assessable to income tax only on net rental income remitted to the UK.

On the sale of the overseas property, any gain will be subject to capital gains tax if the owner is UK-resident or ordinarily resident and domiciled. If he is not UK-domiciled, however, the gain is only taxable if the proceeds are remitted to the UK. Any foreign tax paid on the capital gain can be offset against the UK liability.

Professional advice is essential if it is intended to own the overseas property through a company or other structure. An arrangement designed to minimise one tax (in the UK or abroad) may give rise to a liability of a different type elsewhere, or exposure to allegations of tax avoidance.

5:5 Time-sharing and multi-ownership

Time-sharing schemes have become popular as a more convenient and cheaper method of financing a holiday home, particularly when outside the UK. Under such a scheme, a person acquires a right to occupy holiday accommodation for an agreed period each year, either indefinitely or for a set number of years, depending on the particular legal requirements in the country concerned. It is achieved by payment of a capital sum at the start of the scheme followed by an annual management or service charge. Properties can be purchased in the UK, many countries within Europe and the United States. To improve flexibility for the time-sharer, weeks can be exchanged from one property to another so that the individual is not tied to a particular holiday destination. Properties may also be sub-let if required. Schemes are organised in a number of formats, including clubs, corporate schemes, licences or leases. The latter two are more common in the United States than in Europe.

The taxation of income (depending on whether the property is in the UK or overseas) and capital gains is as described in previous sections. If, however, there are less than 50 years outstanding on a lease at the date of sale, only a proportion of the cost can be deducted, depending on the period still outstanding.

Most time-share investors purchase for their personal use and thus the opportunity for creating income is limited. The annual maintenance charge is likely to rise with inflation and as the properties get older. The quality of management is all important. The investment may not be easy to realise and should be regarded as a medium- to long-term asset.

5:6 Commercial property

Commercial property represents by far the largest sector in the property market. It includes:

(a) retail – high street shops, out of town centres and retail warehouses;

(b) offices;

(c) commercial – hotels, public houses, nursing homes, etc; and

(d) industrial – factories and warehouses.

The principal investors in commercial property are the listed property companies, life assurance companies and pension funds. Private investors may also buy property directly, and as all four types of commercial property can be found in all parts of the country, there is an enormous variety of buildings and locations to choose from.

Income and capital gains from a commercial property are taxed in the same way as let residential property and interest on a loan taken to finance a purchase can be deducted in calculating the owner's taxable income.

For the average private investor, however, exposure to commercial property is best obtained through some form of collective investment. The following are available.

(a) *Property company shares.* Although not strictly a collective investment, the shares of a listed property company are easy to buy and sell. The prices of such shares, however, tend to move more in line with share prices generally than with property values and can for long periods stand at a discount to the value of the company's property portfolio.

(b) *Insurance bonds.* Most insurance companies include a property fund in their range of unit-linked funds. The portfolio will usually be widely spread between the main sub-sectors. The funds vary considerably in size and performance, but details about the underlying holdings and their returns are not readily available, making selection difficult.

(c) *Investment trusts.* Although there are only three authorised investment trusts in the 'property' sector, they mainly hold property company shares. Only one has direct property, representing about 20% of its assets. The share prices of these trusts normally trade at a discount to the net value of their portfolios.

(d) *Authorised unit trusts.* The discount problem does not arise in the case of unit trusts, the value of whose units is based on the value of their assets. The two authorised unit trusts investing in property are however permitted to hold no more than 70% of their funds in directly owned property, with the other 30% in readily realisable assets such as listed property company shares and cash deposits.

(e) *Unauthorised unit trusts and OEICs.* This group includes enterprise zone property trusts (see **5:7**) and specialist funds investing in, for example, residential property and freehold ground rents. They have more freedom in their choice of investments than authorised unit trusts and may in some cases be able to borrow to enlarge their portfolios. Dealings in their units or shares is likely to take place once a month, rather than on a daily basis.

The tax treatment of each of these types of investment is covered in **Chapter 3**. No tax relief is given on interest on a loan taken for the purpose of buying collective funds (except enterprise zone property trusts) or property company shares.

5:7 Enterprise zone property

Enterprise zones are areas designated by the Government under the Local Government, Planning and Land Act 1980. Typically, they are located where the local economy was heavily dependent on a major industry which had fallen into decline (e.g. ship-building, steel-making, mining and, in London, the docks). The area is, therefore, in need of regeneration and the various benefits of designation as an enterprise zone are intended to attract developers, new industries and both institutional and private investors to finance it.

The principal benefit of investing in an enterprise zone is the 100% industrial buildings capital allowances given on the cost of a qualifying industrial or commercial building. The allowances are not given on the cost of the land element, which may be up to 20% of the total cost. The capital allowances can, if the investor wishes, be taken in the year the investment is made and offset against the rental income from the property and his other income to reduce his overall income tax liability. If he prefers, part of the allowances may be taken in the first year and the balance subsequently.

This type of investment was very popular in the healthy property market of the 1980s, when over 20 zones were designated. The general decline in the market in the 1990s, the expiry of many of the earlier zones (designation lasts for only ten years) and the significant problems encountered by some of the enterprise zone trusts have made it less attractive. Only a few zones remain and there is little property available for retail investors. Partly as a result of this, rental yields have fallen to around 6% per annum.

An investor would need at least £100,000 to buy a reasonable building (although smaller units were available in the 1980s). As the owner, he would be responsible for finding a tenant and managing and maintaining the building. For most investors, however, the more practical ways of acquiring an interest are through a syndicate or a trust. In both cases, a manager finds a suitable property, markets the fund to potential investors and uses their subscriptions to buy the property. Syndicates and trusts are, therefore, available for only a limited period of up to six weeks. The manager then finds a tenant (sometimes a property is pre-let before the fund is launched), collects the rents, pays the expenses, and distributes the net rents to investors. Both structures are transparent for income tax, so, instead of the fund being taxed, each member is taxable on his proportionate share of the net rental income and has the benefit of his share of the total capital allowances.

Enterprise zone syndicates and trusts differ in two main respects.

(a) Syndicates consist of a relatively small number of wealthy individuals, who are required to subscribe at least £50,000 (sometimes £100,000). The minimum subscription for a trust, however, is normally £5,000 and there are, therefore, likely to be many more investors.

(b) The financing of a syndicate includes a bank loan, which is arranged by the manager. This and the tax relief result in the actual cash outlay by a syndicate member being a relatively small percentage of his total subscription. Trusts do not borrow, although the manager usually arranges for a bank to provide a loan facility for investors who wish to make use of it.

Because in both cases the interest can be deducted from the rental income for tax purposes, this is an attractive option, which 'gears' the capital and income returns. If, however, the tenant defaults or one is not found, the investor is left to pay the interest out of his other income.

Potential investors in enterprise zone syndicates and trusts need to be aware of the following potential problems and risks:

(a) the price at which an enterprise zone property is acquired from a developer is typically higher than its open market value. This is a way of allowing the developer to share the benefit of the capital allowances given to investors;

(b) the tax relief given through the capital allowances becomes repayable (through a balancing charge) if:

  (i) the property is sold or a capital payment is received within seven years of acquisition;

  (ii) the property is sold between seven and 25 years from acquisition. If, however, a lesser interest is disposed of (e.g. a long lease is created out of a freehold), the allowances are not reclaimed, because the owner retains his original interest; or

  (iii) the investor disposes of his shares in a syndicate or trust.

  After 25 years the allowances cannot be clawed back;

(c) the investment is potentially very long term. Though trust and syndicate managers will normally seek to sell the property at some stage between seven and 15 years after purchase, this cannot be guaranteed and will depend on conditions in the property market in general and in the enterprise zone in particular. The purchasers will not have the benefit of the initial capital allowances;

(d) at least 75% of the members must agree to the sale or a major alteration to the fund. No one member has control and the members are therefore very reliant on the integrity and efficiency of the manager;

(e) a sound tenant – backed if necessary by a bank or parent company guarantees or rental deposits – is essential. If the rent ceases, not only do the members have no income, they may also be called upon to pay the expenses, in addition to any loan interest. Again, the investors have to rely on the manager to carry out appropriate due diligence.

Any gain on the sale of an enterprise zone property (or shares in an enterprise zone trust) will be subject to capital gains tax, with indexation and taper reliefs applying as appropriate. On the disposal of a property by an enterprise zone trust, and the subsequent distribution of the proceeds to the shareholders, capital gains tax is charged both on the trust and (on the net proceeds paid out) on the individual shareholders.

5:8 Farmland

Investment in farmland can be made in two ways.

(a) By purchasing the land outright and commencing a farming business either personally or in partnership. Although the day-to-day running of the business can be delegated to a manager or to a contract farmer, a degree of personal involvement will be necessary. Returns from agriculture have historically been low and changes brought about by EU regulations and the low prices of some produce have pushed many farming businesses into losses. Any profits are taxable as earned income and there are provisions for profits of consecutive years to be averaged if there are severe fluctuations. Trading losses can be set against other income of the same or the previous year, but this relief may be restricted if losses are made for more than five consecutive years. On a sale, business asset taper relief, retirement relief and roll-over relief may apply when calculating the capital gains tax liability.

(b) By purchasing tenanted farmland. This is a pure investment, like any other in let property, the income deriving from the rent charged to the tenant. This is unearned income, from which relevant expenses and loan interest may be deducted for tax purposes. Any gain on sale will not benefit from the reliefs mentioned in **(a)** above.

5:9 Woodlands

Investment in woodlands was popular with high earning individuals before April 1988 because of the income tax relief given (at the investor's marginal rate) on planting expenditure. Since then, the rate of establishment of new woodlands has dropped and most investment is now made in young and semi-mature plantations by those seeking the capital gains tax and inheritance tax benefits. Some also buy for the pleasure of owning a piece of the British countryside, especially if the property has other amenities such as a holiday home, fishing or stalking. There is also some investment in new woodlands on agricultural land for which special grants are available.

Since conifers take 40 years to mature and deciduous trees over 100 years, woodlands are a long-term investment. Properties are, however, available with crops at differing ages and it is possible to buy a property to suit particular needs for capital growth or income (from the proceeds of felling part of the timber each year).

The principal value of a property is in the growing timber; the land value is relatively low. Most woodlands are purchased through specialist estate agents or forestry management companies. Ownership may be as follows.

(a) *As an individual.* The owner then has complete control of and responsibility for the property. He is likely to engage a manager or management company to ensure that the timber crop is properly looked after.

(b) *As a member of a forestry syndicate.* Each syndicate member contributes a proportion of the initial cost of purchasing a property and then participates pro rata in the expenses, income and eventual sale proceeds. A manager deals with all the administration and the care of the trees.

(c) *As a unitholder in a forestry trust.* From time to time, forestry managers set up unit trusts to raise capital to purchase woodland properties. These are open for subscriptions for only a limited period and normally for a specific capital growth or income objective. There is often a fixed winding-up date.

Following the reform of the taxation of woodlands in the Finance Act 1988, income from the sale of timber and fellings from woodlands run on a commercial basis is exempt from income tax and there is no relief for expenses. Grants are available, subject to conditions, to offset the costs of planting and maintenance.

The proceeds of timber sales are also exempt from capital gains tax, which is, however, chargeable on any appreciation in value of the land element when the property is sold. The capital cost of the woodland (i.e. the land and any capital works, for example, roads) qualifies as a business asset for the purpose of roll-over relief following the sale of a previous business asset.

If woodlands are the subject of a gift or are owned at death, and have been owned for at least two years, business property relief (currently at 100%) will apply, so that no inheritance tax is charged. If tax is payable, an election can be made to defer payment on the timber (but not on the land element) until it is sold. Inheritance tax is then charged on the sale proceeds, not on the value at death.

6 Higher risk and alternative investments

6:1 Introduction

The investments discussed in this chapter are principally those which offer the opportunity of above average returns in exchange for a higher risk of loss. In some cases the potential returns are enhanced (or the potential loss reduced) by the presence of tax reliefs. It is these reliefs which attract many investors to the Enterprise Investment Scheme and venture capital trusts, but each proposition must be evaluated primarily on its investment merits and not pursued for the tax reliefs alone.

Investments in Enterprise Zone property and woodlands (see **Chapter 5**) should also be regarded as high risk.

6:2 Reinvestment relief

Although capital gains tax reinvestment relief is not an investment, it should be borne in mind when considering overall investment strategy. Originally introduced in 1993, it was enhanced in 1994 and merged with the EIS relief with effect from 6 April 1998, so that, to qualify for both reliefs, shares must satisfy the same tests (see **6:4**). Investments in EIS shares up to £150,000 now qualify for both the initial income tax relief and for CGT reinvestment relief, with investments over this limit attracting reinvestment relief only. There is no upper monetary limit for reinvestment relief.

The relief applies where, on realising a chargeable gain on any asset, the investor buys new ordinary shares in a trading company carrying on a qualifying trade or in a venture capital trust. It allows the payment of tax on the realised gains to be deferred, up to the amount of the reinvestment. Reinvestment must be made within one year before the date the gain is realised or:

(a) within one year after, if reinvestment is into a venture capital trust; or

(b) within three years after, if reinvestment is into a trading company.

It should be noted that these time limits are not related to tax years.

Companies whose shares qualify for reinvestment relief have to satisfy a number of conditions. In particular they must carry on a qualifying trade for at least three years from the date of investment.

There are five routes to reinvestment relief.

(a) *Shares in private companies.* Investors may have the opportunity to buy new shares in small private or family-owned companies. This route will appeal to 'business angels', who are able to bring their expertise to assist the business and who may, following their investment, become a director. 'Passive' investors also qualify. Potential investors are responsible for carrying out 'due diligence' on the company and for agreeing an appropriate value for the shares to be issued.

(b) *Shares in public EIS companies.* Many EIS companies invite subscriptions by issuing a public prospectus. The costs of preparing the prospectus make this a relatively expensive course if less than about £1.5 million is to be raised, but it does attract a large number of investors. The information in the prospectus about the company's management and business will enable the prospective investor to form a judgement about its potential for success.

(c) *Personal companies.* Some sponsors of EIS companies also offer the facility to form a 'personal' company for investors seeking reinvestment relief for £400,000 or more. They will provide a qualifying business (usually one conducted by one of their existing EIS companies, and with the same management team), and issue all the shares to the investor. Because his shareholding exceeds the 30% limit for EIS, the investor does not obtain the initial 20% income tax relief, but this does not affect his reinvestment relief. Once the company has carried on its qualifying trade for three years, it is free to conduct any type of business in future (it could, for example, merely hold an investment portfolio). So long as the investor holds his shares the payment of tax on his realised capital gains is deferred, and as he is the sole shareholder he has complete control over the company and its activities.

(d) *AIM shares.* Shares traded on the Alternative Investment Market or the unofficial OFEX market are, for the purposes of reinvestment relief and inheritance tax, regarded as unquoted. Investments into new shares on these markets therefore qualify for reinvestment relief, provided that the company meets all the requirements.

(e) *Venture capital trusts.* These are discussed in more detail at **6:5**.

6:3 Business Expansion Scheme

The Business Expansion Scheme (BES) was introduced in 1983 to encourage private investment in companies seeking equity finance to start or expand their business. In 1988, the list of qualifying trades was extended to include companies investing in property to be let on 'assured tenancies', a new type of tenancy arrangement which was designed to encourage the provision of housing for residential letting. The attraction of investing in relatively risk-free properties severely limited the amount of BES money going into genuine trading companies. Sponsors then developed the 'arranged exit' scheme, under which an institution (commonly a bank, building society or university college) undertook to purchase the BES companies' properties at a price which would provide a fixed return to investors. The major risk of this type of investment was thus removed. This persuaded the government to abolish the BES with effect from 31 December 1993 and most investors will by now have disposed of their shares. The principal tax reliefs were:

(a) income tax relief at the investors' marginal rate on the cost of qualifying ordinary shares (maximum £40,000);

(b) provided the income tax relief was intact after five years, exemption from capital gains tax on disposal; and

(c) if the shares had been held for two years and the company was an unquoted trading company, business property relief (currently at 100%) for inheritance tax.

(b) and (c) will still apply to any remaining BES shares.

6:4 Enterprise Investment Scheme

The Finance Act 1994 introduced the Enterprise Investment Scheme (EIS) as a successor to the Business Expansion Scheme for which the CBI and other business organisations had pressed since the announcement of the ending of BES on 31 December 1993. Like the original intention of BES, the objective is to help small companies to raise equity finance and, in a departure from the BES approach, to encourage investors who wish to become involved in their management. It applies to shares in qualifying unquoted companies issued after 1 January 1994. The EIS was amended in the Finance Act 1998, to make it the basis for capital gains tax reinvestment relief from 6 April 1998. The principal features of the EIS are as follows.

(a) Qualifying companies:

(i) The company must carry on a qualifying trade. Among businesses specifically excluded are leasing, financial and legal services, property investment and those which require a significant property element (e.g. farming, forestry, nursing homes and hotels).

(ii) It must have gross assets of less than £15 million before it raises new capital and no more than £16 million afterwards.

(iii) It must be unquoted (but the shares may be dealt in on the Alternative Investment Market (AIM) or OFEX).

(iv) The company may be incorporated and resident outside the UK, but must carry on business in this country.

(v) There are limits on the periods within which the money raised must be put to use and trading must start.

(vi) There must be no arrangement in place at the time the shares are issued for the disposal of the shares or the business, the cessation of trade or to provide protection against loss for investors. This is intended to exclude the 'arranged exit' schemes which became a feature of the BES.

(b) The investment:

The investment must be in the form of a cash subscription for fully paid *new* ordinary shares (i.e. with no preferential rights to income or assets).

(c) The investor:

(i) The initial income tax relief and the CGT exemption on the sale of the EIS shares are only available to individuals.

(ii) The investor must not be entitled to more than 30% of the issued ordinary share capital, the loan and issued share capital, the voting power in the company or the assets available in a winding up.

(iii) The investor must not be 'connected' with the company, including as a director or employee. He may, however, become a director *after* the issue of his shares.

(iv) He must not receive 'value' from the company (apart from specific exemptions and payments of less than £1,000) during the five-year period starting two years before the issue of the shares.

(d) The tax reliefs:

(i) Income tax:

- Initial income tax relief of 20% of the cost of the shares (maximum £150,000 in each tax year), given as a tax credit, irrespective of the investor's marginal tax rate. The relief cannot be greater than the income tax otherwise payable in the year.
- If a subscription is paid between 6 April and 5 October, up to 50% of it (with a maximum of £25,000) may be carried back for income tax relief in the previous year (subject to that year's £150,000 maximum).
- If the shares are disposed of, or the company breaches any of the conditions, within three years, the initial income tax relief (and the CGT exemption on disposal) is lost and will be recovered by the Inland Revenue.
- A loss realised on the disposal of EIS shares (calculated on the basis of their net cost) may be claimed against income, instead of against capital gains.

(ii) Capital gains tax:

- A gain on the disposal of EIS shares is exempt from CGT, provided that the shares have been held for three years and the income tax relief has not been withdrawn.
- Reinvestment relief (see **6:2**) may also be claimed on subscriptions to an EIS qualifying company above the limit of £150,000 for income tax relief. The combination of 20% income tax relief and 40% CGT deferral means that the initial tax relief on an EIS subscription can be as high as 60%.
- Where an investor acquires EIS shares after 5 April 1998, sells them in less than three years at a gain and reinvests in other EIS shares, he is entitled to claim taper relief on the disposal of the second shareholding by reference to the holding period for both EIS investments. This is intended to encourage 'serial entrepreneurs'.

(iii) Inheritance tax

Although business property relief for inheritance tax is not specific to EIS companies, it is likely that EIS shares will qualify for this relief (currently 100%). The shares must have been held for two years and other conditions apply.

The following risks inherent in EIS investment make it an opportunity needing careful consideration.

(a) Investment in young, unquoted companies carries a particularly high risk because of the difficulties of establishing new businesses.

(b) If the company fails to establish itself successfully, the whole investment could be lost.

(c) There is usually no market for EIS shares (although, as noted above, they can be dealt in on the AIM or the unofficial OFEX market), so they are difficult to dispose of.

(d) The investor can be called upon to make a further investment.

(e) The initial tax relief can be withdrawn through no fault of the investor (e.g. if the company breaches one of the many EIS conditions).

The many failures in the early years of BES demonstrated that the risk of investing in an unquoted trading company was high. Many potential investors will probably consider that income tax relief at 20% is not, on its own, a large enough incentive to justify those risks. The EIS may, however, be attractive to those who wish to invest in a business in which they will take an executive role (sometimes called 'business angels') or to obtain reinvestment relief. Potential investors should proceed with extreme caution.

6:5 Venture capital trusts

Venture capital trusts (VCTs) were introduced in the Finance Act 1995 as a further incentive to private investors to finance unquoted companies. Their design was the result of consultations between the Inland Revenue, the Stock Exchange and the venture capital industry. Venture capital trusts are companies and have the same constitution as conventional investment trusts. They are subject to particular constraints and offer a number of tax benefits. To qualify as a venture capital trust the following conditions apply.

(a) The company must be listed on the Stock Exchange and approved by the Inland Revenue as a VCT.

(b) Within three years of first issuing shares, it must invest 70% of its assets in qualifying unquoted companies. Of this 70%, 30% (i.e. 21% of the total assets) must consist of ordinary shares; the remainder may be preference shares and loan stock. The other 30% of the assets may be 'non-qualifying' investments such as listed securities (both equity and fixed interest) and cash deposits. Most VCTs aim to invest 80% of their assets in qualifying shares and securities.

(c) From 2 July 1997, at least 10% of the VCT's total investment in a company must be in ordinary shares, and guaranteed loans and securities cannot form part of the 70% of assets invested in qualifying companies.

(d) The VCT must invest in unquoted companies which have gross assets of not more than £15 million before its investment or £16 million afterwards. These companies must only have qualifying subsidiaries, must not be controlled by another company and must carry on a qualifying trade (dealing in land or securities and providing financial services are excluded, as are businesses which require a significant property element (e.g. farming, forestry, nursing homes and hotels)).

(e) There is a limit of £1 million on investments in one company in any financial year.

(f) The VCT must not hold more than 15% of its investments in any one company or group.

(g) It is required to distribute not less than 85% of its income.

The tax benefits for investors in venture capital trusts are as follows.

(a) Income tax relief of 20% is given on the cost of new ordinary shares, up to a maximum of £100,000 in each tax year. To retain this relief, the shares must be held for five years.

(b) Capital gains tax reinvestment relief is given on the cost of new ordinary shares. Gains realised after 5 April 1995 can be deferred by investment in a venture capital trust and reinvestment must take place within 12 months before or 12 months after the date the gain was realised.

(c) A capital gain realised on the sale of the ordinary shares of a VCT is exempt from capital gains tax, provided the shares were purchased on issue and have been held for three years. Conversely a loss on such shares is not an allowable loss.

(d) Dividends are exempt from income tax.

(e) Capital gains realised by a venture capital trust on its investments are exempt from corporation tax. Unlike ordinary investment trusts, venture capital trusts are permitted to distribute their capital gains to their shareholders.

The benefits at **(d)** and **(e)** are also available to investors who buy VCT shares in the market.

The success of a venture capital trust will depend upon the skill of its managers, who have to be experienced in raising finance for private companies, helping them to develop and arranging their disposal. An assessment of their past record will be an important part of the process of selecting a VCT investment.

6:6 Film finance schemes

Legislation designed to encourage the British film industry was first introduced in 1992. In 1997 this was improved to permit 100% of the cost of qualifying films to be written off as a revenue expense in the year the expense was incurred or the film purchased. A 'qualifying film' is one so certified by the Department of Culture, Media and Sport and the principal requirements are that the total cost of the film is less than £15 million, the producer is based in the UK or EU and the required proportions of the total costs and the labour content are met. The time limit for qualifying expenditure was 1 July 2000, but this has since been extended to 1 July 2005. In the 2002 Budget the Chancellor proposed to restrict the relief to films made for the cinema, thus excluding those made primarily for television.

In March 1998 the Inland Revenue issued a Statement of Practice setting out guidance on the way in which it expected the arrangements to work, covering not only production companies but also other companies and individuals purchasing completed films in order to lease them back and so benefit from the tax relief.

For private investors there are two main types of scheme – sale and leaseback partnerships and film production partnerships. A partnership structure is used because the individual investor has to be carrying on a trade (which includes the purchase and leaseback of films) in order to qualify for the loss relief. Under both arrangements:

(a) the investor's trading loss may be offset against his income for the same tax year or the previous three years, or (if all income is relieved) against capital gains in the current or previous years; and

(b) because the relief is based on the total cost of the films purchased by the partnership, whereas most of the partnership finance is borrowed, the tax repayment received by an investor typically exceeds the amount of capital he contributed, giving rise to a positive cash flow in the first 12 months. Since, however, the tax relief is merely a deferral, it is important to invest this cash wisely, to help fund the later tax payments.

6:6.1 Sale and leaseback partnerships

Since this type of arrangement does not expose the investor to the commercial risk that a film may be a box-office failure (that risk remains with the producer), it is more popular than film production schemes. On the other hand, there is virtually no potential to benefit from a successful film.

The investor borrows about 80% of the capital he subscribes to the partnership and contributes about 20% from his own resources. The partnership buys films and leases the distribution rights back to the producers in return for lease rental payments for 15 years. These payments, which are guaranteed by a bank, repay the investors' loans and interest. As partnership income, they are taxable, so that the initial loss relief is gradually recouped by the Inland Revenue.

The minimum investment in sale and leaseback schemes is £100,000, of which around 80% can be borrowed under the terms of the scheme. Some schemes allow the investor's 20% contribution to be borrowed as well.

6:6.2 Film production schemes

The return from film production schemes is more directly linked to the commercial success of the films. There is therefore the potential to participate in the profits of a successful production, as well as the risk of loss.

Individual investors subscribe a proportion (20%–40%) of the capital of the partnership, which borrows the remainder, secured on the future revenues of the films. The partnership buys films which it believes will be successful, and investors receive the benefit of revenues in excess of those charged to the lending bank. The proceeds of the first series of films may be invested, up to three years later, in a second series, so that investors may not see a return for six to seven years. Again, the initial tax relief (based on the total cost of the films) exceeds the amount subscribed by the investor, but, when the scheme comes to an end, a tax liability of a similar amount becomes payable.

The minimum investment in film production schemes is £25,000.

6:6.3 Risks of film finance schemes

Both types of scheme are for more sophisticated investors with a high income. A decision on investment involves an assessment not only of their overall financial position but also of their recent earnings (and, possibly, capital gains) to ensure that the loss relief is optimised.

Both schemes are subject to the usual commercial risks of partnerships (especially unlimited liability – although some use limited liability partnerships) and will be less effective if tax rates rise. Investors in sale and leaseback arrangements need to consider their position over the next 15 years. Those subscribing to film production schemes must be fully aware of the risk of losses if their films are unsuccessful. In both cases, independent professional guidance should be sought from an adviser familiar with the operation of such arrangements.

6:7 Options and futures

An option is a contract which gives its owner the right – but not the obligation – to buy or sell a quantity of a particular asset. Originally designed for the benefit of commodity producers wishing to protect themselves from price fluctuations, option contracts are now also dealt in by investors (and speculators) as assets in their own right. Their particular value to investors, however, is their use to protect a portfolio, or particular securities, against loss or to reduce the overall risk of a portfolio. Contracts are available not only for commodities (e.g. metals and soft commodities like wheat, coffee, etc) but also for specific securities and for intangible assets like share indices, interest rates and currencies.

The purchaser pays a premium to acquire an option to buy or sell at a specified price (the strike price) on or before a specified date. If he buys a 'call' option (one for a purchase) and the 'spot' price of the asset (i.e. the current market price, for dealings 'on the spot') rises, he will exercise the option; if the price falls, the investor can buy the asset more cheaply and he will allow the option to lapse. His only loss is the cost of the premium. Conversely, he may buy a 'put' option (the right to sell), which he will exercise if the 'spot' price falls.

Futures contracts are also available for a wide range of assets. They differ from options in that the investor is obliged to buy or sell at the specified price on the specified date. Futures contracts for physical commodities are therefore likely to expire in the hands of professional traders or businesses dealing in those commodities.

Options and futures contracts for commodities can be dealt in through a commodity broker. As well as arranging transactions in individual contracts, brokers run discretionary accounts for clients.

Options on shares and securities on the FTSE-100 Index can be bought and sold through a bank, stockbroker or investment manager. They do not have to be held to maturity but can be traded at any time during their life. Because the price of an option is only a small percentage of the price of the underlying shares, large percentage gains can be obtained from fairly small changes in the share price. Similarly, large percentage losses can be incurred, but the maximum loss is limited to the cost of the option. Because a futures contract *has* to be fulfilled, however, the risk of substantial loss is far higher.

6:8 Spread (or index) betting

Financial bookmakers offer the opportunity to bet on the potential movement (both up and down) of a wide range of commodities, indices, financial instruments and exchange rates. For each 'asset' the investor is quoted the current buying and selling prices (the 'spread'); he then places a bet on the price movement and wins a fixed amount for each point the price moves in his chosen direction. The wager can be closed at any time to realise a profit (or cut a loss). A deposit of between 4% and 15% of the value of the bet is paid at the outset, depending on the type of commodity or index chosen. Price changes on the total bet can, therefore, be significant in relation to the outlay and both gains and losses can be considerable. In isolation, therefore, this activity is highly speculative.

One attraction of spread betting is that all returns are exempt from income tax and capital gains tax and no stamp duty or VAT is payable.

6:9 Gold, silver or platinum

Gold has long been regarded as the universal currency, particularly recognised as a store of value in times of crisis. During periods of high interest rates and high inflation, however, its appeal as an investment diminishes, as it provides no income. As with all commodities, the returns are dependent on price movements.

Gold can be purchased as bullion, coins or jewellery. Coins can be bought through banks or stockbrokers, and the most common are Krugerrands and British sovereigns. Other countries have also minted gold coins. Older coins may have a numismatic value and so can trade at a considerable premium over their gold content.

Platinum is also available in modern coins and bars of various weights. Investments in all three metals can be bought through commodity dealers.

VAT is chargeable if the asset is bought in the UK, so it is usual to arrange for the purchase, storage and sale to take place in the Channel Islands and other offshore centres.

6:10 Collectors' items

The essential return from the assets in this section is likely to be the enjoyment of seeking, acquiring and owning them. Substantial capital gains are unlikely, but not impossible; in many cases there will be maintenance and insurance costs.

Examples of assets for which there is a collectors' market are:

(a) antiques and works of art;

(b) stamps;

(c) rare books and old maps;

(d) old coins and bank notes;

(e) medals;

(f) old toys;

(g) postcards and playing cards;

(h) old bond and share certificates; and

(i) veteran and vintage cars.

All of these can be bought and sold through specialist dealers and at auction and, although the investor may have some knowledge himself, it would be advisable in some cases to seek independent advice.

Although not strictly a 'collectors' item' there is one other asset which in some (but relatively few) cases can prove profitable – racehorses. Most owners, however, participate because of their enjoyment of the sport, recognising that the expenses are likely to outweigh the prize money and betting winnings.

Investment may be in horses in training or in stallions. Typically, a horse in training is owned by a syndicate of up to 12 people. The members have to be approved by the Jockey Club. Most syndicates appoint a professional syndicate manager to be responsible for the day-to-day administration.

An alternative form of investment is through an ownership club, which requires less outlay than a syndicate. This too must be approved by the Jockey Club and has considerably more members than a syndicate. The subscription normally covers the cost of the horse and training, etc, for a two-year period, at the end of which the horse is sold and any surplus funds distributed among the members.

Some horses in training are owned by companies, whose shares can be purchased by investors.

Stallions are normally owned by a syndicate of 40 members run by a committee. There are no restrictions as for horses in training.

7 Membership of Lloyd's

When Edward Lloyd opened his first coffee house in 1687 to provide a market place for shipowners, captains and other businessmen who were prepared to consider sharing the risk of marine ventures, he could never have expected that his name would have such a lasting effect on the insurance market. 'Lloyd's' was first incorporated by an Act of Parliament in 1871 and the members of Lloyd's now underwrite UK and international insurance risks within the modern 1986 building in London.

Historically, only individuals (Names) were able to become members of the Lloyd's insurance market and, as sole traders, had to accept the potentially huge disadvantage of unlimited liability. The insurance business is underwritten through syndicates which traditionally specialised in particular classes of business, such as marine, aviation and motor, although composite syndicates now tend to write a mixture of all classes of business.

Since 1 January 1994, corporate members have been allowed to join the market, which has meant that individuals have also been able to invest in quoted corporate members, with investment trust status, as an alternative to full membership of Lloyd's. In addition, since 1996 individual members have been able to consider conversion to either corporate or partnership membership, both with limited liability.

7:1 Financial considerations

The overall capacity of the Lloyd's market is around £12 billion and the vast majority of this is now supported by corporate members. Individual members with unlimited liability have dropped in number to less than 2,500, from the peak of over 30,000 during the late 1980s. The concept of the 'Means Statement' for new members was abolished from the 2001 year of account, but the minimum Funds at Lloyd's entry requirement for new members was £300,000 for 2001 and £350,000 for 2002. Lloyd's is now regulated by the Financial Services Authority so that members' agents must conform more positively to the 'know your client' principle and ensure that only those for whom it is appropriate invest in Lloyd's.

For existing Names, the minimum capital requirement was reduced from 2001 to 40% of the overall premium limit of the member. Thus, the 2002 minimum of £350,000 supported a premium limit of £875,000.

There is also a risk-based capital ratio, relevant to the risk analysis of the syndicates with which the member is involved, and if this exceeds the 40% minimum Funds at Lloyd's requirement, additional funds will need to be introduced.

Some individuals find it convenient to provide part of their Funds at Lloyd's by way of a letter of credit secured on other assets. Lloyd's have now relaxed the rules concerning the use of the principal private residence as security, but only on the proviso that the members' agent is satisfied that this is a matter of convenience and not out of necessity.

Costs of membership can be substantial for the individual Name but, with the volatility of the market, the rewards can also be high. There is an entrance fee of £4,700 plus VAT and associated legal costs, treated as capital expenditure. Annually, there will be agents' fees, profit commissions, subscriptions to Lloyd's Central Fund contributions, bank guarantee charges (if the funds at Lloyd's are provided in this way), stop-loss premiums, estate protection premiums, accountancy charges and other expenses of joining Names' associations. All these are allowable deductions for tax purposes.

Lloyd's business is carried on by professional underwriters who exercise their particular skills in taking on risks for an appropriate premium. They work for managing agencies and the capacity for their operation is determined by the number of members, whether individual or corporate, whose support is recommended to syndicates by members' agencies and Lloyd's advisers.

Syndicates prepare accounts for each calendar year at the end of a three-year period in order to allow time for claims to be made, or for there to be sufficient knowledge of likely claims to enable the outstanding risks to be reinsured into the account of the following year. Thus, a Name who is involved with a syndicate for the 2002 year of account will have to wait until the spring of 2005 to be told whether that syndicate has made a profit or a loss.

An average Name for 2002 may be writing £750,000 premium income and be involved with a considerable number of different syndicates, all of which will be seeking to generate a profit for their Names. Funds at Lloyd's of at least £350,000 must be lodged by this average Name, although any investment income or capital appreciation from these funds will continue to belong to the individual and be treated as part of the trading result for tax purposes.

An individual member of Lloyd's who commences underwriting activities on 1 January 2002 must have had all the financial requirements in place in the autumn of 2001 and, as a pay-out will not be received until the summer of 2005, must be prepared to bear considerable costs in the meantime, which could conceivably amount to £35,000. Membership on this basis should normally only be considered for a long-term period of, say, ten years.

7:2 Advantages of membership

The main attractions of individual membership are as follows.

(a) The Names' assets work twice for them; once earning dividends, interest and capital appreciation, but also as collateral for the underwriting business.

(b) The Name is deemed to be carrying on a trade from which the profits are earned income while, conversely, any losses can be set against other income for tax purposes.

(c) After membership for two years, the total Lloyd's connected assets qualify for 100% inheritance tax relief as business property, as long as the Funds at Lloyd's are not out of all proportion to the level of business being written.

(d) There is a tax-efficient Special Reserve fund into which Names may transfer up to 50% of annual commercial profits, until this fund reaches a value of 50% of premium income. All amounts transferred are tax deductible and the fund itself grows in a tax-free environment. Taxable withdrawals must be made from the fund to pay losses or calls from the underwriting business. However, transfers to this fund must only be considered as tax-efficient deferrals of income tax because ultimately, on cessation of membership, the full market value of the assets in the fund will be brought into charge to income tax for the final year. As part of the overall Lloyd's interest on death, these assets would also attract business property relief.

(e) Pension planning can be considered for all individual Names on profits, but not for partners of Scottish Limited Partnerships or those members involved with corporate membership.

(f) Syndicate participations must be acquired at a cost in the annual auctions and, over a period of time, value will be achieved from good syndicate capacity allocations. On disposal, any proceeds are taxable under the capital gains tax regime and retirement relief may also be due for those over 50 years of age who make a material disposal of business assets, until this relief is finally phased out by 5 April 2003. Otherwise, as business assets, the gains can be rolled over or accepted, with the benefit of the more favourable taper relief.

7:3 Disadvantages of membership

The main disadvantages of individual membership are threefold:

(a) the risk of unlimited liability;

(b) the lack of control over the business being carried on; and

(c) the further deterioration in gearing that has followed the introduction of risk-weighting each syndicate, which could in some cases increase the Funds at Lloyd's ratio to more than 50%.

7:4 Corporate capital

From 1 January 1994, incorporated members, with a minimum paid-up capital of £1.5 million, were introduced to the Lloyd's market. They pay much higher entrance fees and originally had to deposit 50% of their premium income as Funds at Lloyd's. This requirement has now been reduced to 40% plus any risk-based weighting, to come into line with individual Names. Many of these corporate vehicles operate with investment trust status and are quoted so that individuals now have the option of investing in shares of corporate members. For the first time, therefore, individuals can invest in Lloyd's without the high liability risk that previously applied. The main disadvantage is that their investment is not direct into the Lloyd's market, so that their return will be diluted by corporate management charges and profit retentions. There has also been a recent growth of unquoted corporate vehicles dedicated to a particular syndicate or managing agency. These provide capacity for specific syndicates and can detract from the capacity available to individual Names.

7:5 Conversion opportunities

Existing Names have been able to consider converting to limited liability membership in recent years, whether via Scottish Limited Partnerships or individual and collective NameCos. Lloyd's Publications Office provides a Conversion Guide for those who may be interested, as do all Members' Agents.

7:6 Summary

The Lloyd's market has had a turbulent time during the last 15 years, with losses far outweighing profits during this period. The horrendous losses of the late 1980s and early 1990s have now been reinsured separately into Equitas, a reinsurance company set up by Lloyd's specifically for this purpose. All outstanding liabilities for the 1992 and prior years were transferred into Equitas and the Reconstruction & Renewal Settlement engineered by Lloyd's enabled the market to survive, whilst assisting those Names who were badly hit, as well as many others, to extricate themselves from the market at that time. The ongoing structure appeared to be better organised, certainly better regulated and without the downside brought on by some of the poorer syndicates, agencies and active underwriters. Three or four moderately profitable years followed but the market has now returned to a further period of heavy losses, culminating in 2001 with the implications of the terrorist attack on the World Trade Centre. It seems certain that one effect of this disaster will be to create considerable profits in the Lloyd's market for the next two to three years with the increases in premiums that are now being charged.

It is some years since new unlimited liability individuals were attracted to the market but, with most of the tax breaks still intact, this is a venture that may be of interest to some. Most agents now have corporate arrangements, either for converting Names or new entrants, whereby a degree of control can still be exercised within a personal or family NameCo. Lloyd's will provide contact details for anyone who is interested in joining the market at this time.

The Chairman of Lloyd's commissioned a strategy group during 2001 with a view to finding ways to change the structure or method of operating within the market to ensure that it is more profitable in future. Most of the suggestions have already been discarded as being impractical for one reason or another but Lloyd's hopes that it may be possible to obtain support for some ongoing initiatives which could assist the market in future years.

8 Pension arrangements for directors and executives

The remuneration package awarded to business owners, directors and other key corporate executives often contains a generous company-funded pension element that reflects the seniority of these individuals. Retirement benefits provided by companies to their senior executives are usually (but not always) funded in advance by means of one or more tax-approved pension schemes, held separately from the company under a trust arrangement.

This chapter looks at the special types of pension schemes set up by companies for their executives. It also looks at some issues relating to the benefits that executives will have built up as a result of their membership of pension schemes in the past. State pensions or the group pension arrangements used by companies to provide retirement benefits for employees below executive level are not covered. It should however be noted that employees are often entitled to benefits from these group arrangements. Personal pensions are discussed in **Chapter 9**.

The tax treatment of company-sponsored, or 'occupational' pension schemes, the options open to people who leave pension schemes before retirement (normally on a job change) and the various types of pension schemes available to company executives who are seeking to maximise their retirement benefits are also examined.

8:1 Tax position of approved pension schemes

In order to encourage long-term saving for retirement, a succession of governments have provided generous tax concessions to companies that provide retirement benefits for their employees, through a tax approval process for the pension scheme. The concessions apply in the form of tax relief for the company's contributions and the tax-favoured investment of the assets in a pension scheme. Relief is also given to the employees themselves in relation to any pension contributions they make and the various lump sums payable tax-free on retirement or death. The main conditions for tax approval are set out in section **8:2** and the tax treatment of approved schemes is summarised as follows.

(a) Investment income and capital gains accumulate within an approved pension scheme free of UK income and capital gains tax, except on UK dividend income. Pension schemes have not been able to recover tax credits attaching to UK equity dividends after 1 July 1997.

(b) Pensions in payment are treated as earned income, taxed under PAYE.

(c) Lump sum benefits arising on death and at retirement are normally received tax-free.

(d) The company's contributions to approved pension schemes are not taxable on the scheme member as a benefit in kind.

(e) Regular pension contributions payable by a company are allowed as an expense for corporation tax purposes. However, the contribution should be paid and cleared through the company's bank account before the end of its accounting year in order to obtain tax relief in that year.

(f) Corporation tax relief is also given to companies for their *special* pension contributions (those which are not regular contributions). These are typically made to purchase additional benefits for a member in respect of past service. The maximum special contribution on which tax relief will be given in a single year is normally £500,000, but this amount is increased if the special contribution does not exceed the employer's regular contribution to the scheme in any particular year. If the amount of the special contribution exceeds the limits, the period over which the tax relief is spread is determined by the size of the aggregate special contribution, as follows.

Special contribution	*Period of spread*
£500,000 – £1,000,000	2 years
£1,000,001 – £2,000,000	3 years
over £2,000,000	4 years

Tax relief for the contribution is spread evenly over the period.

Spreading is not normally required where a contribution is required solely to finance inflationary increases for pensioners.

(g) Contributions by a member of up to 15% of remuneration in any tax year are treated as allowable deductions for income tax purposes. Remuneration for this purpose must not exceed the earnings cap for those affected by the Finance Act 1989 capping provisions (£97,200 in the 2002/03 tax year, see **8.2.3**).

(h) Although not strictly a taxation advantage, no national insurance contributions are payable on either pension contributions made by a company to an approved pension scheme or on the resulting pensions.

8:2 Conditions for tax approval

In order to qualify for the above tax treatment, a pension scheme must be approved by the Inland Revenue. To gain approval, a scheme must be set up under trust for the *sole purpose* of providing benefits for the beneficiaries upon their retirement or death. The trust must contain provisions (normally in the form of scheme rules) that limit the benefits that can be paid out, normally by reference to the members' 'final remuneration' (see **8:3**). This in turn has an impact on the amounts that can be contributed to a scheme by a company, and hence the amount of tax relief obtained. This is particularly relevant to company executives, for whom companies frequently wish to provide benefits at a high level, close to or at the Inland Revenue prescribed maximum.

A further condition for approval is that the company must make a contribution and written details of this and the scheme benefits are given to the scheme members. There is no formal requirement for a minimum level of company contribution, but it is generally accepted that the company should contribute at least 10% of the total contributions payable.

There are three different tax regimes applicable to occupational pension schemes. The latest regime was introduced in the 1989 Finance Act and applies to individuals joining (or rejoining after more than a temporary absence) a scheme on or after 1 June 1989. This legislation introduced a limit (known as the 'earnings cap') on the maximum amount of an individual's remuneration that can be regarded for the purpose of calculating the maximum benefits payable under an approved pension scheme. The cap changes each tax year normally in line with price inflation. It started at £60,000 in the1989/90 tax year and has increased to £97,200 for the 2002/03 tax year.

Before the 1989 Finance Act, the previous limits regime was introduced in the 1987 (No 2) Finance Act which increased the time needed to accrue the maximum pension (from ten years to 20 years) and applied a cap of £100,000 on the earnings that can be used for calculating the tax-free cash sum payable at retirement. It affects those who joined (or rejoined) an occupational pension scheme between 17 March 1987 and 30 June 1989.

Prior to that a more generous tax regime, consolidated in the 1970 Finance Act, applied to approved pension schemes.

The maximum benefits payable under each regime are summarised as follows.

8:2.1 Pre 1987 regime

The maximum benefits that may be provided under an approved pension scheme for individuals subject to the pre 1987 regime are as follows.

(a) The maximum retirement pension is two-thirds of a member's final remuneration provided that ten years' pensionable service has been completed by the normal retirement date. For shorter periods, an 'accelerated accrual' scale applies, as shown below.

Years of service to normal retirement age	*Maximum pension (fraction of final remuneration)*
1 to 5	1/60th for each year
6	8/60ths
7	16/60ths
8	24/60ths
9	32/60ths
10 or more	40/60ths

Notes

1. Fractions of a year may be interpolated into the scale.

2. Where an accrual rate in excess of 1/60th for each year is applied, benefits provided from previous occupations (retained benefits) must generally be taken into account to ensure that the total pension does not exceed two-thirds of final remuneration.

3. Early retirement is possible on ill-health grounds or from age 50, provided the scheme's normal retirement age is not earlier than 60. The maximum pension is reduced, in cases other than ill-health, by applying the formula 'n/ns', where 'n' is the period from the date the individual joined the scheme to the date of leaving, and 'ns' is the period from the date of joining the scheme to the normal retirement date.

(b) The maximum lump sum on retirement is 1.5 times final remuneration, provided that 20 years' pensionable service has been completed by the normal retirement date. However, if a lump sum is taken, the member's maximum retirement pension is reduced. Based on the maximum lump sum of 1.5 times final remuneration being provided and a 'commutation rate' of £12 to £1 per annum, the reduced pension would be approximately 54% of final remuneration. For shorter periods of service, an accelerated scale applies, as shown below.

Years of service to normal retirement age	*Maximum cash sum (fraction of final remuneration)*
1-8	3/80ths for each year
9	30/80ths
10	36/80ths
11	42/80ths
12	48/80ths
13	54/80ths
14	63/80ths
15	72/80ths
16	81/80ths
17	90/80ths
18	99/80ths
19	108/80ths
20 or more	120/80ths

Notes

1. Fractions of a year may be interpolated into the scale.

2. Where an accrual rate in excess of 3/80ths for each year is applied, benefits provided from previous occupations (retained benefits) must generally be taken into account to ensure that the total cash sum does not exceed 1.5 times final remuneration.

3. Early retirement is possible on ill-health grounds from age 50, provided the scheme's normal retirement age is not earlier than 60. The maximum cash sum is reduced, in cases other than ill-health, by applying the formula 'n/ns', where 'n' is the period from the date the individual joined the scheme to the date of leaving, and 'ns' is the period from the date of joining the scheme to the normal retirement date.

(c) The maximum spouse's pension payable on the death of a member in retirement is two-thirds of the maximum pension that could have been approved for the member before any reduction for lump sum benefits.

(d) The maximum spouse's pension payable on the death of the member in service or in deferment (i.e. after leaving service but before commencement of benefit payments) is two-thirds of the maximum pension that could have been approved for the member had he retired at the date of his death. This pension can take into account the whole of the potential service up to the normal retirement date, providing that the member was in service at death.

(e) Pensions for dependants (other than spouses) are also payable in the event of the member's death before or after retirement. These, together with the spouse's pension, may not exceed the amount of the member's maximum approvable pension (up to two-thirds of final remuneration).

(f) The maximum lump sum death-in-service benefit is four times final remuneration (or £5,000 if greater). A refund of the member's contributions can also be paid, with interest.

(g) Increases may be given to all pensions in payment in line with the greater of the rise in the cost of living as measured by the RPI or 3% per annum. A pension that started below the maximum at retirement may be increased by a greater annual amount than inflation, provided the increased pension is no more than the maximum pension that could have been paid at retirement, increased by the RPI or 3% per annum over the period.

8:2.2 1987-1989 regime

From 17 March 1987, the following changes were applied to all new schemes and arrangements set up prior to 14 March 1989 and to new members of existing schemes joining before 1 June 1989.

(a) The 'accelerated accrual' scale for pension benefits was replaced by a new scale permitting a pension of two-thirds of final remuneration after 20 years' service (previously it was possible to qualify for a maximum of two-thirds of final remuneration after ten years' service). For shorter periods, a 'straight line' maximum accrual rate of 1/30th of final remuneration for each year of service is allowed. The n/ns formula applies on early retirement (see **Note 3** in **8:2.1**).

(b) The accelerated accrual rate for the tax-free lump sum, with a maximum of 1.5 times final remuneration after 20 years' service, can be used only if pension benefits accrue on the new accelerated scale. Otherwise the rate of accrual of the lump sum is directly related to the rate of pension accrual. For example, if pension accrues at the rate of 1/60th of final remuneration for each year of service (with a maximum of 40) cash accrues at the rate of 3/80ths.

(c) Final remuneration for the purpose of calculating the tax-free lump sum on retirement is restricted to £100,000 and so the maximum amount payable may not exceed £150,000.

8.2.3 Post 1989 regime

Further changes were introduced in the Finance Act 1989, affecting all new schemes set up on or after 14 March 1989 and those joining existing schemes from 1 June 1989. These were as follows.

(a) The benefits that can be provided, both pensions and lump sums, are based on earnings, subject to the 'earnings cap' (£97,200 for the tax year 2002/03).

(b) Employees with at least 20 years' service may retire on a pension of two-thirds of final remuneration at any time from age 50 onwards. For shorter periods, 1/30ths of final remuneration for each year of service is allowed.

(c) The maximum tax-free lump sum payable on retirement is calculated as either 3/80ths of final remuneration for each year of service (subject to a maximum of 40) or 2.25 times the annual pension (before reduction for the lump sum), whichever is the greater. The maximum cash sum permissible for those affected by the 1989 regime is currently £145,800 (1.5 times remuneration of £97,200).

Employees not affected by the 1989 regime may nevertheless elect that their benefits be subject to the maxima shown above, but this would include accepting the earnings cap restriction in **(a)** above. For employees otherwise subject to the pre 1987 regime, the ability to make this election must be permitted by the rules of the scheme.

As a consequence of the changes which have occurred since 17 March 1987, many older and highly paid employees may now be reluctant to change jobs since their pension and/or lump sum expectation may be reduced.

8:3 Final remuneration

The most usual definition of final remuneration is the basic salary for any one of the five years preceding the normal retirement date. However, where fluctuating emoluments arise, such as overtime, commission or bonuses, they would usually be taken as the average of three or more consecutive years ending on the last day of the basic pay year used. Directors' fees may rank either as basic pay or as fluctuating emoluments according to the basis on which they are taxed.

In the case of a controlling director (a director who, either on his or her own or with associates, is able to control 20% or more of the ordinary share capital of the company), benefits cannot be based on one year's earnings. Instead, final remuneration is defined as the yearly average of the total emoluments for any three or more consecutive years over a period ending not earlier than ten years before the normal retirement date.

In either case, remuneration may be increased in proportion to the increase in the cost of living for the period from the end of the year on which the remuneration was received up to the date of calculation of benefits. This increase is known as 'dynamisation'. Dynamised final remuneration may not be used to increase the lump sum retirement benefit unless the pension is also being increased.

Benefits in kind may be taken into account in the final remuneration calculation but only if they are assessed to income tax as emoluments under Schedule E. They are normally regarded as fluctuating emoluments and therefore need to be averaged.

On 17 March 1987, a number of changes were made to the calculation of final remuneration applicable to new pension schemes and to new members of existing schemes. These were as follows:

- the definition of final remuneration excludes income and gains from share option schemes (this applies to all share options granted after 17 March 1987);
- employees earning more than £100,000 and any employee who has at any time within ten years prior to retirement been a controlling director have final remuneration defined as if they were controlling directors (see above).

For members of schemes set up on or after 14 March 1989 and those joining existing schemes from 1 June 1989, final remuneration cannot exceed the earnings cap (£97,200 for the 2002/03 tax year).

8:4 Normal retirement date

All approved pension schemes must specify a normal retirement date. This is the date when scheme members are expected to retire and may normally be any age between 60 and 75. Members may retire earlier or later than the scheme's normal retirement age but there is no scope to delay the commencement of benefits beyond age 75 except for those members who joined a scheme prior to 1 June 1989.

Following the *Barber* judgment of the European Court of Justice, all occupational pension schemes have been required to equalise the normal retirement ages for males and females with effect from 17 May 1990.

An individual may continue to work after the normal retirement date. Members subject to the post 1989 benefits regime must normally start to receive benefits upon leaving service after the scheme's normal retirement date (or at age 75, if earlier). This is not the case if an individual is not subject to the post 1989 regime. Such an individual who remains in service after normal retirement date may elect to receive their pension and/or cash benefits upon attaining normal retirement age or at any later date before actual retirement, as an alternative to deferring payment of benefits until retirement.

Retirement earlier than the scheme's normal retirement date is allowed on grounds of incapacity, whatever the age, or if the individual is within ten years of the normal retirement date. In the case of certain occupations the Inland Revenue will approve earlier normal retirement ages than is the norm, for example, footballers at 35. However, each case has to be considered according to its own individual circumstances. It is generally not permitted, however, for an individual to receive their retirement benefits before normal retirement age if they are still in company service. This could lead to the taxation of the retirement lump sum.

Changes of normal retirement date are possible provided the member has not yet reached the current date and provided also that the new date is within the acceptable range (60 to 75). For individuals who are not subject to the post 1989 regime, unless there is a period of at least five years from the date of change to the new retirement date, such changes require Inland Revenue approval.

8:5 Contracting-out

From April 1978, it has been possible for a company to pay, and collect from its employees, national insurance contributions at a reduced rate, if it provides employees with a pension scheme that either provides a minimum level of benefits or is funded by a minimum level of contributions. As a result of the reduction in national insurance payable, the earnings-related component of the State Pension is reduced for the employees concerned. This is known as 'contracting-out'. The reduction in State Pension corresponds with the employees' entitlement to SERPS (the State Earnings-Related Pension Scheme) pension that they would have built up if they had not been contracted-out. SERPS was replaced by the State Second Pension ('S2P') from April 2002.

The reductions in national insurance contributions applicable in the 2002/03 tax year as a result of contracting-out are as follows:

	% of 'band earnings'
Employee's contracted-out rebate	1.6%
Employer's contracted out rebate (defined benefit schemes)	3.5%
Employer's contracted out rebate (defined contribution schemes)	1.0%

Age-related rebates are also payable to defined contribution schemes in certain circumstances (see **8:5.2**).

'Band earnings' are those between the lower and upper limits for national insurance contributions. In 2002/03 the lower earnings limit was £75 per week and the upper limit £585 per week.

Pension arrangements used solely for executives are rarely used for contracting-out of SERPS. However, it is likely that many executives will have been contracted-out as a result of their membership of an occupational pension scheme in the past, or of a current scheme which covers the wider workforce.

The main conditions that an occupational pension scheme must meet before it can be used to contract-out of SERPS are summarised as follows.

8:5.1 Defined benefit pension schemes

Defined benefit (sometimes known as 'final salary' or 'salary-related') schemes must provide a 'Guaranteed Minimum Pension' (or 'GMP') for contracted-out service between April 1978 and April 1997. A GMP is broadly equivalent to the SERPS pension that would have built up if the employee had not been contracted-out, based on band earnings in each tax year. From April 1997, defined benefit schemes have had to provide 90% of the eligible employees with comparable benefits to those payable by a 'reference scheme'. This provides a pension payable at age 65 which must be at least 1/80th of 90% of band earnings for each year of service, of which 50% must be inheritable by a surviving spouse. The pension must increase in payment by the lower of RPI inflation or 5% in any year.

8:5.2 Defined contribution schemes

It has been possible for an employer to use a defined contribution (sometimes known as 'money purchase') scheme to contract-out since April 1988. To enable the reduced rate of national insurance contributions to be paid, the company must make a minimum level of contributions to the scheme. This minimum is equal to the reduction in national insurance contributions applicable if the employer has a contracted-out pension scheme (see the table in **8:5**). From April 1997, an age-related national insurance rebate is also paid by the Inland Revenue directly to the pension scheme. The amount of age-related rebate in 2002/03 ranges from 0.1% of band earnings for a 17 year old employee to 7.9% of band earnings for an employee over age 51. The funds built up from the minimum contributions and the age-related rebates are known as 'protected rights' and must be accounted for separately from funds deriving from the other contributions paid by the company or the scheme member. When taking benefits (which can be no earlier than age 60), the protected rights may only be used to provide a pension and cannot be commuted for a lump sum. The pension must increase in payment in line with the RPI, up to an annual ceiling of 3% or 5% depending on when the contributions were paid. Also, 50% of the pension must be inheritable by a surviving spouse.

8:6 Early leavers: preserved pension options

If an individual leaves employment before normal retirement date and does not wish to take early retirement, a number of options are available in relation to his preserved pension rights.

It is possible that the benefits of leavers with less than two years' pensionable service may not be preserved at all. In these circumstances, the only benefit payable is a refund of the individual's contributions, possibly with interest, less a share of the costs of reinstatement to SERPS/S2P and a deduction for tax of currently 20%. Benefits are preserved if an individual has been a member of an occupational pension scheme for at least two years, although some schemes preserve benefits for shorter periods of membership.

If an individual has a defined benefit entitlement, legislation introduced in 1985 and strengthened in 1990 requires the preserved pension to be 'revalued' in line with the increase in the Retail Prices Index between the date of leaving and the normal retirement date, subject to a 5% annualised limit over the period. If the individual has a GMP (see **8:5.1**) as a result of being contracted-out of SERPS, this pension will also be revalued, but at a different rate to that applicable to the non-GMP benefit. The rate of GMP revaluation depends on when the individual left service and the revaluation method adopted by the scheme.

If an individual leaves service with an entitlement to benefits from a defined contribution pension arrangement, the accrued contributions continue to reflect investment returns but payment of further pension contributions would cease.

As an alternative to leaving benefits preserved in a company pension scheme, a leaver normally has a right to transfer them to another approved pension arrangement. There are a number of different types of arrangement that could receive the transfer payment (see **8.6.2**). Many complex issues need to be taken into account when deciding whether or not an individual should transfer pension rights, and to where, with the issues being evaluated in the light of the needs of the transferor.

8:6.1 Pension transfers – issues to be considered

Advice on pension transfers may only be given by individuals who are regarded by the Financial Services Authority as qualified to give specialist advice in this area. Before advising whether pension rights should be transferred, an adviser must have a complete understanding of the individual's entire financial position. It is inappropriate to advise on a pension transfer without a good understanding of the financial impact that such a transfer would have upon the individual.

The advice process starts by gathering information about the preserved pension entitlement and the transferring pension scheme generally. This includes obtaining details of the current 'transfer value' available. A transfer value is a capital sum offered in lieu of the benefits under the scheme and, if the transfer option is exercised, it may only be transferred to an approved pension arrangement. If the individual has a defined benefit entitlement, an assessment (known as a transfer value analysis) needs to be made to compare the transfer value with the scheme benefits that would be forgone. Amongst other things, this calculates the annualised investment return that the transfer value needs to obtain in order to match the benefits that would have been paid by the scheme at the date of the individual's retirement. The amount of the break-even rate of return required (sometimes known as the 'critical yield') should be discussed with the individual in the light of the investment risk that he is willing to tolerate. Obviously, if the critical yield requires a high-risk investment strategy to be pursued, a transfer will not be suitable for a cautious investor.

If a transfer is financially viable, a number of further points need to be considered and discussed before a transfer is made. These include:

- the benefits payable by the current scheme, in lump sum and pension form, on the individual's death before or after payment of retirement benefits commences;
- how these benefits would compare with those payable following a transfer;
- the individual's entitlement to ancillary benefits under the current scheme (such as ill-health early retirement pensions or lump sum death benefits) and the cost of replacing these following a transfer;
- the individual's state of health and life expectancy;
- the significance to the individual of the loss of *guaranteed* pension benefits (if the current scheme is a defined benefit arrangement) that would result from a transfer;
- the amount of any increases (statutory, guaranteed and discretionary) awarded by the current scheme to pensions in payment and in deferment, and the extent to which they can be matched following a transfer;
- the solvency of the current scheme (if defined benefit) and the likelihood that any surplus could be used to augment scheme benefits;
- the impact of the earnings cap for those subject to the post 1989 Inland Revenue limits regime (see **8:2.3**);
- the importance of pension arrangements in the context of the individual's overall wealth;
- the benefits provided by a new employer's pension scheme in return for the transfer value (if applicable);
- the proximity of the benefits in the current scheme (pension and lump sum) to the Inland Revenue maximum;
- the terms on which retirement ages for men and women have been equalised following the *Barber* judgment in 1990 (see **8:4**);
- any 'transfer club' benefits that which may be lost if the individual transfers out of a public sector superannuation scheme.

Since July 1999, members of defined contribution occupational pension schemes have had the option (provided the scheme rules permit it) to receive their pension income directly from the fund instead of purchasing a pension annuity. This makes occupational pension schemes similar to personal pensions in this regard (see **9:12.3**). It is, however, often preferable to transfer to a personal pension as this permits the staggered drawing of benefits and removes the Inland Revenue's limits on occupational scheme benefits.

8:6.2 Transfer options

The following transfer options are available to an individual who wishes to transfer deferred pension rights.

8:6.2.1 Transfer to a new employer's scheme

If an individual changes jobs and joins a new employer's pension scheme, it may be possible to transfer pension rights to that new scheme. The benefits that a new scheme would grant in exchange for the transfer value should be carefully evaluated. There are three main ways in which transferred-in pension rights may be dealt with by a new scheme.

- If it is a defined benefit scheme, it may provide a number of additional years and months of pensionable service, depending on the amount of the transfer value.
- Alternatively, a defined benefit scheme may provide a guaranteed fixed amount of pension at the normal retirement date in return for the transfer value.
- Thirdly, and perhaps most commonly, the receiving scheme (whether defined benefit or defined contribution) may provide additional retirement benefits in respect of the transfer value, on a money purchase basis, depending on the value at the date when benefits are to be taken.

If a scheme is prepared to offer added years, this might initially appear to be a poor deal. However, it should be borne in mind that the benefit payable at retirement will be based on final remuneration. The future value of this benefit should therefore be carefully assessed, especially if the individual plans to stay with the new employer for a long time and expects a higher rate of salary increase than that assumed when the added years were calculated.

If the transfer value is invested on a money purchase basis, consideration should be given to the charges applicable and investment options available under the new scheme.

8:6.2.2 Transfer to a buy-out bond (often called a section 32 policy)

A buy-out bond is an insurance contract arranged on a money purchase basis, to which a transfer value may be paid. It is subject to the normal Inland Revenue limits applicable to occupational pension schemes, calculated by reference to the period of the member's service with, and his final remuneration from, the former employer. Care needs to be taken if the individual's preserved benefit is already close to the Inland Revenue maximum limits within the current scheme. If this is the case, there may be little to gain from transferring to a buy-out bond as the individual would not get the benefit of any surplus.

If the benefits being transferred include an entitlement to a GMP (see **8:5.1**), this guaranteed benefit must be preserved by the buy-out bond. Benefits accrued in a contracted-out defined benefit scheme after 5 April 1997 form protected rights when transferred to a buy-out bond and must therefore be earmarked separately to provide the benefits at retirement specified in **8:5.2**.

Under a buy-out bond, the maximum tax-free cash sum payable is calculated by the current scheme's administrators, by reference to the member's service with, and final remuneration from, the former employer. The amount calculated at the date of leaving is then increased in line with RPI until benefits are to be taken. This may lead to a higher tax-free lump sum than that allowed under a personal pension arrangement where the tax-free cash is limited to a maximum of 25% of the fund.

Consideration should be given to transferring to a buy-out bond if the individual is in poor health. A bond may be able to pay a higher tax-free lump sum than a personal pension on death before benefits are taken.

8:6.2.3 Transfer to a personal pension

As with a buy-out bond, a personal pension arrangement (see **Chapter 9**) operates on a money purchase basis. However, personal pensions differ from buy-out bonds in that no part of the final benefit is guaranteed. The transfer monies relating to any transferred-in GMP or protected rights in the transferring scheme form protected rights in the personal pension plan and the benefits eventually payable depend on the value of the fund and the amount of pension that can then be provided at that time. The accumulated protected rights fund may only be used to provide pension benefits, payable no earlier than age 60, as specified in **8:5.2.**

From April 2001, regulations were introduced which limit, for 'regulated individuals', the amount of certain lump sum benefits payable from personal pensions where the source of the benefit is a transfer payment from an occupational pension scheme.

A regulated individual is one:

- who is, or was at any time during the period of ten years prior to the date of transfer, a controlling director (see **8:3**); or
- whose annual remuneration is, or was for any year in the six years prior to the date of transfer, more than the earnings cap for the tax year in which the proposed transfer falls (see **8:2.3**), *and* who was aged 45 or over at the date of transfer.

Retirement lump sums are limited, for regulated individuals only, to the amount calculated by reference to the individual's final remuneration from, and service with, the former employer (up to a maximum of 1.5 times final remuneration), increased in line with the RPI up to the date of calculation. If this is greater than 25% of the value of the fund, the cash sum is restricted to 25%. The maximum lump sum benefit is limited to 25% of the personal pension fund if a regulated individual dies leaving a spouse (or nominated dependant) before retirement benefits are taken.

More information about personal pensions is given in **Chapter 9**.

8:7 Types of pension scheme for directors and executives

There are three main types of pension scheme used specifically for directors and executives. These are insured schemes, small self-administered schemes (SSAS) and unapproved schemes. Their main features are as follows.

8:7.1 Insured schemes

Insured pension schemes for directors and executives are usually defined contribution (money purchase) arrangements and are commonly referred to as 'Executive Pension Plans' (or EPPs). Historically, they were used to top-up key employees' retirement benefits provided by a staff pension scheme.

EPPs are normally individual arrangements for one executive, although group plans do exist. An insurance company is responsible for all aspects of the operation of the scheme, including the provision of scheme documentation, communication of details about the scheme (including the mandatory annual benefit statements) to members, securing Inland Revenue approval and the collection and investment of contributions.

EPPs are typically either invested in the unit-linked funds offered by an insurance company (or with links to the funds of other specialist fund managers) or in with-profits funds. Older plans may be invested on a deposit administration, or a non-profit basis but these are increasingly rare. The main features of unit-linked and with-profits pension investments are as follows.

(a) *Unit-linked*

Insurance companies offer a wide range of suitable tax-exempt unit-linked funds for the trustees of EPPs to invest in. They vary from numerous risk-graded managed funds to specialist sector funds (classified as in section **3:4.1**). The value of a unit-linked pension investment fluctuates with the value of the underlying assets on which the price of the units is based. Consequently, unit-linked policies usually involve volatility in the value of the fund, but can produce investment returns that are substantially in excess of inflation.

Some providers offer a 'lifestyle' option which switches investments progressively in the period up to anticipated retirement, out of UK or global equities into fixed interest securities and cash. This can protect the scheme member against sudden falls in equity markets over the period immediately prior to retirement and provides a good match with the investments that underlie the annuity to be purchased at retirement.

(b) *With-profits*

The benefit of a with-profits investment is that investment returns are 'smoothed' over the duration of the policy. Each year, the insurance company declares and pays an annual bonus which, once credited, cannot be taken away. Insurance companies aim to maintain a consistent level of bonus year-on-year in order to continue to attract new money for investment. After making deductions for the company's administrative and other expenses, the investment returns it makes are applied partly towards the payment of bonuses and, in years when investment returns have been favourable, towards the reserves it maintains. These reserves can be used to pay bonuses at levels that may not have been justified by the investment returns made in periods when investment conditions are less favourable.

In addition to the annual bonuses, insurance companies pay 'terminal' bonuses when a policy matures or on early surrender. The amount of bonus is mainly based on the capital appreciation over the term of the policy. If there has been no (or negative) capital return or if annual bonuses have been less than justified by the investments made, an insurance company may reduce the value of the with-profits investment upon early surrender, by applying a 'market value adjustment'.

Insurance companies have generally now 'unitised' their with-profits funds so that investors hold units which increase in value as bonuses are added.

When benefits are due to be paid by either type of EPP, it is customary for an annuity to be bought using the proceeds of the insurance policy. The annuity can either be bought from the EPP provider or from a different company under an 'open market option'. Purchasing an annuity ensures that the executive's pension is maintained at an agreed level for the remainder of his lifetime. However annuity rates have fallen substantially in recent years. Individuals with larger EPP funds have tended to prefer deferring the purchase of their annuity, and instead have either received their retirement income directly from the EPP funds or, more commonly, have transferred to a personal pension and made use of income drawdown facilities (see **9:12.3**).

It is now normal practice, in the case of all types of insured schemes, for an open market option to be available without penalty at retirement age. The amount normally transferred is the fund after payment of any retirement lump sum. It is usually worthwhile for several quotations to be obtained at retirement from leading life assurance companies in the annuity market and then for the annuity to be bought from the company offering the best value.

8:7.2 Small self-administered schemes

Small self-administered schemes (SSAS) are popular for directors, particularly of owner-managed businesses. The main difference between insured and self-administered pension schemes is that the administration and the management of the investments are undertaken by the trustees, who can be nominated by the company, so that control of the assets of the scheme is not passed to an insurance company. Also, SSAS are not required to use their assets to purchase an annuity for retired members until they attain age 75. In the meantime, their pension and lump sum benefits can be paid from the scheme's assets. SSAS trustees should however take professional advice on the most opportune time to purchase an annuity and keep deferral under continuous review.

Pension schemes have been available for controlling directors (see **8:3**) since the 1973 Finance Act. However, it was not until February 1979 that the first proper guidance was given on SSAS. They are now governed by the Retirement Benefit Schemes (Restriction on Discretion to Approve Small Self Administered Schemes) Regulations 1991 (SI 1991 No. 1614).

Since 1979, many insurance companies have brought out their own 'hybrid' SSAS which are part-insured and part self-administered.

A 'small' scheme is one with fewer than 12 members and in this interpretation, the Inland Revenue will ignore relatively low-paid employees who have been included (often with derisory benefits) in a SSAS in order to bring the total membership to 12 or slightly more. Schemes will also not be regarded as 'small' if no members are 'connected' to any other member, to the employer (normally as a director) or to the trustees. An insurance company scheme established under self-administered documentation but with all its assets fully insured is not regarded as a small self-administered scheme.

Every SSAS must have a 'pensioneer trustee' (an independent individual or body, widely involved with occupational pension schemes and considered appropriate to act as a SSAS trustee by the Inland Revenue). The pensioneer trustee must give an undertaking that he will not consent to any improper termination of a scheme of which he is a trustee. It must also jointly own the assets of a SSAS with the other trustees and must give written agreement before any funds can be paid out of a SSAS. The resignation or replacement of the pensioneer trustee must be reported to the Inland Revenue within a specified timescale.

There must be an actuarial valuation of the cost of funding the scheme's liabilities (normally the Inland Revenue maximum benefits for the scheme members) at its inception and thereafter, taking into account the assets already accumulated in a scheme, at three-yearly intervals. Contributions cannot be paid to the scheme unless justified by the latest actuarial valuation.

In order to obtain Inland Revenue approval for a SSAS, its sole purpose must be pension provision and not tax avoidance. A company is only permitted to have one SSAS. It should be noted that to comply with the provisions of the Financial Services and Markets Act, all members should be trustees.

8:7.2.1 SSAS investments

A major feature of SSAS, and reason for their attractiveness to owner-managers, is their ability to invest in 'employer-related' assets such as:

- loans to the company;
- shares in the company; or
- property that is leased to the company and used for its business.

Employer-related investments must be arranged at arm's length on fully commercial terms.

SSAS trustees may only invest a maximum of 25% of the scheme's assets in shares in or loans to the employer during the first two years of the scheme. The valuation of the scheme's assets in this period cannot include assets arising from the payment of a transfer value or held because the trustees have deferred purchasing annuities for retired members.

After the initial two-year period, the trustees may invest up to 50% of the total market value of the scheme assets (excluding those from deferring annuity purchase) in the aggregate of loans to and shares in the employer. Any loans to the employer must be at a commercial rate of interest (typically 3% per annum above bank base rate).

If the trustees of a SSAS wish to invest in shares in any unlisted company, they cannot invest more than the 25%/50% limits described above. In addition, they cannot purchase shares which carry more than 30% of the voting rights in the company or entitle the trustees to more than 30% of any dividends declared by the company.

If a company property is sold to a SSAS (or paid as an 'in specie' contribution) and leased back, the company receives a corporation tax deduction for the rent paid, which is received in the SSAS fund with no liability to tax. When the property is sold, any gain in the property value is free from capital gains tax.

The trustees may invest in a wide range of assets that are not employer-related, excluding personal chattels such as yachts or works of art and (except in specific circumstances) residential property.

Special arrangements apply to schemes where the trustees held investments prior to 15 July 1991 (the date of implementation of the regulations).

The administrator of a SSAS must report the following transactions to the Inland Revenue within 90 days:

(a) the acquisition or disposal of land, including buildings or other structures;

(b) any loans to an employer or associated employer;

(c) the acquisition or disposal of shares in the employer or associated employer or in an unlisted company;

(d) any borrowing by the trustees; and

(e) the purchase, sale or lease from or to an employer or associated employer of any asset other than as described in **(a)** or **(c)** above.

8:7.2.2 Suitability

A SSAS can be suitable where:

(a) the amount of contributions is significant, as the costs of setting up and maintaining a SSAS are high compared to an insured scheme. Annual contributions should be at least £10,000 and if a special contribution is paid it should be at least £100,000; or

(b) it will be used to make specific, typically employer-related investments.

The main advantages of a SSAS compared to an insured scheme are as follows:

(a) *investment flexibility* – the trustees (generally the scheme members and the pensioneer trustee) have direct control of the investments of a SSAS and any changes of investment manager can be made easily by the trustees;

(b) *investment choice* – the range of investment options is wider than with an insured scheme;

(c) *costs* – insurance company charges if based on a percentage of the pension fund can be higher than with a SSAS; however a SSAS can have comparatively higher set-up costs in view of the need for bespoke documentation and an actuarial valuation;

(d) *employer-related investments* – the ability to make investments such as property leased back to the company.

The principal disadvantage of SSAS is that they involve more administration than insured schemes, often requiring the involvement of company management. They involve greater set-up costs and there is a need for a triennial actuarial valuation. Depending on the investments made, the ongoing costs may be greater or less than those involved with a comparable insured pension scheme.

Although SSAS can be quite complex pension arrangements, they can be well suited to the requirements of many executives and business owners. Specialist assistance should be sought when considering a SSAS.

8:7.3 Unapproved schemes

Employers are able to provide more generous benefits than those allowed for tax-approved pension schemes but the usual tax advantages will not apply. This can be done by establishing an unapproved top-up scheme, which can be funded or unfunded.

Benefits from a funded unapproved retirement benefits scheme (known as a 'FURBS') are tax free if paid as a cash sum, but taxed if paid as a pension. For this reason, FURBS benefits are normally paid as a cash sum. Contributions to a FURBS are taxed as income of the employee and they are also subject to national insurance contributions. A key feature of FURBS, compared with the payment of bonuses to the individual, is that investment income is not taxed at the higher (40%) tax rate. Income on FURBS investments is taxed either at 20% or 22% (at 2002/03 tax rates) depending on its source. Capital gains are taxed at an initial rate of 34% with taper relief reducing the effective tax rate to 20% on disposal of an asset after ten years or more. There is an annual capital gains allowance of one-half of the individual allowance (i.e. £3,850 in 2002/03).

There is no tax payable in relation to an unfunded unapproved scheme until benefits are paid. At that point, the benefit, whether pension or cash, is taxed at the marginal rate of income tax applicable to the recipient. Unfunded schemes are effectively a promise to an individual by his employer to pay a benefit upon his retirement, out of the company's resources. There is no certainty that benefits would be paid, for example if the employer became insolvent.

Because they are not subject to the benefit limits or other requirements for tax approval, these schemes are attractive to executives and other high earners who are subject to the earnings cap introduced by the Finance Act 1989 (see **8:2.3**). Since this legislation was introduced there has been a significant growth in the popularity of unapproved schemes, particularly FURBS.

8:8 Main uses of pension arrangements for directors and executives

Formal pension arrangements, whether approved or unapproved, are primarily used by business owners, directors and key executives to ensure that they have an adequate level of income in retirement. SSAS, EPPs and unapproved schemes are used to supplement the state pension and the benefits payable to executives under any wider employee pension scheme.

Other uses include the following.

(a) *Mitigating the company's corporation tax liabilities* (see **8:1**). Large pension contributions can have a significant effect on a company's taxable profits. It is possible for a company to retain control over some or all of the amount contributed if payments are made to a SSAS which then makes an employer-related investment.

(b) *Reducing the value of a company.* The value of a company for both capital gains tax and inheritance tax purposes can be reduced as a result of the payment of significant pension contributions. This is particularly beneficial at the time of disposal of a company by a business owner.

(c) *Inheritance tax planning.* A good pension arrangement provides a continuing income for the member and his or her spouse in retirement. It is therefore possible that a business owner may be willing to dispose of personal assets during his lifetime and thereby benefit from inheritance tax exemptions. Also, lump sum death-in-service benefits may be provided free of inheritance tax for the benefit of children and dependants, by way of an 'expression of wish letter' to the trustees of the pension scheme. This letter should be regularly reviewed in case it becomes appropriate to change the individuals nominated.

(d) *Funding for cash.* Individuals eligible for the pre 1987 Inland Revenue limits regime (see **8:2.1**) are able to receive their entire pension fund as a tax-free cash sum (within Inland Revenue limits) if they have sufficient service and earnings from the company.

8:9 Maximising benefits

Due to the considerable tax concessions given to company pension schemes, it will be beneficial to directors and executives if their pension arrangements can be maximised (without overfunding). The following are some of the ways in which this can be done.

(a) Dynamising past salaries. As mentioned in **8:3**, remuneration may be 'dynamised' in proportion to the increase in the cost of living for the period between the end of the year on which the remuneration is based and the date of retirement. Therefore, when the rate of inflation has exceeded the actual increases in remuneration, notional final remuneration should be calculated by taking the actual remuneration for an earlier period and applying the increase in the RPI up to the retirement date. This will then produce a larger amount on which pension benefits can be based than the final remuneration actually paid.

(b) Arranging for the normal retirement age to be the earliest allowed by the Inland Revenue. As a result of this, larger contributions would be required for the pension fund to build up to produce the required benefits, due to the shorter period available and fewer contributions payable. In addition, a larger fund would be required to provide the pension benefits as they would normally be payable for a longer period. The current retirement date can be changed, if necessary, to achieve this (see **8:4**).

(c) Funding for post-retirement pensions to escalate by the maximum permitted (the greater of the increase in the cost of living, as measured by the RPI, or 3% per annum).

(d) Maximising all death-in-service benefits.

(e) Some business owners can employ their spouse (as a director if appropriate). In this way, the spouse can be paid a salary and be provided with pension benefits in their own right. The Inland Revenue will however need to be satisfied that the spouse is a genuine employee actively working on a regular basis in the business.

9 Personal pensions and AVCs

9:1 Introduction

This chapter looks at personal pension arrangements (including stakeholder pensions) for self-employed individuals and for employees who are not covered by an occupational pension scheme, and 'Additional Voluntary Contribution (AVC)' arrangements for pension scheme members who wish to top-up their benefits by making further personal contributions.

Personal pensions were introduced in the Finance (No 2) Act 1987 and came into effect on 1 July 1988, replacing section 226 retirement annuities (see **9:8**). Stakeholder pensions are a new type of low-cost personal pension introduced from 6 April 2001.

Contributions to stakeholder or personal pensions can be made by anyone with 'relevant earnings' (see **9:2**). These individuals can be:

- self-employed (including sole traders or partners in a partnership);
- employees who are not in an occupational pension scheme (because their employer does not provide one or because they have opted not to belong to it); or
- employees who are members of an occupational pension scheme, but for death benefits only.

Contributions up to an amount known as the 'earnings threshold' may be paid by individuals with no relevant earnings or (subject to certain restrictions) by individuals who are also accruing pension benefits under an occupational pension scheme. The earnings threshold for 2002/03 is £3,600. To qualify, a pension scheme member cannot be a 'controlling director' (see **8:3**) and must have P60 earnings that are less than a 'remuneration limit' (currently £30,000) in the tax year.

Personal pensions may be provided by life assurance companies (including friendly societies), building societies, banks and unit trust management groups.

Unlike company pension arrangements where contribution limits are determined by final remuneration and length of service, the benefits available from personal pensions are not subject to monetary limits. The only restriction is on the maximum amount that may be contributed in a tax year (see **9:2**).

Precise notes on the operation of personal pension schemes can be found in the Inland Revenue booklet IR76 (see: www.inlandrevenue.gov.uk/pensionschemes/ir76.rtf).

AVC schemes are subject to the legislation applicable to occupational pension schemes (see **Chapter 8**) and are used to provide additional benefits to those payable under an employer's pension scheme. There are two main types, 'in-scheme' and free-standing (FSAVC) arrangements. More information about both types of AVC is given in section **9.9**.

9:2 Personal pension contributions

If an individual contributes to a personal pension arrangement, the amount that may be paid in a tax year is limited to a percentage of the individual's 'net relevant earnings' in the year. The maximum percentage varies according to the age of the person concerned on 6 April in the tax year. Relevant earnings are defined as any income chargeable to UK tax for the tax year in question that is:

- an emolument chargeable under Schedule E from an office or employment held by the individual (unless pensionable under an occupational pension scheme);
- income from any property which is attached to or forms part of the emoluments of an office or employment held (unless pensionable);
- income which is chargeable under Schedule D and is immediately derived from the carrying on or exercise of a trade, profession or vocation, either as an individual or as a partner acting personally or in a partnership; or
- income from patent rights treated as earned income.

Appendix 4 contains a list of various types of income and states whether or not it is defined as *relevant* earnings. A precise definition can be found in section 644 of the Income and Corporation Taxes Act (ICTA) 1988.

Net relevant earnings are an individual's relevant earnings for the tax year in question less the various deductions made in computing taxable income. They are limited in any year to the amount of the earnings cap applicable. This cap was introduced in the Finance Act 1989 and limits the earnings that can be used for calculating maximum contributions to a personal pension. The initial level of the cap was set at £60,000 and the intention was that this would rise in line with RPI, although the uplift was missed in 1993/94.

The earnings caps have been as follows:

Tax year	*Earnings cap* £
1989/90	60,000
1990/91	64,800
1991/92	71,400
1992/93	75,000
1993/94	75,000
1994/95	76,800
1995/96	78,600
1996/97	82,200
1997/98	84,000
1998/99	87,600
1999/00	90,600
2000/01	91,800
2001/02	95,400
2002/03	97,200

Where an individual wishes to pay more than the earnings threshold (£3,600 in 2002/03) in a tax year (see **9:1**), the maximum allowable personal pension contributions are as follows:

Age at beginning of tax year	*Maximum contributions (% of net relevant earnings)*
35 or less	17.5
36-45	20
46-50	25
51-55	30
56-60	35
61-75	40

An individual may, from 6 April 2001, nominate the year that they wish to be used as the 'basis year' for their net relevant earnings. This year may be:

- the current tax year, or
- any of the *previous* five tax years. The individual did not need to have been a member of a personal pension plan during the basis year, but they must have had net relevant earnings in that year.

When calculating how much to contribute, an individual must use their net relevant earnings from the basis year and (if applicable) the earnings cap from the current year.

The net relevant earnings in the basis year may be used as the basis for calculating contributions over the earnings threshold not only in the basis year itself, or the current tax year, but also in the five years *following* the basis year. It is possible to change the basis year, for example if earnings increase, in which case the new basis year may be used to calculate contributions in that year and the five following tax years.

The effect of this is that when net relevant earnings cease, the rules allow the earnings of the basis year to be used for contributions for a further five years.

Example 6

A man aged 46 wishes to maximise contributions for the foreseeable future. He nominates 2001/02 as the basis year and is therefore able to contribute £21,250 (i.e. 25% of his basis year earnings of £85,000) for five years until 2005/06, and £25,500 (30% of £85,000 because he has reached age 51) for one year. After his earnings cease in 2006/07, he can continue to contribute the appropriate percentage of the basis year earnings for the five post cessation years. He therefore continues to pay £25,500 for four years and £29,750 for the one remaining qualifying post cessation year (as he is then aged 56 at the beginning of 2012/13). From April 2013 the amount of his contributions reduces to the earnings threshold (currently £3,600).

Tax year ending 5 April	*Age at beginning of tax year*	*Net relevant earnings*	*Maximum contributions (% of net relevant earnings)*	*Maximum contributions*
		£		*£*
2002	46	85,000	25	21,250
2003	47	70,000	25	21,250
2004	48	73,000	25	21,250
2005	49	65,000	25	21,250
2006	50	52,000	25	21,250
2007	51	63,000	30	25,500
2008	52	0	30	25,500
2009	53	0	30	25,500
2010	54	0	30	25,500
2011	55	0	30	25,500
2012	56	0	35	29,750
2013	57	0	35	3,600

Where a personal pension has been effected by an employee, it is also possible for a contribution to be paid by his employer, although the overall limits shown above must not be exceeded. Minimum contributions and age-related rebates paid by the DSS for an arrangement that is used to contract-out of S2P (see **9:4**) are not included when determining the maximum contributions payable.

From 6 April 2001, the maximum contributions qualifying for tax relief in respect of the provision of new death-in-service benefits are limited to 10% of contributions paid towards retirement benefits. Previously the limit was 5% of net relevant earnings and this continues to apply for arrangements in force on 6 April 2001. The contributions paid reduce the maximum contributions available to provide the benefits **(a)** to **(d)** in **9:3**.

9:3 Main benefits

The following are the main benefits that can be provided by a personal pension arrangement.

(a) *Retirement pension*. This will normally commence at a minimum age of 50 with the maximum age at which the pension must be taken being 75. However, for certain professions and occupations, the Inland Revenue has agreed earlier retirement ages (see **Appendix 3**).

As an alternative to a full pension, a tax-free lump sum may be taken together with a reduced pension. The pension and lump sum must be taken simultaneously (unless income drawdown is used – see **9:12.3**). The maximum cash sum allowed is 25% of the overall fund excluding the value of the 'Protected Rights' fund (see **9:4**).

In practice, it is generally worthwhile to take the lump sum together with the reduced pension as the lump sum can (if required) be used to buy a 'purchased life annuity'. If this is done, a higher net income is normally obtained than from the full pension, as part of the purchased life annuity is tax free. In addition, taking the lump sum provides liquid funds, a facility not offered by an annuity.

(b) *Dependant's retirement pension* (this must not exceed the amount of the individual's pension) payable to a spouse or other person financially dependent on the retired person.

(c) *Annual increases* in the individual's and dependant's retirement pensions.

(d) *Lump sum death-in-service benefit* with the maximum allowed being the value of the pension fund at the time of death.

(e) *Supplementary death-in-service benefits* to provide a cash lump sum or pension for any named individual. These benefits can be provided only by an insurance company or friendly society.

9:4 Contracting-out

Employed persons, including those in contracted-in occupational schemes, can use a personal pension to contract-out of the State Second Pension (S2P). Personal pensions used in this way are known as 'appropriate personal pension schemes'.

Such schemes receive a compulsory minimum contribution, equal to the national insurance contracting-out rebate (see below) and payable by the Inland Revenue (National Insurance Contributions Office) directly to the pension provider chosen by the individual. The fund built up by these contributions forms Protected Rights, the benefits from which may be taken only from State pension age or later and in a prescribed manner (see **8:5.2**).

For the 2002/03 tax year, the combined national insurance rebate for employer and employee was 2.6% of 'band earnings', which are earnings between the Class I national insurance lower and upper earnings limits (£3,900 and £30,420 per annum for 2002/03). Since 6 April 1997, an age-related national insurance rebate has also been payable. The amount of the age-related rebate is determined by a complex formula which depends on age and earnings.

The levels of rebate are calculated by the Government Actuary every five years and are calculated to provide benefits from a personal pension that match those payable under S2P. The calculations take account of the expenses that would be levied by personal pension providers.

9:5 Personal pensions – taxation position

As with company pensions, the provision of personal pensions is regarded very favourably by the Inland Revenue, with the taxation position being broadly as follows.

(a) Contributions up to the maximum permitted are effectively allowed against the highest income tax rates payable in the tax year in which the contribution is paid. For the self-employed, contributions made on or before 5 April 2001 were paid gross with the tax relief being claimed from the Inland Revenue, either using form PP120 or via the tax return. For those in employment, employee contributions are paid net of basic rate tax, so for example an individual who wishes to pay a personal pension contribution of £100 need only pay £78 in the 2002/03 tax year. The plan administrator (normally an insurance company) claims the remaining £22 from the Inland Revenue. Any claim by an individual for higher rate tax relief is made via the tax return or by using form PP120. From 6 April 2001, all contributions made by the self-employed and by the employed are paid net of basic rate tax, with higher rate relief (if applicable) being given by means of the tax return. Employer contributions are paid gross. Prior to 6 April 2001, contributions could not exceed an individual's taxable earned income for the year in which relief was claimed. Since then all contributions attract a minimum of 22% tax relief irrespective of the tax actually paid. Where an individual pays higher rate tax on either earned or investment income, further relief of 18% will be available.

(b) By election, a contribution paid in one tax year may be treated for tax purposes as having been paid in the previous tax year. This is known as 'carry back'. It is particularly useful if an individual (particularly a self-employed individual) wants to pay the maximum permitted contribution but does not know the amount of his net relevant earnings for the year (perhaps because his accounts have not been finalised). From 6 April 2001, a contribution must be paid by 31 January in the following tax year to be eligible for 'carry back' treatment. An election for this treatment must be made before or at the time the contribution is made.

(c) Investment income and capital gains accumulate within the pension fund free of all UK tax. However, since 2 July 1997, pension schemes have been unable to recover tax credits attaching to UK dividends.

(d) The resulting pension is treated as earned income.

(e) The lump sum benefit on retirement is tax-free.

(f) The lump sum death-in-service benefits are free of income tax. These benefits, apart from any amount payable in respect of the Protected Rights fund, are usually paid at the scheme administrators' discretion (it is normal for the policyholder to nominate to whom he would like the benefits paid) and are therefore free of inheritance tax liability. It is also possible to make all lump sum death-in-service benefits the subject of an individual trust and this will again remove any inheritance tax liability.

9:6 Options available

Personal pensions are very flexible contracts, with the following options often being available.

(a) Regular contribution contracts can allow payments to be increased, decreased, temporarily stopped and restarted or entirely omitted. However, depending upon the charging structure of the contract, penalties may arise on reduction or cessation of regular contributions. Contracts may also be set up with 'one-off' single contributions.

(b) Switching facilities are now available within the same pension plan whereby both the existing fund and/or future contributions can be switched from a with-profits basis to a unit-linked basis and vice versa (under these plans, with-profits funds are themselves on a unitised basis).

(c) Until 5 April 2001, waiver of contributions under regular contribution contracts could be arranged by the payment of small additional contributions. These qualify for tax relief in the same way as the normal pension contributions. Consequently, if the person concerned is unable to work due to a prolonged period of sickness or disability, the contributions falling due are waived, thus enabling benefits to be maintained. Without the waiver of contribution option, benefits could not be maintained due to the lack of net relevant earnings, even if the individual had the necessary money to pay the contributions. This option is particularly important when the tax-free lump sum on retirement is to be used to repay a loan. Where waiver existed prior to 5 April 2001 or an option to take out the benefit existed, the benefit can continue or be initiated.

    From 6 April 2001, those wishing to insure the continuity of their contributions have to take out a separate policy. A personal pension scheme may nevertheless allow a member to elect that up to 25% of the contribution may be used to pay premiums under an insurance contract providing ill-health early retirement benefits. The benefit is an annuity for an individual who retires early as a result of incapacity, the amount of which is equal to the annuity that would have become payable if the individual had retired at his normal retirement date.

(d) In the event of death before retirement, the contributions paid can be returned, either with or without interest. Alternatively, the full value of the pension fund can be returned.

(e) An open market option is generally available whereby the pension fund can be built up with one pension provider but the actual pension taken with a different company if this offers higher annuity rates at retirement.

Although the open market option can be very important, it is the general level of interest rates prevailing at the time the pension is taken that is likely to have an even greater influence on the actual amount to be received.

(f) At retirement, it is usually possible for a person to elect for his pension benefits to be guaranteed for a period of up to ten years or be taken on a joint life, second death basis. This can be particularly useful if he is not in good health at that time. If the individual has only a short life expectancy, it may be worthwhile for him to delay taking his benefits. In these circumstances, the amount payable on death before retirement will often exceed the guaranteed retirement benefits. Alternatively, an 'impaired life' annuity can be purchased; however, detailed medical evidence will be required.

(g) An option is often available for the pension benefits to be taken in stages rather than the entire benefits commencing at the same time. This 'phased' retirement is normally arranged by the pension plan being divided into multiple policies which can then be dealt with independently.

(h) Instead of taking level pension benefits, it is possible to arrange for them to increase in accordance with one of the following methods:

   (i) by a fixed percentage annually;

   (ii) on a with-profits basis (the pension is dependent on bonuses credited);

   (iii) in line with the RPI;

   (iv) in line with the value of the underlying fund in the case of a unit-linked policy (under this method, the amount of the pension can also decrease).

Where an increasing pension is taken, it will generally commence at a significantly lower amount than the corresponding level pension and consequently it will usually take several years (often more than ten years) before the amount of the level pension is reached. Therefore, unless the person concerned believes he has an above average life expectancy or expects the increasing pension to rise rapidly, a level pension can be more attractive.

(i) Term assurance can be taken out with tax relief effectively allowed at the individual's highest rates of income tax payable. The benefits can be written under trust to pass free of inheritance tax to any dependant.

If net relevant earnings should cease, some life companies may permit the conversion of the policy into a term assurance policy with no medical evidence required.

(j) Loan facilities are often available prior to the proposed retirement date (the main advantages of loan facilities are discussed at **9:16**).

(k) The benefits under a personal pension may be transferred to most other types of pension arrangement but special conditions apply to the benefits, if any, in the Protected Rights fund. Transfer payments from any pension arrangement may be made to a personal pension, although in certain cases it may be necessary for additional restrictions to be imposed and guarantees may be lost.

9:7 Stakeholder pension schemes

From April 2001, individuals have been able to contribute to a new type of pension arrangement known as a stakeholder pension. This scheme has been introduced with the aim of encouraging a greater number of individuals to save for their retirement. To qualify as a stakeholder pension, a pension scheme must satisfy a number of minimum conditions:

- it must be a money purchase arrangement;
- management charges in each year must not amount to more than 1% of the total value of the fund and are taken from the fund;
- as well as the 1%, the law allows pension providers to recover costs and charges they have to pay for certain other things such as stamp duty or other charges for buying and selling investments for the fund;
- any extra services and any extra charges not provided for by law must be optional. Extra services must be offered under a separate arrangement with clearly defined costs for the services being offered;
- the scheme must accept transfers in, and there must be no additional charge for transferring to a different stakeholder pension;
- the minimum contribution to a stakeholder pension cannot be set higher than £20 (schemes may set a lower minimum contribution if they wish). Contributions can be paid weekly, monthly (or at other intervals), or they can be a single one-off contribution;

- to look after the interests of their members, schemes must have either trustees or stakeholder managers;
- for trust-based schemes, one-third of the trustees must be independent;
- schemes must appoint a scheme auditor or a reporting accountant to check the annual declaration made by the trustees or managers to ensure that the scheme complies with the relevant regulations;
- schemes must have a statement of investment principles;
- schemes must have a default investment option.

In certain circumstances, employers are required to nominate a stakeholder scheme for eligible employees and deduct from pay any contributions those employees may want to make. Employers are not required to contribute (at present). Such schemes do not have to be made available where:

(a) an employer has less than five employees;

(b) an employee has earned below the national insurance lower earnings limit during the last three months;

(c) an employee has been employed for less than three months;

(d) an employee is eligible to join an occupational pension scheme after a waiting period of not more than 12 months;

(e) an employer has agreed to contribute to a personal pension plan for all employees over age 18, with a minimum contribution of 3% of basic salary.

Another aspect of stakeholder pensions is the fact that contributions may be paid to them by (or for) individuals (such as children or non-working spouses) who have no relevant earnings. As a result, they are likely to become increasingly used for personal tax planning.

9:8 Section 226 retirement annuities

Prior to 1 July 1988, pension arrangements for the self-employed and those in non-pensionable employment were covered by section 226 of the Income and Corporation Taxes Act 1970 (which was consolidated as section 620 of the Income and Corporation Taxes Act 1988). Contracts in force before that date remain governed by this legislation and most allow for contributions to continue even where only single contribution contracts have been arranged.

Most of the personal pension details in this chapter apply equally to section 226 contracts, with the following exceptions.

(a) The Finance Act 1989 earnings limit (see **9:2**) does not apply to section 226 contracts but the percentage contribution limits have not been increased. The limits applying to section 226 contracts are as follows.

Age at beginning of year of assessment	*Maximum contributions (% of earnings)*
Up to and including 50	17.5
51–55	20.0
56–60	22.5
61 or more	27.5

The limits for personal pension contributions will apply in place of these limits in any tax year in which the investor pays a contribution to a personal pension arrangement, including personal pension term assurance.

(b) The definition of relevant earnings for retirement annuities is different to that for personal pensions. A full definition can be found in section 623 of the Income and Corporation Taxes Act 1988. The main difference relates to the treatment of:

(i) share option proceeds;

(ii) golden handshakes and payments on removal from office; and

(iii) emoluments of controlling directors.

(c) The retirement pension cannot normally commence before age 60. As an alternative to a full pension, a tax-free lump sum on retirement may be taken together with a reduced pension. The maximum lump sum allowed is three times the amount of the remaining pension (it is permissible for the calculation to be on the basis that the pension is payable yearly in arrears with no guaranteed period, thus increasing the lump sum available). This formula normally produces a lump sum of between 25% and 40% of the fund. The precise figure is dependent on the level of interest rates and the age of the person at the time the benefits are taken.

(d) For each contract started on or after 17 March 1987, the maximum lump sum allowed is £150,000.

(e) A transfer payment can be received only from another section 226 contract.

(f) Complex calculations of the maximum contributions payable can arise where a person has section 226 contracts and personal pensions, especially where net relevant earnings are in excess of the earnings 'cap'. Generally, it is advantageous to ensure that contributions to only one type of contract (and not both) are paid in each tax year. Computations of available reliefs, where the carry forward of unused relief is combined with the payment of both personal pension and retirement annuity contributions, are also complex. Reference should be made to the Inland Revenue booklet IR76.

(g) A section 226 arrangement cannot be used to contract-out of S2P.

(h) The funds in a section 226 arrangement can be transferred to a personal pension plan. This is particularly useful if the investor wishes to draw his benefits between the ages of 50 and 60 or defer the purchase of an annuity by using the income drawdown provisions. In some circumstances such a transfer also enables greater tax-free cash lump sum benefits to be paid.

(i) The ending of carry forward provisions for unused relief from 5 April 2001 in respect of personal pensions does not apply to retirement annuity contracts. Where retirement annuity contributions paid in a fiscal year are less than the maximum contributions permitted, the difference (known as unused relief) may be carried forward for up to six years. Relief will be given in the year in which the excess contribution is paid, or deemed to have been paid, at the tax rates applicable for that year.

9:9 Additional voluntary contribution arrangements

Individuals who are provided with benefits under an occupational pension scheme may increase these benefits by making additional voluntary contributions (AVCs). The maximum permitted AVC is 15% of remuneration in a tax year, less the amount of the individual's contribution to the scheme that is required as a condition of membership. 'Remuneration' for this purpose must not exceed £97,200 in 2002/03 for those affected by the post 1989 benefit limits (see **8:2.3**).

Scheme members are able to pay 'free-standing' (FSAVC) contributions to the pension provider of their own choice (only one per tax year), or contribute to the AVC facility which must be provided within an employer's pension scheme. The latter is generally to be preferred if costs can be spread across the scheme members, unless the range of funds available is restricted or has an unsatisfactory investment performance record. Because of concern that free-standing AVCs had been mis-sold in circumstances where an employer's scheme was more appropriate, the Financial Services Authority has ordered a review of such contracts.

Individuals paying FSAVCs are able to deduct basic rate tax from the contribution, before paying the AVC to the pension provider. Higher-rate taxpayers can claim a further 18% relief through their tax return.

Benefits provided by FSAVCs have to be taken in the form of pension rather than a lump sum. This also generally applies to contributions under 'in-scheme' AVC arrangements entered into by employees on or after 8 April 1987. Employees who were already in such arrangements on 7 April 1987 may still commute pension benefits for a lump sum, subject to the Inland Revenue limits described in **Chapter 8**.

Although no part of the benefits secured by AVC arrangements effected on or after 8 April 1987 can be taken in the form of cash at retirement, the scheme can take into account the total benefits available from the scheme when calculating the maximum tax-free cash sum at retirement. This may give an advantage to AVCs paid within the scheme rather than FSAVCs, unless the scheme also takes into account the benefits from FSAVCs alongside any normal AVCs.

There are reporting procedures for FSAVCs, known as 'headroom checks' which are designed to prevent the payment of contributions to provide benefits in excess of the benefit limits. For FSAVC contributions of up to £2,400 a year, the pension provider carries out a small number of simple checks which do not involve the employer. Further checks before retirement are not normally necessary unless the contributions exceed this amount.

If, despite these checks, benefits at retirement (either from an in-scheme AVC or an FSAVC) exceed the Inland Revenue limits, the surplus funds are returned to the employee subject to a tax charge. The rate of tax deducted reflects the tax relief received on contributions and on the build up of funds.

The payment of AVCs may be worthwhile in the following cases.

(a) Where the benefits offered by a company pension scheme are low. Although commutation from the AVC scheme may no longer be allowed, it might still be possible to increase the overall pension benefits by the payment of AVCs and then take the maximum tax-free lump sum at retirement from the main scheme. However, this would cause a reduction in the pension provided from the main scheme and consequently post-retirement increases may be lost, although the AVC fund can be used for this purpose.

(b) The pension scheme may have been introduced late in the individual's working life with the result that he may receive only low pension benefits at retirement.

(c) A change of job may not allow an individual sufficient time in his new pension scheme to build up the maximum pension.

(d) Earnings for the purposes of the pension scheme may not reflect an individual's total earnings, with commissions or bonuses not having been taken into account.

(e) No provision may have been made in the pension scheme for escalation of post-retirement pensions earned before 6 April 1997.

However, before an individual decides to pay AVCs, he should bear in mind that the fund built up from the AVCs is locked in until retirement. A relaxation was announced in July 1999 enabling AVC benefits to be taken at any time between age 50 (or earlier in the event of incapacity) and age 75. If taken before the main scheme benefits, they may not be taken in lump sum form, even if contributions started before April 1987.

Many employers are introducing a facility to enable employees' pension contributions to be made by salary sacrifice. Under this arrangement an individual's salary is reduced, or rights to a bonus waived, but the company pays an additional pension contribution for their benefit. In many cases, the employer also passes on some or all of the national insurance saving made by the employer as a result of the reduction in the employee's earnings. It should be borne in mind that under this type of arrangement any excess funds cannot be returned to the member at retirement and must remain within the scheme for the benefit of other members. Also, life assurance benefits, mortgage limits or even maximum retirement benefits could be reduced as a result of the salary sacrifice.

There are conflicting factors operating in the choice between AVCs and salary sacrifice and the decision should be considered carefully.

9:10 With-profits policies

The main types of insured schemes available for personal pensions are similar to those for company pension arrangements for directors and executives and have already been considered in **Chapter 8**.

The following are the principal types of with-profits policies together with their characteristics.

(a) *Funding for cash.* Under this type of contract, a cash fund is built up by the addition of reversionary bonuses to the guaranteed basic sum. A terminal bonus, representing mainly the investment surplus earned over the lifetime of the policy, will also often be added to the pension fund when the policy proceeds are taken. At retirement, if beneficial, the open market option can be exercised. The contract may be arranged on a unitised basis.

(b) *Deferred annuities with guaranteed cash conversion rates.* Unlike the funding for cash contract, this type of arrangement provides a guaranteed basic pension to which pension additions are made in the form of reversionary bonuses and a terminal bonus, if applicable. At retirement, guaranteed conversion factors from pension to cash are applied based on the age and sex of the person concerned. The open market option can then be applied to the converted cash sum. The level of benefits under this contract generally tends to be less volatile than in the case of the funding for cash contract.

(c) *True deferred annuities.* This type of arrangement operates in a similar way to **(b)** above, except that there are no guaranteed conversion rates with the pension being unaffected by the rates of interest at the time of retirement. The pensions receivable under this contract are likely to be more predictable than for the more common with-profits contracts shown under **(a)** and **(b)** above.

9:11 Unit-linked policies

The main considerations relating to unit-linked policies are as follows.

(a) The amount of the pension benefits receivable under a unit-linked policy (and also largely under a with-profits policy) will partly depend on the cash fund at retirement, which results from:

   (i) the amounts and dates of the contributions paid;

   (ii) the performance of the investment fund;

   (iii) the charges levied by the life office.

   It will also be influenced by the translation of this fund into pension, which depends on:

   (i) the sex of the individual and the age at retirement;

   (ii) the level of annuity rates at the time the pension commences;

(iii) the form in which the benefits are taken – cash/pension and such factors as guaranteed period, escalation rate and provision of a dependant's pension.

(b) Although unit-linked policies are normally of a higher risk/higher reward nature than with-profits policies, this need not necessarily be the case. For example, by switching, as retirement approaches, into a gilt and/or a deposit fund where the pension fund is credited with a rate of interest, the value of the fund cannot fall but must increase with interest additions. A switch to a gilt fund will broadly 'purchase' the annuity at the time the switch is made. This is because movements in the value of the fund should match annuity market movements.

(c) Investment market conditions are reflected more immediately in the value of unit-linked policies, whereas there is a 'smoothing' effect in the case of with-profits policies.

(d) It is normally possible to switch at low cost both the amount already accumulated and future contributions between the available underlying investment funds.

(e) Equity-linked funds are often suitable when it is possible to have flexibility in choosing a retirement date in order for it to coincide with a time when stock market values are considered high. However, if this flexibility is not available, consideration should be given to switching into a deposit fund shortly before retirement at a time when stock market values are considered high.

(f) Charges on unit-linked policies can be incurred in the following ways:

(i) policy fees;

(ii) bid/offer spread or other initial charge;

(iii) unit allocations;

(iv) capital levy, applicable under some contracts, for example on units allocated during the first one or two years;

(v) periodic fund management charge;

(vi) early retirement penalties which represent the outstanding balance of the capital levy;

(vii) transfer penalties;

(viii) fund switch charges.

9:12 Drawing benefits

9:12.1 Phased encashment

For those in corporate arrangements, the drawing of pension benefits is usually a one-off event; however, personal pension policyholders have always had the opportunity to phase encashment, by drawing benefits from their various policies when extra income is required. This is particularly useful for the self-employed or business owners who are often able to reduce their workload gradually as retirement approaches. Pension benefits can then be used to top-up income as earnings reduce.

The main advantages of phased encashment are:

(a) there is flexibility over the amount of income that can be drawn;

(b) there is an opportunity to obtain different types of annuities;

(c) there is an opportunity to defer annuity purchase if annuity rates are low and expected to rise;

(d) the unused pension investments remain invested in a tax-free environment; and

(e) the unused pension investments remain available for return to the estate or a trust in the event of death.

The main disadvantages are:

(a) the tax-free cash lump sum becomes phased;

(b) the 'open-market' option (if it is to be used) must be carried out each time a policy is encashed – as a result the pension becomes potentially payable from several offices;

(c) annuity rates could worsen as mortality improves or long-term interest rates worsen.

9:12.2 Staggered vesting

Personal pension administration systems allow policies to be divided into a number of segments (typically 1,000) to enable benefits to be taken progressively rather than all at once. As a result retirement can become more flexible. Whenever income is needed, a number of segments are encashed, through the cancellation of units, to produce income and tax-free cash benefits. The cash element of each policy is used to enhance the income, enabling a part of the income to be paid tax-free. The balance of the fund remains in a tax-free environment until further income is required.

The advantages and disadvantages of staggered vesting are similar to those for phased retirement. However, staggered vesting does have the disadvantage of leaving all invested funds with one pension provider. If necessary this can be overcome by taking out plans with more than one provider when consolidating a pension portfolio at outset, although this does increase the administrative burden. Staggered vesting is the only option in cases where a pension portfolio is not sufficiently well spread to enable phased retirement to take place.

9:12.3 Deferral of personal pension annuity purchase – 'income drawdown'

The Finance Act 1995 introduced the option of deferring the purchase of a personal pension annuity whilst drawing benefits. The option has the following features.

(a) The option allows a policyholder to delay the purchase of an annuity and instead withdraw an income based on upper and lower limits set by the Government Actuary. Currently after tax-free cash has been taken, such income must be between 35% and 100% of the amount of single life level annuity that could have been purchased each year.

(b) The level of income taken each year can vary (within the limits prescribed) to meet the varying personal cash-flow needs of an individual. The option could also be a useful tool in planning, as a means of reducing income tax liabilities on a year-by-year basis.

(c) The upper and lower limits are re-calculated at three-yearly intervals. This ensures that the original purpose of the pension fund (to provide an income throughout retirement) is being maintained, i.e. that the level of income withdrawals is not excessive and may comfortably be supported by the remaining pension fund.

(d) The policyholder must purchase an annuity by his 75th birthday. If a policyholder dies before an annuity has been purchased, a greater level of flexibility is now available to the widow(er) or dependants in relation to the fund that is being used to provide income. These options are:

   (i) take the remaining fund as cash. A 35% tax charge is levied on a total withdrawal; or

(ii) purchase an annuity; or

(iii) continue with the drawdown until the earlier of when the original policyholder would have reached 75 or the 75th birthday of the survivor or dependant. On the death of the survivor, the remaining fund can be passed on as cash, subject to the 35% tax charge and possibly inheritance tax. An annuity can be purchased at any time.

If the beneficiary is neither the spouse nor a financial dependant, payment must be made as a lump sum less the 35% tax charge.

(e) The option of a tax-free cash lump sum is still available upon retirement at the rate applicable to all personal pensions (25% of the 'non-protected rights' fund). Once the lump sum has been taken, income drawdown must start.

(f) After the tax-free cash lump sum has been taken and income drawdown has begun, no additional contributions can be made to the income drawdown plan. However, the fund itself will still benefit from the tax-free status of pension funds.

(g) One of the reasons behind the introduction of income drawdown was to give personal pension holders an alternative to annuities, which in recent years have provided disappointing income levels. Regrettably, a pensioner then has to live with these disappointing returns for the remainder of his or her life.

(h) For income drawdown to be worthwhile, the rate of return from the plan needs to be at least equal to that which could have been obtained from an annuity. This rate of return needs to be after expenses and the ongoing costs of professional advice and investment management.

(i) The 'mortality drag' effect means that individuals who do not buy an annuity when first able to do so may lose some of the cross subsidies available in an insurance company's annuity fund when other annuitants die earlier than anticipated. As a result annuities (other things being equal) become more expensive over time. This further increases the investment return required for drawdown to match the return from an annuity. It is likely that for an adequate return to be achieved by the income drawdown plan, it will have to be invested in equities. This requirement automatically restricts the potential users of the option to those with a relatively high investment risk threshold and a substantial fund.

(j) With larger funds, a reasonable amount of investment diversification can be obtained and the transaction costs are reasonable in the context of the funds at issue. Due to the risks involved in deferring the purchase of an annuity, the option will be more suitable for those who are younger and able to ride out short-term volatility within equity markets. It will therefore not suit those approaching age 75, the point at which an annuity must be purchased.

(k) The key decision is choosing the right moment to switch to an annuity. The optimum time will be when equity markets are high and annuity conversion rates are good.

(l) The basic cost of the option far exceeds the charges incurred in arranging an annuity. Annual investment management charges, along with the professional advice needed on a continuing basis, increase the rate of return needed to better the return from an annuity. If this option is taken, the individual should be comfortable with the continuing involvement of professional advisers.

Individuals benefit from the introduction of income drawdown in that it provides a further choice as to how benefits are taken. Specific beneficiaries are likely to be:

(a) those wishing to delay the purchase of an annuity, in the expectation of annuity rate rises;

(b) those who believe the fund remaining invested will produce a return materially in excess of the return available from a portfolio of long-dated gilts (on which annuity rates are based). For this reason a tolerance to and an understanding of the risks inherent in equity investment is essential for those using the option;

(c) those who are already investing in self-invested personal pensions, as the option is a natural extension of that concept;

(d) those with much younger spouses wishing to maintain flexibility over the level of the survivor's benefits;

(e) those wishing to dovetail income drawdown with their State benefits. This would entail taking a higher income level at outset and reducing it once State benefits become available;

(f) those with substantial pension portfolios who wish to maintain an equity market exposure for as long as possible, perhaps having purchased an annuity with part of their fund;

(g) those for whom the benefits available to the family on death before purchasing an annuity are equally or more important than the level of pension. The death benefits can play a useful role in estate planning.

Inevitably there will be those for whom the cost of and the risks inherent in taking up the option will not match the benefits of additional flexibility. Categories who may not benefit are:

(a) those who are cautious, do not require flexibility or consider annuity rates to be at a reasonable level;

(b) those with smaller funds, where the contract costs and the cost of ongoing professional advice are likely to outweigh any benefits or flexibility;

(c) those in retirement annuities and company schemes, when the transfer to a personal pension causes a material reduction in the tax-free cash lump sum;

(d) those not requiring the lump sum or income until near age 75; and

(e) those who do not wish to be involved in monitoring their funds or continuing professional advice.

Pensioners who are contemplating this option should be very clear that, unless they expose themselves to a substantial amount of investment risk, they are unlikely to exceed the return from an annuity. The option should therefore be regarded as a means of providing flexibility, rather than improving the total retirement income.

While the income drawdown plan must be provided by and administered by a pension provider, it is possible for the investor to appoint his own investment manager. It is recommended that income drawdown plans are established as self-invested personal pensions (see **9:18**), so that the investor is able to change the investment manager if he becomes dissatisfied with the performance of his fund, without having to change plan provider.

9:13 General principles

Before any firm pension recommendations can be made, it is necessary to consider the exact circumstances of the person concerned. These include:

(a) the age of the person;

(b) the number of years until the pension is to be taken and whether the pension date is flexible;

(c) the degree of risk the person is prepared to take;

(d) the likelihood of the person remaining self-employed or not joining an occupational pension scheme;

(e) the extent to which earnings are likely to fluctuate;

(f) the state of health of the person;

(g) the family circumstances of the person;

(h) the extent of surplus income.

Subject to the particular requirements and circumstances of the person concerned, the following general principles will normally apply.

(a) The ability to vary the amount of the payments can be extremely important.

(b) The more volatile funds available under unit-linked policies are usually more appropriate for younger persons, unless the retirement date is flexible.

(c) With-profits, fixed interest and cash deposit funds are often more suitable for persons within five years of the intended date of annuity purchase.

(d) In many cases, it is most appropriate to pay single contributions rather than start regular contribution policies. Contributions paid on a single-premium basis often carry far lower charges than annual premium contracts. They also allow an element of flexibility, as a decision can be taken each year as to the company to which additional contributions are to be paid.

(e) It is normally recommended that contributions should be paid to several different companies, in order to obtain a spread of investment management.

(f) Due to the higher charges made by some companies in respect of longer-term annual contribution contracts, policies should often be written to age 50 as the retirement age. Late retirement rarely incurs a penalty, whereas early retirement does. In addition, many life companies offer regular contribution policies costed on a single premium basis.

9:13.1 The cost of delay

It is generally advantageous to start the payment of contributions to a personal pension at the earliest possible age. By so doing, the amount of the pension to be received is usually considerably enhanced.

This is illustrated in the following examples.

Example 7

Two men aged 39 next birthday and 40 next birthday with a retirement age of 60 pay pension contributions of £1,000 per annum for 21 and 20 years respectively.

	Man aged 39 next birthday paying 21 contributions	*Man aged 40 next birthday paying 20 contributions*
	£	£
Illustration of benefits at age 60		
Cash value of pension fund	40,000	36,800
Tax-free lump sum	10,000	9,220
Annual pension	2,380	2,190
Increase in illustrated pension fund by payment of additional contribution	8.7%	

Notes

1. The figures shown in **Examples 7** and **8** are based on the rules laid down by the Financial Services Authority and assume that contributions, before allowing for a deduction for expenses, grow at 7% per annum. Immediate annuity rates are based on an interest rate of 6% per annum.

2. In the event of death before retirement, the full value of the pension fund would be paid.

3. The pension is non-increasing and payable monthly in advance for a guaranteed period of five years.

Example 8

Two men aged 39 next birthday and 40 next birthday with a retirement age of 60 each pay a single contribution of £2,000.

	Man aged 39 next birthday	*Man aged 40 next birthday*
	£	£
Illustration of benefits at age 60		
Cash value of pension fund	7,130	6,700
Tax-free lump sum	1,780	1,670
Annual pension	424	398
Increase in illustrated pension fund by earlier payment of contribution	6.4%	

9:13.2 Immediate vesting

Where other resources are available at retirement, it is often preferable to take the pension benefits as late as possible due to the favourable taxation treatment of the pension fund and improved annuity rates at older ages. However, it may be that an individual only wishes to pay a contribution if the pension benefits are received immediately. Such an arrangement (known as an immediate vesting personal pension) can be advantageous, particularly for higher rate taxpayers, but is subject to the following requirements:

(a) the individual must be aged between 50 and 75 when benefits are to be received;

(b) the individual must have sufficient tax relief available to make the payment;

(c) the amount to be paid must not exceed taxable earned income in the year of payment, even if there are sufficient available reliefs;

(d) preferably, the individual should be in good health so that he is likely to live for a longer period than that for which the pension is guaranteed.

The following example illustrates an immediate vesting personal pension for a man paying tax at the higher rate.

Example 9

A man aged 59 years 11 months subject to tax at 40% pays a single contribution of £10,000 and chooses to take the pension benefits at age 60.

		Net cost
	£	£
Gross contribution		10,000
Tax relief at 40%		4,000
		£6,000
Benefits provided		
Tax-free lump sum payable at age 60 (25% of £10,000)		£2,500
Gross annual pension	515	
Less: tax payable at 40%	206	
Net pension (per annum)		£309

Notes

1. The pension is non-increasing, payable monthly in arrears for life, but in any event guaranteed for five years. Therefore, the man or his estate would receive in the first five years after retirement, based on present tax rates, a total amount after tax of £4,045 (lump-sum of £2,500 plus annual net pension of £309 payable for five years).

2. The net cost of the single contribution of £10,000 would be recovered in full within ten years and five months (one month after payment, a lump sum of £2,500 is receivable, followed by a net monthly pension of £25.75 for 11 years four months, assuming the man survived for that period). If his top rate of tax payable should fall below 40% after retirement, the net cost of the single contribution would be recouped more quickly.

3. The annual pension represents a return of 8.8% per annum on the net cash outlay of £3,500 (the gross contribution of £10,000 less the tax relief and the tax-free lump sum).

9:14 The employment of spouses

It is often worthwhile for a self-employed individual to employ a spouse in the business and pay them a salary. As a result, he or she could then be provided with pension benefits in the same way as an employed person under a company arrangement. Moreover, if the salary was not greater than the amount at which national insurance contributions commence (currently £4,615 per annum), no liability for national insurance contributions would arise. In addition, the resulting pension would be free of income tax up to the amount of the spouse's personal allowance, subject to them having no other income.

The work performed for the business by the spouse must be such as to justify the salary paid. As an alternative to the spouse being an employee, it may be advantageous for them to be taken into partnership with similar results to the above except that higher remuneration can often be justified.

9:15 Personal pension term assurance

The provision of term assurance under a personal pension contract may, after tax relief, be cheaper than conventional life assurance contracts. The market for the latter is, however, far more competitive and this has driven premium levels down; for younger ages it is possible for a conventional policy to be cheaper than a pension term assurance, even allowing for the tax relief.

It should also be remembered that the contributions payable to provide term assurance under a personal pension contract have to be included within the overall contribution limits permitted (see **9:2**). Therefore, if a person wishes to pay the maximum possible contributions for pension benefits, it is generally expedient for any term assurance to be obtained through a life assurance contract.

9:16 Loan facilities

Loan facilities are available in association with many personal pensions on the market. It must be stressed that pension funds are not being 'borrowed back' but that life companies (particularly bancassurers) are offering their policyholders the opportunity to borrow funds.

The following points should be noted:

(a) there need not be any restrictions over the purpose of the loan and borrowing can be arranged as and when required;

(b) the company lending will normally require the loan to be secured, usually on a property;

(c) life cover will probably be required;

(d) the loan will probably be 'interest only';

(e) the amount that can be borrowed will normally be limited to the value of the tax-free cash payable under the policy;

(f) the rate of interest attaching to the loan is likely to be above the prevailing base rate.

It may be preferable to consider other sources of finance before resorting to this type of borrowing, particularly as it is likely that security will be required.

9:17 Regular or single contribution policies?

Where a person is eligible to pay personal pension contributions, it will be necessary to decide whether regular contribution or single contribution policies should be effected. The main advantages of regular contribution policies are as follows:

(a) higher minimum guaranteed pensions are provided by some with-profits investments;

(b) due to the ongoing nature of the contract, there may be a greater personal commitment to maintain the regular payment of contributions, thereby providing larger pension benefits;

(c) the need to shop around each year for a particular policy is avoided, with the consequent saving in time;

(d) the accumulation of a large number of policies is avoided.

The principal advantages of single contribution policies are as follows.

(a) Greater flexibility is provided. This is particularly important in the following cases:

    (i) the risk of overpayment is reduced;

    (ii) if a person suffers a reduction in earnings, ceases to be eligible to pay contributions or if adverse future legislation is introduced, he can reduce or stop the payment of contributions without penalties being incurred. This is often not the case with a regular contribution policy if it is varied or made paid up.

(b) A series of single contribution policies effected with one insurance company will usually produce better results than a regular contribution policy arranged with the same company. This is mainly due to the higher initial charges of the latter contract, principally caused by the payment of larger introductory commissions and the longer investment term.

(c) The individual has the ability to assess the market each year and choose investment managers likely to produce above-average returns. Contributions can also be avoided to managers whose investment performance is deteriorating.

9:18 Self-invested personal pensions

Joint Office Memorandum 101 introduced greater investment freedom for personal pension investors. Investors are now able to establish vehicles that allow them to select and control their investments rather than rely on the provider for investment management.

The permitted investments for self-invested personal pensions are:

(a) stocks and shares (including gilts and debentures) quoted on the UK Stock Exchange including securities traded on the Alternative Investment Market;

(b) unit trusts, OEICs and investment trusts;

(c) stocks and shares traded on a recognised overseas stock exchange;

(d) insurance company managed funds and unit-linked funds;

(e) deposit accounts;

(f) commercial property; and

(g) second-hand endowment policies.

Certain investments are prohibited.

(a) Scheme funds must not be used to provide loans to a member or any persons connected with a member.

(b) Schemes must not enter into any investment transactions with a member or any person connected with a member. This means that the transfer of an existing investment portfolio or commercial property is expressly prohibited. It also follows that a member cannot acquire scheme assets.

(c) Schemes must not hold residential property or land connected with such a property or chattels capable of personal use.

The one exception to the above is that once commercial property has been acquired within the regulations, it can be leased to a business or partnership connected with the member. The lease, including the rent payable, must be on commercial terms, supported by a professional valuation.

Self-invested personal pensions are likely to be most attractive to:

(a) investment professionals who wish to manage their own funds;

(b) those with substantial transfer values;

(c) those hoping to acquire commercial property in future;

(d) those wishing to consolidate a number of different pension policies; and

(e) those whose funds are in income drawdown (see **9:12.3**).

9:19 Personal pensions or company pension arrangements?

If a company director or executive is in non-pensionable employment, it may be that he or she has the option to effect their own personal pension or alternatively to be provided with pension benefits through the company. There are advantages to both options.

9:19.1 Advantages of personal pensions

(a) Personal pensions are simpler to set up. There is less documentation and no delay in obtaining Inland Revenue approval.

(b) Greater flexibility is provided, for example, the contributions paid can be varied more easily. In addition, it is unnecessary for personal contributions to be paid before the end of the current tax year due to the relating back provision. It should be noted that employer's contributions cannot be related back.

(c) In certain circumstances, personal pensions may allow higher benefits. Unlike an arrangement made through a company where a minimum of 20 years' service by retirement is necessary in order to obtain maximum pension benefits, the benefits received under a personal pension are not affected by length of service or final remuneration.

(d) A personal pension may be preferable if the period of employment is likely to be relatively short. Contributions can continue if the investor moves to a new job.

9:19.2 Advantages of company arrangements

(a) It is often possible for greater pension benefits to be obtained with the actual amounts receivable being based on final remuneration.

(b) The whole or a substantial part of the amount in the pension fund can, in some cases, particularly those eligible for the pre 1987 Inland Revenue limits regime (see **8:2.1**), be taken in the form of a tax-free cash sum.

Where an option is available between the two types of arrangement, all the circumstances need to be considered before a decision can be reached. However, in general, if large or maximum benefits are required or there is a substantial period until retirement, a company arrangement is likely to be more appropriate.

It will very rarely be appropriate for employees to opt out of their company pension schemes, unless an equivalent employer contribution is to be made to the personal pension. If this is offered, consideration needs to be given to whether it is worthwhile for an employee to opt out.

The main points are set out in **9:19.3**.

9:19.3 Advantages of personal pensions for employees

(a) There is considerable personal control and freedom of choice.

(b) If an employee is proposing to change jobs frequently, a higher ultimate pension is possible as transfer penalties will be avoided.

(c) It is easier for employees to take their pensions with them if they change jobs.

(d) Personal pensions will be preferable for those employees whose earnings will peak during their middle years of employment, rather than close to retirement.

9:19.4 Disadvantages of personal pensions for employees

(a) There may be no contributions from the employer.

(b) The final benefits are dependent on investment returns and are not related to final salary (this can also be an advantage).

(c) Economies of scale and/or cross subsidies are not available as in a group pension scheme, particularly a defined benefit scheme.

In addition, much will depend on:

(a) the level of employer contributions to the pension scheme;

(b) whether the person concerned is likely to change jobs, and if so, the period remaining to retirement after the change;

(c) future salary increases and the impact of the earnings cap;

(d) future investment returns;

(e) the level of pension scheme benefits provided; and

(f) whether or not the employer will allow the employee to rejoin the company scheme in the future.

10 Life assurance policies as investments

The principal purpose of this chapter is to discuss the two main types of regular premium investment policies which can be particularly useful in personal financial planning. These are with-profits endowment contracts and maximum investment plans. Also discussed are friendly society plans, some of the more usual methods of funding a life policy from capital and investment in second-hand endowment policies.

10:1 With-profits endowment policies

Under this type of policy, an insurance company promises to pay a fixed amount (the basic sum assured) on the maturity of the policy or on the death of the life assured, if earlier. To this reversionary bonuses are added, normally on an annual basis, with terminal bonuses also being paid by most insurance companies. A with-profits endowment policy is therefore likely to offer an individual a low-risk investment medium with capital appreciation and guarantees. However, the choice of the right life assurance company will be of the utmost importance in determining the benefits ultimately received. For example, for policies maturing on 1 February 2002, contracts with the best results over ten years and 25 years paid out 40% and 72% more respectively than the contracts with the worst results (based on a male aged 30 at the start of the policies).

Before consideration can be given to the selection of a particular contract, certain basic information, such as the person's age and state of health and the date when the policy is required to mature, will be needed. It will then be possible to consider the particular company with which the contract should be taken out with careful attention being paid to:

(a) past performance;

(b) surrender values;

(c) underwriting;

(d) other considerations.

10:1.1 Past performance

The following matters should be borne in mind when considering past performance.

(a) It is normally worthwhile to select a life company which has produced consistently good returns over a reasonable period. However, it should be remembered that good past performance is no guarantee of good future results.

(b) The trend of past performance is very important, but it should be remembered that, with a long-term policy, the results could be largely based on earlier conditions which no longer apply. This could be due to changes in investment managers, investment policy or charging structure.

(c) The mutual offices have tended (with exceptions) to produce better results than the proprietary companies, as all profits of a mutual office are retained for the benefit of policyholders, whereas, in the case of proprietary companies, up to 10% of distributable profits are allocated to shareholders. However, if additional capital is required for future development, proprietary companies are likely to have greater flexibility.

(d) Large companies with greater financial strength have usually produced results superior to those of small companies.

(e) Terminal bonuses are much more volatile than reversionary bonuses, which are largely based on a company's investment income and, once declared, cannot be taken away. Terminal bonuses mainly reflect a company's investment surplus at the time policy benefits are paid. However, sometimes a proportion of terminal bonus is also paid when a policy is surrendered. Despite this, it should be remembered that bonuses reflect investment returns, with no absolute distinction between income and capital appreciation.

Some companies have regularly paid large terminal bonuses, while others have not paid any, or only small ones, or bonuses which have shown major fluctuations in accordance with market conditions at the time the policies have matured.

Recent industry trends have been, in general, to increase the proportion of total benefits paid via terminal bonuses and to weight reversionary bonuses towards longer dated policies. The combined effect of these trends has been to reduce yields on ten-year policies and increase them on longer-term policies.

(f) A company may have declared a special reversionary bonus out of successful investment operations which are not expected to recur. Such a bonus, unlike the terminal bonus, cannot be withdrawn once it has been declared and added to the policy. A special reversionary bonus is less of a burden to a life company than a reversionary bonus since there is no commitment to make the same ongoing payouts. Special bonuses have also been paid in recent years when a mutual company has been acquired by another company.

(g) The average results of ten-year with-profits endowment policies maturing on 1 February 2002 compare very favourably with the underlying rate of inflation over the same period and with other types of investment offering the same degree of security. In addition, life assurance cover is provided by the policy.

10:1.2 Surrender values

Although a life assurance policy would not normally be taken out as a short-term savings contract, unforeseen circumstances can occur which require the policy to be surrendered before its maturity date. It is for this reason that surrender values are important and, in order to provide some guide to the treatment by life companies of policies surrendered prematurely, the actual surrender values offered over different periods should be considered.

It should also be borne in mind that on surrendering a policy a charge to higher-rate tax could arise (the tax would be calculated in a similar way to the charge on investment bonds – see **Chapter 3**).

Due to the relatively low values normally offered on surrender, especially in the early years, a policy should be maintained to maturity if possible. This applies particularly to policies effected before 14 March 1984, whose premiums enjoyed a measure of income tax relief. Accordingly, where it is necessary to raise capital, a loan against the policy may be appropriate. Most companies will lend up to 90% of the surrender value, with interest rates normally in line with market rates.

Another possible alternative to surrendering a policy is to make it paid-up: no further contributions are payable and the benefits on maturity or death are reduced accordingly. However, if this course of action is taken, a charge to higher-rate tax may arise when the benefits are subsequently received.

Where a decision has been taken that a policy should be surrendered, it is useful to bear in mind that there are several organisations which specialise in arranging the sale of second-hand life policies. In these cases, the price fetched will often exceed the surrender value offered by the life company, with the taxation position being the same as if the policy was actually surrendered. This market is discussed in more detail at **10:5**.

10:1.3 Underwriting

The degree or level of underwriting required by life assurance companies varies considerably. This can have an important bearing on the selection of a particular contract, as, generally, the more demanding companies have tended to produce the better results due to their more favourable mortality experience.

Therefore, before a particular policy is selected, details of the person's occupation, recreational pursuits and state of health, including smoking habits, should first be obtained and the information considered before proceeding further. If there are health problems, a medical examination can often be arranged for the use of more than one company.

In recent years, the medical information requested by life companies has generally been considerably reduced other than for larger proposals, mainly due to the expense and time involved. An example of this is that many companies allow an endowment policy to be arranged within defined limits for the purpose of repaying a mortgage and seek only the minimum medical evidence. The main exception is in respect of individuals whose health or lifestyle might increase the chances of them being victims or carriers of AIDS. In these cases, blood tests or full medical examinations are usually required.

10:1.4 Other considerations

In choosing a particular company, the following points are also important.

(a) The financial strength of the life company. It should be remembered that bonuses will be paid from the surplus of a life company and this will largely depend on the investment performance, together with the level of the company's expenses. The stronger the company, the more flexibility it has to invest in equities and, therefore, the better its long-term returns are likely to be. The stockmarket falls in 2000 and 2001 and other factors such as guaranteed annuity liabilities have seriously eroded the financial strength of most UK life companies.

(b) The service provided by the life company.

(c) It is unlikely that policies taken out now will enjoy the returns produced by policies invested during the 1980s and 1990s. Policyholders therefore need to have realistic expectations of the sum that the endowment will ultimately produce.

10:1.5 Low-cost endowment policies

Low-cost endowment policies are a variation of the with-profits endowment policy and are usually a combination of a normal with-profits endowment and a decreasing term assurance (see **11:1.2**). These policies are thus designed as endowment assurances which contain a guaranteed minimum death benefit at a level higher than that used for bonus purposes. They are often used as the repayment medium for mortgages, where the guaranteed minimum death benefit is equal to the amount of the mortgage outstanding.

10:2 Maximum investment plans

Maximum investment plans are unit-linked qualifying life assurance policies and thus incorporate the usual tax advantages. Therefore, income accruing within the life fund is taxed at a maximum rate of 20% and the policy proceeds are normally completely free of any personal liability to income tax and capital gains tax, provided that premiums have been paid for a minimum period of ten years (or three quarters of the term, if less, in the case of an endowment-type policy).

The main characteristic of these plans is that they are essentially investment vehicles which have the minimum amount of life cover necessary to retain qualifying life policy status. Part of each premium pays for the life assurance cover and the balance is invested in units in an investment fund. There is normally a higher allocation to units for larger premiums.

Although policy charges are important, it is the investment performance of the underlying fund that will normally determine whether a particular policy will prove to be good value.

10:2.1 Options available

To enable him to maximise investment performance, the policyholder is normally given the option to switch both the existing fund and/or future premiums between the different funds available. The choice of funds available is the same as for investment bonds – see **3:4.2** – although not all life companies offer a fund in every sector. In order to provide maximum flexibility, virtually all life companies writing maximum investment plans permit a plan to be divided into a number of identical cluster policies.

At the end of ten years (or the agreed period, if longer), the following options are generally available to policyholders:

(a) to take the accumulated fund as a tax-free lump sum;

(b) to stop paying premiums but leave the capital to accumulate within the policy;

(c) to continue paying the premiums in full for a further ten years (a higher investment allocation than that provided at the outset of the policy is generally given);

(d) to continue paying a nominal premium to maintain the policy and encash segments to provide a tax-free income.

The option to take a tax-free income after ten years can be particularly advantageous and is especially suitable in the following cases:

(a) to increase the net spendable income of a higher rate taxpayer;

(b) to supplement a pension;

(c) to provide for education fees.

In the two latter cases, it is normally expedient that the policy should be linked to a stable fund rather than a volatile one.

By taking a tax-free income instead of a tax-free lump sum which is then reinvested, a higher rate taxpayer avoids the tax that would have been payable on the investment income, although the income arising within the life fund would still be taxed at life assurance company rates (20%). In the case of a husband and wife, a policy written on a joint life, last survivor basis should be considered. This has two advantages over a policy written on a single life basis:

- the policy would continue until the second death – as a result, the tax-free income facility could continue after the first death;
- a higher investment allocation would usually be obtained, as the death benefit payable by the life company would normally be postponed.

It should be noted that, for many individuals who wish to invest on a regular basis in equities, an ISA savings plan directly into a unit or investment trust is likely to produce superior results to a unit-linked life policy. This is due to there being no tax payable either on capital gains or on dividend income and no cost of life assurance cover.

10:3 Friendly society plans

Due to their advantageous tax treatment, these plans should generally produce satisfactory results, although the maximum premiums which can be paid are very low. Their main characteristics are as follows.

(a) They are written as ten-year savings plans (sometimes for longer).

(b) Policyholders must be between the ages of 18 and 74 (although plans can be written for the benefit of children of any age).

(c) Investment income and capital gains accumulate within the friendly society investment fund free of all UK tax (this can be particularly advantageous where the main purpose of the fund is to produce a high income).

(d) The maximum annual premiums payable are £270 (£300 if premiums are payable more frequently than annually). However, some societies permit a lump sum to be paid at outset to cover the first premium and to purchase an annuity to fund all the premiums after the first. It is also possible to combine a friendly society plan with a conventional policy, which may provide a saving in expenses compared with two completely separate policies.

(e) The charges made on friendly society plans are frequently high in relation to the premiums paid.

(f) Although it is no longer necessary that a minimum of 50% of the underlying investments of the fund should be in narrower-range investments, some friendly societies have not changed their practice. Any such restrictions can inhibit investment performance.

(g) At the end of ten years, the policyholder is usually provided with certain options (similar to those under maximum investment plans), but this will depend on the particular plan.

(h) If the plan is surrendered within seven and a half years when written as an endowment policy, or within ten years when written as a whole life policy, the penalties can be severe.

10:4 Funding a life policy from capital

In addition to paying premiums from income, a life policy can be funded from the investment of a capital sum by one or more of the following methods (these packages are generally known as capital conversion plans or, colloquially, 'back-to-back' schemes).

(a) *Temporary annuities.* These have the main advantages of guaranteeing returns and of simplicity and convenience. The disadvantages are that capital is locked in, the investment return is often not competitive (particularly in the current era of low interest and annuity rates) and the annuity ceases on early death.

(b) *A series of guaranteed growth bonds.* Again, these have the advantages of having returns guaranteed and of convenience, but the disadvantage of an uncompetitive investment return in the early years.

(c) *Investment bonds.* The principal advantage of this method is that the return could be very competitive, as the underlying investments are not restricted to fixed-interest investments. In addition, some insurance packages are administratively easy to operate. The main disadvantage is the risk of the need to provide funds from other resources to pay the premiums if the value of the investment bond fails to show sufficient growth.

A further method would be to realise capital from existing investments on a regular basis to meet the premiums as they fall due.

The actual method selected would depend upon all circumstances of the case, including the return on the various investments at the particular time and the financial and tax position and age of the person concerned.

Capital conversion plans can also be used to generate an income for ten years with a subsequent return of capital at the end of that period. In this case, only part of the total amount arising each year from the capital sum is used to fund the life assurance premiums, with the balance being available as spendable income.

10:5 Second-hand endowment policies

Reference was made at **10:1.2** to the facility which now exists for a with-profits endowment policyholder to sell his policy instead of surrendering it. There are two options:

- to sell the policy at auction; or
- to sell the policy to a market-maker.

The proceeds of a sale at auction will depend upon the demand for the policy from those attending it. The seller can set a reserve price, but cannot be sure that it will be reached. A market-maker will offer a firm price, which the seller may accept or refuse.

The success of the second-hand (or traded) endowment policy market is the result of the appreciation by investors of the advantages of such policies. These are:

(a) the fact that the heaviest expenses are borne by the policy during the first five years of its life; by buying the policy second-hand they avoid these expenses;

(b) much of the appreciation in the value of a policy arises at its maturity in the form of the terminal bonus;

(c) the risk of loss is limited to the difference between the purchase price and the surrender value, since the latter is the price which the insurance company would pay for the policy;

(d) endowment policies are low risk investments whose returns have historically been well in excess of the rate of inflation.

When a policyholder sells his policy it is assigned to the purchaser, who becomes responsible for paying the premiums. The original owner remains the life assured, however, and if he were to die before the maturity date of the policy, the life assurance company will, on presentation of his death certificate, pay the claim value to the purchaser. For this reason, market-makers arrange for referees to be appointed to whom the purchaser can refer, to ascertain whether or not the original policyholder is still alive.

Policies are priced by reference to a discount rate applied to the estimated maturity value of the policy. This value is calculated on the assumption that annual and terminal bonuses will continue at their present level – which, in view of the lower investment returns experienced in recent years and expected in the future, may not be the case. The market-makers will provide potential investors with a sensitivity chart showing the different returns which will be achieved on the basis of different assumptions about the level of bonuses.

Generally there is a 'turn' of about 6% (similar to the bid/offer spread of unit trust prices) between the price which a market-maker pays a seller and the price at which he sells to a new investor.

An alternative to direct investment in second-hand policies is the purchase of shares in one of the OEICs or investment trusts owning a portfolio of such policies.

The taxation position of the purchaser of a second-hand policy is as follows:

- if the policy is a qualifying policy, he will be subject to capital gains tax on the maturity proceeds. He will be entitled to the indexation allowance on both the purchase price and on the premiums he has paid up to 6 April 1998 and to taper relief thereafter;
- if the policy is non-qualifying, he will be subject to income tax at the higher rate (if he is a higher rate taxpayer in the year the proceeds are paid). The calculation is similar to that for investment bonds in **Chapter 3**.

Not all endowment policies are 'tradeable' in this way. The market-makers do not accept all insurance companies' policies and require the policy to have been in force for at least five (in some cases seven) years and to have a minimum surrender value of £2,000. In addition to with-profits endowment policies, many market-makers will also deal in with-profits whole of life policies and guaranteed income bonds. One specialist area is 'viatical settlements' – the sale of life policies by those diagnosed as having a terminal illness. While it benefits them by providing funds to enable them to enjoy their last months, this practice requires great care and sensitivity.

11 Protection through life assurance

In the previous chapter, life assurance policies were considered as investments. However, their original purpose was to provide protection and it is this application that is now discussed. For most individuals, subject to their state of health, appropriate protection policies should be arranged in order to provide the required level of cover before investment is considered. These policies can normally be effected cheaply, with UK insurance companies offering amongst the most competitive rates in the world.

Although it is not always possible to distinguish completely between protection and investment policies (this can be seen later in this chapter when flexible unit-linked whole life policies are discussed – see **11:2.1**), better results can often be achieved if the protection and investment needs are dealt with separately.

The amount of life cover required will vary depending on the individual circumstances. For example, a man approaching retirement would normally need less cover to protect his family than a younger person with dependent children, although it is more likely that he will wish to effect a policy for inheritance tax purposes. In any event, before a particular type of policy can be selected, the following matters should be considered:

(a) the purpose of the policy and the exact needs of the individual's and/or their dependants;

(b) the ages of the individual and their dependants;

(c) the health of the individual, including their smoking habits;

(d) the resources to pay for the cover;

(e) the existing level of cover, if any, and to whom it is payable;

(f) the existing estate after inheritance tax which would be available to the dependants in the event of the life assured's death.

The two main broad categories of protection policies are term assurance and whole life. These policies can usually be effected in the following ways:

(a) on a single life basis;

(b) on a joint life basis, payable on the first death;

(c) on a joint life, last survivor basis, payable on the second death.

Where a policy is arranged in order to provide protection for the family of the life assured, it is normally beneficial for it to be written in trust for the spouse or children or, alternatively, on a life of another basis. The particular method will depend on the precise circumstances.

11:1 Term assurance policies

Although there are several classes of term assurance, they all have the same principal purpose of providing a tax-free lump sum if death should occur within a preselected period. If the individual concerned survives until the end of that period, the policy automatically expires without value. There are no surrender values or paid-up values on term assurance policies. If premiums cease, the policy automatically lapses, with the insurance company having no further liability.

For each of the types of term assurance mentioned below, there is no personal liability to income tax or capital gains tax on the benefit payable from the policy. However, unless the policy is written under a suitably worded trust (see **Chapter 16**), the proceeds could form part of the deceased's estate for inheritance tax purposes. Therefore, it is advisable, in most cases, to write this type of policy under trust, in order to avoid the proceeds enhancing the deceased's estate, with the resulting adverse inheritance tax consequences. This also has the advantage that the proceeds can be paid to the trustees on production of the death certificate; they do not have to wait until probate has been granted to his executors.

The following are the most common types of term assurance policies (death-in-service benefits under company pension arrangements and personal pensions have already been considered in **Chapters 8** and **9** respectively):

(a) level term;

(b) decreasing term;

(c) mortgage protection;

(d) increasing term;

(e) convertible term;

(f) convertible, renewable term;

(g) family income benefit.

11:1.1 Level term

This is the most straightforward type of term assurance, enabling a tax-free lump sum to be provided in the event of the death of the life assured within the preselected period. Apart from making provision for the death of the bread-winner, one of its most usual practical applications is in connection with a bank or other loan arranged on an interest-only basis, where the life of the borrower would be insured for the full amount of the loan. If the lender requires assignment of the policy, it cannot be placed in trust.

11:1.2 Decreasing term

Under this assurance, the amount of the life cover reduces each year (or lesser period) by predetermined amounts throughout the duration of the policy. Like level term assurance, decreasing term assurance is often effected in conjunction with a loan, but one whose principal is being repaid by equal instalments. The life cover provided then decreases in line with the amount of the loan outstanding.

Decreasing term assurance is also used to insure lifetime gifts between individuals which exceed the nil rate band where an inheritance tax (IHT) liability would crystallise on the death of the donor. The cover reduces in such a way as to match the reducing tax liability over a seven-year period, namely:

Years	*Cover as a % of initial IHT liability*
up to 3	100
3–4	80
4–5	60
5–6	40
6–7	20

11:1.3 Mortgage protection

This is a form of decreasing term assurance, where the amount of life cover is designed to be sufficient to repay the outstanding mortgage at death. Since the cover reduces more slowly in the early years than under a decreasing term assurance, the cost of a mortgage protection policy is normally greater.

Mortgage protection policies usually match the outstanding capital when a loan is being repaid by regular instalments of capital and interest. Any deviation from the original terms of the loan may upset the relationship between the capital outstanding and the cover provided.

Before a mortgage protection policy is arranged, it is worthwhile investigating the options available and particularly the position should mortgage interest rates rise substantially. If this were to happen and the policy lacked flexibility, the individual could find themselves under-insured. Where the mortgage repayments depend upon the joint incomes of a husband and wife, it is often advantageous for two single life policies to be effected rather than one policy written on a joint life, first death basis, especially if the couple have dependent children. This then provides two sets of benefit if both parents should die within the term, usually at little extra cost. In addition, in the event of divorce or separation, matters are considerably simplified.

11:1.4 Increasing term

Because of the effect of inflation, a fixed level of cover under a policy may become inadequate. Some companies therefore offer the option to increase cover by a fixed amount or by the rate of inflation each year. The premium is raised correspondingly.

11:1.5 Convertible term

This type of policy is similar to level term assurance except that the policyholder has the option to convert to another type of life policy throughout the term, subject to conversion taking place before a maximum age of normally 60 or 65, regardless of the assured's state of health at the time the option is exercised. The premium rate applicable to the new policy is based on the individual's age at the time of conversion.

Before a person decides on a specific policy, it is important to consider whether they are likely to exercise the conversion option and, if so, into what type of policy. Policyholders will normally be allowed to convert into whole life or endowment contracts, while other options often include unit-linked or level term policies. Consequently, the competitiveness of the policy after conversion can be of greater significance than the initial cost of the term assurance itself. Convertible term assurance can be a particularly useful contract for a younger person who requires immediate life cover but cannot afford the cost of a more permanent policy at the time the convertible term assurance is effected. By subsequently being allowed to switch into, say, a whole life or endowment contract, irrespective of their state of health at that time, a very valuable option is offered at a relatively low cost.

11:1.6 Convertible, renewable term

These are usually short-term policies, typically of five years' duration, offering maximum flexibility but with minimum commitment. Two basic options are provided: to convert the policy into another contract and to renew the policy at the end of the original term.

The conversion option under this contract operates in a way similar to the option provided under a normal convertible term assurance policy. The conversion option can be taken up at any time during the term of the contract, with many insurance companies also allowing partial conversion. The renewal option allows the policyholder to renew the policy at the end of each term without further medical evidence normally until the age of 60 or 65. The premium will usually increase at renewal in line with the rates for their age at the time.

This policy therefore enables an individual to obtain guaranteed life cover in most cases until retirement age, at low cost. In addition, they are provided with the opportunity to convert the policy into a different contract more appropriate to their needs.

Due to the number of variations in the terms offered, it is important to compare like with like, as far as this is possible, when selecting a particular contract. The options which are likely to be exercised in the future should also be considered, bearing in mind that some contracts may offer very competitive rates at lower ages but uncompetitive rates at higher ages. Therefore, if the original intention is to renew the policy throughout, the cheapest contract at the outset may not necessarily be the most suitable.

11:1.7 Family income benefit

This policy is a form of term assurance where a tax-free income is provided from the date of death of the life assured to the expiry of the preselected term (an option is also often available to commute the future income payments into a cash lump sum). A family income benefit contract is therefore effectively a decreasing term assurance.

Although termed ‘income’, the payments are actually instalments of the sum assured under the policy, and therefore do not create any personal liability to income tax or capital gains tax. Policies which provide increasing payments to combat the effects of inflation are also available but these require higher premiums.

Although a family income policy may be effected on the joint lives of a husband and wife with the benefits payable on the first death, it is often preferable to take out two single life policies instead, especially where the couple have young children. If the husband should die before the children are financially independent, there could be considerable hardship for the rest of the family. Consequently, it is usually advisable that a policy should be effected at the time of the birth of a child for the period of likely dependence.

A husband and wife should also consider arranging a family income benefit policy on the life of the wife where she looks after the children or where he is dependent on her earnings. If the wife should die prematurely, the husband may need additional income, either to pay for home help and the supervision of the children while he is at work or to replace her lost earnings.

Due to the reducing nature of the life cover and to the death benefit only being paid in instalments (unless a cash lump sum is taken in commutation), this contract provides higher initial life cover for the same premium than other types of term assurance policy. Consequently, because of this and the important need it serves, a family income benefit policy is an essential requirement for many families.

The following example illustrates some of the more competitive rates for effecting the principal types of term assurance policies.

Example 10

Two men, aged 30 and 40 next birthday respectively, both in good health and non-smokers, arrange £100,000 initial life cover over a period of 20 years through the main types of term assurance policies. Premiums are to be paid annually.

	Man aged 30 next birthday Annual premium	*Man aged 40 next birthday Annual premium*
	£	£
Level term	75	154
Decreasing term (7 years for inheritance tax)	60	80
Mortgage protection	63	113
Increasing term (escalating at RPI)	94	180
Convertible term	95	193
Convertible renewable term	101	206
Family income benefit (see **Note**)	60	95

Note

The family income benefit assurance provides a tax-free income of £5,000 per annum, payable monthly from the date of death to the end of the 20-year period.

11:2 Whole life policies

Unlike term assurance policies where the sum assured only becomes payable if death should occur within a predetermined period, the benefit from a whole life policy is payable whenever death occurs. In addition, a whole life policy acquires both a surrender value and a paid-up value, except generally in the first two years of the contract. Due to the certainty of eventual death, a whole life policy is considerably more expensive to arrange than a term assurance policy. The following are the more usual types of whole life policies:

(a) whole life with-profits;

(b) low-cost whole life;

(c) flexible unit-linked whole life.

Whole of life assurance used to be written on a with-profits basis (with annual and terminal bonuses like an endowment policy), a non-profit basis, (with a fixed sum assured), and on a 'low-cost' basis. A low-cost policy was a combination of with-profits whole of life and term assurance, which, as the name implied, was cheaper than a full with-profits policy. Now, however, almost all companies only offer whole of life assurance on a unit-linked basis. This has the advantage of flexibility and lower cost.

11:2.1 Flexible unit-linked whole life

This modern type of whole life policy (often known as a flexible or universal life policy) combines a mix of insurance and investment and is designed to cover an individual's life assurance needs throughout his or her life.

A wide degree of flexibility is offered as to the extent to which the emphasis can be varied between protection and investment during the term of the policy. There are normally at least three options – minimum, standard and maximum cover – for the specified level of premium. Minimum cover allows a high proportion of the premium to be invested, as only a small sum is required for the life cover. Most of a maximum cover premium will be spent on providing the life assurance, with only a small amount invested. Standard cover is the level of life assurance the company calculates it will be able to provide if the invested portion of the premiums grows at a reasonable rate; if this growth is achieved, it should not be necessary to increase the premiums. Maximum cover premiums, however, are reviewed after the first ten years and are then likely to be considerably increased, if the level of cover is to be maintained, in view of the policyholder's greater age; no further medical evidence is required.

A flexible unit-linked whole life policy works as follows.

(a) Premiums are paid to the insurance company from which charges are deducted for the setting up and administration costs. The balance of each premium is then invested in units in one or more of the insurance company's unit-linked funds with the normal switching facility usually being available. This type of policy can also be effected on a single premium basis.

(b) Units are encashed each month to pay for the life cover, with the actual number depending on the value of the units allocated to the policy at the time, the amount of cover chosen and the age and sex of the policyholder. The units remaining provide the investment element of the policy; 'protection' cover is required for the difference between their value and the agreed sum assured.

(c) The insurance company sets the maximum amount of cover that can be chosen by assuming a growth rate for the value of the units, usually around 6.5% per annum. Some insurance companies base this maximum on the level of cover that could be maintained throughout the policyholder's life. Other companies call this maintainable level of cover 'standard cover', and offer a considerably higher maximum on the basis that it is maintained only for the first ten years of the policy, after which time the cover or premium may need to be adjusted.

(d) The premiums and life cover are reviewed at the end of the first ten years and at regular intervals thereafter (generally every five years, but usually more often for elderly policyholders). Between reviews, the insurance company agrees not to seek to change the amount of the premiums or life cover. However, the policyholder is still normally provided with the option to increase their cover each year without waiting for the next review date, although, in some cases, evidence of health may be required.

    At each review, the insurance company looks at both the value of the remaining units and the current premium level in order to decide whether they are sufficient to maintain the chosen level of cover until the next review. If they are not sufficient, either the premiums have to be increased or the level of cover reduced.

    If the value of the units has increased at a rate higher than that assumed, many insurance companies allow this to be used in order to obtain a greater level of cover, although medical evidence is generally required. However, only a small minority of companies permit a reduction in the amount of the premiums.

(e) On the death of the life assured, the policy will pay out the greater of the chosen amount of life cover and the value of the units.

(f) If the payment of premiums continues for a minimum period of ten years, similar options to those applicable with maximum investment plans will be available (these options have already been considered in **Chapter 10**). Alternatively, life cover can continue to be provided, subject to the value of the units being sufficient to meet the costs involved.

(g) Where premiums are paid for less than ten years, any value attaching to the policy can be used to take a lump sum, although a charge to higher rate tax may arise. As further options, the units can be left to accumulate or be utilised to pay for continued life cover, assuming they have sufficient value.

The main advantages of flexible unit-linked whole life policies are therefore as follows.

(a) The convenience of having only one policy to serve both the protection and investment needs of an individual, together with the flexibility to make changes without excessive administration.

(b) Competitive premium rates. By regularly reviewing the progress of a policy and having the facility to make adjustments when considered appropriate, an insurance company need not use the same conservative actuarial basis as when a guaranteed sum assured is provided for a fixed premium over a very long period. As a result, it is possible for a less cautious approach to be adopted, with the consequent beneficial effect on premiums.

(c) A choice of funds and switching facilities are generally provided. If mortality trends improve, this can be taken into account when making reviews. Conversely, if the trends are worse than anticipated, this is likely to be a disadvantage.

Despite the above advantages, improved investment results may often be obtained if separate insurance policies are effected to provide the required life cover, with the balance of the funds available being used exclusively for investment in, for example, shares, ISAs, OEICs, unit or investment trusts.

Where an individual does decide to effect a flexible unit-linked whole life policy, its exact purpose should clearly be borne in mind before a specific contract is chosen, due to the varying terms and different options available. In addition, if the main purpose of the policy is to provide life cover, the investment link should be a relatively stable fund, such as a managed fund, rather than a volatile fund.

The following example illustrates competitive rates for effecting a whole of life policy.

Example 11

Two men aged 30 and 40 next birthday respectively, both in good health and non-smokers, arrange £100,000 initial life cover through flexible, unit-linked whole of life policies. Premiums are to be paid annually throughout life.

	Man aged 30 next birthday Annual premium	*Man aged 40 next birthday Annual premium*
	£	£
Standard cover	397	829
Maximum cover	102	170

Note

Standard cover premiums are calculated to remain unaltered throughout life on the assumption that the price of the underlying units grows by 6% per annum. The maximum cover premiums are fixed only for the first ten years.

11:3 Back-to-back arrangements

A further use of whole life policies has been in connection with back-to-back arrangements which combine purchased life annuities with regular premium whole life policies written under trust for named beneficiaries. The arrangements were mainly designed for elderly higher rate taxpayers in reasonable health, with their main purposes being to increase the net spendable income of the policyholder and the net estate available to the beneficiaries.

To ensure that the arrangements are not challenged by the Inland Revenue as 'associated operations', it is necessary that:

- the life policy is issued after full medical underwriting of the life assured, following the normal requirements and limits set by the particular insurance company; and
- the terms on which the life policy is issued should have no regard to the purchase of the annuity. (It is therefore usually advisable to arrange for the two contracts to be effected with different life assurance companies.)

Generally, for the payment of annual premiums not to be subject to inheritance tax as gifts to the trustees of the life policy, they must fall within one of the specified exemptions. In order to qualify as 'normal expenditure out of income', the following conditions must be satisfied:

(a) the payments must be part of normal expenditure, namely they must be habitual; in the case of a life assurance policy, it is accepted that this is covered by the nature of the contract to pay regular premiums;

(b) the payments must be made out of taxed income; the capital element of an annuity does not count as income for this purpose;

(c) after allowing for all payments forming part of normal expenditure, there must be sufficient income to maintain the usual standard of living.

If the normal expenditure exemption is not appropriate, the other annual exemptions could be utilised (see **Chapter 12**).

Due to the very low level of annuity rates at the current time, it is difficult to generate additional net spendable income by this method. However, should annuity rates improve in the future, this may again prove to be a viable option.

11:4 Other insurance contracts

Although not strictly life assurance policies, other insurance contracts can be arranged for protection purposes. The most usual of these contracts are as follows:

(a) permanent health insurance;

(b) personal accident and sickness insurance;

(c) hospital insurance;

(d) private medical insurance;

(e) critical illness insurance;

(f) long-term care insurance.

11:4.1 Permanent health insurance

The purpose of permanent health insurance is to provide an income for an individual during prolonged disability following sickness or accident. Although far fewer permanent health insurance policies are arranged in comparison to many types of life assurance policies, they nevertheless serve a very important need. According to available statistics, a breakdown in health lasting more than six months before age 65 is ten times more likely than death before that age.

The following are some of the more important characteristics of individual permanent health insurance policies.

(a) The contract cannot be cancelled by the insurance company after it has been effected (hence the word 'permanent') nor can the company refuse to renew the contract if the health of the policyholder should deteriorate.

(b) There are different definitions of disability. Some insurance companies are very harsh in their interpretation, while others take a more lenient approach. It is therefore very important to investigate a company's attitude to claims before effecting one of its policies.

(c) Some occupations are not normally acceptable to insurance companies, while others may attract special terms or restrictions.

(d) Benefits are not usually payable immediately from the time of disablement but after a deferred period (normally after a minimum of four weeks and a maximum of 52 weeks). The longer the deferment period, the lower the premiums will be. Policies are usually written to age 60 or 65. Benefits generally cease at the age selected even if disability continues.

(e) The maximum amount of benefit which can be received may be restricted, for example to 50%–60% of earnings less State Incapacity Benefit. Stricter limits are generally applied where the individual has a high level of earnings.

(f) The level of insured benefits may be arranged at outset to remain constant or increase on an annual basis by a fixed percentage or in line with the RPI. Where benefits increase, usually the premiums will also rise each year. Benefits following a claim can likewise be arranged to increase annually, usually by a fixed percentage of 5% or RPI.

(g) Benefits are not taxable.

11:4.2 Personal accident and sickness insurance

The purpose of this contract is to enable a person to insure against accident or sickness, the benefits being in the form of either a lump sum or an income. The lump sum could become payable on death, loss of sight or a limb or on permanent total disability.

The following are some of the more relevant features of personal accident and sickness insurance policies.

(a) The contract is of an annual nature and subject to state of health each year. It can therefore be cancelled or special provisions made at the option of the insurance company at each renewal date.

(b) The amount of the premiums depends mainly on the level of benefits to be insured and the occupation and sex of the person concerned.

(c) In the case of sickness insurance, benefits are normally payable after one week. However, there is usually an option for the benefits to be deferred for a longer period, with a consequent reduction in premiums.

(d) The amount of benefit is usually restricted to a percentage of earnings, usually 50–60% thereof.

(e) Benefits are normally paid for a maximum of up to two years if the person is unable to work as a result of an accident or illness.

(f) Lump sum benefits are generally not taxable. The income benefits are not taxable.

Mainly due to the ability of the insurance company to cancel the policy each year, this type of contract is not generally of prime importance for many individuals. It is mainly encountered as part of a travel insurance policy.

11:4.3 Hospital insurance

The purpose of hospital insurance is to provide the policyholder with funds to mitigate the loss of his earnings while he is in hospital and also to cover incidental expenses, such as the cost of relatives' travel to and from the hospital. In addition, the plans usually provide further benefits, such as a lump sum for a loss of a limb or eyesight.

Some of the more important aspects of hospital insurance plans are as follows.

(a) The premiums on these policies are written on a renewable annual basis. Depending on the premiums, which are normally limited, the policyholder obtains a predetermined sum for each day or night that he stays in hospital.

(b) No medical evidence is required before a plan is effected. However, there may be problems when a claim is made, as a result of the exclusion clauses in the policy.

(c) The policy conditions require careful consideration due to their varying terms; for example, most companies will not pay out the benefits during the first two years of the policy if the claim relates to a recurrence of an illness which the policyholder had before the policy was effected.

(d) Neither the lump sum nor income benefits are taxable.

Unless an individual thinks that he is likely to suffer ill-health, these policies are not normally a priority. The premiums paid could usually be better applied elsewhere to provide the additional funds which might be required to meet the costs of a stay in hospital.

11:4.4 Private medical insurance

The purpose of being a subscriber to a private health insurance scheme is to enable medical treatment to be arranged privately, rather than through the National Health Service, for an individual and their family. This will usually provide the following advantages:

(a) there are effectively no waiting lists;

(b) the patient can choose the time for their treatment;

(c) the patient can select a hospital for their own convenience and often choose a particular surgeon;

(d) miscellaneous benefits are provided, such as a private room with better amenities and more flexible visiting hours;

(e) some health insurance schemes provide a daily cash benefit to pay for incidental expenses while in hospital, such as telephone calls.

Despite the benefits of being a subscriber to a private health insurance scheme, a material proportion of those who use private medicine in the UK still finance the costs out of their own funds without medical insurance. The view taken by many of these people is that it is less expensive to meet the costs of private medicine directly, as and when necessary, than it is to pay the subscription to an insurance scheme each year. They prefer to invest an amount equal to the cost of the premiums into other savings media. Whether this proves to be the right decision will depend on the extent of the private medical treatment required by the individual and his family.

In recent years, due to the mutual benefits provided, it has become increasingly common for private medical insurance to be arranged by a business for its staff and their families (it should be noted that this is regarded as a 'benefit in kind' and therefore a personal tax liability will almost always be incurred by the employees on the notional premium paid by the employer for their membership). The dramatically cheaper rates available for group schemes normally make this a much more attractive route than taking out cover personally.

11:4.5 Critical illness insurance

The purpose of this insurance is to provide a lump sum payment in the event of the insured person suffering a critical illness. It can either be provided as an addition to a life assurance or permanent health insurance policy or as a stand-alone policy. The range of illnesses covered includes heart attack, cancer, stroke, conditions necessitating coronary by-pass surgery or major organ transplant, kidney failure, multiple sclerosis, paralysis, paraplegia, loss of sight or limbs, brain tumours, serious burns and motor neurone disease.

There are no income or capital gains tax implications for critical illness policy claims. Payments made from life policies are not taxable as they fall outside the chargeable events legislation. The Inland Revenue has also confirmed that payments are not subject to capital gains tax.

The principal tax problems relating to critical illness cover are in connection with inheritance tax. A claimant's estate may be increased just before his death and it makes sense to try to mitigate the inheritance tax consequences. This is normally achieved by the use of trusts, but, to be effective, any trust requires the policyholder to be excluded from being a potential beneficiary. Where critical illness cover is provided as an addition to a life assurance policy, it may be difficult to draft appropriate trust wording for the separate benefits. An easier solution is to arrange critical illness and life assurance in separate policies.

11:4.6 Long-term care insurance

There is a growing need for contracts that assist in meeting the cost of professional care in later life. The statistics are persuasive. By 2020, the number of people over the age of 85 will have increased by 50%, whilst over the next 40 years, the number is expected to double. It is likely that the State will not be able to meet the full cost of care and individuals will be required to be responsible for a far greater level of private provision than they are currently.

There are two types of long-term care contracts. The first type are insurance policies. These insure the costs of long-term care for either a single lump sum or regular monthly premiums.

The second type of contract is arranged at the time care is needed. A lump sum purchases an annuity which provides the care costs. Because the individual is, by definition, in poor health, the rates are much better than for a healthy person.

Claims are paid when a level of incapacity, requiring long-term care, is reached. Most insurance companies measure this on the basis of the policyholder's ability to complete 'activities of daily living (ADLs)'. Typically, these are washing, dressing, feeding, toileting, mobility and transferring (from a wheelchair to a bed). A claim will normally be paid when two or three of these ADLs cannot be completed without assistance. Most policies will also pay out on cognitive impairment, such as senility or Alzheimer's disease.

All claims paid on long-term care policies are free from tax.

A variant on the two approaches outlined above involves an investment bond. Units are purchased in an investment bond fund and monthly premium deductions are made from the value of the bond. This approach enables the lump sum invested to continue providing an investment return.

When the policyholder makes a claim, premium deductions cease and care payments (made directly to the nursing home) begin. The policyholder must decide at the outset the extent to which the value of the bond is used to finance the payments. To the extent that there is value in the bond at death, it passes to the heirs.

The caveat of mixing insurance and investment obviously applies in this case. It is particularly important to quantify whether the investment vehicle is appropriate and whether growth will be sufficient to fund increasing care insurance premiums or whether capital erosion is likely.

11:5 Underwriting

Underwriting in connection with investment policies has already been discussed in **Chapter 10**. As far as protection policies are concerned, underwriting will generally be of greater relevance due to the extra risks involved, arising from the higher level and longer periods of life cover normally required. Consequently, life assurance companies are likely to take a more detailed approach to obtaining medical information.

A particular example of this concerns smoking. Many insurance companies now provide two different levels of premium rates for their protection policies, one for smokers and one for non-smokers (the definition of this can vary widely). The discount offered to non-smokers can be as much as one-third off the rates for smokers.

Consideration of the risks of contracting AIDS and associated medical problems has had a much greater effect on protection policies than on investment contracts. Many insurance companies have ceased to write convertible or increasable contracts, or have made such options subject to fresh enquiry into the AIDS risk at the time of the options being exercised. Generally, premiums have increased substantially, particularly for the younger age groups.

New policies for permanent health insurance, personal accident and sickness, hospital insurance and private medical insurance generally exclude the AIDS risk (the possible exception to this is for group permanent health schemes, where greatly increased premium rates would usually be applied).

Where a medical examination is conducted as part of the underwriting process, the life assured has the right to see any medical report sent to the life company under the Access to Medical Reports Act 1988. If there are errors, the life assured has the right to request rectification.

11:6 Taxation position

Life assurance premium relief was abolished for all life policies effected after 13 March 1984. The position for policies arranged on or before 13 March 1984 which provide for the benefits to be increased or the term extended after that date, is as follows:

(a) where a policyholder exercises the option to increase or extend cover, such as in a convertible, renewable term assurance, the tax relief is lost on all subsequent premiums;

(b) where a policy has an in-built automatic increase for which the policyholder contracted at the outset, the premiums still qualify for tax relief;

(c) where the mix of insurance and investment within one policy can be altered without a change in the amount of the premiums, such as in a flexible unit-linked whole life policy, the policyholder continues to obtain life assurance premium relief, even if they choose to increase the life cover.

With effect from 6 April 1989, life assurance premium relief was reduced from 15% to 12.5%. Consequently, the net premium payable in respect of these policies is now 87.5% of the gross premium.

11:7 Some specific uses of protection policies

The following are some specific uses of life assurance protection policies:

(a) funding for inheritance tax;

(b) partnership and share purchase assurance;

(c) keyman assurance.

11:7.1 Funding for inheritance tax

Life assurance protection policies written under trust for the benefit of nominated persons are often required in funding for inheritance tax liabilities. The circumstances in which they may be used together with the appropriate type of policy are shown below.

(a) To meet the inheritance tax payable on death – a whole life policy.

(b) To meet the inheritance tax payable on the death of a surviving spouse – a whole life policy written on a joint life, last survivor basis.

(c) To meet the inheritance tax payable if death should occur within seven years of a potentially exempt transfer (PET) when the nil rate IHT band has already been used – seven-year decreasing term assurance.

(d) To meet the extra inheritance tax liability on a donor's death, resulting from adding back to their estate any PET, as reduced by taper relief (see **Chapter 12**), made in the seven years preceding death – seven-year level term assurance. This arises where the original PET was within the donor's nil rate IHT band.

(e) To meet any extra inheritance tax payable on death, which arises on a transfer that was chargeable during lifetime but the tax is recalculated as death occurs within seven years – a specially tailored decreasing term assurance.

11:7.2 Partnership and share purchase assurance

The purpose of partnership and private limited company share purchase life assurance arrangements is to assist in providing the funds required by the surviving partners to buy the shares of a deceased partner or by the remaining shareholders to buy a deceased's shareholding. Partnership assurance enables the necessary funds to be received by the surviving partners, with the following advantages:

(a) it removes the need for the surviving partners to borrow, liquidate assets or use existing funds already earmarked for other purposes to provide the money to buy the deceased's share;

(b) less attractive solutions, such as finding a new partner with capital or the widow becoming involved in the business, are avoided;

(c) those entitled to the deceased's estate will be able to benefit from readily available funds.

Since partnerships and companies can vary considerably in their constitution and organisation, each case should be considered on an individual basis. The following information should be ascertained before a life policy is effected:

(a) the number of partners or directors, together with their ages, sex, state of health and smoking habits;

(b) the likelihood of future changes in the composition of the partnership or the shareholders;

(c) the current resources available;

(d) the value of the partnership shares or shareholdings;

(e) whether there are any relevant provisions in the partnership agreement or articles of association;

(f) whether there are any existing life assurance arrangements.

The main policies which can be suitably used in partnership or share purchase assurance to provide life cover for the appropriate period, normally up to the anticipated dates of retirement, are shown below:

(a) level term assurance;

(b) convertible term assurance;

(c) convertible, renewable term assurance;

(d) term assurance provided under personal pension plans;

(e) flexible unit-linked whole life policies.

Policies may be written on a 'life of another' basis so that the individuals paying the premiums can obtain direct benefit from them. This can considerably simplify matters both with regard to inheritance tax and also by ensuring that the cost of the arrangement is on an equitable basis. Such arrangements can, however, be very rigid. Therefore it may be preferable to use the own life route using a flexible trust wording in favour of the other partners/shareholders, especially where frequent changes are a possibility.

11:7.3 'Keyman' assurance

The purpose of keyman assurance is to cover the loss of profits to an employer arising from the death of a key employee. This assurance could therefore be required where:

(a) the owner has only provided the capital but the keyman has detailed knowledge of the business;

(b) the keyman has important personal and business connections;

(c) any other situation where the loss of the keyman's services will be critical to the business, and will result in a financial loss to the business or an extra burden, such as costs of recruiting a replacement or loss of orders.

The premiums payable will be allowed as a business expense providing the following conditions are met.

(a) The sole relationship of the life assured to the company is that of employee to employer. The employee must not be a significant shareholder.

(b) The assurance is intended to meet the loss of profits resulting from the loss of the keyman's services. The Inland Revenue will accept a level of cover, normally up to a maximum of ten times the keyman's salary, but this will particularly depend on their status within the company and can be any amount actually justifiable in the given circumstances.

(c) The life policy is an annual or short-term assurance. This can normally be defined as not exceeding five years, although, in exceptional circumstances, terms of up to ten years or more may be acceptable.

The company should agree the tax position with the Inland Revenue at the outset. Each case will be considered on its own facts but, in principle, if the premiums are allowed as an expense for corporation tax, the proceeds will be taxed as income. If, on the other hand, the premiums are not allowed, the proceeds may not be taxed. The company does not have the option to select one alternative or the other. The Inland Revenue's ruling will need to be taken into account when arranging the policy (e.g. in determining the sum assured or arranging for the proceeds to be paid over a period of years rather than in a single amount).

Qualifying policies taken out by companies on or after 14 March 1989 are treated in the same way as non-qualifying policies for the taxation of policy gains. Consequently, in the case of a whole life policy, if the surrender value at the time of payment of any benefit is greater than the premiums paid, the gain is liable to corporation tax.

In addition to the benefits payable on the death of a keyman, it is also possible to arrange for them to be paid if they should become disabled. This will then provide the company with the resources to seek a replacement for the keyman or for any other required purpose. Again, if the critical illness or permanent health policy has a surrender value, a taxable policy gain could arise.

One particular consequence of arranging this type of assurance is that, where benefits are received on the keyman's death, the value of the business may be inflated by the cash received. Therefore, where the keyman is a shareholder, the value of their shares may be increased, with the result that their estate may be subject to a larger inheritance tax liability.

12 Tax planning

Tax plays an extremely important part in financial planning for an individual since the main objective of most people is to increase their capital and/or income after tax. However, saving tax should generally be of secondary importance to personal, practical and investment considerations. Many of the tax saving and planning aspects for individuals are discussed in the chapters to which they relate. The purpose of this chapter is to mention some of the other more important matters which have not been covered elsewhere. These can be shown under three main headings:

(a) income tax;

(b) capital gains tax;

(c) inheritance tax.

12:1 Income tax

The following matters should be considered in relation to income tax.

(a) All personal allowances and reliefs to which an individual is entitled should be claimed. Elections, where appropriate, should be made within the relevant time limits.

(b) A husband and wife are taxed independently for both income tax and capital gains tax purposes. For income tax, each has a separate personal allowance. The married couple's allowance has been abolished from 6 April 2000 onwards other than for taxpayers aged 65 or over.

Significant planning opportunities are, therefore, available to transfer assets between spouses to enable income to be taxed at lower rates. If one spouse is a higher rate taxpayer and the other is not, consideration should be given to transferring income-producing assets to the latter to enable him or her to use the personal allowance, lower and basic rate tax bands. This can be done free of capital gains tax (and also usually inheritance tax), but, to be effective, there must be an outright unconditional gift of the asset.

(c) If assets are held jointly, income is normally divided equally for tax purposes, irrespective of the actual division of ownership. If jointly held property is not held in equal shares a declaration may be made to the Inland Revenue so that each spouse is taxed on the income to which they are actually entitled, provided that this corresponds to their beneficial interest in the property. Such a declaration will lead to savings if the lower rate taxpayer or non-taxpayer is entitled to a greater share of the asset.

(d) Deductions such as annual payments should be paid by the spouse with the higher marginal tax rate.

(e) In any situation involving separation or divorce, there is from 6 April 2000 no relief for maintenance payments under arrangements set up on or after 15 March 1988 other than for taxpayers aged 65 or over. Consequently, the most tax-effective way of providing for a former spouse is now usually by way of a capital settlement, as the income from it will be taxed at a lower rate. However, this may not always be possible and, in any event, the payer does not obtain tax relief.

It should also be borne in mind that because maintenance payments are free from tax in the recipient's hands, it may be possible to settle on a lower annual payment to recognise the tax-free status of the payments.

(f) If it is desired to transfer income to a person with unused allowances, it is necessary to make an outright gift of a capital sum to generate sufficient income, or to create a settlement with a similar sum in favour of the individual concerned. This will not be effective in the case of a settlement by a parent in favour of a minor unmarried child. Before it is decided to set up a trust, it should be remembered that there may be both capital gains tax and inheritance tax consequences. Therefore, the total position must be considered.

(g) The 'accrued income scheme' is designed to combat 'bondwashing', which was the practice of converting income accruing on certain fixed-interest securities into capital so that it was exempt from tax as a capital gain rather than taxed as income. Broadly, the intention of the accrued income scheme is to treat interest on securities, such as gilts, local authority bonds and non-convertible company debentures and unsecured loan stocks, as accruing on a day-to-day basis between interest payment dates and separately from the capital value of the investment. Interest accrued at the date of sale is taxable as income and, in the case of a purchase, accrued income bought is offset for tax purposes against interest subsequently received. The accrued income scheme applies to all UK residents, except for those holding securities with a nominal value of £5,000 or less.

(h) Favourable income tax treatment can be obtained by individuals on certain transactions and investments. Shown below are some of those which are especially advantageous:

(i) National Savings Certificates (see **2:2.5**);

(ii) investments under the Enterprise Investment Scheme and in Venture Capital Trusts (see **Chapter 6**);

(iii) individual savings accounts (see **4:2**);

(iv) additional voluntary contributions (see **Chapter 9**);

(v) personal pension contributions (see **Chapter 9**);

(vi) school fees composition schemes (see **14:2.3**);

(vii) gifts to charities;

(viii) Lloyd's Underwriters (see **Chapter 7**);

(ix) purchase of an interest in an industrial or commercial building in an enterprise zone, either directly or through one of the property trusts or syndicates set up for this purpose (see **Chapter 5**);

(x) in certain situations, income arising to an offshore trust where the settlor or his spouse is not a beneficiary can be free of UK income tax. These situations are rare, following law changes in 1991 and 1998; and

(xi) investment in certain qualifying film finance schemes.

(i) Investments in Enterprise Investment Scheme shares, Enterprise Zone property (and trusts and syndicates), venture capital trusts and individual savings accounts must all be made before 5 April to qualify for the reliefs or allowances for the current tax year. Where possible, it is sensible to make VCT and ISA investments early in the tax year in order to enjoy the potential for tax-free income and growth at the earliest opportunity. If an Enterprise Investment Scheme investment is made before 6 October, some relief can be claimed in the previous tax year (see **6:4**).

(j) Non-taxpayers (i.e. those whose income is covered by their personal allowance) should invest in assets which pay gross income (including ISAs), to avoid the need for repayment claims. For example, interest on British Government stocks, National Savings Income Bonds and Pensioners' Income Bonds is paid gross and non-taxpayers can complete Inland Revenue form R85 to register for the payment of bank and building society interest without deduction of income tax.

(k) As well as enjoying capital gains tax exemptions (see **12:2**), a gift of shares or securities to a charity after 5 April 2000 qualifies for income tax relief. The value of the gift can be claimed as a deduction from income. This relief is extended to gifts of land and buildings to charity after 5 April 2002.

12:2 Capital gains tax

The following are the main considerations for the planning of capital gains tax.

(a) Timing of disposals is of the utmost importance:

(i) if a disposal is postponed until shortly after 5 April, the payment of any capital gains tax is delayed for one year;

(ii) the Finance Act 1998 radically reformed CGT for individuals, trustees and personal representatives by freezing indexation allowance on the base cost and replacing it with taper relief. This treatment applies to disposals made by them after 5 April 1998. For these disposals, indexation allowance will be given in accordance with the increase in the Retail Prices Index up to April 1998 but not beyond. For disposals after 5 April 1998, the chargeable gain will be progressively reduced (tapered), according to the length of time the asset has been held after 5 April 1998, plus one extra year for assets held at 17 March 1998 in the case of non-business assets.

The taper relief in respect of business assets was increased in the Finance Acts 2000 and 2002, and the table below relates to disposals on or after 6 April 2002.

The maximum taper relief for non-business assets is 40% (60% of the gain being chargeable), when the holding period is ten years or more. The relief operates more rapidly and more generously for business assets. The following table provides details of all taper percentages.

No. of complete years after 5 April 1998 for which asset held	*Percentage of gain chargeable for business assets*	*Percentage of gain chargeable for non-business assets*
0	100	100
1	50	100
2	25	100
3	25	95
4	25	90
5	25	85
6	25	80
7	25	75
8	25	70
9	25	65
10 or more	25	60

Thus, delaying the disposal so that an additional complete year of ownership since 5 April 1998 or the date of purchase, if later, is reached may considerably reduce the chargeable gain.

The effective rates of tax on gains realised by a higher rate taxpayer are, therefore, 10% (40% x 25%) after only two years' ownership of a business asset and 24% (40% x 60%) after ten years' ownership of a non-business asset.

The distinction between business and non-business assets is therefore very important. From 6 April 2000 business assets are, broadly:

(i) assets used for the purposes of a trade;

(ii) all shares and securities in unlisted trading companies;

(iii) all shares and securities in a listed trading company where the investor is an employee or officer (including part-time employees); and

(iv) all shares and securities in a listed company (whether or not trading) where the investor is an employee or officer (including part-time employees) provided the investor holds 10% or less of the voting rights; and

(v) all shares and securities in a company where the investor is able to exercise at least 5% of the voting rights.

Prior to 6 April 2000, more stringent rules applied and shares and securities only qualified if they were in trading companies and the individual could exercise at least 25% of the voting rights, reduced to 5% for a full-time working employee or officer of the company.

The following example demonstrates how chargeable gains are now calculated.

Example 12

An asset was purchased in 1988 for £40,000 and sold on 31 July 2002 for £100,000. Indexation allowance for the period from 1988 to April 1998 is calculated at £12,000. The holding period for taper relief is five years for a non-business asset but four years for a business asset.

The chargeable gain is computed as follows:

	£
Proceeds	100,000
Less: Cost	(40,000)
	60,000
Less: Indexation allowance	(12,000)
	£48,000

If the asset is non-business:

Percentage of gain taxable 85% x £48,000	£40,800

If the asset is a business asset throughout:

Percentage of gain taxable 25% x £48,000	£12,000

If an asset is partly a business asset and partly non-business during the period of ownership, complex time apportionment rules apply.

(iii) if disposals are spread over more than one tax year so that the realised gains in each year, after adjusting for indexation or taper relief, do not exceed the annual exemption (£7,700 for 2002/03), no capital gains tax liability arises (in the case of most trusts, the annual exemption is £3,850 for 2002/03);

(iv) if realised gains (as adjusted for indexation or taper relief) in excess of the annual exemption have been made in a tax year, consideration should be given to disposing of assets showing a loss. The losses can then be offset against the gains made, thereby reducing or eliminating the potential capital gains tax liability. Losses brought forward from previous years can also be used in a similar manner. In this instance, such losses will be used only to reduce realised gains before taper relief to £7,700, the exemption limit, with any unused balance being again carried forward. The interaction of losses and taper relief is complex, and careful consideration needs to be given to the time of disposal. Losses should be set against gains qualifying for the *lowest* rate of taper relief. Losses cannot be carried back to an earlier tax year; they can only be offset against chargeable gains realised in the current tax year or subsequent years.

Despite the availability of these timing opportunities, it should be borne in mind that disposals should first be considered from an investment viewpoint. As previously mentioned, a poor investment even with good tax planning is unlikely to produce a satisfactory result.

(b) Every person, including a minor, is entitled to his or her own exemption. Consideration should therefore be given to husbands and wives spreading the ownership of investments in a family so that each member is able to realise tax-free gains.

The income tax rule which treats a child's income from a parental gift as the parents' if it exceeds £100 per annum in total is not mirrored in the capital gains tax legislation. Parental gifts should therefore be invested in assets providing capital growth and no income, for example the capital shares or zero dividend preference shares of split capital investment trusts.

(c) Each spouse has an annual capital gains tax exemption. In order to make maximum use of this, it may be worthwhile for them to transfer shares to each other. In addition, as capital gains are aggregated with income to determine the rate of tax, gains should be crystallised by the spouse with the lower top rate of tax. For example, one spouse may have losses brought forward. These cannot be used directly to offset a gain to be made by the other spouse. However, if the asset to be realised is first transferred between the spouses, the necessary offset is achieved. No stamp duty would be payable on such gifts, but all the formalities of transfer of ownership should be carried out before any sale. Any such transfer must be unconditional.

(d) 'Bed and breakfasting' (the sale and subsequent repurchase of shares, generally on the following day) was widely used to crystallise capital gains or losses for set off purposes or to utilise the annual exemption.

This practice has been stopped for disposals made on or after 17 March 1998. Sales will now be identified with purchases made within 30 days of the disposal. Alternative techniques for avoiding being 'out of the market' with a particular share or collective investment could include:

(i) immediate repurchase of an identical holding by the spouse;

(ii) immediate repurchase of a similar investment;

(iii) repurchase within an ISA; or

(iv) purchasing an option to protect against a price increase during the 30-day period (this will only be possible with shares and could be prohibitively complex and expensive).

(e) Gains and losses arising on the disposal of gilts and other qualifying corporate bonds (this includes local authority bonds and non-convertible company debentures and unsecured loan stocks) are completely exempt from capital gains tax. Consequently, investors are largely able to pursue a policy for such assets based entirely on investment criteria without being concerned with the tax consequences of any decision. The accrued income scheme (see **12:1(g)**) should, however, be considered.

(f) Since capital gains tax is not payable on death, it is often advisable for a person with a very short life expectancy to avoid realising substantial gains during the remainder of their lifetime, to benefit from the tax-free step up on death.

(g) Careful attention should also be paid to the effect of the taper relief rules on the capital gains tax position. In choosing which investments to sell, particular note should be taken of the holding period and the type of asset, to ensure that taper relief is maximised. Enhanced taper relief is available on business assets as defined above.

(h) If an individual wishes to make a large gift to a charity, it is usually beneficial, where it can be arranged, for the gift to be in the form of a chargeable asset showing a sizeable capital gain and not the equivalent cash value. Since gains arising on gifts to charities are completely exempt from capital gains tax, the potential tax liability would be avoided. From 6 April 2000, an income tax deduction is also available for the value of the shares, making such a gift extremely tax efficient. From 6 April 2002, this deduction is extended to gifts of land and buildings to charity.

(i) Where an individual becomes the owner of two homes, they should, within two years of acquiring the second home, make an election as to which home is to be treated as their main private residence. Since only one residence is exempt from capital gains tax, they should usually select the home likely to show the greater gain on sale (see **5:2**). A married couple may have only one exempt private residence between them.

(j) Where an individual owns an asset, such as shares, which becomes of negligible value, a claim can be made to have the loss treated as if it had been crystallised without an actual disposal being necessary. The loss can be used in any of the two tax years preceding the year of the claim, providing that the asset was also of negligible value at the earlier date.

(k) A capital loss on the disposal of subscriber shares in an unquoted company can be set against income in certain circumstances.

(l) Where a person is the owner of 5% or more of the shares in a trading company and works full-time in it as a director or employee, or is a sole trader, or a partner in a firm, he or she is entitled to capital gains tax retirement relief on all or part of a gain not exceeding £50,000 (for the year ending 5 April 2003) if the business is sold (or gifted), provided the individual is at least age 50, or has to retire earlier due to ill-health.

Retirement relief is being gradually phased out from 6 April 1999, and will not be available from 6 April 2003 onwards. However, taper relief is available at enhanced rates for business assets, and a maximum of 75% of the gain will be exempted when the shares have been held for only two years.

The retirement relief exemption is reduced proportionately where the business or shares have not been owned for the whole of the previous ten years before the date of sale or, in the case of a company, where the director or employee has not been a full-time working director or employee for that period.

One-half of the gain in excess of £50,000 (or the proportionately reduced figure, if applicable) up to a maximum of £200,000 is also eligible for relief for the year ending 5 April 2003. If the disposal is of shares in a company, the gain qualifying for relief would be in the proportion of the company's chargeable business assets to the total chargeable assets (chargeable assets are all assets on which a chargeable gain or allowable loss would arise if the company disposed of them). Thus, the holding of chargeable non-business assets within a company should be minimised where possible.

In order to maximise retirement relief, it is usually worthwhile for the following action to be taken by an individual, when practicable:

(i) postpone the disposal of the business until age 50 and also, in the case of a company, continue to work in it until that time;

(ii) postpone the disposal of the business until it has been owned for ten years; and

(iii) arrange for the spouse to work full-time in the business and to own part of it. He or she will then also obtain retirement relief against their own gains on disposal of the business.

As retirement relief will only be available up to 5 April 2003, it may be worth ensuring that planned disposals take place before that date to secure the relief. However, this needs to be considered in conjunction with optimising the holding period for taper relief purposes.

In all cases, it is recommended that detailed professional advice is obtained, as the conditions which have to be satisfied can be complex.

(m) As capital gains may arise where a person becomes absolutely entitled to trust assets, consideration should be given to prolonging the life of the settlement if the beneficiary is prepared to receive the income but not the capital. This can be achieved by conferring on the beneficiary an interest in possession at age 25 instead of absolute entitlement. By this means, liability for capital gains tax is deferred, sometimes indefinitely.

(n) Capital gains can be deferred by an investment in EIS or VCT companies (see **6:2**). Provided the sale proceeds are used to subscribe for shares in a qualifying company, the capital gain can be deferred until a subsequent disposal. The rules are detailed and complex, and professional advice is recommended.

12:3 The taxation of savings income

From the year 1996/97 onwards, savings income (excluding dividend income) of basic and lower rate taxpayers has generally been taxed at the 20% rate. This includes interest from banks and building societies, interest distributions from unit trusts, interest from gilts and other securities including corporate bonds, and purchased life annuities. It does not, however, include savings income from overseas taxed on a remittance basis for non-domiciled individuals.

The income tax implications are that:

(a) those exempt from tax or not liable to tax may claim a refund of the tax credit or tax deducted at 20%;

(b) those liable to tax at 10% may claim a partial refund;

(c) those liable to income tax at the savings rate of 20% will have no further tax to pay;

(d) those liable to tax at the basic rate will not be required to pay further tax; and

(e) those who are liable to the higher rate of income tax will be taxed at 40% on the net income received grossed up at 20%, but with a credit for the 20% deducted at source.

For these purposes savings income is taken as the 'top slice' of an individual's income.

Different rules apply to dividend income, as the tax credit on dividends from UK companies was reduced to 10% from 6 April 1999. Lower and basic rate taxpayers have no further liability; higher rate taxpayers pay tax at 32.5% on such income but with a credit for the 10% tax credit, so that their effective rate of tax is the same as that on other savings income. Non-taxpayers will not be able to reclaim the tax credit.

As regards capital gains tax, where an individual's income is over the higher rate threshold, all chargeable gains will be taxed at 40%. For those whose income is less than the higher rate threshold, it is possible that receipt of dividend and savings income will cause difficulties in determining the appropriate marginal rate at which capital gains are taxed. Professional advice should be sought in this situation.

12:4 Inheritance tax

IHT is a tax on certain lifetime gifts and on an individual's estate on death. It operates on a cumulative basis and, subject to certain exemptions and reliefs, is chargeable on the cumulative total:

(a) at death, on certain lifetime gifts made within the previous seven years;

(b) at death, on lifetime gifts with reservation (see **12:4.3**);

(c) of gifts into discretionary trusts, whether in lifetime or on death;

(d) of the value of the assets passing on death.

For transfers made on or after 6 April 2002, the first £250,000 (for 2002/03) of cumulative chargeable transfers (the nil rate band) is exempt from IHT and any excess is taxed on death at a rate of 40%.

To some extent, IHT can be described as a voluntary tax due to the many exemptions and reliefs available. With early planning, it is often possible to reduce or eliminate potential IHT liabilities entirely, and this is helped by a husband and wife each having their own exemptions and rate bands. However, all assets are potentially liable to IHT on death, with only estates (including cumulative transfers) within the nil rate band not giving rise to a tax charge at all. Since an individual's house must be included in calculating the value of his assets, IHT may affect many individuals who otherwise have only relatively modest estates.

For the purpose of calculating the value of a lifetime transfer, it is the loss suffered by the donor on the transfer, rather than the benefit received by the donee, which is relevant for IHT.

12:4.1 Classes of transfer

Transfers can be broadly classified as follows:

(a) exempt (see below);

(b) potentially exempt;

(c) chargeable.

A potentially exempt transfer (PET) is a lifetime gift made on or after 18 March 1986 by an individual to one of the recipients shown in **(a)**, **(b)** and **(d)** below – in the case of **(c)**, the relevant date is on or after 17 March 1987:

(a) another individual;

(b) an accumulation and maintenance trust;

(c) an interest in possession trust;

(d) a disabled person's trust.

A PET is treated as an exempt transfer on which no IHT is payable at the time of the gift and, if the donor survives for seven years after the gift is made, no tax will be payable. If the donor dies within those seven years, the PET is treated as a chargeable transfer at the time it was made and IHT may become due at the date of death. However, a PET will still provide the benefits listed below.

(a) Although the PET may have become chargeable, the amount on which the charge is based is the value at the time of the actual gift and not the value at the date of death when the charge arises. If the property gifted has increased in value, this 'freezing' of its value will often be advantageous. Where the value of the property has fallen since the gift, the lower value may be used in most circumstances.

(b) Payment of IHT is postponed until after the death of the donor, rather than becoming payable shortly after the gift is made.

(c) IHT is charged at the rates in force at the date of death, where they may be different to those applying at the time of the gift. If the gift is made more than three years before the date of death, the tax payable is subject to taper relief as shown in the following table.

Time between gift and death	*% of full rate payable*
Up to 3 years	100
3-4 years	80
4-5 years	60
5-6 years	40
6-7 years	20

It should be noted that it is the tax payable, not the value of the gift, which is tapered. If no tax is payable because the gift is covered by the annual exemption and the nil rate band, taper relief will not apply.

The IHT due on a PET is payable by the donee.

A lifetime gift which does not qualify as an exempt transfer or a PET (typically a gift to a discretionary trust) is regarded as a chargeable transfer at the time it is made, and, subject to the nil rate band, is immediately liable to IHT at one-half of the death rates in force at the time. For this purpose, any chargeable transfers which have been made in the previous seven years are taken into account in calculating how much of the nil rate band remains unused. If the donor survives seven years, there are no further IHT consequences. However, if he or she does not, the tax charge is recalculated using the full rates in force at the date of death but reduced by any taper relief. If this produces a higher charge than the tax already paid on the lifetime transfer, a further liability arises. Where the calculation shows a lower charge, the difference is not repayable.

When making a chargeable transfer, the options below are normally available:

(a) the donor pays the tax based on the value of the transfer plus the tax; or

(b) the donee pays the tax calculated on the transfer value only. In this case, the tax does not decrease the donor's estate and, consequently, both the amount of the transfer and the inheritance tax are lower.

12:4.2 Exemptions and reliefs

The following are the main IHT exemptions.

(a) Transfers between husband and wife, whether made during lifetime or on death. The exception to this is where a husband or wife, domiciled in the UK, makes a transfer to a foreign-domiciled spouse. In these circumstances, only the first £55,000 is exempt.

(b) Lifetime transfers in each tax year up to £3,000 (per donor). Any unused part of the exemption may be carried forward for one year only for use in the following tax year after the exemption for that following year has been utilised.

(c) Outright lifetime gifts to any one person not exceeding £250 in each tax year with no limit to the number of recipients. However, this exemption cannot be claimed in respect of gifts to a particular person where more than £250 is given to that person in a tax year.

(d) Normal expenditure out of income. This covers transfers of net income after tax, provided that they form part of normal expenditure and leave sufficient income for the donor to maintain his usual standard of living. For this purpose, the capital element of a purchased life annuity is not treated as being part of the donor's income. Following recent case law, 'normal' is interpreted as expenditure according with the transferor's settled pattern of expenditure, either by reference to past habits, or a prior commitment as to the future.

(e) Gifts in consideration of marriage. The following amounts are exempt:

   (i) £5,000 from each parent;

   (ii) £2,500 from each grandparent;

   (iii) £2,500 from one party of the marriage to the other;

   (iv) £1,000 from any other person.

(f) Lifetime gifts for the support and maintenance of children and dependant relatives, including a former spouse.

(g) Gifts to charities both during lifetime and on death. This exemption can be of particular relevance to individuals with no relatives who prefer their favourite charities to benefit rather than the Crown.

Business property relief applies at 100% in respect of interests in unincorporated businesses and holdings of shares in unquoted trading companies, subject to certain conditions. Similarly, relief of 100% is available against agricultural land and woodlands. Thus no inheritance tax is payable on the value of these assets at the date of gift or death, providing the conditions are met.

12:4.3 Gifts with reservation

Anti-avoidance provisions relating to gifts with reservation exist with the aim of counteracting 'have your cake and eat it' schemes such as inheritance trusts. The rules on gifts with reservation are essentially the same as the old estate duty provisions, with gifted property subject to a reservation if either the donee does not assume full possession and enjoyment of the property at the time it is gifted or at least seven years before the donor's death; or if the donor retains a benefit or enjoyment from the property at any time in the last seven years of his or her life.

The consequences of a gift with reservation depend on whether or not the reservation ceases during the donor's lifetime, or whether it is still in existence at the time of death. If the donor releases the reservation before death, he or she is treated as having made a PET of the gifted property at the time the reservation is released. Where the donor dies without releasing the reservation, the gifted property is treated as part of the estate at death. IHT is charged according to the value of the property at that time. The original gift may also be charged as a lifetime gift in certain circumstances.

The gift with reservation provisions particularly affect many individuals with medium-sized estates who may now feel unable to pass on their property before death.

12:5 Inheritance tax planning

The following matters are of the utmost importance in IHT planning.

(a) Subject to the individual circumstances, it is often beneficial from an IHT viewpoint for the assets of a husband and wife to be divided between them so that they are both able to take advantage of the various exemptions and the nil rate band. However, care should be taken to ensure as far as possible that the 'associated operations' rules do not apply, in order to avoid the transfer between the husband and wife, and the subsequent transfer from the recipient, being treated as one transaction.

In practice, the Inland Revenue is unlikely to use the associated operations provisions where a husband shares capital with his wife who then chooses to make gifts out of the money she has received. The exception to this is where there is a blatant case of a husband's gift to his wife (or vice versa) being made on condition that she should at once use the money to make gifts to others.

(b) Maximum advantage should be taken of the opportunity to make gifts within the various exemptions available. In this way, a considerable amount can be transferred from an estate over a period of years without any IHT liability.

(c) In addition to exempt gifts, an individual with a large estate should consider making further outright lifetime gifts, rather than waiting until death, for the following reasons:

   (i) cumulative chargeable lifetime gifts may be made within the IHT nil rate band (£250,000 for transfers made on or after 6 April 2002). Gifts made more than seven years previously drop out and, consequently, further gifts can be made within the nil rate band without attracting IHT;

   (ii) if the gifts were treated as PETs, the benefits mentioned earlier in this chapter would apply. Accordingly, it will often be particularly advantageous to gift those assets which are likely to increase in value. In particular, the spouse with the longer life expectancy should make PETs and this may involve transferring assets from one spouse to the other prior to making a PET, subject to the associated operation rules set out above.

   However, as capital gains tax holdover is now only available for gifts of business assets, the capital gains tax implications of such gifts must also be considered.

   Any tax payable by the donee if death occurs within seven years should be covered by decreasing term assurance (see **11:1.2**).

(d) In appropriate circumstances, it may be beneficial to 'skip' a generation and make gifts (or legacies) to grandchildren rather than to children. There will then be no charge to inheritance tax on the children's deaths. The grandchildren's interests could be held in an accumulation and maintenance trust.

(e) An inheritance tax saving will be made if an amount equal to the nil rate band is left away from the spouse, so that this exemption is not wasted. In order to avoid redrafting a will each time the nil rate band changes, the will can be drawn up on the basis that an amount equivalent to the current nil rate band, less any chargeable gifts made within the previous seven years, is left in this way. A common provision is for a discretionary trust for the widow(er) and children, thus enabling the whole of the surviving family to benefit from this gift (see **Chapter 16**). Care should be taken, however, to ensure that a share in the family home does not become an asset of the trust. If the surviving spouse continues to live there, he or she is likely to be regarded as having an interest in possession in the whole property, with the result that its value will be included as part of their estate on their death.

(f) As previously mentioned, it is the loss suffered by a donor on a transfer, rather than the benefit received by the donee, which is relevant for IHT purposes. Therefore, an individual should be aware of the circumstances where a gift providing a small benefit for the donee can give rise to a large potential IHT liability, for example, a gift of 2% out of a 51% family company shareholding. Although, in this case, the gift may be of little value to the recipient, the donor would lose control of the company, with the result that a large reduction in the value of the estate would be likely. Under current legislation, however, 100% business property relief is likely to be available on such a transfer.

(g) If appropriate, advantage should be taken of business property relief and/or agricultural property relief. Where relief is available, the transfer will be assessed for IHT purposes at a nil, or reduced value. It must be borne in mind, however, that the donor will not qualify for the relief until he or she has owned the property for two years. In connection with agricultural property relief, it is very important that ownership of a farmhouse should not be retained without some of the farmland, otherwise it will not enjoy agricultural property relief. For transfers within the last seven years of life, there are also conditions which the donee must satisfy in order to secure an exemption when the PET becomes chargeable.

(h) If a loan is obtained, it should be secured against non-business assets where possible. A loan secured against business property will reduce the amount of business property relief available.

(i) The setting up of a trust may be especially useful to pass capital to children, grandchildren or other dependants, but at the same time enabling some flexibility and control over the assets to be retained. The particular type of trust would depend on the exact circumstances, although a typical arrangement might be a discretionary trust up to the amount of the nil rate band.

(j) Funding for IHT through life assurance policies (see **Chapter 11**) is now likely to play an even greater role in IHT planning, due to the treatment of gifts with reservation and the lack of capital gains hold-over relief for most gifts.

(k) Where a life or pension policy is arranged in order to provide protection for the family of the life assured, it is often advisable for it to be written in trust or under nomination to pass free of IHT to the dependant concerned.

(l) Even after death, a variation of a will or a disclaimer may be effected. These can produce considerable IHT savings (see **Chapter 15**).

(m) On certain assets, an option is provided to pay an IHT liability by interest-free instalments over ten years. Where this is permitted, it is usually beneficial to exercise the option. In other cases, the IHT liability may also be paid by instalments but interest would be payable. In this connection, the order of gifts made in a lifetime can be critical. If a PET becomes chargeable, it is important that, where it is a gift of an asset on which tax can be paid by instalments, it is not the part of the estate which is within the nil rate band.

12:6 Overriding considerations for tax planning

Although this chapter has been written from a tax planning viewpoint, the following overriding considerations should be borne in mind.

(a) Personal and family happiness is of greater importance than saving tax. The possibility of children being financially immature or having unsatisfactory marriages should be taken into account.

(b) Although tax considerations are often vital in making a financial decision, the investment aspects will normally be paramount – the tax tail must not wag the investment dog.

(c) Advice which may be suitable for most people will need to be adapted to the practical circumstances of the particular case. For example, in IHT planning, assets should generally only be passed to children or grandchildren provided the surviving spouse has been left with sufficient capital and/or income on which to live. It may also be unwise to pass assets of high value to relatively young children until they are more responsible. It might also be unwise to split the ownership of the family home on the death of the first spouse as this may severely affect the future well-being and lifestyle of the surviving spouse.

(d) In the light of court cases and Inland Revenue statements in recent years, considerable caution should be exercised before proceeding with certain tax mitigation schemes.

(e) It is usually advisable to keep matters simple and for any scheme to be as flexible as possible. It should be remembered that not only do individuals' family and financial circumstances change, but also governments and tax legislation.

(f) Income and capital should not be considered separately for tax planning purposes. Frequently, a higher net return can be obtained by making capital gains than by creating income.

(g) A course of action should be considered from the viewpoint of all forms of tax and not just one tax in isolation. For example, while a lifetime gift may be advantageous for IHT purposes, the benefit could be outweighed by the capital gains tax payable.

(h) Tax planning can be very complicated. It is therefore generally worthwhile for an individual to obtain professional advice before entering into any arrangement where a large sum of money is involved.

13 Mortgages

Apart from the personal satisfaction and enjoyment of owning one's home, it has, in many periods, been one of the best investments an individual could make. In order to finance the purchase, it is quite usual for a mortgage to be obtained from a building society, bank or other lender.

13:1 Guidelines on the amount which can be borrowed

The maximum loan which can be obtained will normally be limited by reference to the size of the borrower's income and the value of the property. This is discussed below.

13:1.1 The size of the borrower's income

(a) Lenders usually base their loans on a multiple of income. For a single person, the multiple normally varies from 3 times to 3.75 times income.

(b) In the case of couples, both of whom are earning, the basis of the loan would often be the greater of:

(i) three times the main income plus the second income; or

(ii) $2^1/2$ times the joint income.

(c) Some lenders operate low-start schemes (usually for first-time buyers), whereby a higher multiple of income is accepted. However, such schemes usually result in larger repayments being made over the total term of the mortgage.

(d) The definition of 'income' varies between lenders. As a general rule lenders take into account 50% of overtime, bonuses, commission, etc if they are not guaranteed.

(e) For the self-employed, the loan is usually based on the income of the previous year. The lender will also normally wish to examine audited accounts for the last three years.

(f) Directors who have a controlling interest in their business will generally be treated as if self-employed.

13:1.2 The value of the property

(a) The normal maximum amount that a building society or bank will lend varies between 85% and 100% of the agreed purchase price or valuation, whichever is the lower. Since the property is used as security for the loan, the lender will wish to ensure that its value is adequate and will appoint its own valuer for this purpose.

(b) If the loan required is very large or it is to be used to purchase an older or less common type of property, there may be a further restriction on the percentage offered.

13:2 Taxation position

In order to encourage private home ownership, successive governments provided assistance to individuals in the form of tax relief on mortgage interest and an exemption from capital gains tax on the profit made from the sale of the main home. The latter continues but interest relief was ended on 5 April 2000 (for the exception, see **13:8**).

13:3 Main types of mortgage

The method selected to repay a mortgage will depend on the exact circumstances of the individual, including his age, state of health, income and tax position. The main types of mortgage are:

(a) repayment mortgages;

(b) endowment mortgages;

(c) pension mortgages;

(d) PEP and ISA mortgages; and

(e) flexible mortgages.

13:3.1 Repayment mortgages

Under this method, both interest and part of the capital of the outstanding loan are paid to the lender monthly. In addition to the monthly loan repayments, most lenders strongly advise that the borrower pays premiums to a mortgage protection policy or other term assurance in order to provide life cover for the outstanding mortgage.

With this type of mortgage, an increasing proportion of the regular payments is applied each year to reduce the capital outstanding. Most lenders offer 'constant net repayment' mortgages. These mortgages are costed so that, if interest rates remain static throughout the mortgage term, the monthly repayments remain the same.

13:3.2 Endowment mortgages

Payments made under an endowment mortgage consist of two separate parts: interest to the lender (in most cases, this will be at the same rate as for a repayment mortgage) and life assurance premiums to an insurance company. The interest is payable throughout the term of the mortgage and will only vary with movements in interest rates.

The proceeds from the life policy are used to repay the mortgage at the end of the term, with any surplus arising being available to the borrower. Both unit-linked and with-profits policies can be taken out to repay a mortgage. Although unit-linked endowments are offered by almost all life companies, with-profits policies are normally more appropriate because there is less fluctuation in the value of the plan.

The main type of with-profits policy which is used to repay a mortgage is a low-cost endowment policy. Occasionally, a full with-profits endowment policy may also be suitable (these policies were considered in **10:1**).

Most low-cost endowment policies are effectively a combination of with-profits endowment assurance and decreasing term assurance, but, since future bonus rates are not known, the life cover from the term assurance is not defined. In reality, these policies are endowment assurances with a guaranteed death benefit which is higher than the amount on which bonuses are declared. A low-cost endowment policy can also be a combination of a with-profits endowment policy and a level term assurance.

Since the total death benefit from the low-cost endowment policy is normally set equal to the amount of the mortgage, the policy should provide sufficient cover to repay the loan in the event of the death of the borrower while the loan is still outstanding.

During the 1990s, competition in the mortgage market led to a reasonably relaxed approach by many lenders to the growth rate assumed for a low-cost endowment taken out to repay an interest-only mortgage at the end of the term. This and the reductions that all life companies have had to make to their bonus rates has resulted in some borrowers being told by their life assurance companies that the projected maturity proceeds of their policies will be insufficient to repay their loans. They have, therefore, had to increase their premiums or start a new savings plan to fund for the shortfall. Policyholders who are a considerable way into their policies should not be concerned as they will have enjoyedsome years of excellent returns. Premiums for new policies now reflect the companies' expectation that future investment returns will be lower than in the recent past.

The main advantage of a low-cost endowment policy, when compared with a full with-profits policy, is that it is much cheaper, due to part of the initial cover being provided by term assurance. Against this, the longer the period, the greater will be the difference in the amount of the proceeds of the two policies.

However, even where an individual has sufficient resources to be able to afford to repay a mortgage by way of a full with-profits endowment policy, it is not usually advisable to do so. Instead, it would normally be advantageous to effect a low-cost endowment to repay the mortgage and arrange an additional savings plan, such as an ISA for the uncommitted funds. In this way, the additional plan will not be charged to the lender and can be stopped at any time and the proceeds used for other purposes. It will also be more tax-efficient.

It should be noted that the high charges and lack of flexibility inherent in endowment policies has recently caused them to lose favour with borrowers as a means of repaying a mortgage.

Alternatives to a with-profits endowment policy are:

(a) *a unit-linked policy.* Because its value will be more subject to stockmarket movements than a with-profits policy, it is reviewed at intervals to check the performance of the fund. If it falls short of the value deemed necessary to produce the required amount, the level of premiums will be increased. However, in this case, care must be exercised to avoid the policy becoming non-qualifying, otherwise a tax charge may arise when the proceeds are received. It may be better to start a separate plan.

(b) *a unit trust, OEIC or investment trust regular savings plan.* Again, the plan will be reviewed at intervals to check that the savings rate is adequate, or to release capital if the performance of the underlying funds is greater than that assumed at the time the mortgage was arranged. This type of repayment vehicle should only be considered if the borrower is already taking advantage of his full ISA allowance. Appropriate life assurance cover should be arranged separately.

13:3.3 Pension mortgages

These mortgages, which are usually arranged by the self-employed or employees not in an occupational pension scheme, have similarities to endowment mortgages. A personal pension policy is effected instead of a life assurance policy and the tax-free cash lump sum is used to repay the mortgage. However, while an endowment policy can be assigned to a lender, this is not possible with a personal pension policy providing retirement benefits. Consequently, the lender will normally require a separate term assurance policy, which can be written under personal pension rules, to be assigned to it to cover the borrower's death before the loan is repaid. It is also possible for a pension mortgage to be taken out by a director, executive or other person through a company pension arrangement.

The main advantage of a pension mortgage, compared with the other methods, is the favourable tax position in respect of both the contributions paid and the pension fund itself. As mentioned in **Chapter 9**, contributions up to the maximum permitted are effectively allowed against the highest income tax rates payable by the individual. The pension fund grows free from capital gains tax, and attracts no additional income tax charge, although since 2 July 1997 pension funds are no longer able to reclaim the tax credit on UK dividend income. As a result, pension mortgages are particularly advantageous for higher rate taxpayers.

However, against these advantages, only a proportion of the amount in the pension fund at retirement can be taken in the form of cash, with the balance being taken by way of pension. Despite the attractions of a pension mortgage, the following matters should be considered before a decision is taken to use this method to repay a loan:

(a) it will not normally be possible to repay the mortgage or receive the pension and any surplus cash before age 50 (access to retirement annuity funds can be obtained through switching to personal pensions);

(b) by using the tax-free cash to repay the mortgage, the cash benefit available for retirement purposes is reduced (this is particularly important where maximum contributions are already being paid);

(c) if earnings are volatile, there may be a restriction in poor years on the level of contributions which can be paid;

(d) if the person concerned should cease to be self-employed or become a member of an occupational pension scheme, he would be ineligible to pay contributions into the existing contract and, consequently, would have to make alternative arrangements.

Pension mortgages are mainly suitable for those who are able to predict their future with a reasonable degree of certainty. These will largely be high-earning, self-employed professional people who are unlikely to work for an employer in the future, or directors and executives who are able to utilise their potential benefits under a company pension scheme or individual pension arrangement. In any event, before the pension method is decided upon, consideration should be given to the position which would arise if, at a future date, contributions cannot be maintained. It is also important to remember that legislation could be introduced to reduce the tax advantages of a pension mortgage, perhaps restricting or taxing the lump sum available when benefits are taken.

13:3.4 PEP and ISA mortgages

These mortgages are similar to pension mortgages, except that a PEP or ISA is used as the repayment medium. Although the plans (see **Chapter 4**) do not enjoy tax relief on subscriptions, the funds currently roll up tax free. In addition, all of the accumulated funds can be used to repay the loan. Surrender penalties do not apply on the cessation or reduction of a PEP or ISA investment and this may be attractive if the intention is to reduce the mortgage before the end of the term.

Separate term assurance will be required to cover the possibility of the borrower's death before repayment. Borrowers taking out ISAs should be prepared for volatility in the value of their investments; however, over a 25-year period this should not be of great concern. To an extent, volatility can be reduced by opting for an OEIC or unit or investment trust ISA.

The fact that the maximum annual subscription to an ISA is £7,000 per annum could cause problems for borrowers with large mortgages.

The following example illustrates various ways of repaying a mortgage

Example 13

A man aged 40 next birthday, paying tax at 40%, takes out a £50,000 mortgage repayable over 25 years. He is in good health and a non-smoker.

The gross interest rate charged under each type of mortgage is 5.75%

	Repayment mortgage	*Low-cost endowment mortgage*	*Pension mortgage*	*ISA mortgage*
	£	£	£	£
Monthly payments				
To lender	318	240	240	240
To insurance company:				
term assurance premiums	6		6*	8
endowment premiums		84		
pension premiums			164*	
To ISA provider				86
	£324	£324	£410	£334

**Net of tax relief at 40%*

Illustrative benefits at end of mortgage term				
Assumed growth rate	–	6%	7%	7%
Illustrative value of life policy/ pension fund/ISA	–	£50,000	£50,000	£50,000
Annual gross pension	–	–	£9,120	–

Notes

1. The illustrative values of the life policy, pension fund and ISA fund are based on the rules laid down by the Financial Services Authority (FSA) and assume that contributions, after allowing for a deduction for expenses and the cost of life cover (in the case of the life policy), will be invested to earn 6% per annum net of tax, 7% and 7% respectively. For the purpose of calculating the annual gross pension, immediate annuity rates are based on an interest rate of 6% per annum, 3% per annum escalation and a 50% spouse's benefit.

2. The term assurance premiums relate to a mortgage protection policy in respect of the repayment mortgage, a level term assurance effected under a personal pension policy in respect of the pension mortgage and level term assurance for the ISA mortgage. The pension policy would also repay the accumulated value of the fund in the event of death before retirement.

3. Comparisons between the different house purchase methods will vary with the age of the person concerned and the level of interest rates.

13:3.5 Flexible mortgages

A recent development in the mortgage market is flexible mortgages. These are available both on an 'interest only' basis (with the repayment medium left to the borrower's choice) and on a capital repayment basis. These flexible mortgages also permit 'payment holidays', lump sum repayment at any time and often carry a cheque book facility which permits borrowers to re-access funds repaid (up to the original amount borrowed).

Newer plans offer the facility to offset the balances on current or savings accounts with the lender against borrowings on a mortgage, personal loan or credit card account, for the purpose of calculating the interest payable.

13:4 Early repayment of a mortgage

From a financial viewpoint, it can be advantageous to repay a mortgage if a lump sum should become available to do so. However, it is sometimes possible to obtain a greater return by investing the lump sum than the net saving which could be achieved by repaying the mortgage. A further factor is that, once a borrower has made an early repayment, the capital so used cannot be applied for other purposes, with the result that liquidity and flexibility are lost. It should also be borne in mind that interest rates on most other forms of finance are higher than those on mortgages.

However, following the abolition of mortgage interest relief, early or partial repayment of a mortgage is generally worthwhile in the circumstances below.

(a) Where both spouses are fully utilising their personal allowances, with income generated from sources other than the cash sums being considered for the repayment.

(b) Where a building society mortgage is near the end of its term. In these circumstances, the effective rate of interest charged can be very high if it is based on the amount of capital outstanding at the beginning of a year with no account being taken of the capital subsequently repaid during that year.

Even if it is not financially expedient to repay a mortgage early, many people prefer to do so from an emotional viewpoint. If this is the situation, it should be remembered that an individual's personal requirements are generally of prime importance, even to the point where financial returns are not maximised.

If it is proposed to make a significant partial repayment, the lender should be asked the optimum date for this to take place. This is because interest is sometimes calculated only on periodic balances, and there could be some time before the repayment is taken into account for the calculation of future interest.

Before the final payment on a mortgage is made to a building society, whether by early repayment or otherwise, it should be remembered that it is often worthwhile to leave a nominal amount unpaid, for the following reasons:

(a) the building society will continue to store the title deeds free of charge;

(b) if a further advance is required, the individual may not incur further legal fees; and

(c) in the event that the society is taken over or converts to a public limited company, mortgage holders are likely to benefit from a cash bonus or an allotment of shares.

However, against these advantages, a higher rate of interest is often charged for further advances.

13:5 General principles in choosing a mortgage

The following general principles will often apply in choosing a particular type of mortgage.

(a) If the individual's main requirement is to keep the monthly outgoings to a minimum, a repayment mortgage is often most appropriate.

(b) A repayment mortgage is normally more flexible than the other types of mortgage. However, against this, if a person sells a property in the early years of a mortgage, only a small proportion of the capital will have been repaid. Many new mortgages are taken out with the same term as the previous repayment mortgage, which may mean that the final repayment is delayed beyond the date originally anticipated.

   In the case of endowment, pension and ISA mortgages, the investments can usually be continued if a new loan is subsequently arranged. Consequently, the mortgage will be repaid within the original term selected.

(c) If a person is in poor health, he may not be able to arrange an endowment mortgage since underwriting will generally be required.

(d) Endowment mortgages may not be available to older borrowers and, in the case of a pension mortgage, the amount of the loan may be restricted because of the limits on contributions.

(e) For a self-employed person or an employed person not in an occupational pension scheme, a pension mortgage is likely to produce the best results, although it requires the highest contributions.

(f) As ISAs are generally equity-based, they are prone to short-term volatility. If markets fall, their value will be reduced, which may mean that they are not adequate to repay the mortgage at the desired time.

13:6 Other mortgage considerations

The following are other matters which should be borne in mind.

(a) The type of property may restrict the choice of lender or method of repayment. This includes timber-framed houses and older or listed buildings.

(b) The Consumer Credit Act 1974 does not apply to any loan, regardless of size, if it is used to finance house purchase. However, the Act is applicable in all other cases of loans of £25,000 or less, except where the loan is required for property improvements or repairs and there is an existing mortgage which was originally taken out with the same lender to buy the property.

(c) All lenders are required to show the annual percentage rate (APR) of interest in all advertisements and personal quotations. This rate is calculated according to a statutory formula and is designed to show in a single figure all of the different elements of the cost of a mortgage. It is therefore important to compare APRs rather than the quoted interest rates when considering a mortgage, as this is likely to provide a more reliable indication of the total costs involved.

(d) It is often possible to arrange a remortgage. This can then be used to repay an existing mortgage and provide additional capital for home improvements or a further property purchase, perhaps at a lower interest rate. However, the amount used for purposes other than repaying the existing mortgage might be treated as a further advance and consequently may attract a higher rate of interest. Some building societies charge a higher rate of interest on the entire amount of the remortgage.

(e) If an individual has financial problems in meeting his mortgage repayments, it is generally advisable to inform the lender as soon as possible. Very often, a temporary arrangement can be made to assist the borrower over a difficult period.

13:7 Mortgage variations

The following are types of mortgage which have been recently developed and are generally variations of those previously mentioned.

(a) A fixed interest mortgage can be arranged where the rate of interest charged remains constant for the first few years of the mortgage term, regardless of movements in the general level of interest rates. This type of mortgage can be suitable where a borrower considers that interest rates are likely to rise on average over the term for which the rate of interest is fixed or requires certainty of the level of monthly payments.

(b) Low-start or deferred payment mortgages provide for deferment of part of the interest or capital payments in the early years, the payments rising either in steps or at the end of an agreed period. Unpaid interest is added to the debt so that the overall cost will be higher. Another form of low-start mortgage involves an endowment or low-cost endowment policy on which the premiums rise in steps over a five-year period. This type of scheme is now rare.

(c) LIBOR mortgages have their interest rate linked to the London Inter-Bank Offered Rate for three-month loans between the major banks. Due to the short-term nature of the rate, the interest on the mortgage is likely to fluctuate more than with a building society loan, although, in most cases, interest is only adjusted quarterly.

(d) Discounted mortgage rates are offered by a number of banks and building societies. The discount usually runs for between one and five years and is relative to the provider's normal variable rate. These rates are offered to attract new borrowers or remortgage business and can offer very competitive short-term rates.

With many discounted rate mortgages, there is a redemption period which may extend several years beyond the discounted period. This effectively ties the borrower into the provider's standard variable rate for a number of years because if the loan is repaid before the end of the redemption period, a penalty (often substantial) will be charged.

(e) Another method used by providers to attract new business is to offer a 'cash-back' lump sum to the borrower when the mortgage is first taken out. As with discounted rate mortgages, there will usually be a redemption period to prevent the borrower repaying the mortgage for a number of years without a substantial penalty.

(f) 'Caps' and 'Collars' limit the borrower's exposure to mortgage rate movements. With a cap, the mortgage rate cannot move higher than the capped level during the period to which the cap applies. With a collar, there is a limit below which the rate cannot fall, as well as an upper limit.

The lower limit is clearly of no direct benefit to the borrower but may enable the lender to provide a more attractive upper limit by sharing some of the benefit of a fall in rates with the borrower.

(g) Foreign currency mortgages are simply loans in a foreign currency such as Swiss francs or euros. Interest is payable at the rate applicable to that currency. Such loans are often superficially appealing where interest rates are lower than those in the UK. This may reflect the fact that the currency is regarded as stronger than sterling and the risk of exchange loss should not be overlooked. The exchange rate between the selected currency and the pound sterling will vary, so that the sterling value of the debt will increase if the pound weakens, and vice versa. The sterling value of the interest payments will also vary to the same extent.

In view of the possibility that adverse currency movements could dramatically increase the size of the mortgage, these loans are only for the most sophisticated investor. This type of mortgage could be of use to borrowers whose earnings are not in sterling, and who will be able to borrow in that currency to hedge their position against adverse fluctuations.

A further variation of this form of lending is the managed currency loan, which represents a basket of currencies. As a result, the risk from exchange rate fluctuations in a single currency is reduced.

It should be remembered that unit-linked, unit trust, ISA and foreign currency mortgages carry a greater risk that the capital accumulated at the end of the mortgage term may not be sufficient to repay the loan. However, if the underlying investments perform well, then either the overall cost will be less or the return at the end of the mortgage term will be greater than originally projected.

13:8 Raising income from the home

Various schemes are available to help older homeowners to raise capital or generate income through the mortgage or deferred sale of their property. The development of these schemes (generally known as 'equity release schemes') reflects the plight in which some elderly homeowners find themselves, having little by way of realisable assets and inadequate income. In many cases, their largest asset is their house, the real value of which can only be unlocked by the upheaval and cost of a move to less expensive property, with any balance of the sale proceeds being invested to generate income. These schemes enable elderly homeowners to continue to live in their homes, whilst realising at least a proportion of the value, which can be used to generate income.

Apart from raising capital or generating income, these schemes can often be advantageous in inheritance tax planning. This is because the mortgage or deferred sale causes a reduction in the estate.

Whether or not it is worthwhile to arrange one of these schemes can only be decided after all circumstances have been considered. These will include the health and age of the person or couple, whether there are any close relatives and whether other resources are available. In any event, before an arrangement is made, professional advice should be obtained on both the financial and legal consequences.

13:8.1 Home income plans

The basis of these schemes is for the homeowner to be granted a mortgage on their home and the loan used to purchase an annuity. This will provide a monthly income for the remainder of their life or, in the case of married couples, until the death of the survivor. At that time, the mortgage will be repaid either from the sale proceeds of the property or other sources. Consequently, the benefit of any capital appreciation on the home will be retained.

Before income payments are made to the homeowner, two deductions are normally made. These are interest payments on the mortgage and savings rate tax on the income element of the annuity. The operation of these schemes is considerably simplified when the MIRAS system applies, as the deduction for mortgage interest is made net of basic rate tax.

Only loans of up to £30,000 arranged under a home income plan set up before 9 March 1999 still qualify for income tax relief on the interest paid. The other conditions are that:

(a) the homeowner must have attained the age of 65 or, in the case of a joint scheme, both annuitants must have reached a combined age of 130;

(b) a minimum of 90% of the loan must have been applied to purchase an annuity, only the remaining 10% being retained by the borrower;

(c) the loan must be secured on property in the UK or Eire owned by one of the annuitants;

(d) the property on which the loan is secured must be the only or main residence at the time the interest is paid.

Income tax relief on the interest paid under home income plans is 23%. The income element of the annuity is normally paid after deduction of savings rate tax. However, it is possible for a non-taxpayer to arrange for the annuity payments to be paid gross without this deduction being made.

There are other considerations to be taken into account.

(a) The home must be a freehold or long leasehold, have no tenancies and be in reasonable condition.

(b) It is preferable for the property to be free of all mortgages. Consequently, any existing mortgages should be repaid before a home income plan is arranged.

(c) Like the annuity, the loan interest rate is normally fixed, with the result that the homeowner will usually know the amount of income which will be provided by the plan throughout their lifetime, subject to changes in tax rates and allowances.

(d) Apart from any contribution made by the company offering the home income plan, the homeowner is responsible for the legal and valuation costs involved in arranging the scheme.

The income produced by arranging a home income plan will mainly depend on the following factors:

(a) the amount of the annuity purchased;

(b) the age of the homeowner when the plan is taken out (the older the person or persons concerned, the greater will be the annuity);

(c) the tax position of the homeowner;

(d) whether the annuity is arranged on a single life or joint life basis;

(e) the level of interest rates at the time the plan is effected;

(f) whether the whole amount of the loan is used to purchase an annuity or whether a part is taken in cash;

(g) whether the annuity is taken out on a capital-protected basis in order to reduce the loss in the event of early death.

The following example shows the increase in net spendable income that can be obtained by arranging a home income plan.

Example 14

A woman aged 75 obtains a mortgage of £30,000 (50% on a house valued at £60,000) with an interest rate of 7.5%. She uses the money to buy a level annuity on a non-capital protected, non-guaranteed basis:

Income tax rate	*Nil %*	*22%*	*40%*
	£	£	£
Annual gross annuity	3,214	3,214	3,214
Less: savings rate tax on income element	–	172	172
Net annuity	3,214	3,042	3,042
Less: mortgage interest	(2,250)	(2,250)	(2,250)
Less: higher rate tax on income element of annuity	(–)	(–)	(172)
Increase in net spendable income	£964	£792	£620

The combination of lower annuity rates and the removal of tax relief for new plans has made this type of contract much less beneficial than in the past. A better return than that shown in the example may be obtained by agreeing to surrender a percentage of the future appreciation of the property's value in exchange for a lower interest rate on the loan. Some plans do not require regular payments of interest; instead the interest is rolled up and is recovered by the lender out of the proceeds of the sale of the property. The amount which can be borrowed under this arrangement is lower than for plans where interest is paid.

Before making a final decision to proceed with a home income plan, the following matters should be borne in mind.

(a) Where there are no capital resources other than the home itself, it will be necessary for the property to be sold on the death of the individual (or individuals, in the case of a joint life plan) in order for the outstanding loan to be repaid. Therefore, the home cannot be left to children or other dependants.

(b) Once the contract has been established, there is no scope for an individual to change his mind and encash the annuity.

(c) When the individual dies, the annuity ceases. Consequently, if death occurs immediately after effecting the contract, the beneficiaries are just left with an outstanding loan and no compensating benefit. As a result, a home income plan is not normally suitable for those in poor health. Despite this, if the homeowner is prepared to receive a lower net income, they can choose a capital-protected annuity so that, in the event of early death, some of its cost is repaid.

(d) The annuity payments can affect eligibility for means-tested benefits, such as housing benefit and income support (age allowance, however, is not reduced as the interest paid on the mortgage will exceed the taxable income received). Consequently, the advantage of increased income from a home income plan can partially be lost by a reduction in other benefits.

13:8.2 Home reversion schemes

An alternative method for a homeowner to raise capital from their home is to enter into a reversion scheme. Under these contracts, the property (or a proportion of it) is sold at a discounted value, depending on the age and sex of the person concerned, with the homeowner normally being allowed to live in the home at no cost for the remainder of his or her life. When the property is sold, the proceeds are shared between the company owning the reversion and the homeowner (or his estate) in their due proportions. Usually, it is required that the capital raised be invested in an annuity for life, either on a single or joint life basis. A major disadvantage of these schemes is that the homeowner loses the benefit of any future capital appreciation on the home.

A variation on the home reversion scheme is the instalment reversion, where the property is sold in stages over a ten-year period.

As with home income plans, the annuity payments can affect eligibility for means-tested benefits but, in addition, may affect age allowance.

13:9 Other factors

Some lenders offer roll-up plans to elderly homeowners, where loans are made without interest or capital repayments being needed. Interest is rolled up and added to the loan, with the final debt being satisfied by the sale of the property on the death of the occupant (or occupants). As interest is chargeable on both the capital and accrued interest, the debt can escalate rapidly, outpacing the increase in value of the house and leaving the borrower vulnerable. Consequently, these schemes should be regarded with great caution.

There is no question that home income plans properly used have a valuable role to play in financial planning for the elderly. Potential borrowers should restrict themselves to plans offered by SHIP (Safe Home Income Plans), an association of the leading companies in this market.

14 Providing for education fees

Next to purchasing a house, the cost of educating children privately and at university is likely to be a family's largest financial commitment. Fees at an independent boarding school can currently be as much as £18,000 per annum for one child, with further expenses for other activities. In many cases, provision for the costs of university education is a growing concern, and references to 'school fees' in this chapter apply equally to university costs.

There is no magic formula in providing for school fees. The most successful planning is a combination of early recognition and careful identification of the most practical and cost-effective method. Each case must be considered individually, with the purpose of making the necessary monies available on the required dates in order to pay the fees. School fees provision is therefore very much an investment problem, but with due regard being given to the taxation consequences of any plan and the commitment being undertaken.

Before a school fees scheme can be properly considered, the individual's asset and income position should be assessed, together with the overall situation.

14:1 Assessing the situation

Before embarking on private education, a proper evaluation should be undertaken to decide whether this is possible at all. A detailed schedule should be produced to show the estimated funds required to pay the school fees, together with the dates when they fall due, with allowance being made for extras and future increases (these usually exceed the rate of retail price inflation). After this schedule has been prepared, it will be necessary to consider the possible sources of funds from which the school fees can be paid. These sources may be broadly classified as:

(a) capital;

(b) income; and

(c) other (such as grandparents' gifts).

In practice, it will often be necessary to draw upon more than one source to provide the funds required.

If a decision is then taken to educate a child privately, the following matters should be considered before a school fees scheme is implemented:

(a) the choice of school;

(b) the possibility of the child not attending the chosen school or any other private school;

(c) whether the child will be a day pupil or a boarder;

(d) the possibility of the child changing to a different school mid-stream;

(e) the possible death or incapacity of the child;

(f) possible increases in costs due to inflation or government action;

(g) a deterioration in the parents' financial circumstances;

(h) the possible death of the parents;

(i) the availability of scholarships and bursaries;

(j) possible special needs if the child is gifted (academically or artistically) or handicapped; and

(k) eligibility for grants and allowances.

If it is intended that the child will attend university or other further education, provision should also be made for parental contributions to tuition fees and to augment student maintenance grants to cover living costs during term-time (the annual contribution payable would mainly depend on where the student lives and the income of the parents, unless the student is classed as independent). The student loan scheme is an additional source of finance, but leaves the student in debt at the conclusion of his or her course. Further education is likely to prove increasingly costly for the family from now on. Many students get no grant at all.

14:2 Funding from capital

Apart from paying school fees directly out of capital as and when they fall due, the following are the six principal methods by which capital can be applied for school fees purposes:

(a) investment portfolios;

(b) family trusts;

(c) school fees composition schemes;

(d) educational trusts;

(e) back-to-back arrangements; and

(f) loan arrangements (see **14:4**).

14:2.1 Investment portfolios

Establishing an investment portfolio, using unit and investment trusts, ISAs, government stocks, the zero dividend preference shares of investment trusts, National Savings products, investment bonds and/or building society accounts, is often the easiest, and certainly the most flexible, way of providing for school fees from capital. This approach has the following advantages:

(a) maximum advantage can be taken of all tax-efficient investment opportunities;

(b) the funds can be used for other purposes, if necessary, without penalty;

(c) the funds need only be realised when there is a shortfall in the income providing the fees.

A single premium investment bond may in some circumstances be an appropriate vehicle. For a higher rate taxpayer, the facility to withdraw 5% per annum of the initial premium, with no immediate charge to income tax, may be attractive. This fixed limit may, however, be exceeded in time by the amount of the fees, which are likely to increase each year. For larger withdrawals, a multi-segmented policy would enable an appropriate number of segments to be encashed each year. This would avoid the problems which can arise from partial withdrawals and a basic rate taxpayer would have no additional income tax liability, unless the gain on the bond took his total income for the year over the threshold for higher rate tax (see **3:13.1**).

14:2.2 Family trusts

If the student or one of his parents is a beneficiary of a family trust, it may be appropriate for the trustees to release capital or income to assist with the payment of the student's educational fees. The trustees should consider the tax and legal implications of such a distribution, particularly if the trust is located offshore.

If the family's finances permit, it may be particularly beneficial for grandparents to create an accumulation and maintenance settlement (see **Chapter 16**) with a view to providing for their grandchildren's educational costs. The transfer of assets into the trust is a potentially exempt transfer which will reduce the settlors' estates (although not completely for seven years) and bypass the parents' estates. When income is applied for a child's benefit, the child will, if his or her gross taxable income is less than the personal allowance, be able to reclaim some or all of the income tax paid by the trustees.

Grandparents may, alternatively, place assets in a bare trust for the student, perhaps administered by the parents. Again, the child may be able to reclaim income tax deducted at source; preferably investments should be made in assets which pay income gross.

14:2.3 School fees composition schemes

School fees composition schemes are essentially deferred annuity contracts, allowing a lump sum to be paid in advance at a discount to the total fees to be funded. The following are the main characteristics of school fees composition schemes.

(a) The terms which the school will offer largely depend on the length of time before the fees become due and interest rates prevailing when the lump sum is paid.

(b) As the school has the status of an educational charity, the scheme is particularly attractive to a higher rate taxpayer, since there would be no liability to either income or capital gains tax on the investment of the lump sum by the school. Furthermore, if the lump sum is paid by a parent or guardian and a trust is declared under section 11 of the Inheritance Tax Act 1984, this is exempt from inheritance tax. A section 11 trust enables parents and (in restricted circumstances) other donors to make dispositions for the education, maintenance or training of a child, without liability to inheritance tax.

    However, if the payment was made by a person not covered by the restrictions, a chargeable transfer arises, although this may be within their annual or other inheritance tax exemptions or the nil rate band (£250,000 for 2002/03).

(c) One of the main advantages of school fees composition schemes is that they are simple and convenient. Against this, a major disadvantage is that they are often inflexible. The following matters, which may be open to negotiation, should be investigated before a scheme is arranged to see what would happen if:

    (i) the child does not attend the school (normally, a repayment is made, but on unattractive terms);

    (ii) the child leaves the school or dies before completing his education;

    (iii) the tax advantages relating to educational charities are abolished.

(d) The competitiveness of a school fees composition scheme will depend, to a large extent, on the rates offered at the particular time. Consequently, a quotation specifying individual requirements should be obtained and the investment return in percentage terms compared with possible alternatives.

(e) It should be noted that a payment to a school fees composition scheme does not necessarily guarantee a place at the chosen school.

14:2.4 Educational trusts

Educational trusts were effectively independent versions of the fees composition schemes operated by schools. Their returns depended largely on their charitable status, but this was withdrawn for new plans in 1997.

14:2.5 Back-to-back arrangements

Capital may be applied to purchase a temporary annuity or other suitable funding medium which will provide the required premiums for appropriate life assurance policies. The maturity proceeds from the life policies can then be used to pay the school fees.

14:3 Funding from income

Unless the school fees are paid directly out of net income as they fall due, it will usually be necessary for the payments to be spread over a period longer than the period of education. It is therefore worthwhile, wherever practicable, for appropriate action to be taken at the earliest possible date, not only to prevent the payment period extending beyond the time the child leaves school or university, but also to minimise the cost involved.

Consideration should also be given to the position should the provider's main source of income cease. This could arise if he or she was to die early, become disabled or be made redundant. Adequate life assurance and permanent health insurance should always be in place to cover the first two eventualities.

The following are the principal methods of funding school fees out of income:

(a) life assurance schemes;

(b) unit trust, OEIC and investment trust regular savings plans; and

(c) a series of individual savings accounts.

14:3.1 Life assurance schemes

Although there are several different types of qualifying life assurance policies available, they all enable the proceeds to be received with no personal liability to income tax and capital gains tax provided that premiums are payable for a minimum period of ten years (or three-quarters of the term, if less, in the case of an endowment-type policy). Accordingly, where premiums are started in sufficient time for them to be paid for this period before the school fees commence, the policies outlined below would normally be most suitable.

(a) A series of with-profits endowment policies maturing in successive years over the period of the child's education at a senior school. This method has the advantage of generally providing a competitive and relatively secure return, particularly for higher rate taxpayers, with scope to receive increasing maturity proceeds each year in order to cover the higher education costs caused by inflation.

(b) Flexible endowment policies where the parent can choose the date when the policy proceeds are received. However, this flexibility does not come without cost and therefore these policies are in general less attractive than the more usual with-profits endowment policies.

(c) Unit-linked policies (such as maximum investment plans) offering a tax-free income facility after ten years. Where a policy is issued for school fees purposes, it is prudent to invest in a stable fund rather than in a volatile one.

(d) Friendly society policies (see **10:3**).

(e) Non-qualifying life policies, such as five-year endowments, can, for basic rate taxpayers, provide a shorter-term alternative to qualifying endowments.

If there are any existing life assurance policies, it is possible that these could also be used for school fees provision.

Using life policies as a method of providing for school fees offers a number of advantages.

(a) The regular premiums are spread over a long period.

(b) If circumstances change, the policy proceeds can be applied for other purposes without any penalty being suffered.

(c) The death benefits provided would normally be available to pay the school fees should the parents die prematurely.

(d) The policyholder can borrow against the policy once it has acquired a surrender value.

The recent trend towards weighting with-profits bonuses more in favour of longer term policies has made the returns on the 10–15-year policies suitable for school fees planning less attractive. The greater emphasis on terminal bonuses also means that the maturity values are less predictable than in the past.

14:3.2 Unit trust, OEIC and investment trust regular savings plans

These plans, which were considered in **3:20**, represent direct investments into unit trusts, OEICs and investment trusts on a regular (usually monthly) basis. They have many of the characteristics of unit-linked life policies investing in equities, although the taxation position is different. As no life cover is provided, consideration should be given to effecting a separate term assurance policy in order to safeguard the future provision of fees in the event of the early death of the parents.

Unit trust, OEIC and investment trust savings plans provide even greater flexibility than unit-linked life policies and may be terminated at any time without penalty. This is particularly important for parents whose disposable income fluctuates. Such plans are also likely, in many cases, to produce results superior to those of a life policy investing in the same fund (see **Chapter 10**). It is generally desirable for the savings plan to be linked to a broadly based fund rather than to a more volatile one to reduce the risk of the plan having a low value at the time the proceeds are required to pay the school fees. Index-tracking trusts may be particularly appropriate.

Capital gains tax may arise on the sale of the units or investment trust shares, although, if these are being sold gradually, they will usually fall within the annual capital gains tax exemption unless substantial funds are realised. If the holdings are in the names of both parents, then both their annual exemptions will be available.

14:3.3 A series of individual savings accounts

As stated in **4:2**, a UK resident aged 18 or over may invest up to £7,000 per tax year into an individual savings account. Like unit-linked life policies and unit trust, OEIC and investment trust regular savings plans, the choice of underlying investments should be conservative, to reduce the risk of the ISA having a low value at the time the school fees become due. A separate term assurance policy should be considered, as life cover is not provided by the ISA.

A series of ISAs is a very tax-efficient method of providing for school fees, since there is no tax to pay either on capital gains or on dividend income. Consequently, if an individual decides to arrange a unit trust, OEIC or investment trust regular savings plan, this is likely to be more advantageous within, rather than outside, an ISA. However, as previously mentioned, any account should be regarded as a medium- to long-term investment.

14:4 Funding from loan arrangements

There are several methods by which borrowings can be made to pay for school fees, but the interest on the loan is not allowed as an expense for tax purposes. This course may be the only one available where earlier planning was not possible, but the cost of the interest can increase the overall cost considerably.

The following ways of raising funds may be particularly suitable in appropriate circumstances:

(a) a parent who owns their own business may be able to increase their drawings and then arrange a loan to replenish working capital, so tax relief is then obtained indirectly on the amounts withdrawn to meet the school fees;

(b) if the parent cannot afford the cost of both personal pension contributions and school fees, it may be worthwhile to pay the contributions and then arrange a loan under the pension policy, so tax relief would effectively be allowed on the premiums against the parent's highest income tax rates, even though relief would not be obtained on the loan interest paid;

(c) if the parent lives in a house with no mortgage or only a relatively small mortgage, it may be possible to obtain a larger mortgage, either by moving house, or remortgaging, or under an 'equity release' scheme offered by some banks. Again, no tax relief would be given on the interest paid and provision would have to be made to repay the loan at some future date;

(d) where there is insufficient time for premiums to be paid to a life assurance policy for the minimum qualifying period before the school fees fall due, it may be worthwhile to obtain loans from the insurance company against the surrender value of the policy in order to pay the school fees. The loans are then repaid out of the policy proceeds at maturity. It is therefore important at outset to obtain a positive commitment from the insurance company that loans will be available together with the relevant terms and conditions. The rate of interest on policy loans is often lower than a bank would charge.

14:5 Funding for university costs

With the phasing out of maintenance grants and the introduction of parental contributions to tuition fees, the need to provide for the costs of a student's three or four years at university affects a growing number of parents. The costs will vary considerably, but an annual budget could be around £6,500. This can partly be financed by a student loan, which carries a low rate of interest and is repayable only when the student starts earning a reasonable income.

Where parents are funding a minor child's education, the planning should take into account the fact that, if the child's income from parental gifts exceeds £100 a year, that income is aggregated with the parents'. This does not apply once the child reaches 18, however, so that the capital from parental gifts can be invested to produce an income after that age which will be taxable on the child and, in all probability, covered by his or her personal allowance. (Many students these days do, however, have part-time jobs, and the amount of their earnings must be taken into account.)

One investment where the tax treatment is beneficial for this situation is the offshore roll-up fund (see **2:3.4**). If investments are made for the benefit of the child during his minority, no income tax is payable on the accumulated income. Gains ('offshore income gains') realised on encashments after the child reaches 18 will be subject to income tax but can be arranged so as to be covered by the child's personal allowance and thus be tax free. It should be noted, however, that the taxation treatment of offshore roll-up funds may change following the Inland Revenue's review during 2002.

The child will also have the use of his own annual exemption for capital gains tax to cover gains realised from capital growth investments.

14:6 Conclusion

For many parents, considerable sacrifices will have to be made in order to send their children to private schools. These sacrifices, however, can often be mitigated by making the best use of the facilities that exist in the circumstances. In particular, it should be remembered that:

(a) while the best results are generally achieved by early action, taken as soon as possible after the child is born, even a late contribution is usually worthwhile;

(b) a well designed scheme will have a considerable amount of in-built flexibility – this is of the utmost importance in view of the uncertainties that may lie ahead.

15 Wills

15:1 Intestacy

Although many people delay making a will, the consequences of this can be very serious. If a person dies without having made a will, their estate will be distributed according to the laws of intestacy (see **Appendix 5**), subject to any post-death variation. The main disadvantages of dying intestate are listed below.

(a) The estate may not necessarily be distributed in accordance with the individual's wishes. In particular, the surviving spouse is likely to be disadvantaged; if there are children the widow(er)'s entitlement is limited.

(b) The appointed administrators may not be those whom the individual would have chosen.

(c) It may take longer for the estate to be distributed. When a will has been made, an executor can take up his duties immediately after death occurs.

(d) The costs may be greater.

(e) There may be an unnecessary inheritance tax liability.

(f) Children will receive capital automatically at the age of 18; it may be the individual's wish that capital should be paid at a later age. Furthermore, assets such as the family home may have to be sold in order to raise the capital.

(g) A testamentary guardian is not appointed for young children.

(h) Trusts may arise under an intestacy which can produce complications, including statutory restrictions on the trustees' power to invest and advance capital. These restraints might be particularly onerous where the estate wishes to hold shares in private companies.

15:2 The need for professional advice

In order to avoid the danger of having a will which is uncertain as to the intentions of the testator, or having a will which proves to be invalid, it is essential that its wording should be clear and precise and that the wording and execution of the will should conform with various formalities. Consequently, it is generally advisable that the will should be drawn up by a solicitor and that other professional advice be obtained where appropriate, for example, to minimise inheritance tax. In this way, the following common mistakes should be avoided:

(a) failure to dispose of all the estate, resulting in partial intestacy;

(b) specific gifts that are free of tax could dissolve the residuary estate unintentionally;

(c) uncertainty as to where the burden of tax should lie where the residuary estate is left to a tax-exempt beneficiary (such as a UK spouse) and a non-exempt beneficiary (such as a child) in equal shares;

(d) gifts being made to witnesses or their spouses (as a general rule, these are legally ineffective and therefore the person concerned would not be able to receive his or her legacy);

(e) alterations being made to the will at or before the time it is signed without being sufficiently authenticated and therefore having uncertain validity;

(f) no consideration being given to the possibility of a beneficiary dying before the testator or not surviving long enough to enjoy any real benefit;

(g) failure to consider the effects of the testator's divorce and/or remarriage;

(h) being unaware of the rights of certain family members and dependants to make a claim against the estate if reasonable financial provision has not been made for them;

(i) failure to appreciate that the word 'children' includes legitimate, illegitimate and adopted children but not normally stepchildren.

15:3 Important matters before drawing up a will

The following are some important matters which should be attended to before a will is drawn up.

(a) Consideration should be given to the disposal of the body on death, including bequests for scientific research.

(b) Agreement should be obtained from the persons to act as executors and trustees.

(c) If there are young children, consideration should be given to the appointment of a guardian (and his or her consent obtained) to cover the event of the testator's early death. This is particularly important if only one parent is still alive.

(d) An estimate must be made of the value of the estate by calculating the market value of assets and deducting any liabilities. A list of these assets would also be desirable. (**Appendix 6** is a detailed 'dying tidily' log which should be completed and filed with the individual's private papers.)

(e) A list of the persons (including charities) to benefit under the will should be compiled, showing any particular assets to be passed to specific beneficiaries.

(f) Trust provisions, including the powers given to the trustees, should be specified.

(g) Consideration should be given as to whom the assets should pass if a beneficiary dies before the testator.

(h) Where a testator owns property overseas, in general it is preferable that this should be dealt with by a will drawn up under the terms of the local law. Care is required that it should not inadvertently be revoked when making a new UK will (and vice versa) and that the provisions are consistent.

15:4 Executors

The responsibility of an executor is to collect in the estate of the deceased and deal with the distribution of the estate according to law. This can involve arranging the funeral and generally taking over the deceased's affairs, including being responsible for the payment of all debts and taxes due in respect of the estate. In order to preserve the estate, the executor should consider taking immediate possession of any valuables in order to secure their safety and should arrange insurance where appropriate. Although an executor's responsibility commences from the time the deceased dies, it will still be necessary for the will to be proved and the appointment confirmed by a grant of probate.

The choice of an executor, who may also be a beneficiary, is very important as a considerable amount of work and responsibility may be involved. The following matters should be borne in mind before an appointment is made.

(a) It is often advantageous for co-executors to act, such as the spouse (or if not alive, a friend or relative), together with a person in professional practice, such as an accountant or solicitor.

(b) The ideal number of executors is two or three. Probate will not be granted to more than four, but this number (or more) is likely to be unwieldy in practice.

(c) An executor should preferably be younger than the testator, although a minor cannot obtain probate.

(d) It is often worthwhile to include a substitute executor, in the event of the appointed executor dying before the testator or being unwilling or unable to act.

(e) If the will includes a trust, it will usually be expedient for the trustees to be the same as the executors. A testator should endeavour to ensure that the executors know his or her wishes and can be relied upon to carry them out. It is common for him to leave a letter of wishes with his will to guide them in the exercise of their judgement.

(f) The will can be written so that the final decision over the distribution of some or all of the estate is postponed until after death. The executors can then make a decision as to how to distribute that property based on all the circumstances. This can be achieved by including what are known as discretionary trust provisions in the will. This will only be suitable if a testator is confident of the executors' judgement.

15:5 Variations and disclaimers

At the present time, a beneficiary can tax-efficiently redirect certain property to another person within two years of the deceased's death. This is effected by means of a written variation, referring to the relevant statutory provisions for inheritance tax and capital gains tax. It used to be necessary to make a separate election to the Inspector of Taxes for capital gains tax purposes and the Capital Taxes Office for inheritance tax purposes within six months of the date of the variation. But for deeds of variation made on or after 1 August 2002, separate elections are not necessary if the deed of variation states the tax provisions which are intended to apply. A beneficiary can also, within the same two-year period, disclaim an inheritance which has not previously been accepted.

Variation of a will can be particularly appropriate where a deceased may for instance have gifted the entire estate to his widow without having made use of the inheritance tax nil rate band, or where the beneficiary does not wish to receive the inheritance. A variation is also possible under an intestacy.

While similar in many respects to a variation, a disclaimer has several important differences, which are set out below.

(a) Under a disclaimer, the beneficiary can merely disclaim or waive their entitlement without making any election to the Inspector of Taxes or Capital Taxes Office.

(b) The terms of the will or intestacy should be examined in order to discover who benefits in lieu, whereas, in the case of a variation, the assets can pass as agreed; for example, a widow who has benefited under her husband's will can effectively rewrite it to benefit the children.

(c) A disclaimer will normally relate to the whole gift, whereas a variation can be made either in respect of the whole or only part of it.

(d) In the case of a disclaimer, the beneficiary must not have received any previous benefit from the gift, such as receipt of income.

Variations and disclaimers can be very helpful in both capital gains tax and inheritance tax planning, mainly due to changing circumstances, especially tax, and the testator not always being aware of the wishes of the various beneficiaries. However, their use would arise less often if wills were properly prepared at the outset. They should also not be regarded as a substitute for proper estate planning. Infants cannot consent to a variation; if the will has made gifts to infants, a variation may not be possible or its effect may be limited.

One further point is that a variation must genuinely vary the inheritance made under the will. For example, if on a father's death his entire estate passes to the children who, by variation, re-route their inheritance to their mother, the mother could subsequently make a potentially exempt transfer of the property back to her children. In such a case, the Inspector of Taxes and/or Capital Taxes Office will enquire as to whether the variation was genuine or artificial.

15:6 Other matters

The following are other matters relating to wills which should be borne in mind.

(a) The will should be kept in a safe place, such as in a bank or with a solicitor or accountant, and the executors advised of its location.

(b) Marriage (or remarriage) will automatically revoke a will unless it states that it was made in expectation of that particular marriage.

(c) Divorce (decree absolute) or annulment of marriage (unless the will states otherwise) automatically disinherits the spouse from receiving any defined interest under the will and prevents the spouse from acting as an executor or trustee of the will. The will takes effect as if the spouse died on the divorce or annulment.

(d) The will should be reviewed at regular intervals (say, not less than every five years) in order to take into account changes in the testator's circumstances and in tax legislation.

(e) If a person wishes to alter their will, this is usually possible by way of a codicil. However, in almost all cases it is preferable for a new will to be made which reflects the required changes.

Note

This chapter has been written based on the law in England and Wales. It must be remembered that the position may be different in Scotland and Northern Ireland.

16 Trusts

Trusts, in various forms, have been in existence for centuries. However, their concept is strange to many people and their uses, particularly following recent changes in tax legislation, are not widely appreciated. The principal purpose of this chapter is to discuss some of the terms of English trust law, the differences between the various types of trust, and the uses to which the more common forms of trust can be put.

16:1 What is a trust?

A trust is a separate legal entity, usually set up with a formal document or under a will. Trusts are often referred to as 'settlements' and for all practical purposes the two words are interchangeable. There are five main constituents of a trust:

(a) *the settlor* – the person who sets up the trust, usually by passing assets to the trustees;

(b) *the trustees* – the people (usually two, three or four in number) in whose name the assets are registered and who control them in accordance with the terms of the trust deed;

(c) *the trust deed* – the legal document which instructs the trustees how to administer and distribute the trust fund (unless the trust is established by will);

(d) *the trust fund* – the assets of the trust, including the original property given to the trustees, and assets transferred to the trustees subsequently, the capital growth on the assets, and any income retained by the trustees on behalf of the beneficiaries;

(e) *the beneficiaries* – the people, whether specifically named or not (but who must be identifiable with reasonable certainty), who can benefit from the trust fund under the terms of the trust document.

Thus, although the trustees have legal ownership of the trust assets, they have no personal interest in them, unless they are also beneficiaries of the trust. Trusts are used in a wide variety of situations, including charities, employees' pension schemes, life assurance policies and the maintenance of historic buildings. However, this chapter is limited to the use of trusts for the financial benefit of an individual's family, relatives and friends.

16:1.1 The settlor

The settlor often wishes to dispose of capital for the benefit of members of his or her family, but for practical reasons, may not wish to give them outright control of the capital. For instance:

(a) the settlor might not wish to lose effective control of the capital;

(b) the beneficiaries may be children or young adults;

(c) the settlor may not know specifically whom he or she wants to benefit;

(d) the beneficiaries may not have the experience, time or ability to look after the capital;

(e) the settlor may wish to protect the capital in the event of a bad marriage, a death or a bankruptcy.

The settlor can himself be a beneficiary of a trust, but there are no tax benefits in this case. Indeed, there can be tax disadvantages, particularly in connection with the reservation of benefit rule.

16:1.2 The trustees

Although the trustees have to administer and distribute the trust fund in accordance with the terms of the trust deed, in modern trusts they are usually given very wide discretionary powers. It is therefore important that trustees are chosen carefully. Settlors cannot directly impose their wishes on the trustees, but, in practice, they can strongly influence them by:

(a) making themselves a trustee (normally the first-named);

(b) writing a 'letter of wishes' to the trustees at the time of setting up the trust;

(c) reserving the power to appoint new trustees and remove existing trustees.

Although trustees have to act unanimously (unless otherwise specified in the trust deed), where votes on a company's shares are concerned, these are exercisable only by the first-named trustee.

The role of a trustee can sometimes be onerous, particularly in the cases of larger complex trusts or where trustees might have to make difficult choices in dealing with beneficiaries who are close members of the family. For this reason, the appointment of an independent professional trustee can often be advantageous. It is also important to explain the responsibilities involved to a lay trustee before they accept appointment.

16:1.3 The trust deed

Trusts can be set up either during the settlor's lifetime or under the terms of a will on death. Trusts set up in lifetime are often referred to as 'settlements', those under a will as 'trusts', but these are not set in stone.

It is not essential to have a written trust deed. However, without this, the trustees are limited in the way they can act, and doubts can arise in later years as to what the settlor intended. For maximum flexibility, it is advisable to have a modern form of trust deed drafted by a solicitor who has a good working knowledge of trusts.

Trust deeds tend to be lengthy and are often difficult to understand. Much of the text is of a technical nature and deals with the various powers given to the trustees. As a guide, the legal costs involved in setting up a trust range from £750 to £2,000, depending on complexity and the variations required from standard precedents.

Depending on the type of trust (see below), a good modern trust deed will generally give the trustees wide discretionary powers, including:

(a) the power to determine the extent to which a beneficiary will benefit from the trust, if at all;

(b) the power to determine the age at which a beneficiary will benefit;

(c) the power to invest the trust fund in any form of investment, whether or not producing income, including the purchase of a house for a beneficiary;

(d) the power to set up subsidiary trusts for beneficiaries;

(e) the power to borrow and lend.

Some (particularly older) trusts do not contain all the powers that trustees ideally need and want to run a flexible trust. The Trustee Act 2000, which came into force on 1 February 2001, cures this to a certain extent. It confers a number of new powers on trustees, and it applies to trusts established both before and after its enforcement date. The new statutory powers include wide investment powers and powers of delegation and insurance. However, the Act also imposes some new duties on trustees. For example, in exercising their investment powers (whether pursuant to the Act or not), trustees must obtain and consider proper advice about the way their investment powers should be exercised. Furthermore, trustees are required to adhere to a new statutory duty of care whenever exercising any of the powers conferred by the Act. Notwithstanding the Act, it remains very useful for a trust deed to contain the whole range of powers that the trustees might need during the life of the trust.

Unless the trustees act fraudulently, they are usually protected from any personal financial liability.

16:1.4 The trust fund

A trust is often set up with a nominal amount of, say, £100 and further capital is usually gifted subsequently. The trust fund consists of two elements.

- *Capital* – the original and subsequent gifts, plus any growth in the value of the assets.
- *Income* – arising on the capital assets. Except in the case of interest in possession trusts (see below), if income is not distributed to beneficiaries, it is accumulated in the fund, usually by way of a transfer to capital.

As mentioned above, the trustees are usually given extremely wide powers to invest in any form of asset. These can include land, life assurance policies, shares (including shares in family companies), paintings and overseas assets. In some cases, there may be restrictions on the particular type of asset in which an investment can be made.

16:1.5 The beneficiaries

Other than in specific types of trust, such as those set up under the Married Women's Property Act 1882, there is no restriction on who can be a beneficiary of a trust. The person does not need to be specifically named in the trust document, but does need to be in a specified class of beneficiary, such as grandchildren. However, in some cases, it is possible to add a beneficiary where he was not originally included. Many trust documents provide for substitution so that, in the event of a beneficiary dying, his children acquire his interest in the trust fund.

Depending on the type of trust, trustees are often given the maximum flexibility in deciding to what extent, if at all, a beneficiary should benefit from the trust fund, in terms of both annual income and capital.

Where appropriate, children can benefit from trusts from the day they are born, often with significant income and capital gains tax advantages.

16:2 Tax position of trusts

16:2.1 Setting up a trust

Changes in tax legislation have made it extremely cheap, in terms of tax, to set up a trust. If:

(a) unquoted shares in a trading company are transferred to a trust; or

(b) any assets are transferred to a discretionary trust,

no capital gains tax is chargeable on the disposal by the settlor and the trustees are deemed to acquire the assets at the original cost to the settlor. Stamp duty on gifts has been abolished (apart from a nominal £5 in some cases). The present inheritance tax legislation is comparatively liberal and the exemptions reasonable. In larger cases, where tax liabilities do arise, they are likely to be substantially less than they would ultimately be if no action was taken.

Provided gifts are not deferred until too late in life (at least seven years before death), a husband and wife can dispose of substantial amounts of capital, even more so where business or agricultural assets are concerned, without paying large amounts of inheritance tax. By the use of trusts, they can often at the same time keep effective control over the assets.

16:2.2 The trust

(a) *Inheritance tax.* The extent to which there is a liability to inheritance tax on creation or during the life of a trust depends upon the particular type of trust (see **16:3**).

(b) *Income tax.* Generally, when a trust has been created, income which arises from the assets put into trust is treated for all purposes as the income of the trustees. This is completely separate and independent of their own personal tax affairs and those of the settlor. The main exceptions to this rule are where the settlor has included himself or his spouse as a beneficiary, or where income is distributed to the settlor's children while they are under 18 and unmarried. In such cases, the income is treated as that of the settlor for tax purposes.

    The tax liability on the income of the trust again depends upon the type of trust. Where a beneficiary has a right to income, the trust will pay tax at the Schedule F rate (10% in 2000/01) on dividends, at the savings rate (20% in 2002/03) on savings income and at the basic rate (22% in 2002/03) on certain other types of income such as property or trading income. If a beneficiary is liable to tax at the higher rate (40% in 2002/03), he will be responsible personally for the extra tax on the trust income.

    If the beneficiary has no right to income, but the amount he receives is determined at the discretion of the trustees, the trust income (other than dividends) is subject to tax at the trust rate (34% for 2002/03) in the trustees' hands. Dividends are taxed in the trustees' hands at the

Schedule F trust rate (25% for 2002/03). When income is distributed to beneficiaries at the trustees' discretion, it carries a tax credit of 34% which, depending on the tax position of the beneficiary, may be recoverable, either in whole or part, or further tax may be payable if the beneficiary is liable to the higher rate of tax. However, because the 10% dividend tax credit suffered by the trustees is not repayable, it is not available to frank the 34% tax credit carried by the income distributions. The effect of this is to reduce the maximum possible distribution of dividend income to beneficiaries.

(c) *Capital gains tax*. Trustees are liable to capital gains tax at 34% on realised gains (less losses), subject to indexation allowance and taper relief and an annual exemption (£3,850 in 2002/03, which in appropriate circumstances may have to be divided between all the settlements made by the same settlor). However, as with the income tax rules, gains made by trustees will be charged to tax upon settlors who retain or give their spouse any interest in the trust. As mentioned earlier in this chapter, it may be possible for a gain arising on the transfer of specific assets into a trust to be deferred. Similarly, it may be possible for a gain arising on specific assets leaving a trust, which are also subject to a tax charge, to be deferred.

16:3 Types of trusts

There are six main types of trust which are described below:

(a) interest in possession trusts;

(b) voluntary trusts;

(c) accumulation and maintenance trusts;

(d) discretionary trusts;

(e) bare trusts;

(f) charitable trusts.

16:3.1 Interest in possession trusts (also known as life interest or fixed interest trusts)

16:3.1.1 General description

In broad terms, an 'interest in possession' is defined as a right to receive the income arising from the trust assets. Thus, an interest in possession trust exists where the income arising on the trust capital is payable to a named beneficiary, the life tenant, usually for his or her lifetime. The beneficiary may also have the use of the property within the trust if, for example, a house was settled upon trust giving the beneficiary the right to occupy it for life. The capital remains under the trustees' control and, on the death of the life tenant (or early termination of their interest), the capital can pass to other beneficiaries (the remaindermen) as specified in the trust document (or, if the trust document permits, to those nominated by the life tenant).

The trustees are often given a discretionary power to advance capital to the life tenant.

16:3.1.2 Uses

Interest in possession trusts are most suited where beneficiaries are over the age of 25 and a settlor does not wish to pass outright ownership of assets to them, but wishes the beneficiaries to enjoy the income generated by the assets. Such trusts are particularly useful where:

(a) shares in family companies are involved, since any voting rights remain with the trustees;

(b) the settlor considers the beneficiary might not want the responsibility or be able to look after the capital;

(c) the settlor wishes to protect the capital in the event of, say, a bad marriage or the premature death of a son or daughter;

(d) the settlor wishes to remove an asset from his or her estate and yet does not wish the beneficiary to be entitled to the capital until the settlor's death;

(e) the settlor wishes to create an inheritance tax-free fund payable on death, which can be used by the beneficiaries to pay the inheritance tax due or to replace the inheritance tax paid from the estate.

16:3.1.3 Tax position

(a) *Inheritance tax.* Transfers by an individual into an interest in possession trust qualify as a potentially exempt transfer (PET) and do not attract a charge to inheritance tax, provided that the settlor survives seven years from the time of the transfer. Similarly, on most transfers from interest in possession trusts (such as the life tenant surrendering their interest in favour of another individual), no charge arises if the transferor survives seven years.

On the death of a life tenant, a charge to inheritance tax arises, as the life tenant is deemed to own the underlying trust assets on which they have been receiving income. On such occasion, tax is chargeable at the full rate.

(b) *Income tax*. The trustees pay income tax at the basic rate, either direct to the Inland Revenue (for example, on rental income), or by deduction at source (for example, on interest from government stocks). As with individuals, most savings income is taxed at the 20% savings rate. Dividends are taxed at the 10% Schedule F ordinary rate. After deducting expenses (which are set off in the first instance against the income with the lowest tax credits), the trust income is added to the beneficiary's other income and, if liable to the higher rate of tax, the beneficiary pays the extra tax. If the beneficiary does not have sufficient income to cover his or her personal tax allowance, a tax repayment can be obtained.

(c) *Capital gains tax*. Capital gains are taxed at 34%, after the deduction of the appropriate annual exemption (see **16:2.2(c)**). If a beneficiary becomes absolutely entitled to trust assets, this is a disposal at market value by the trustees, giving rise to a capital gains tax charge. This can, however, be held over if the assets are unquoted shares in a trading company.

16:3.2 Voluntary trusts

16:3.2.1 General description

This is any trust made without consideration, including a trust which an individual makes for his or her own benefit by transferring assets to trustees, who then pay the income to the settlor during his or her lifetime, with the capital remaining in trust, normally for the settlor's children.

16:3.2.2 Uses

Voluntary trusts are used when the individual wishes to protect himself from wasting his own capital or where he does not want the responsibility of managing it. Voluntary trusts can be particularly useful if the settlor is non-resident for a period.

16:3.2.3 Tax position

There are no tax advantages during the lifetime of such trusts. Although no inheritance tax liability arises on the transfer of funds to the trustees, or from the trustees to the settlor, capital gains tax could be payable on such transfers depending on the asset transferred. The settlor is assessed to tax on the trust income and gains as if they continued to own the trust assets. In addition, the settled property remains part of the settlor's estate for inheritance tax purposes.

16:3.3 Accumulation and maintenance trusts

16:3.3.1 General description

Accumulation and maintenance trusts are normally established for the maintenance, education and benefit of children under the age of 25, including those not yet born. While the children are under that age, the trustees may be able to accumulate income (i.e. add it to trust capital) or it can be used to pay the children's living expenses (such payments would normally be made to a beneficiary's parents or guardian while the children are minors). Capital may also be advanced to a beneficiary at the discretion of the trustees. Trustees can be given complete discretion over the allocation of both capital and income between beneficiaries while they are under the age of 25. Thereafter, trustees can retain control of the capital, paying only income to a beneficiary, but reserving the right to advance capital to him or her at any time.

For a trust to qualify as an accumulation and maintenance settlement for tax purposes, the following conditions must be satisfied:

(a) one or more of the beneficiaries must become entitled to an interest in the capital or income of the trust before reaching a specified age not more than 25;

(b) there is no interest in possession (i.e. a right to be paid the income) and income must be accumulated if it is not applied for the maintenance, education or advancement of the beneficiaries; and

(c) not more than 25 years have elapsed since the trust was set up or all the beneficiaries are or were:

   (i) grandchildren of a common grandparent; or

   (ii) children, widows or widowers of such grandchildren who have succeeded to a deceased beneficiary's entitlement.

16:3.3.2 Uses

These trusts are mainly of use to a parent or grandparent who wishes to benefit their issue under the age of 25, both during minority and in later years. They are also very beneficial in tax planning, for example, where a grandparent wishes to provide funds to meet school fees, or where a parent wants to give children shares in the family company, but does not know at the time which children will take an active interest in the company. Accumulation and maintenance trusts provide flexibility, without the inheritance tax charge normally associated with discretionary trusts.

16:3.3.3 Tax position

(a) *Inheritance tax.* A gift by an individual into an accumulation and maintenance trust is treated in the same way as an outright gift to another individual and qualifies as a potentially exempt transfer (no inheritance tax is chargeable on the gift if the settlor survives for seven years). These trusts are also not liable to tax when a beneficiary becomes entitled to capital or income and are not subject to a ten-year charge as in the case of discretionary trusts (see below).

(b) *Income tax.* Income (other than dividends) is subject to tax at the trust rate (34% for 2002/03) in the trustees' hands. Dividends are taxed in the trustees' hands at the Schedule F trust rate (25% for 2002/03). When income is distributed to beneficiaries at the trustees' discretion, it carries a tax credit of 34% which, depending on the tax position of the beneficiary, may be recoverable, either in whole or part, or further tax may be payable if the beneficiary is liable to the higher rate of tax. However, because the 10% dividend tax credit suffered by the trustees is not repayable, it is not available to frank the 34% tax credit carried by the income distributions. The effect of this is to reduce the maximum possible distribution of dividend income to beneficiaries.

Where income is distributed to the settlor's children while they are under the age of 18 and unmarried, the income is treated as that of the settlor for tax purposes. Where a beneficiary is specifically entitled to income, for example, where they are over the age of 25, the income tax treatment is the same as for an interest in possession trust (see above).

(c) *Capital gains tax.* The rate of capital gains tax for this type of trust is 34% after deduction of the appropriate annual exemption (see **16:2.2(c)**). A gain arising on the transfer of any asset out of an accumulation and maintenance settlement to a beneficiary can be held over, the beneficiary effectively taking over the trustees' base cost.

16:3.4 Discretionary trusts

16:3.4.1 General description

A discretionary trust is one set up for a number of designated beneficiaries or classes of beneficiaries, in which distributions of capital and income during the trust period are entirely at the discretion of the trustees. The trustees have no obligation to distribute income to all beneficiaries and, subject to certain restrictions, any income not distributed can be retained in the trust fund.

16:3.4.2 Uses

Discretionary trusts are very flexible and can be used in a number of different situations, including the following:

(a) where a settlor wishes to give away capital to his or her family but does not know at the time whom they want to benefit;

(b) where the settlor wishes one class of beneficiary to receive income, but another class to receive capital;

(c) where one spouse wishes to pass capital to the next generation, but wants the surviving spouse to have the opportunity of receiving income and/or capital if required.

16:3.4.3 Tax position

(a) *Inheritance tax.* Although discretionary trusts are the most flexible type of trust, they are the least favourable for inheritance tax purposes. The creation of a discretionary trust attracts a charge to inheritance tax if the value of the assets gifted, together with the value of any other gifts by the settlor that were not PETs made within the seven preceding years, exceeds the amount of the nil rate band (£250,000 for 2002/03). This charge is at one-half of the normal rate, so it is 20% in 2002/03. A further charge, generally at very low rates of tax, may be made on capital distributions from such trusts or on each tenth anniversary of their existence. The latter (generally known as the 'periodic charge') is subject to a maximum of 6% of the capital value of the trust. This should be compared, however, to the rate of 40% which would apply to assets held at death, either personally or in an interest in possession trust.

(b) *Income tax.* Income (other than dividends) is subject to tax at the trust rate (34% for 2002/03) in the trustees' hands. Dividends are taxed in the trustees' hands at the Schedule F trust rate (25% for 2002/03). When income is distributed to beneficiaries at the trustees' discretion, it carries a tax credit of 34% which, depending on the tax position of the beneficiary, may be recoverable, either in whole or part, or further tax may be payable if the beneficiary is liable to the higher rate of tax. However, because the 10% dividend tax credit suffered by the trustees is not repayable, it is not available to frank the 34% tax credit carried by the income distributions. The effect of this is to reduce the maximum possible distribution of dividend income to beneficiaries.

(c) *Capital gains tax.* On the creation of a discretionary trust, the settlor and the trustees may elect that the capital gains on the assets transferred are 'held over', so that they pass to the trustees. The trustees, therefore, take the assets at their base cost when acquired by the settlor. The rate of capital gains tax on gains realised by discretionary trusts is 34% after the appropriate annual exemption (see **16:2.2(c)**).

Any capital gain which would normally arise on the distribution of assets to a beneficiary can be held over.

16:3.5 Bare trusts

16:3.5.1 General description

Assets transferred to a bare trust are held by trustees for a named beneficiary who has an absolute and unconditional title to both the capital and the income. In effect, the transfer is an outright gift with the trustees holding assets in name only; the beneficiary can insist at any time that the assets are transferred to him or her.

16:3.5.2 Uses

Generally, a bare trust is used when an individual wishes to make a gift to a minor, an overseas beneficiary or an elderly beneficiary who has difficulty in managing his own affairs.

16:3.5.3 Tax position

(a) *Inheritance tax*. Assets held on bare trusts are deemed for inheritance tax purposes to belong to the beneficiary and offer no additional tax advantages over outright gifts.

(b) *Income tax*. The income on the assets is assessed on the beneficiary and taxed at his or her appropriate rate of tax. Where, however, a parent transfers assets into a bare trust for their own children, who are under the age of 18 and unmarried, the income is treated as the parent's if it exceeds £100 in a tax year.

(c) *Capital gains tax*. Gains of trustees will be assessed on the beneficiary and taxed at his or her appropriate rate of tax.

16:3.6 Charitable trusts

16:3.6.1 General description

Wealthy investors may wish to establish a trust whose assets and income are applied solely for charitable purposes. The settlor will probably be one of the trustees and will thus be able to recommend support for causes which he particularly favours. As well as satisfying the requirements for the tax benefits of a charitable trust, the trust deed must be approved by the Charity Commission, to which annual reports must be submitted. The trustees need to be aware of, and to receive professional advice on, the current legislation governing charities and the conduct and reporting of their activities.

16:3.6.2 Uses

Charitable trusts are normally set up where the settlor has capital assets surplus to his anticipated requirements which he wishes to devote to charitable purposes. By doing so, he benefits from a number of tax reliefs and retains flexibility over the selection of beneficiaries.

16:3.6.3 Tax position

(a) *Inheritance tax.* Transfers of assets to and out of a charitable trust are exempt from inheritance tax.

(b) *Income tax.* The income of a charitable trust is normally exempt from income tax.

(c) *Capital gains tax.* Where assets are transferred to a charitable trust, the disposal is exempt from capital gains tax. (If the assets transferred are quoted securities or land, the settlor can also claim the value of the assets as a deduction for income tax purposes.) Gains realised by the trust are also exempt.

16:4 Non-resident trusts

Prior to the Finance Act 1991, a popular way of holding investments was via a non-resident trust. A trust created since 19 March 1991, or an existing trust which has received additional capital since that date, is subject to a special tax regime, where the settlor is domiciled in the UK and either resident or ordinarily resident in the UK. Briefly, if the settlor, or his wife, or his children (including adult children), can benefit from the trust, all income (see below) and capital gains are taxed on the settlor. There is, therefore, no income tax or capital gains tax advantage. For all other trusts, mainly those created before 19 March 1991, therc were, until the 1998 Finance Act, still capital gains tax and income tax advantages. Those advantages have now largely been removed.

16:4.1 Tax position

(a) *Inheritance tax*. For a trust made by a UK-domiciled settlor, the inheritance tax treatment is the same as for a resident trust. For a settlor who establishes a settlement whilst he is not either domiciled or deemed domiciled for inheritance tax purposes, non-UK situs assets held within the trust will not form part of his UK estate for inheritance tax purposes, nor that of any beneficiary of the trust.

(b) *Income tax*. If the settlor or their spouse cannot benefit from the trust, foreign income can be accumulated free of UK income tax by the trust. However, UK-resident beneficiaries will be taxable on any income distributed to them, or on the value of any benefits provided out of trust assets. UK resident beneficiaries who are non-domiciled will be taxable only on income remitted to the UK.

(c) *Capital gains tax*. For capital gains tax purposes, a trust will be non-resident if the trustees, or a majority of them, are not resident in the UK and the administration of the trust is carried out abroad. The effect of such non-residence is that the trustees are not liable to capital gains tax and trust gains are only taxed if they are paid to a UK resident and domiciled beneficiary, or benefits are provided to the beneficiary out of trust assets. For example, if non-resident trustees make capital gains of £8,000 and a beneficiary receives a capital payment of £12,000, that beneficiary would be liable to capital gains tax on £8,000. Therefore, if the trustees reinvest such gains, whether in UK or overseas assets, it is possible to defer capital gains tax indefinitely (it is also possible entirely to avoid capital gains tax if the beneficiary whom it is desired to benefit ceases to be resident *and* ordinarily resident in the UK (to the satisfaction of the Inland Revenue) and then receives such payments of capital out of the trust). However, the rate of tax payable by a beneficiary depends on the number of years that have elapsed since the gain was made and can be as high as 64%.

The 1998 Finance Act introduced a number of further restrictions on the use of non-resident trusts for the purposes of capital gains tax planning:

(i) gains of pre-19 March 1991 settlements made by a UK domiciled settlor from which the settlor, his spouse and his children can benefit will be taxed on the settlor as they arise for tax years 1999/2000 onwards, unless the only beneficiaries are children of the settlor aged under 18 at the start of a tax year;

(ii) gains of trusts set up by a UK domiciled settlor on or after 17 March 1998 from which the settlor's grandchildren can also benefit will be taxed on the settlor. Existing trusts which receive additional capital after 17 March 1998 will also fall within the charge.

(iii) prior to 17 March 1998, UK-resident and domiciled beneficiaries were only taxable on capital payments received from a settlement with a UK-resident and domiciled settlor. For capital gains arising and capital payments received on or after 17 March 1998, the status of the settlor will be irrelevant.

It is seldom advisable to set up a non-resident trust, unless substantial tax savings can be achieved, as its administration must be in a tax haven in order to avoid local tax. Management expenses can also be very high.

16:5 Trusts and life assurance policies

Life assurance policies are frequently subjected to trusts in order to provide a fund outside the estate of the settlor to pay inheritance tax on death. Usually, the settlor will pay all premiums. If the premiums are large, to ensure they are PETs where they are paid to an accumulation and maintenance trust or interest in possession trust, the cash should be gifted to the trustees who should pay the premiums. Where the assured is the settlor, a fund can be built up outside their estate with no tax payable on death. At that time, the fund can be used by the beneficiaries to pay inheritance tax, allowing the assets of the estate to be distributed intact.

Where the trust is in the form of an interest in possession trust, it will often provide that any proceeds can be advanced to the beneficiaries absolutely to enable the tax to be paid. If the trust is in the form of an accumulation and maintenance trust, the power to advance capital, before or after the beneficiaries attain the age of 25, will generally provide sufficient flexibility to enable any policy proceeds to be used to fund the payment of inheritance tax. However, the trustees of neither trust can compel the beneficiaries to use the monies to pay inheritance tax, nor can the trustees pay it on behalf of such beneficiaries.

The 1998 Finance Act introduced measures to ensure that where the settlor is either dead or not UK-resident at the time of encashment, the gains arising can be taxed on either any UK-resident trustees or UK-resident beneficiaries. This applies to chargeable events on or after 6 April 1998.

16:6 Modern day use of trusts

Modern trusts are normally very flexible and are used for a wide variety of purposes. A large proportion of the country's wealth is held upon trust, for example, pension funds. Family trusts have played an important part in personal financial planning for a considerable time and, with today's complex tax legislation, they are now even more useful.

Family trusts are used for many purposes in tax planning, but their principal purpose is not in tax mitigation, but the retention of wealth within the family and the management of capital and income for beneficiaries. However, significant tax advantages are usually available. There is generally a trust suitable for most situations but, before creating a trust, it is essential to seek professional advice from an adviser who is experienced in current trust law and taxation.

Appendix 1

Useful addresses

The Financial Services Authority
Financial Services Authority
25 The North Colonnade
Canary Wharf
London E14 5HS
Tel: 020 7676 1000
Website: www.fsa.gov.uk
Consumer helpline:
(including queries about the Central Register) 0845 606 1234

The FSA co-operates with the following:

- HM Treasury – Responsible for legislation and the general framework of regulation
- The Bank of England – Working together to maintain financial stability
- The Department of Trade and Industry – Responsible for company and insolvency law
- The Department for Work and Pensions – Responsible for pensions policy and regulating occupational pension schemes
- The Occupational Pensions Regulatory Authority – Responsible for regulating the operation of occupational schemes in the UK
- The Office of Fair Trading – Responsible for consumer credit, consumer protection and competition issues
- The Serious Fraud Office – Responsible for investigating and prosecuting serious fraud
- The National Criminal Intelligence Service – Responsible for leading the fight against serious and organised crime

The Financial Ombudsman Service
The Financial Services Ombudsman
South Quay Plaza
183 Marsh Wall
London E14 9SR
Tel: 0845 080 1800
Website: www.financial-ombudsman.org.uk

The Financial Ombudsman Service provides consumers with a free, independent service for resolving disputes with financial firms. It can help with complaints about most topics, including investment, banking, life and general insurance and mortgages. The Ombudsman will, however, only become involved if the complaint has first been put to the financial firm concerned, and his service offers advice on how to do this. If the firm does not resolve the complaint, application should then to made to the Ombudsman.

The Financial Services Compensation Scheme
7th Floor
Lloyds Chambers
1 Portsoken Street
London E1 8BN
Tel: 020 7892 7300
Website: www.fscs.org.uk

The purpose of The Financial Services Compensation Scheme is to compensate investors if an authorised firm is unable to pay claims against it, usually because it is insolvent or has gone out of business. The Scheme is funded by the financial services industry and covers investments, deposits and insurance. It replaced (with effect from 1 December 2001) eight previous compensation and protection schemes covering these areas. For claims lodged before 1 December 2001, the rules of those schemes will apply, although the cases will be handled by the Scheme.

Trade bodies

The Association of British Insurers
51 Gresham Street
London EC2V 7HQ
Tel: 020 7600 3333
Website: www.abi.org.uk

The Association of Investment Trust Companies
Durrant House
8–13 Chiswell Street
London EC1Y 4YY
Tel: 020 7282 5555
Website: www.aitc.co.uk

The Association of Policy Market Makers
The Holywell Centre
1 Phipp Street
London EC2A 4PS
Tel: 020 7739 3949
Website: www.apmm.org

The Association of Private Client Investment Managers and Stockbrokers
112 Middlesex Street
London E1 7HY
Tel: 020 7247 7080
Website: www.apcims.co.uk

The Investment Management Association
65 Kingsway
London WC2B 6TD
Tel: 020 7831 0898
Website: www.investmentuk.org

The IMA was formed in February 2002 by the merger of the Association of Unit Trusts and Investment Funds (AUTIF) and the Fund Managers Association.

Financial advisers' bodies

The Association of Independent Financial Advisers
Austin Friars House
2-6 Austin Friars
London EC2N 2HD
Tel: 020 7628 1287
Website: www.aifa.net

The Institute of Financial Planning
Whitefriars Centre
Lewins Mead
Bristol BS1 2NT
Tel: 0117 945 2470
Website: www.financialplanning.org.uk

The Life Insurance Association
LIA House
Chorleywood
Rickmansworth
Herts WD3 5PF
Tel: 01923 285 333
Website: www.lia.co.uk
OR www.find-an-adviser.co.uk

The Society of Financial Advisers
20 Aldermanbury
London EC2V 7HY
Tel: 020 8989 8464
Website: www.sofa.org

Designated professional bodies

The Association of Chartered Certified Accountants
29 Lincoln's Inn Fields
London WC2A 3EE
Tel: 020 7242 6855
Website: www.acca.org.uk

Institute of Actuaries
Staple Inn Hall
High Holborn
London WC1V 7QJ
Tel: 020 7632 2100
Website: www.actuaries.org.uk

Institute of Chartered Accountants in England and Wales
PO Box 433
Chartered Accountants' Hall
Moorgate Place
London EC2P 2BJ
Tel: 020 7920 8100
Website: www.icaew.co.uk

Institute of Chartered Accountants in Ireland
11 Donegall Square South
Belfast BT1 5JE
Tel: 02890 321 600
Website: www.icai.ie

Institute of Chartered Accountants of Scotland
CA House
21 Haymarket Yards
Edinburgh EH12 5BH
Tel: 0131 347 0100
Website: www.icas.org.uk

The Law Society of England and Wales
The Law Society's Hall
113 Chancery Lane
London WC2A 1PL
Tel: 020 7242 1222
Website: www.lawsociety.org.uk

The Law Society of Northern Ireland
Law Society House
98 Victoria Street
Belfast BT1 3JT
Tel: 02890 231 614
Website: www.lawsoc-ni.org

The Law Society of Scotland
The Law Society's Hall
26 Drumsheugh Gardens
Edinburgh EH3 7YR
Tel: 0131 226 7411
Website: www.lawscot.org.uk

Collective funds rating services

The following websites provide performance and other statistics, analysis and comment on unit trusts, OEICs and other collective funds. They may assist investors in selecting suitable funds for their portfolios.

- Standard & Poor's: www.funds-sp.com – Fund research ratings (AAA, AA and A) based on quantitative and qualitative research.
- Lipper Leaders: www.lipperleaders.com – Ratings based on: (a) consistent return (stability and strength of past performance) and (b) preservation (a fund's ability not to lose money).
- Morningstar: www.morningstar.co.uk – Analysis of performance charges, style, risk and market sector (small, medium or large companies).
- FT Fund Ratings: www.ft.com/fundratings – Ratings based on charges (total expense ratios), risk profile and past performance.
- Forsyth – OBSR Fund Ratings: www. forsyth-obsr.com – For professional intermediaries only.

Appendix 2

Personal financial planning questionnaire

1. Personal and family details

Self

Name	Title Surname	
	Forenames	
Address	Home	Correspondence (*if different*)
	Postcode	Postcode
Date and place of birth		
Telephone numbers	Home	Business
	Mobile	E-mail
Fax numbers	Home	Business
Business details	Occupation	Employer
Marital Status		

Partner

Name	Title Surname	
	Forenames	
Date and place of birth		
Business details	Occupation	Employer

1. Personal and family details (*continued*)

Children and other dependants

Full name	Relationship	Date of birth	Financially dependent on you? Yes/No

2. Residence and domicile

	Self	Partner
Country of residence (*for tax purposes*)		
Country of domicile (*country you regard as your permanent home*)		
Nationality		
Nationality of children (*if different from parents*)		

3. Income details

Please attach a copy of your most recent tax return(s) or give details below of your and your partner's income.

Earned income	**Self**	**Partner**
Basic salary	£	£ ....
Bonuses	£	£ ....
Taxable benefits (*for example company car or private medical insurance*)	£	£ ....
Pensions – state	£	£ ....
– other	£	£ ....
Investment income		
Dividends etc	£	£ ....
Bank/building society interest	£	£ ....
Trust income	£	£ ....
Income from other sources (*please specify below*)		
	£	£ ....
	£	£ ....
	£	£ ....

Please give details below of any substantial changes in your or your spouse's income in the foreseeable future.

4. Value of assets

Please give below the approximate values of assets held by you, your partner and your dependants. Where appropriate please include copies of valuations of investments.

	Self	Partner
Principal residence (*If jointly held specify whether joint tenants or tenants in common*)	£	£ ....
Other properties	£	£ ....
Agricultural land	£	£ ....
House contents and valuables	£	£ ....
Quoted stocks and shares	£	£ ....
Share options	£	£ ....
Lloyd's funds	£	£ ....
Insurance bonds	£	£ ....
Unit trusts	£	£ ....
BES, EIS, VCT and Enterprise Zone property	£	£ ....
Personal Equity Plans, ISAs and TESSAs	£	£ ....
National Savings	£	£ ....
Other savings plans	£	£ ....
Building society deposits	£	£ ....
Bank accounts: Current	£	£ ....
Deposit	£	£ ....
Other assets – please specify (*see note below*)		
	£	£ ....
	£	£ ....
	£	£ ....

Dependants' assets

Name	Type of asset	Value

Note: Business interests, pensions and life assurance are covered in sections 5, 8 and 9.

5. Business interests

Please give below details of you and your partner's business interests. If you do not have any please ignore this section.

Nature of the business

Are you a: sole trader? yes ☐ no ☐

partner? yes ☐ no ☐

director? yes ☐ no ☐

shareholder? yes ☐ no ☐

If sole trader or partner please give estimated value of your share of the business £

Do you own shares in a private company? yes ☐ no ☐

Name of company

Number of shares held and percentage of the total shares issued %

Annual turnover and accounting year end

Please give details below of the principal directors, shareholders, partners or other key people in the business.

Name	Position	% Shareholding

What provision has been made for the death of controlling shareholder(s) or partner(s)?

If you hold any other directorships, please state the name of the company and the size of your shareholding.

6. Liabilities

Regular commitments

	Self	Partner
Expenses	£	£
Savings	£	£

Please give details of your current liabilities, for example mortgages, overdrafts, loans, hire purchase and other debts.

Date incurred	Lender	Purpose	Original term	Amount outstanding	Interest rate	Final repayment date

Outstanding taxes

Date payable	Amount	Type of tax	Self/partner

Please give details of any substantial capital expenditure you or your partner expect to incur in the foreseeable future.

7. Educational fees

Please complete this section if you wish to provide or are already providing fees for your children's or grandchildren's schooling or further education costs.

Child's name	Start date	Educational establishment	Current termly fees (if known)	Number of years fees required

8. Pension arrangements

If you do not have sufficient information available to complete the specific details about your pensions, please provide any relevant records such as a scheme members' handbook or pension policy documents.

	Self	Partner
Your anticipated retirement age	☐	☐
Are you currently contributing to a company pension scheme?	yes ☐ no ☐	yes ☐ no ☐
Have you made any other pension arrangements?	yes ☐ no ☐	yes ☐ no ☐

Company pension scheme – current

Please complete the following section only if you or your spouse are currently contributing to a company pension scheme or if you belong to a non-contributory scheme.

	Self	Partner
Date started	☐	☐
Your gross annual contribution (amount or percentage of your salary)	☐	☐
Additional voluntary contributions	☐	☐
Does your employer contribute to the scheme?	yes ☐ no ☐	yes ☐ no ☐
Is the scheme contracted out of SERPS?	yes ☐ no ☐	yes ☐ no ☐
Retirement age under the scheme	☐	☐
Basis on which pension is earned (*for example, 1/60th, 1/80th or other*)	☐	☐
What life cover is provided on death before retirement? (*please show this as a multiple of your salary, for example 3 x salary*)	☐	☐
In whose favour have you nominated this lump sum?	☐	☐
Dependant's pension on your death (as a fraction of your pension)		
– before retirement	☐	☐
– after retirement	☐	☐

8. Pension arrangements (*continued*)

Pension benefits from previous employments

	Self		Partner	
Are you entitled to pension benefits from previous employments?	yes ☐	no ☐	yes ☐	no ☐

If yes, please give details

Name of company	Years of employment	Amount of pension	Transfer value

Other pension arrangements

Please give details of any other pension arrangements made by yourself or your partner.

Self

Name of company	Policy number	Type of policy	Contributions	Start date	If written in trust, beneficiary's name

Partner

Name of company	Policy number	Type of policy	Contributions	Start date	If written in trust, beneficiary's name

	Self		Partner	
Is the scheme contracted out of SERPS?	yes ☐	no ☐	yes ☐	no ☐

9. Insurance

Please give details of any insurance policies in which you and your partner have an interest.

Life assurance and endowment policies

Life assured*	Type of policy	Company	Policy number	Sum assured	Premium	Date started	Maturity date

*Please mark with an asterisk if the policy has been written in trust for someone else, and give details below.

Other insurance

Do you or your partner have permanent health, critical illness or private medical insurance? If yes, please give details below.

Self/partner	Company	Premium	Benefits

10. Wills and gifts

Wills

Please attach a copy of your will or, if this is not convenient, give brief details of your will. If you have not made a will, briefly describe your wishes for the distribution of your estate in the event of death, including any specific bequests you intend to make.

Self

Date made

Details of the will

Executors

Partner

Date made

Details of the will

Executors

Gifts

Please give details of any substantial gifts including transfers into trust made by you or your partner within the last seven years.

Self/partner	Date	Description of asset	Value	Donee

10. Wills and gifts (*continued*)

Trusts

Also list the names of the trusts of which you are a trustee. If you or your partner are entitled to benefit from a trust please give details.

11. General

Please give any other relevant information, such as early retirement or possible relocation.

	Self		Partner	
National insurance number				
Tax district and reference				
Are you a smoker?	yes ☐	no ☐	yes ☐	no ☐
Are you in good health?	yes ☐	no ☐	yes ☐	no ☐

12. Financial objectives

Please indicate below which of the following financial objectives are most important to you. Please state your priority on a scale of 1 to 5 (1 least important and 5 most important).

Objectives	Priority	Objectives	Priority
Creating or increasing capital	☐	Inheritance tax planning	☐
Increasing net income	☐	Provision for children's or grandchildren's education	☐
Planning for retirement	☐	Financial security for your family	☐
Reducing income tax	☐	Overall financial planning review	☐

Please give details below of any other specific financial objectives you wish to achieve.

Investment risk profile

The answers to the following questions will help us to decide what type of investment to recommend to you. They will be regarded as a general guide rather than absolute criteria.

Please indicate below your attitude to investment.

	You	Partner		You	Partner		You	Partner
Conservative	☐	☐	Balanced	☐	☐	Speculative	☐	☐

(The degree of risk you can accept will vary with different investments and in different circumstances. We will discuss this with you each time we advise on a particular investment).

Please tick the appropriate box to indicate your main investment objective.

	You	Partner
Maximum capital growth	☐	☐
A reasonable balance between growth and income	☐	☐
High income subject to protection of capital value	☐	☐
Maximum income, accepting possible erosion of capital	☐	☐

Other (please specify)

Please state any restrictions you wish to impose on particular areas of investment.

13. Your advisers

Accountant	Name
	Address
	Telephone no. Fax no.
Stockbroker/ Investment manager	Name
	Address
	Telephone no. Fax no.
Solicitor	Name
	Address
	Telephone no. Fax no.

Signatures

Yourself		**Date**	
Partner		**Date**	

Thank you very much for completing this client information form.

Appendix 3

Minimum retirement ages for certain occupations

Retirement ages have been agreed by the Inland Revenue for self-employed persons or persons not in an occupational pension scheme in respect of the following professions and occupations

Profession or occupation	*Retirement age*
Athletes	35
Badminton players	35
Boxers	35
Cricketers	40
Cyclists	35
Dancers	35
Divers (saturation, deep sea and free swimming)	40
Footballers	35
Golfers	40
Ice hockey players	35
Jockeys – flat racing	45
– national hunt	35
Members of the reserve forces	45
Models	35
Motorcycle riders (motocross or road racing)	40
Motor racing drivers	40
Rugby League and Union players	35
Skiers (downhill)	30
Snooker and billiards players	40
Speedway riders	40
Squash players	35
Table tennis players	35
Tennis players (including real tennis)	35
Trapeze artistes	40
Wrestlers	35

Note

The concession to take pension benefits at an early retirement age may be withdrawn if the individual changes occupation but continues to contribute to the same policy. Therefore, when a change of occupation arises before benefits are taken, it may be worthwhile for the old policy to be made paid-up and a new policy effected for subsequent contributions.

Appendix 4

Definition of relevant earnings for personal pension purposes

The following income counts as relevant earnings:

- profits chargeable under Schedule D immediately derived from a trade, profession or vocation;
- salary, wages, bonus, overtime and commission;
- benefits in kind which are chargeable to tax under Schedule E (applies to employees earning over £8,500 per annum, and to directors);
- profit related pay (including the part which is not taxable);
- Statutory Sick Pay (SSP) and Statutory Maternity Pay (SMP) provided it is paid by the employer and chargeable under Schedule E;
- Permanent Health Insurance (PHI) payments paid by the employer whilst the individual is still in employment;
- furnished holiday lettings chargeable under Schedule A;
- salary paid by way of government securities;
- Enterprise Allowance payments chargeable under section 127 ICTA 1988;
- post-cessation receipts which qualify as earned income under section 107 ICTA 1988;
- remuneration paid in the form of units in an authorised unit trust provided it is treated, on receipt, as a taxable emolument of the individual;
- income from woodlands provided it is treated for tax purposes as immediately derived from the carrying on of a trade;
- patent rights treated as earned income under section 529 ICTA 1988;
- sub-postmaster's retirement gratuities;
- payments made to local councillors which are chargeable under Schedule E;
- amounts deducted from salary to purchase partnership shares in a share incentive plan provided they qualify as such under paragraph 83 of Schedule 8 of Finance Act 2000;

- employer contributions to a funded unapproved retirement benefit scheme (FURBS) which are assessable on the employee, provided the FURBS is the only scheme of the employer of which the employee is a member.

The following income does not count as relevant earnings:

- income from an employment which is pensioned under an occupational pension scheme (section 645 ICTA 1988);
- redundancy and termination payments chargeable to tax under section 148 ICTA 1988 (golden handshakes);
- income arising from the acquisition or disposal of shares or an interest in shares or from a right to acquire shares;
- emoluments received by an individual as a controlling director of an investment company;
- earnings falling within section 644(6A) ICTA 1988 (controlling directors who, in certain circumstances, are in receipt of benefits from an occupational pension scheme or a personal pension scheme funded by a transfer payment from an occupational pension scheme);
- pensions (a pension is not remuneration from an office or employment);
- all benefits paid by the State, including Invalid Care Allowance, Working Families Tax Credit and Disabled Person's Tax Credit;
- grants paid by local authorities to foster parents;
- Statutory Sick Pay and Statutory Maternity Pay paid by the DWP;
- except for directors, benefits in kind where earnings from the employment are less than £8,500 per annum (such benefits are not taxable);
- Permanent Health Insurance (PHI) paid directly to the individual by the insurance company after the employment has ceased;
- partnership retirement annuities;
- client's account interest assessed under Schedule D Case III;
- earnings from international organisations which are exempt from UK tax by reason of a statutory instrument, including the United Nations, World Health Organisation and certain other international organisations;

- 'foreign emoluments' chargeable under section 192 ICTA 1988 where the individual is a member of a 'corresponding' overseas pension scheme;
- employer contributions to a funded unapproved retirement benefit scheme (FURBS) where the employee is also a member of an approved occupational pension scheme.

Appendix 5

Distribution of an estate under an intestacy

A summary of the position in respect of the distribution of an estate under the laws of intestacy in England and Wales is shown below. Since 1 January 1996, a spouse must survive for 28 days to become entitled under these rules. It should be noted that the position in England and Wales differs in some respects from that in Northern Ireland and considerably from that in Scotland.

England and Wales

If deceased dies leaving	*Persons who benefit*
1. Spouse, but no issue, parent, brother or sister, nephew or niece	1. Spouse takes everything absolutely.
2. Spouse and issue	2. (a) Spouse takes £125,000 absolutely, plus personal chattels (car, furniture, pictures, clothing, jewellery, etc.), plus life interest (income only) in half of residue. (b) Issue take half residue on reaching age 18 or marrying before that age, plus, on death of spouse, the half residue in which the spouse had a life interest.
3. Spouse, no issue, but parent(s) or brother(s) or sister(s) of the whole blood or their issue	3. (a) Spouse takes £200,000 absolutely, plus personal chattels, plus half residue absolutely. (b) Parents, but, if none, then brothers and sisters (nephews and nieces step into their parents' shoes if the latter are dead) take half residue.

If deceased dies leaving	*Persons who benefit*
4. No spouse	4. Everything is taken by:
	(a) Issue on reaching 18 or marrying under that age; but if none
	(b) Parents; but if none
	(c) Brothers and sisters of the whole blood (nephews and nieces step into their parents' shoes); but if none
	(d) Half brothers and sisters (or failing them, their own respective issue); but if none
	(e) Grandparents; but if none
	(f) Uncles and aunts of the whole blood (cousins step into their parents' shoes); but if none
	(g) Half uncles and aunts (or failing them, their own respective issue); but if none
	(h) The Crown.

Notes

(a) 'Issue' is defined as children (including illegitimate and adopted children), grandchildren and so on. However, it does not include stepchildren.

(b) Where part of the residuary estate includes a dwelling-house in which the surviving spouse resided at the date of death, the spouse has the right to have the dwelling-house as part of the absolute interest or towards the capital value of the life interest under **2(a)** and **3(a)** above.

Appendix 6

Dying tidily log

This log should be completed and filed with your private papers. Your next of kin should be informed of its contents and location. This should assist considerably with the administration of your estate when the need arises.

Information about estate and assets of:

Name	
Address	
Date of birth	
National Health number	
National Insurance number	

1. Will

Date	
Location	
Executors – names, addresses, telephone numbers	

Funeral wishes (burial, cremation, name of cemetery and plot number)

2. Professional advisers, etc.

(state name, address and telephone number) Doctor	

Dentist	
Solicitor	
Accountant	
Bank	
Stockbroker	
Insurance broker	
HM Inspector of Taxes District Reference number	
Others	

3. Assets

Main residence

Address	

Ownership (sole, joint, tenants in common)	
Subject to or free from mortgage	
Mortgagee or lender Address Reference number	

Other properties

Address	
Ownership (sole, joint, tenants in common)	
Subject to or free from mortgage	
Mortgagee or lender Address Reference number	

Business or share of partnership	

Investments (please state if held jointly)

(a) Bank accounts and building society accounts	
Name and address of bank/building society	
Type of account	
Account number	
(b) National Savings	
(c) Guaranteed income bonds/ guaranteed growth bonds	
(d) Fixed interest securities	
(e) Ordinary stocks and shares (equities)	
(f) Unit trusts	
(g) Investment bonds	

(h) Private companies	
(state approximate % holdings, including related holdings)	
(i) Other investments	
(j) Assets held in trust	

4. Liabilities

Bank overdraft arrangements	
Loans	
Other liabilities	

5. Gifts

Details, values and dates of all material gifts made within the last seven years.	

6. Pension and life assurance policies

Name of company	Policy number	Type of policy	On whose life	Sum assured	Name of beneficiaries (if applicable)	Names of trustees (if the policy is written subject to a trust)

7. Location of valuables

(a) Property deeds	
(b) Stock and share certificates, unit trust certificates, National Savings Certificates, building society passbooks, etc.	
(c) Pension and life assurance policies	
(d) Contracts (hire purchase agreements, loan agreements, general insurance policies, etc.)	
(e) Safe deposit box (if any)	
(f) Safe deposit key (if any)	
(g) Personal papers (birth certificates, marriage certificate, partnership agreement, etc.)	
(h) Passports	
(i) Bank statements	
(j) Others (please specify)	

8. Notifications required

(in addition to those mentioned in earlier section)

(a) Employer (name, address and telephone number)	
(b) Membership of occupational pension schemes (including former employers)	
(c) Department of Social Security	
(d) Deeds of covenant ceasing on death	
(e) Standing orders and direct debits	
(f) Credit cards/charge cards (name and number)	
(g) Trusteeships, executorships and guardianships held	

(h) Memberships of associations (name, address, membership number, etc.)

Professional/trade associations

Clubs

Other organisations (AA, RAC, etc.)

(i) Honorary offices held

(j) Contracts (with whom held, renewal date, where kept)

Hire purchase or loan

General insurance	
House	
Contents	
Car	
Other insurances	
Other contracts	
(k) Licences	
Road fund licence (registration number and date of expiry)	
MOT certificate (registration number and date of expiry)	
Driving licence (serial number)	
TV licence (date of expiry)	

Other licences	
(l) Others	

9. Other information

Relevant information not already stated in this log.	

INDEX

This index is in alphabetical, word by word order. Location references refer to chapter number (bold type), followed by a colon and the relevant section number. For example:

Accident insurance.........**11**:4.2

indicates that information on accident insurance can be found in Chapter **11**, section 4.2.

A

C

H

I

T

Born in Britain, Clive Brasnett began a career overseas when he took up a post as a lecturer at the University of Libya in Beghazi in 1961. Subsequently he worked in Syria in the years leading up to the Six Day War, joined the British Council and represented that organisation in India, Malaysia, Kenya and in Lebanon during the Lebanese Civil War. The tales in this collection, all of them true, tell of his encounters with people in those countries over a period of thirty years. Some of those who play a part in these tales are internationally-known figures, others ordinary people mixed up in extraordinary situations. All of them are vividly recalled.

First published in 2009
by Peris Press
34 Beaconsfield Road
London W5 5JE
www.perispress.co.uk

Printed by
Mitchell & Wright Printers Limited
Banastre Road, Birkdale,
Southport, Merseyside PR8 5AL
www.mitchellwright.co.uk

Cover photograph by Adrian Brasnett: Caves at Ellora

Contents

Introduction

The stories that follow took place over a period of forty years leading up to the end of the twentieth century and describe events in Asian and African countries. I call them *stories* rather than *memoirs* because I wanted to tell about the people, mainly Asians or Africans, who took part in them and to talk about myself only in so far as I played a part in their activities. They were all interesting, in many cases remarkable people, though in only a few cases will their names be widely known outside their own countries. Ideally I would like to have remained simply a recorder, like the camera in Isherwood's *Goodbye to Berlin*, but I constantly found myself writing down my reactions, what I thought about what was happening and about the people who were making these things happen.

These thoughts, I now find, were frequently expressed in terms of incertitude - "I wondered why ..., I was at a loss to know whether ..., I couldn't understand what ...". In some cases I was happily able to arrive at some understanding of seemingly inexplicable matters; in others the mystery remained in my mind unresolved. Why was I so often at a loss? I know that one reason is that I found myself operating in situations that were quite different from those I had grown up in, by necessity, and by my own choice, spending most of my working life overseas. If I had spent all those years in one country I might perhaps have been able to claim that I had arrived at a perfect understanding of the local scene, but in fact I found myself being posted at intervals of three, four or five years to a succession of different countries.

I have heard the expression 'culture shock' used to describe the experience of travellers arriving in an unfamiliar environment. It is not a term I like, because it implies something unpleasant whereas to me cultural differences, while they might prove unsettling, were matters of great interest, things to be looked into and appreciated.

Some of the cities I worked in were largely unknown to my fellow countrymen at the time my family and I lived there. I don't recall seeing tourists in, for example, Benghazi, Damascus or in the Indian city of Hyderabad. These places are now on the tourist map, even if only as stopping off places on the way to equally exotic places. In retirement here in London I am always delighted when friends tell me they have been there on holiday. Here's a chance to compare notes, to find out whether their experiences reflect my own happy memories of these places. On occasions I have been taken aback by how thoroughly in the space of a fortnight they have come to terms with societies which had me baffled for years. One friend had extended a ten day tour of India's Golden Triangle to spend a day in Hyderabad, visiting Golconda Fort, gazing down on the Ktub Shahi tombs and taking a look at the old British Residency, now a women's college, so graphically described by William Dalrymple in *White Mughals*. (In this college the redoubtable principal, Mrs Jussawala, had at one time invited us to evenings of *ghazals*, old Hyderabadi love songs.) What most impressed me in my friend's report on his holiday, however, was the comprehensive insight he appeared to have obtained into Indian society and recent history. After two lengthy periods of residence in India I had managed to arrive at no such understanding of matters in that vast and complex country, but when I compared the views I had formed with those being recounted by my friend I noticed strange discrepancies. The picture he painted was somehow distorted, as though the subject had been strangely slewed.

He ended by saying: "Our guide, Mr Singh, was an excellent guide."

Here perhaps was the explanation. Whereas there may well be Sikh academics ready and able to give a scholarly and detached view of Indian history it must be difficult for members of the Sikh community in general to be unmindful of the unhappy sequence of events which led to armed intervention by Government forces in the Golden Temple in Amritsar during Mrs Gandhi's administration. Might this have coloured Mr Singh's words to his charges?

When I retired and became a foreign tourist rather than a foreign resident I came to appreciate the critical role of tour guides, how much information is filtered through these travelling companions. Apart from waiters they may be the only natives of the country we speak to. We take their information on trust but we know little of their background. A guide in Egypt, a man deeply informative about antiquities, held extremely harsh views on Shia Muslims and Copts. We assumed that he himself was a Sunni Muslim, though not necessarily a typical one. There are also guides who tell their customers what they assume they would wish to hear or endorse what they believe to be received opinion - the elderly guide who assures Britons that his country folk yearn for the return of the British raj, the Greek guide confirming that her menfolk are congenitally lazy. But encountering contrary evidence - Greek shopkeepers working all the hours God gives or veterans of the Quit India campaign recalling old grievances - is confusing, leads to thoughts like Lao-Tzu's that "The further one travels the less one may know."

To be absolutely confident about foreign places it is perhaps an advantage not to have been there at all. In a discussion on international relations the host of a BBC phone-in radio programme came up with: "Let's take one of these crackpot states, say Syria." His choice of terminology struck me as singular. 'Crackpot' applied to an individual implies a person so deranged as to be incapable of functioning. While Syria is a nation the majority of whose citizens subscribe to a religion other than the official religion here, people subject to a government more authoritarian than our own, in many ways the country functions perfectly well - it has health, education, post, telephone and transport services, people produce and market agricultural goods, furniture and other necessities much in the way of people in many other countries. Nobody phoned in to query Jeremy Vine's judgement - or if somebody did her words were not broadcast - so it may be that his view is widely accepted as authoritative.

I was even more taken aback when attending the AGM of an organisation concerned with the fostering of international good will by the words of a man who was holding forth to a group of fellow invitees before the formal proceedings began. He was a substantial man, a member of the House of Lords. As I joined the group he declared, with great conviction: "In my view the whole of Africa is a basket case."

I am not a violent man but, when I thought of the Africans I had worked with in Kenya, I had to suppress a strong desire to hit him. On reflection I see that this would have been unkind. He was no doubt talking about macroeconomics, whereas I was bogged down in memories of personal relationships, thinking about my work with Lorna Wandera and Ben Odiambo on a comparatively small-scale operation.

Not that personal relations between people of different nations are necessarily straightforward. When I told friends recently that I was thinking of taking a trip through Portugal, all of them who had been there assured me that the Portuguese are kind people. I found, with the exception of two rather brusque encounters, that this was perfectly true, but it would be hard to establish whether the general level of kindness was any higher there than elsewhere. Even in London I have seen natives going out of their way to direct bewildered foreign visitors, sometimes even venturing to address them in their own language. Generalisations, however, are the stuff of travellers' tales.

A coachload of us were once approaching Knossos at nine in the morning. One of our party, observing a stream of local people walking in the opposite direction, remarked: "Cretans are not a smiley people." Indeed they were not smiling but it might well have been because they were on their way to work. I have noticed a similar lack of cheeriness in the faces of tube travellers in London at the same hour and it may be a universal phenomenon. Nevertheless, if our fellow traveller reports back to her friends on her observation it may well become widely accepted that the people of Crete are lacking in high spirits.

In an article in the *Independent on Sunday* Christopher West expresses his dislike of the 'Funny Foreigner school of travel writing.' In my experience funny foreigners have been my fellow countrymen who have failed to come to terms with overseas countries in which they find themselves. An Englishman, temporarily resident in Damascus, decided to take his family to visit those parts of the Holy Land which at that time formed part of the Hashemite Kingdom of Jordan. Driving to the southern outskirts of the city he cried out of his car window "King Hussein? King Hussein?" but passers-by failed to reply, looking at him in amazement. He lamented bitterly: "You'd think these people would have heard of King Hussein and know where he lives."

The existence of non-British eccentrics, however, cannot be denied. A few, recognised even by their fellow nationals, have found their way into the following pages. It would be churlish to leave them out; their disconcerting presence enlivened our otherwise humdrum lives.

In listing these causes of incertitude which beset the expatriate - untried preconceptions., unreliable informants, dubious generalisations, ex cathedra pronouncements, unpredictable eccentrics - I have sought to excuse the inconclusive nature of my stories. In cases where I have had the opportunity to revisit scenes of action, sometimes after many years, I have tried to resolve perplexing concerns, to tie up loose ends - usually without success. Some place names - Bombay, Madras, King Fuad I street - have been officially altered in recent years. In sticking to the names they bore when the stories took place I hope I have not added further confusion to the mental uncertainties I have expressed at many points.

Mr Nirmal's Guru

I first became aware of Mr Nirmal when he appeared on the stage and thrust a book into our distinguished guest's hands. However, our English Studies Officer, Dr (Miss) Willy Engineer, told me he'd been spotted at every previous reading William Golding had given throughout India. A devoted fan, then, and a considerable traveller, too. Still, he shouldn't have got up on to the stage. Our arrangements were supposed to protect our guest from the public after a reading. He wanted things that way and who can blame him. He put a lot of himself into those readings. Frankly, I was surprised to see Mr Nirmal up there, blocking our escape route through a side door into the library. Perhaps Golding was, too, but he carried it off well, with a firm "Thank you", a side step and barely a pause before exiting.

After Bombay it was Poona, for a book signing and another reading. Willy went with the Goldings and brought them back safely to Bombay.

"It was hell," she said, "the crush in Manni's bookshop."

"And the reading?"

"Oh, that went down very well. It was in the Sivaji Hall at the University. The microphones worked and so did the loudspeakers."

"Who was there?"

"Everybody who was supposed to be. Mr Nirmal was there, too."

"Who *is* Mr Nirmal?"

"I don't know, but I can find out if you like."

It was a quiet weekend. We offered the Goldings a tour of the city, but they sensibly opted to rest up in the air-conditioned luxury of the Oberoi Hotel. On Monday morning they'd have to fly up to Aurangabad for yet another reading - the last of a lengthy All-India tour, demanding at any age, but probably exhausting for septuagenarians. At least we'd programmed time off for visits to the caves at Ajunta and Ellora. Greta and

I would act as guides there.

On the up-country flight Willy went through the programme. She'd planned it immaculately, as always. The reception committee, the small English faculty at the University, was lined up at Aurangabad airport, as expected. Less expected was the solitary figure standing apart demurely making the palms-pressed-together *Namaste* greeting.

"It's Mr Nirmal," said William Golding.

"Who *is* Mr Nirmal?" I hissed at Willy Engineer.

"I've got to get the cases. I'll tell you at the hotel."

"This Mr Nirmal has been a very constant supporter," said Ann Golding. "Do you think you could possibly include him in tomorrow's dinner party?"

"Yes, you're right. Why don't you invite him personally. He'd appreciate that."

After the greetings and the garlandings we were driven to the hotel. The airport is some distance from town and the road dusty in the hot season. Our car put up some of this dust over Mr Nirmal as he stood by the roadside *namasteing*. He was smiling benignly.

"He seemed very pleased with the invitation," said Ann Golding. "D'you know, this is his home place, so I told him to bring his wife as well."

I looked back. Mr Nirmal could be seen making good progress townwards on foot behind us, but he was soon lost to sight.

I can thoroughly recommend the Rama Hotel in Aurangabad. It is some way out of town, but has fine views from the roof over the plain towards the hills to the north-east. The manager had kept a large suite for the Goldings, at no extra charge. The suite had a well-stocked bar and was a good place to relax after a journey or a speaking engagement.

Before dinner Willy Engineer filled me in on Mr Nirmal. "He's a PhD student and his thesis is on Golding's novels. That's why he's been following the tour."

"Has he actually spoken to Golding?"

"No, only to say *Namaste*."

"I wonder why he keeps coming to the readings. The passages are usually the same and the question and answer sessions don't vary much either. D'you think he wants something?"

"No. He just hopes some of the aura will rub off on him. After all, Golding is a Nobel prize winner. Mr Nirmal calls him his *guru*."

"Golding wouldn't like that. You know what he says, 'Call me Bill.' Very much a plain man's ordinary man."

"*Guru* only means *teacher*."

"It could mean something more than that."

"I shouldn't worry about it," said Willy.

In the event it was Willy who did the worrying. She was first down to breakfast next morning. When Greta and I joined her she was reading a letter balanced on a massive brown paper parcel.

"What's that?" I asked.

"It's Mr Nirmal's PhD thesis. He wants Golding to read it."

"What! You can't bring a Nobel prize winner thousands of miles on a lecture tour with no fee and expect him to read PhD theses."

"It's worse than that. Listen to what Mr Nirmal's written in his letter. Golding's asked me to deal with it."

The letter began ceremoniously and went on to give details of the student's struggles to obtain a doctorate. It was not a pretty story.

"The people who met you at the airport are my enemies. They are trying to kill me. If they have their way, I shall never obtain my PhD while I am alive."

"Do they award posthumous degrees in Aurangabad?" asked Greta.

I was in no mood for frivolity. The evening's dinner party was to be a small one - the Goldings, ourselves, the Department of

English faculty, the man they were trying to murder, and the intended victim's wife; a dozen of us round one big table.

Greta and I agree that of all the wonderful sites we visited during our nine years in India the temples at Ellora are the most awe-inspiring in the majesty of their conception and execution. Most majestic of all is the Kailasa temple ["the noblest Hindu memorial of ancient India," says Murray's Guide], carved out of solid black volcanic rock, immense, over a hundred foot high with a courtyard over a hundred and fifty feet wide and nearly twice as long and every one of its superabundance of carvings and bas reliefs - gods, goddesses, monsters - whether in human or animal form, gigantic or merely life-sized - carved with the utmost intricacy, except where the sculptors' hands were mysteriously arrested, leaving only the incised outlines of wonders that were yet to be. This Kailasa temple is the first to come in sight as the road from Aurangabad rounds the bend.

Only three of us made the journey that morning, William Golding, Greta and I. Ann Golding wasn't feeling too well, but was determined to attend the afternoon's reading at the University. Willy had been toying with the strings of Mr Nirmal's brown paper parcel when we left. The parcel, the letter and the prospect of a disastrous dinner party (Would the faculty seize the opportunity to do away with a troublesome research student or would Mr Nirmal, perhaps, make a pre-emptive strike and denounce his enemies to the authorities during the soup course?) had been much on my mind, but I forgot all that when we saw the Kailasa temple. We walked round together in complete silence, except when I gently rebuffed local guides who wanted to take Golding off to dark corners to see lesser deities doing unspeakably intimate things to one another.

At the end of some hours Golding told us: "In the whole of the Valley of the Kings there's nothing that surpasses what we've seen here today."

Coming from someone whose admiration for ancient Egypt had been almost life-long, we found this immensely gratifying.

On the journey back to the hotel Greta and Golding chatted

about the passing scene. I was silent, thinking again about the dinner party that night after the reading, about a potentially dangerous confrontation between Mr Nirmal and his academic enemies. One of these academics I'd recognised at the airport, a Dr Nihalani, brother of an old friend I'd worked with years before in Hyderabad. The brother, Paroo, had always been very frank with me about academic in-fighting in India. I determined to try to find an opportunity for a word about our present dilemma when we went to the University for the reading.

As it happened, the opportunity presented itself. Dr Nihalani and I found ourselves seated side by side in a corner of the Vice-Chancellor's capacious office where the Goldings were entertained to tea before the reading. I wasn't sure how to broach the matter but, given the shortage of available time, decided to put it bluntly.

"He says you're his enemies and are trying to kill him," I said, after explaining our association with Mr Nirmal.

Dr Nihalani smiled broadly, in a manner that reminded me strongly of his brother. "It isn't quite like that."

"But things have turned rather nasty, I suppose? Is there some bitterness about the thesis? Have you seen it?"

"Oh yes. It was submitted some months ago. We had to send it back, asking for some amendments and additions."

"He says he'll never get his PhD while he's alive."

Dr Nihalani smiled again. "That depends on how soon he re-submits his thesis."

At this point we had to break off to file into the lecture hall with the Goldings and the Vice-Chancellor.

The lecture hall was tight-packed to over capacity. Behind the professors, lecturers and researchers, students pressed narrow shoulder to narrow shoulder. Enterprising ones had hauled themselves up on to window sills and behind them peons craned in through the windows, precariously hanging on to the frames. I wondered whether these last spoke anything other than Marathi or some more local language. They stared at us fixedly as we made our way up to the dais and a susurration of murmured excitement ran through the hall below. As soon as Golding began, this ceased. There was pin-drop silence. Golding had never read better and you could sense the magnetism of the great man. The English voice with its slight West Country burr held professor and peon alike, transfixed, here in the heartland of Maharastra and final resting place of Aurangzebe, just as it had in cosmopolitan Bombay. Possibly the air was even more highly charged, the listening even more intense, here in this stifling up-country atmosphere. I thought again of the proposition I'd put to Willy the day before, that *guru* meant more than simply *teacher* and, thinking of the mystical bond which united guru and acolyte, I peered intently from the dais at the mass of faces below, my eye going carefully along the tight pressed ranks. A most extraordinary possibility: Mr Nirmal might not be there. I checked and double-checked, but saw no sign of him. Of course, in such a mass an individual could easily be overlooked. Even so ..... Could Mr Nirmal's courage have deserted him? This was his enemies' camp, after all, and they were here en masse. And if he had failed to face them here, what odds that he might also fail our feast later that day and social embarrassment, at the least, be avoided? It was a cowardly thought, but I took comfort in it.

Indian audiences' applause is low-keyed compared with what we are used to in the West and the gauge of a successful performance or lecture lies more in the silence of its reception, the attentiveness of the audience while it is going on. By this standard Golding's reading was certainly an outstanding success, but, on this occasion, I was also struck by the intensity of the ovation given at the end. I like to think that it had been a unique occasion in Aurangabad though, as we hurriedly left the hall, an announcement by the convenor made it clear that the event had been one of a series.

"Next Wednesday," he said, "the second secretary of the Yugoslav Embassy in New Delhi will be here to talk about economic developments in Yugoslavia since 1956."

Back in the hotel the Goldings went to their suite to rest before dinner. I consulted Willy in the bar.

"Do you know," I said, "I think Mr Nirmal wasn't there."

"No, he wasn't." She seemed neither surprised not concerned.

"But don't you see, this might mean that he won't tum up for our dinner tonight."

"I wouldn't bank on it. I expect he's gone to his native place, to fetch his wife."

"But this *is* his native place."

"Only in the more general, Indian sense of the expression."

Willy gave me the patient look she always assumed when needing to fill a vast gap in an understanding unperfected despite eight years' residence in her vast and complicated country.

"His native place is about a hundred and fifty miles from here. It's pretty remote. He's the village schoolmaster."

"Then perhaps he won't get back in time. However will he travel?"

"There are buses," she said, "and bullock carts. We shall see."

"Better tell the maitre-d we may be only ten for dinner."

"I've already told him. Ten or twelve, he won't be fussed," said Willy.

It was lucky that the maitre-d was flexible about numbers. After we had changed for dinner we found Willy in the lounge with a family of three, Mr Nirmal, Mrs Nirmal and their daughter, Baby Nirmal, an enchanting ten-year-old girl with her hair in two plaits tied with red bows. She wore a gym-slip which revealed the extreme thinness of her frame and limbs.

"There was no-one in the village they could leave her with," Willy explained.

Mrs Nirmal and Baby Nirmal didn't speak English, but they smiled shyly and seemed content to be included in our dinner party for thirteen.

The Foreign and Commonwealth booklet explaining how to seat guests of honour at dinner parties had been issued many years earlier, but Greta and I continued to find its seating-plan proposals useful. However, on this occasion we were guided by principles other than protocol. We decided we had to keep Mr Nirmal somewhat apart from his perceived enemies.

The three Nirmals should sit at one end of the table with the Goldings and ourselves acting as buffers between them and the Faculty of English. Greta, with her flair for non-verbal communication, was seated nearest Mrs Nirmal, whose scholar husband, placed next to William Golding, would have a chance at last to say something more than *Namaste* to his guru.

"It seems the safest thing," I said in an aside to Willy. "I just hope he doesn't play up this *guru* business too much."

"I shouldn't worry about it," she said. She often said reassuring things like that.

The setting we had chosen for dinner could not, I pride myself, have been better. A long table was set up on the hotel roof and surrounding terracotta pots containing lamps allowed to escape through their interstices a light which was adequate but, because of its subdued nature, did not detract from the enchantment of the starlight in a clear, deep azure sky. Since we were facing away from the city this was sufficient to silhouette the hills beyond the plain. Moonlight might have been a bonus, we thought, but our arrangements looked about as perfect as the Gods permit.

In deference to the Goldings known liking for early nights our university guests arrived promptly and soon after eight we were safely seated according to the prearranged plan. We had allowed no time for mingling before dinner. Despite the idyllic setting and Willy's injunction not to worry, a nagging doubt remained. Would the Nirmals, even Mr Nirmal, since he was basically a simple village schoolmaster, find the occasion totally overawing?

As we started the first course (fruit cup, vegetarian like the rest of the menu designed for a group of scholarly diners almost certain to include Brahmins), I was busy setting up a conversation between Ann Golding and her neighbour about hockey. Luckily he was an enthusiast and Ann a former Kent county player. I was suddenly distracted by a loud exclamation from her husband on the other side of the table. He had raised both hands in protest towards Mr Nirmal, saying loudly: "No! No!"

"Oh dear," I thought, "the *guru* business."

It was worse than that. Golding's exclamation had halted conversation around the table and Mr Nirmal could clearly be heard explaining that the night before he had received a vision of Golding as a God, himself a humble supplicant bending low to kiss his (Golding's) feet. This had occurred while the overnight bus was passing through the Pipalgaon district.

"I must ask you to cast the thought of any such behaviour from your mind," protested Golding, deeply disturbed. "I am simply an ordinary mortal."

Mr Nirmal smiled complacently, indicating that he knew better. "The conjunction of the planets at the time of your arrival in India was correct," he said.

Fortunately he chose not to pursue the subject, simply nodding towards the distant hills, but the incident had blighted conversation and other diners were busying themselves with their fruit cups.

Waiters removing the dishes paused on finding that neither Mr nor Mrs Nirmal had eaten any part of this first course (though Baby Nirmal had cleaned up her dish very nicely) but, after a whispered word, the two dishes were taken away full.

We hoped the next course, mulligatawny soup, would prove more pleasing to the Nirmals' palates. Its arrival was the signal for renewed conversation amongst our academic friends, a professor explaining the Tamil origins of the word *mulligatawny*. A general exchange about English lexical borrowings from Indian languages ensued and I was not sorry that attention had swung away from Mr Nirmal, though rather disturbed when I glanced to their end of the table to note that neither he nor his wife was making any attempt to eat the soup. At first I feared that the elaborate lay out of the cutlery was inhibiting them, but then I saw that Baby Nirmal, seated between them, was setting an excellent example with the correct spoon.

Greta, solicitous hostess, left her seat and, crouching beside

Mr Nirmal, carried on a whispered conversation which I was just able to hear.

"Is there something wrong with the food?"

"No, it looks perfectly wholesome to me."

"Then wouldn't you like to try the soup?"

"No. We are fasting."

It was well within our experience to have guests accept dinner invitations only to sit throughout the meal totally abstinent, observing their fast. I should not have pursued the matter, but Greta astutely asked: "When does your fast end?"

"When the moon rises."

"And when do you think that will be?"

"I don't think. I know; nine o'clock."

Greta, looking thoughtful, returned to her seat. She then passed a whispered message around the table: "Would we please eat our soup slowly so that the Nirmals, at moonrise, could catch up with us."

It was fortunate that the soup was mulligatawny. However cold it grew during the ensuing twenty minutes or so, its peppery flavouring maintained the illusion that we were eating a hot dish, but the tedious process of pausing lengthily between spoonfuls undoubtedly put a damper on the party and nor could there be any doubt that Mr Nirmal, after all a mere afterthought on the guest list, had once again become the focus of attention. Only he and his family faced eastwards. Other guests glanced anxiously sideways or over their shoulders in that direction from time to time. Mr Nirmal himself remained stoically composed, giving alternative nods of approval towards William Golding on his right and towards Baby Nirmal on his left. She alone had not felt constrained to go slow on the soup. Having cleaned her bowl she was eating a bread roll, taking delicate bites with obvious satisfaction.

Holy men in India have been known to disagree about the conjunction of the planets and what this may portend. To what extent Mr Nirmal may or may not have been correct about the cosmic importance of the timing of Golding's arrival in India I could not begin to judge. What I was relieved to discover, however, was that as regards the relative movements of planets earth and moon, insofar as they affected us that night in Aurangabad, Mr Nirmal was spot on. Promptly at nine the moon appeared over the eastern hills. From a clear sky it bathed us all in its beneficence, conferring an especial glow upon the Nirmals, whom it struck full face.

Mr Nirmal looked slowly from face to face around the table. In his moonlit smile there was no trace of any scholarly animosity he might have been expected to feel for the Faculty of English. He raised a spoonful of soup to his lips and it was our turn to nod approvingly, but the harmonious moment was short-lived. One taste was enough.

"I can't eat that," he said, pushing the offending bowl away.

I find it hard to believe that there was anything calculated in Mr Nirmal's behaviour, that he had deliberately imposed himself upon our party as its focal point. However, if calculation there were, at this point there was also misjudgement, a hand overplayed. After a momentary silence of disbelief, all eyes turned away from Mr Nirmal and he played no further significant part in our feast. Instinctively, it seemed, we and the Goldings resumed our conversations with our academic guests. As the moon rose higher it spread its favours more evenly upon us, upon William Golding's venerable locks and on the faces of fellow diners turned towards him, listening to his commonsensical, entirely mortal words of wisdom. Occasionally, from the comer of my eye, I noticed Mr Nirmal continuing to reject the Rama hotel's excellent food, Mrs Nirmal, loyally following suit and Baby Nirmal cleaning successive plates in her delicate but determined manner. Maybe one day she will tell Mr Nirmal's grandchildren of his encounter with the Nobel laureate. Certainly for her the meal must have been a memorable one. They had travelled a long way for it.

Aurangabad 1988.

And Now for the Good News

I am not sure at which point Mohammed Slim appointed himself unofficial Security Adviser. Certainly he took on this burden as cheerfully and efficiently as that of Driver-Projectionist, his official designation.

Recognition of his additional appointment was a gradual process. It had been my practice, on arriving each morning at our Beirut office, to discuss my daily appointments with my secretary. Having recorded them, she would then brief Mohammed on any car journeys required. As I had arrived to fill this post only recently, after an interregnum occasioned by the first phase of the Lebanese Civil War, I was keen to reestablish contacts and make as many calls on people as possible. Plenty of car journeys were predicted every day. Very few of them, however, actually took place.

Mohammed Slim would enter my office, car log book in hand and a smile registering both puzzlement and indulgence on his face.

"This visit to the Ministry of X .....," he would begin.

He would then explain why it could certainly not take place that day. During the night snipers from militia A had killed two men manning a road block for militia B. Militia B were even now bringing reinforcements down from the mountains into the city. Retaliation would be swift and bloody. There was no reason to assume that a British Council officer traversing the route in a non-bullet-proofed Vauxhall saloon, however well-intentioned his mission, would escape maiming or worse in the resultant mêlée.

Similar situation summaries were adduced to explain why projected calls at Charity Foundation Y and the University of Z were equally ill-advised. Mohammed gleaned his information not only from reading the local Arabic, French and English-language press but also from personal witness supplied by a network of drivers he would consult on his way to the office from his home on the airport road. His dire predictions of daily bloodshed and mayhem, sporadic and localised but nonetheless deadly for those involved, intentionally or otherwise, were almost always confirmed by events.

By mutual agreement of all three parties, Mohammed came to supplant my secretary as my first caller of the day. The programme drawn up would then at least have the advantage of being realisable. It had the disadvantage of confining me to the Centre far more than I would have liked. Repeated discussions with Towfiq Jabour, the Administrative Officer, over the relative merits of a rope ladder or a permanently installed external iron stairway as offering the better chance of escape for staff on the first floor in the event of an armed attack on the main entrance proved inconclusive. In theory, a hastily lowered rope ladder had the advantage of not offering an additional fixed access, which would facilitate a two-pronged assault on the building. In practice, however, older members of staff refused to take to the rope ladder in emergency drills. My secretary, having changed into a pair of trousers, shinned down it nimbly enough, as did the two young British directors of studies of the Institute of English. I myself negotiated the descent with some difficulty. Nobody else was prepared to try it, not even Mr Jabour, its staunchest advocate. I spent some time reflecting how bad it would look if, in the event of a disaster, the expatriate staff accounted for three-quarters of the survivors.

Time was also spent looking into the classrooms of the Institute, housed on the ground floor. A dedicated team of experts in teaching English as a foreign language needed little help there. Prominent among the students were 'officers' of the militia which controlled the area in the immediate vicinity of the Centre. Reduced fee lessons had been offered to these as an insurance policy against having to use the rope ladder. I was disconcerted to see that one of these fiercely moustached young men had exchanged his uniform tee-shirt for one bearing the British Council logo. However, he was earnestly repeating after Samia Skaf, his teacher: "Would you like tea, or would you prefer coffee?" - conveying through correct stress and intonation the essence of punctilio.

The library, however, offered me the chance to chat with customers. These were dedicated users of our services. Many of them told me of their gratitude for our keeping the library open throughout the worst days of the fighting in the Civil War's first phase.

"When there was curfew every night, we were very happy staying at home with our library books."

Far from being able to claim any credit for this, having been in Kenya at the time, my understanding was that the whole Centre, including the library, had been officially closed during those months. However, date stamping in the books indicated that many of them had undoubtedly been issued. It was Mohammed who explained the paradox. All other staff having been evacuated or stood off, he and two messengers were left to mount guard over the books, films, office furniture and equipment in the locked and shuttered building. Once the local population had adjusted to life under shellfire, sorties from home were made for shopping and other family business. Several regulars took to beating on the library door, demanding to exchange their books. Mohammed and the messengers were by no means reluctant to provide this service. Unawed by the complexities of library science they had, in better times, grasped by observation the essence of the business - stamping a date two weeks in the future on the issue slip inside the cover of each book in demand. Reduced to this essential procedure the library seemed to have run perfectly well under Mohammed's command. Eventually he was able to hand back authority to the reappointed head librarian, Mr Rafiq, who made it one of his first tasks to organise a stocktaking. Remarkably, losses turned out to be less than in any other period of comparable length. Mr Rafiq's major problem, however, was finding funds for updating stock, an exercise neglected for some fifteen months.

Lack of funding and lack of security, these were the two great problems for all of us. Confined to my office for long periods by the latter, I spent frustrating hours thinking about the former. In normal times British funds, official and otherwise, can be tapped to help countries which have suffered the sort of disasters Lebanon had undergone. However, once the militias, in many cases not more than armed bands of marauders, had seized power from the country's official forces, there was an understandable reluctance to commit funds that might well fall into the wrong hands.

Largely immune from the violent intrusions of the militias, at least at this stage of the war, were the charitable foundations which ran educational and medical services. Regardless of their religious affiliations - Shia, Sunni, Druse, Maronite, Greek Orthodox, Protestant, Armenian - their colleges and hospitals kept their doors open while violence raged about them. To these institutions we devoted such small disbursements of funds as could be diverted from our routine running costs. These were largely token gifts, messages of empathy in present sufferings, symbols of hope for survival and better times to come. One such token gift was the planned provision of nurses' dictionaries, one for each of the fifty trainees at the School of Nursing of the Maqassad Hospital, paid for out of Mr Rafiq's hard-pressed library restocking funds.

The director of the School, a young woman recently graduated in Biology, had asked for a formal hand over. On the morning tentatively arranged for this I arrived early at the office and went through the Beirut newspapers. We had had little sleep the previous night as the noise from shellfire and from bursts of firing from automatic weapons had been almost continuous.

L 'Orient-Le Jour reported overnight shelling of Ashrafieh and Sin el-Fil and a large explosion in Bourj Hammoud. *Es-Safir's* lead story was about close quarter encounters in the Kantari area, but this may not have been more than the playing off of old grudges by armed gangs. So far, so good. There was no reason for our crossing any of these districts en route to the Maqassad Hospital. *Ike* had a report from nearer home, the abduction of a barmaid from an establishment in Sidani Street. This, also, need prove no deterrent, nor should the reported direct hit which had destroyed half the central telephone exchange. Telephone connections had already become so fragmented that we had come to rely generally on messages relayed across the city by hand. Of course, Mohammed's situation appraisal, finalised after the newspapers had been put to bed, might, as on several occasions in the past, demand a last minute cancellation.

Not so, this time. His cheerful demeanour that morning plainly indicated that all would be well. He seemed to be quite as euphoric as I was at the prospect of getting away from the building and about the sort of business which could justify our presence in the country.

"The dictionaries are already in the boot," he said.

The ceremony took place in the School's assembly hall. Beside the presentation table where Mohammed had neatly stacked the dictionaries a hospital bed had been drawn up. It contained a lifelike shop dummy of a woman lying on her back. Alongside her well-coiffured head was placed a plastic doll. Both figures glowed pinkly with evident good health, mother and child representing an augury for a happier future.

The trainee nurses, young women from Sunni Moslem villages around Beirut, were dressed in white overalls and starched white caps. During the initial speeches I noticed that they were being led away one by one into an adjoining room by a white-jacketed man, presumably a doctor from the hospital to which the School was attached, before rejoining the assembly in time to line up to receive their dictionaries. When all of these had been distributed I asked the young Director of Nursing Training why the trainees had earlier been led away.

She explained: "Last night a pregnant woman was brought into the hospital. Normally the midwife would have looked after her in her own village, but she had begun haemorrhaging heavily. She's forty years old and this would be her first baby. There was fighting in the hills but, luckily, the militiamen let our ambulance pass through their lines. Unfortunately, we've been unable to stop the bleeding. She needs blood transfusions, but our blood bank is almost empty. We've had a lot of shrapnel wound cases lately and, in any case, this woman's blood group is rather rare - O-negative. None of the staff in the hospital can supply the blood needed and that's why they've been testing our trainee nurses."

"Any success?" I asked.

"No, none of them is the right group."

"How pregnant is the woman?"

"She's about to give birth."

"What will happen?"

"We don't know. Without a blood transfusion the mother will certainly die. I doubt they can save the baby."

"How much time have you got?"

"Almost none at all. The woman is dying now."

I suddenly remembered that some months previously all the staff at the British Embassy in Beirut, a largish embassy, had been blood tested in case of injury. Somebody there kept a list of the staff's blood groups.

"Can I try your telephone?"

"You can try, but I think all the lines are down. The central exchange was almost wiped out last night."

By totally unexpected good fortune the line between hospital and embassy was not down and I got through in reasonably quick time. The duty officer checked his list, but he had nobody O-negative on it.

"I'll try the US Embassy," he offered. "Hold on." After a minute he told me: "No, I can't get through. I'm going to run along the Corniche to them."

Only four hundred metres separated the two embassies, but the telephone line went dead and I had to leave the hospital being able only to give a vague assurance that the duty officer was doing his best. Chances of success seemed slim.

Mohammed drove me back to the office. His usual high spirits seemed subdued. I think we both felt that our achievement in handing over the dictionaries successfully was overshadowed by our inability to do anything effective for the dying mother. After all, in what until recently had been the most scientifically advanced city in the Middle East, women should not be dying for lack of a blood transfusion. Mohammed had often told me of his intense loathing for the gunmen who had brought his country down and how he, a Shia Moslem, had made it his mission to help any fellow-countryman he could, regardless of creed. His was a rare spirit, but he was by no means unique amongst the ordinary people of Lebanon in those days. However, from various sources I was able in the course of the next two days to piece together the story of what had happened after I had lost touch with my contact at the Embassy.

He had run, as promised, along the Corniche from the British to the US Embassy. There he had an initial setback which neither of us had foreseen. It was American Thanksgiving Day and the Embassy was closed. He managed, however, to raise the US marine on duty. Yes, he had a list of blood groups of members of staff but no, none of them was O-negative. However, there was a second list, of dependents of members of staff and Mary Kinsolving, wife of the Chargé d'Affaires, did have this rare blood group. Fortunately the Chargé and his wife were housed in the penthouse apartment in the building alongside the Embassy.

It was noon when the marine and the British duty officer arrived on Mary Kinsolving's doorstep. She was supervising preparations for a Thanksgiving lunch for fifty guests, those leading members of the Lebanese community who were able to get across the city to West Beirut to attend. All traffic regulations had long since broken down in the city and the US Embassy Chevrolet was able to get the blood donor to the hospital in less than half an hour. The transfusion was made immediately and the hostess was able to return to her lunch party, too late to greet her guests on arrival, but in time to join them in enjoying the pumpkin pie.

Next day the hospital sent a message. Both mother and baby were doing well.

That evening I went to one of those cocktail parties which Beirut society kept going even in the worst of times. Numbers were sometimes depleted by invitees' being unable to cross the green line or get past road blocks created by newly-formed militias, but there was never a falling off in the sumptuous fare offered to eat and drink, delicacies often being brought in through the port of Jounieh and subject to unofficial taxes levied by gunmen established at intervals along the road between there and West Beirut. At the party I met Jim Muir, a journalist long resident in the country and an occasional stand-in for Tim Llewellyn, the BBC's Middle East correspondent, whose voice was often to be heard giving lucid and penetrating reports on the complex and confused situation in the area. I told him the story of the Maqassad Hospital patient and Mary Kinsolving.

"Who was the patient?" he asked. "Some prominent Sunni Moslem lady?"

"No. Just an ordinary village woman."

Jim looked thoughtful. "That *is* a story," he said.

A week later my secretary brought me a copy of the latest issue of *Mideast Events*. A page was devoted to Lebanon, a collection of reports of internecine warfare, brutal killings and abductions, of man's inhumanity to man. Across the bottom of the page was the story of the blood transfusion at the Maqassad Hospital. It was written by Jim Muir and given the headline *And Now for the Good News*.

Beirut 1977

Happy Birthday, Maestro

```
ECYO advises you to proceed to Artillery School
at Deolali and borrow cannons from CO for 1812
Overture.
```

The arrival on my desk in Bombay of this telex message from our Director of Music Department in London reinforced an uneasy feeling that we were in danger of overcommitting ourselves in our collaboration with the European Community Youth Orchestra over their proposed tour of India. Up till that point the orchestra's dynamic secretary-general had more or less carried me with her; everything would be possible. Certainly there was a case for a grandeur of conception in planning a project intended to form a tribute by the youth of Europe to the youth of India in the centenary year of the birth of Jawarhalal Nehru. Why then did I jib at the proposed Deolali expedition? There was no denying that by tradition cannons were a prerequisite for a performance of Tchaikovsky's 1812. Nor was I being asked to transport these armaments throughout the whole of the tour of India, since the 1812 was to form part of the programme only for the final concert in Bombay, a mere 113 miles from Deolali. I believe my misgivings were crystallised by the very word Deolali, associated in popular British parlance with mental derangement since the days when shell-shocked British tommies were sent there for recuperation.

"A mad undertaking." It was difficult not to think in these terms about the orchestra's proposal given that, some forty years after independence, the Deolali garrison was no longer made up of deranged British troops but of perfectly sane Indian gunnery instructors. Would the commanding officer be likely to accede to a request from a foreigner to remove some of his weaponry for musical purposes? Despite the continuing tradition of certain British army practices in the army of the Republic of India, I thought not and nor did 1 think that an assignment I had once undertaken at the behest (relayed to me at several removes) of the then C-in-C, Field Marshal Sam Manekshaw, at the HQ of Southern Command in Poona would carry much weight nearly twenty years after the event. Nevertheless, we were under a vague but compelling instruction to do all in our power to ensure the success of the orchestra's proposed tour.

I was pondering this dilemma when Mr N K Prabhu, our Cultural Activities Officer, made his timely entry. I handed him the telex.

"Leave it to me," he said.

"1 think they're looking for some urgent action."

"I'll go and see about it this afternoon and let you know tomorrow morning."

I had great faith in Mr Prabhu's resourcefulness, but I felt that he might be overreaching himself this time.

"It's a very slow train to Deolali," I reminded him.

"I may not have to go that far." But he left my office immediately, with his usual purposeful air.

A lot of people had been involved in trying to set up this musical tour. I was pleased when Mrs Ratti Mehta, the able chairman of the Time and Talents Club's Concert Committee, was drawn in. She and her committee ladies had successfully collaborated in tours by many leading orchestras, among them the Warsaw National Philharmonic, the English Chamber, the Los Angeles Philharmonic and the New York Philharmonic. Both the US orchestras had been conducted by "Bombay-born" Zubin Mehta, who was to come again, this time with the pick of the young players from the European Community, some hundred and twenty of them, accompanied by twenty officials. The distinguishing feature of this tour was that the orchestra was to play not only in Bombay, with its ready-made audience for Western music, but also in five other Indian cities. Of course, the inclusion in the programme of a sitar concerto by Ravi Shankar, with the composer performing the solo part himself, was a guaranteed crowd puller, but I saw the tour as a vastly ambitious undertaking and was glad our involvement was largely confined to the Bombay end of it. Largely, but not wholly.

It is well known that Bombay, a city of over eighteen million people, pays some forty per cent of the total taxation in a country of over a billion. The percentage may not be exact, but it is the one most often quoted by Bombay businessmen, with a mixture of pride and resentment. Certainly in Indian terms Bombay is an immensely rich city. Not only its cultural organisers, but also its captains of industry are dynamic. However, when Joy Bryer, secretary-general of the European Community Youth Orchestra, arrived from London on our doorstep for the first of a series of flying visits, we had cause to revise upwards our conception of dynamism.

She flew in just in time for lunch with our friends of the Time and Talents Club. Mrs Amersey has hosted many delightfully leisurely luncheons in her elegant residence. This was quite a different affair. By the time we had sampled the first marsala dosas we found that we had agreed to the following propositions: the first Bombay concert would be in the Shanmukhananda Hall but the second would need a much larger venue, the Cricket Club of India's erstwhile test cricket ground (why not?) and yes, there would be not only accompanying cannon fire but also a massive fireworks display and the Time and Talent Club's indispensable acoustic screen would go with the orchestra throughout the whole tour of India and all this would cost an immense amount of money but no-one was to worry about this because not only would all twelve European Community member states cough up but provided we pointed Joy Bryer in the right direction she would ensure that Indian captains of industry and commerce coughed up as well. Before the meal had reached the coffee stage Joy had set off in directions we had confidently assured her would prove to be the right ones.

Once she had gone, the misgivings set in. It is one thing in India to secure financial backing for events with a vast popular appeal, a test cricket series, say, but performances of Westem classical music are quite another matter. Potential audiences form only a tiny minority of the population. Of course, in a country of over a billion such a minority can still provide respectable numbers - but would the event appear large enough to attract big-business backing?

Several flying visits later Joy Bryer had to admit that there was some substance in our misgivings, but her optimism remained unbounded. Finance from the European end was secured - a word with a prime minister here, a foreign minister there - but at the Indian end captains of industry were not to be persuaded. The problem became crystallised. What was needed was one big sponsor who would supply not necessarily ready cash but services in kind - for example, free accommodation for the entire tour.

This seemed to all of us well within the bounds of the possible. The solution, we thought, was here on our Bombay doorstep. Overlooking the Gateway to India and Bombay harbour stands the magnificent multi-domed Taj Mahal Hotel, flagship of the Taj Group hotels throughout India, a group managed by members of the community most strongly attuned to Western classical music in the sub-continent - the Parsees. Maestro Zubin Mehta himself sprang from this community. If there were anyone who would come up with the wherewithal to clinch the orchestra's tour it would undoubtedly be the enlightened management of the Taj hotels. Mrs Amersey's third tour-planning luncheon ended on a note of euphoria as we saw Joy Bryer off to meet them. This time we were sure of her success.

But we were wrong. With the best will in the world the Taj Group could not come up with free accommodation for a hundred and twenty young musicians and the twenty back-up people who travelled with them.

A lesser person would have given up. Not Joy Bryer, though I think I did detect at this time a hint of despondency in the bearing of this indomitable woman. Misgivings suppressed for months reemerged - the iffiness of the whole ambitious enterprise. If no free accommodation, no tour. If not Taj hotels, then what?

On the other side of the isthmus which connects the one-time island of Colaba with the rest of the city, on a piece of land reclaimed from the sea, downtown Bombay's other great hotel, the Oberoi, a modern building, overlooks the seaward side, with views across the Back Bay toward Malabar Hill, to which it is linked by the curving Marine Drive, at night studded with lights and therefore known as the Queen's Necklace. Like the Taj Hotel it has a rightly-deserved five-star rating. Unlike the Taj it is not the headquarters of the group of hotels it belongs to. Nor had we any reason to believe that its management, unlike that of the Taj, would be drawn to sponsoring a Western orchestra. On one of Joy Bryer's early visits to Bombay I had hosted a dinner for her at the Oberoi. Nine months later she returned there for an appointment with the Oberoi Group's Vice-President, Adil Murchandani. As we expected, nothing could be decided in Bombay, though Adil did set up a meeting for her with the group's president, Mr P J Oberoi, in Delhi.

Did the prospect of this meeting dispel that hint of despondency I thought to have detected in Joy Bryer earlier? Perhaps not, or perhaps she was simply tired as she faced yet another flight to Delhi. However, before her departure she asked me about a detail which in all the discussions about fund raising had been pushed to the back of my mind: "Are the cannons secured?" It was good to be able to give a positive answer at the end of what had otherwise been a disappointing visit.

I can claim no credit for success in this matter. That belonged entirely to our resourceful Cultural Activities Officer, Mr N K Prabhu. If there *were* to be a tour culminating with a performance of the 1812 Overture in Bombay, accompanying cannon would be obtained, not as the ECYO had suggested from the Indian Army Artillery School at Deolali but from a source much nearer home. Our centre in downtown Bombay was housed in one of a mass of high-rise blocks of buildings which, standing on land reclaimed from the sea, give the southern part of the city a somewhat fantastic air. Some ten miles to the north is the truly fantastic city of the great studios, Filmi City. Here the mighty epics of the Hindi cinema are shot. To feed the fantasies of millions of moviegoers, on huge cardboard and plaster sets glittering melodramas are enacted. To the essential romantic elements of these epics - love, betrayal, fate and the intervention of the gods in the affairs of mortals - not infrequently battle scenes are added. It was with this in mind that Mr Prabhu had left my office with Music department's telex message in his hand, his unerring instinct leading him to the Filmi City studio of a useful contact. He returned with the promise of "cannons" which, although not authentic weapons of war, could be guaranteed to produce explosive noises loud enough to accompany a spirited performance of the 1812. Furthermore, unlike the cannons from the Army School, there would be no possibility of their causing through an unfortunate error damage to life and property within the Braboume cricket stadium.

Two days after Joy Bryer's departure for Delhi, in a meeting with Mr Prabhu to discuss our current arts activities in Western India, I told him how I had tried to lighten her spirits by reporting on his success with the cannons. Regrettably I had then to resort to a phrase currently in use in bureaucratic circles to describe such efforts, "nugatory activity". I had become convinced that the tour was off. Mr Prabhu agreed that the Taj Hotel Group's refusal was a serious blow, but he remained hopeful. Something of Joy Bryer's indomitable spirit reigned in Mr Prabhu, though it manifested itself in an altogether quieter, less ebullient manner. In our five years of working together I never heard him admit that any project, however bizarre or ambitious, could not be undertaken successfully. That this judgement proved so often to be correct owed much to his own genius for getting things done. During our discussion a telex arrived which proved his optimism once again justified: "ECYO tour definitely on. Orchestra staying at Oberoi hotels throughout India."

What happened in Delhi I do not know. Did Joy Bryer have to summon up extraordinary reserves of persuasive power to convince Mr P J Oberoi? Or did that legendary successful magnate combine a flair for the hotel business with an enthusiasm for Brahms and Beethoven? Even Mr Prabhu could not answer these questions. I thought he knew everybody, but he did not know Mr P J Oberoi. However, we spent little time in speculation, glad to be able to turn our minds to other matters, amongst them a major theatrical tour with attendant difficulties about stage requirements.

In the remaining six weeks lead-in time for the ECYO tour we were not much called upon for assistance. Most communications were merely progress reports. The Indian Council for Cultural Relations had agreed to become involved. The European Community ambassador in New Delhi would travel throughout India with the orchestra. The tour would have a preliminary European stage, with concerts in Paris,

Madrid and London, thus bringing home to the youth of Europe the importance of the Jawaharlal Nehru centenary. I was particularly pleased about this. With the slackening of pressure on our services I had found time to press upon the ECYO the idea of including in the orchestra for their tour a talented young Indian violinist, Joe Pinto, occasional leader of the amateur Bombay Chamber Orchestra and full-time clerk with Indian Railways. With concessionary fares Joe had travelled quite a bit around his own county, but never outside it. It is difficult to assess the impact on him of getting a chance to play with the world's greatest youth orchestra in European capitals. When we gave him the news, Joe reacted in his usual quiet and courteous manner. He said he thought he would be able to get the necessary leave of absence from the railway authorities.

One of the few demands for action on our part was to supply the name of a reputable manufacturer of fireworks in Bombay. From a country where every joyous occasion is celebrated with detonations of fireworks of an intensity unrivalled throughout the world we were able to reply promptly. In the particularly hectic rush of arts activities at that time neither Mr Prabhu nor I had queried the significance of our supplying this information. By then we had realised that our modest groundwork tasks were largely done. The tour had taken on its own momentum. Nevertheless, grateful authorities kept us informed of developments. For instance, the internationally-renowned film actor and matinee idol Shashi Kapoor would *emcee* the final concert in the Braboume Cricket stadium. This, like the fireworks, was intriguing. I could not recall ever having seen an MC in action at a symphony concert.

Speculation about the form of the stadium concert tended to overshadow for us in Bombay interest in the other concerts throughout India. However, once the Indian part of the tour got going, colleagues in New Delhi and Calcutta sent us enthusiastic reports of the orchestra, the brilliance of the young players' performance, their excellence off stage as ambassadors for Europe.

We awaited their arrival with a pleasurable anticipation modified somewhat by concern with a last minute flurry of activity by experts in stage construction, lighting and acoustics engaged for the last night, cricket stadium event. Bombay had witnessed plenty of successful pop concerts in such venues, but never a symphony concert. Mr Prabhu and I dropped in at the stadium on our way to the first of the orchestra's Bombay engagements, which was taking place in the Shanmukhananda Hall, in a northern suburb. The stage carpenters seemed to be making a good job of the platform and its shell-like hood, despite being impeded to some extent by the intricate cables of the lighting and acoustic men. I was puzzled to see one cable being led to the rear of the platform.

Mr Prabhu explained. "That's for the fireworks man. Electrical impulses from the orchestra will set off his fireworks at appropriate moments during the 1812 Overture."

"What sort of fireworks?"

He seemed a bit vague about this. "You know, rockets and bangers."

"Bangers?"

"Yes, they've decided to do without my cannons."

This was a sad reward for Mr Prabhu's enterprising efforts in Filmi City. I congratulated myself on not having made a futile and tiring 226 mile round trip to the Army Artillery School at Deolali.

It is commonplace to describe successful theatrical or musical events as *glittering*, but in India the brilliance of golden bangles and gold-bordered saris worn by the women in the audience and the abundance of frangipani garlands decorating the platform alone justify the epithet. The playing of the orchestra that night was no less brilliant. Bombay boasts a large body of eminent and knowledgeable music critics, some appointed by the national press, most self-appointed. All agreed that the playing coaxed from the ECYO by their erstwhile fellow citizen, maestro Zubin Mehta, from 120 players aged between seventeen and twenty-three, coming from thirteen different countries and having only occasional opportunities for playing together, rivalled anything produced by the world's great symphony orchestras.

Later, at the celebratory dinner in the Oberoi Hotel's ballroom, the players were in a boisterously euphoric mood. Greta and I found ourselves dining at a long table mostly occupied by robust young men from the brass section, students or graduates from the Royal Northern College of Music. We thought this a gratifying and distinctively British contribution to the success of this extraordinary orchestra.

However, I particularly wanted to find a certain young man from the string section, Joe Pinto, to check on his experiences travelling and playing with these young Europeans. Disappointingly, he seemed to be missing from the dinner. A young woman travelling as administrative assistant to Joy Bryer gave us disconcerting news. Joe had not been happy on the tour. However, when she went on to amplify this, we realised that it was a mistaken impression arising out of one of those minor but troublesome cultural differences which sometimes bedevil even those who set out with the intention of getting along together with perfect understanding. In the many group photographs, taken in Paris, Madrid, London or wherever, Joe had presented the only unsmiling face. We explained that Indians facing the camera lens do not feel impelled to display the cheerful grins assumed by Westerners for such occasions. Rather they choose, no doubt unconsciously, to emulate the sensible practice followed by our grandfathers and great-grandfathers in photography's earlier days, letting the camera record for posterity the characteristic expression of their faces in repose. When Joe did finally turn up he left us in no doubt, in his usual undemonstrative manner, that the tour had been the great event of his life.

As the dinner ended there were speeches and presentations, greeted by the young musicians, who were collectively on a very considerable high, with those curious whooping noises I had only previously heard from Americans attending political party rallies or candidate-endorsing conventions.

Seated next to Joy Bryer at the top table was Mr P J Oberoi. She, of course, had been the powerhouse of the whole enterprise, but it had been his late and beneficent intervention which had rescued the tour when plans seemed on the point of falling through. A diminutive, though solidly-built man, seated here in his own splendid Bombay hotel, he looked every inch the successful business magnate and sported a large cigar. Fittingly, he received an impressive-looking presentation. I was pleased to see a similar mark of acknowledgement going to Mrs Ratti Mehta, chairman of the Time and Talent Club's Concert Committee. Nobody in India had worked harder for the enterprise in the long lead-in period than Ratti and her committee and I knew that in addition to the presentation there would be a donation to the funds of her club, to help them with their work amongst the country's most deprived rural poor.

On the other side of P J Oberoi, leaning over to engage him in animated conversation, was the stately figure of Zubin Mehta's wife. The maestro himself arrived later, accompanied by several Bombay ladies, some of them declaring themselves to be his aunts. One of these aunts spread the news that the following day was Zubin Mehta's fifty-third birthday.

The party broke up very late. We marvelled at the stamina of the young players, who faced rehearsals in the morning for the tour's final and most ambitious concert. We had had an impressive demonstration of their skills that night in the Shanmukhananda Hall. In the Brabourne Stadium next day, however, their success would depend in part on the professional skills of other experts.

The scene outside the Brabourne Stadium at nightfall on the day of the concert recalled the stadium's palmy days when it had hosted cricket test matches, before its owners, the Cricket Club of India, fell out with the Indian test cricket authorities. In a game of bluff and counter-bluff over ticket allocations the Club lost and suffered the indignity of seeing Bombay test matches transferred to a stadium newly-constructed for the purpose a few hundred yards up the road. The crowd now assembling there was perhaps the largest since that fateful transference some years earlier. Only two of the many turnstiles around the vast circular stadium had been opened and the resultant queues were prodigious. A totally unexpected feature of these was that no provision seemed to have been made for VVIPs (very, very important persons), a category not normally subjected to the inconvenience of queuing in India.

There they stood, being jostled on the pavement alongside ordinary citizens. I even noticed amidst the throng one or two of those captains of commerce and industry who had been approached in vain for sponsorship funds, though their fate was probably the result of even-handedness rather than vindictiveness.

The stands inside the stadium were rapidly filling up with a crowd much more boisterous than the usual concert-going audience and there was lively animation also amongst those taking the seats on the playing field between the stands and the platform. Nearest the platform were rows of sofas.

These were for VIPs, few of whom had yet turned up, but Mr Prabhu stood there, beside the Sheriff of Bombay, eying the crowds in the stands - a crowd mostly made up of youngsters, many with bottles of limca, thums-up or other soft drinks. We hoped they had not come expecting the kind of loud and feverish *tamasha* provided by western style pop concerts in the city. However, we agreed that, whatever musical tastes they may have developed, they certainly represented a section of the youth of India that the ECYO's tour was intended to pay tribute to. And they, along with their elders, had turned up in their thousands. It was, perhaps, the biggest ever live audience for western classical music in India.

No doubt the youngsters would have found some aspects of the setting for that evening's concert familiar. The platform was lavishly decorated and lighted. Banks of amplifiers faced the audience in the stands furthest from the source of the music. I was glad to see that the electrical cabling, so much in evidence on our visit the day before, had for the most part been decently hidden away under matting. In the shadows to one side but rather behind the concert platform I could dimly make out a lorry.

Articles were being unloaded from this and handed to a figure kneeling on the ground.

"That's the fireworks man," Mr Prabhu explained.

He seemed to bear no resentment that this technician's devices were to supply the effects originally planned to be provided by the cannons he had secured. In fact, Mr Prabhu added a tribute: "An excellent man. Knows his stuff."

Those of us who had attended the previous night's concert had come to this one expecting to be impressed. Our expectations were more than fulfilled. In a tour as well publicised as this it was remarkable how many surprises had been kept in reserve. For a start, the 120 young musicians who had previously appeared in public in conventional dark suits and dresses now filed on to the platform in peach and white outfits, the men in kurta pyjamas, the women in shalwar khamees complete with flowing dapatas.

We soon learned what the function of the MC was. Shashi Kapoor had experience in this role in concerts of quite different music put on for Indian expatriate audiences in the Gulf. Now he rallied the packed audience in the Brabourne Stadium in a mixture of Hindi and English, holding the crowd in pin-drop silence interrupted by outbursts of applause. The loudest of these greeted the introduction of the conductor, "Bombay's own son", Zubin Mehta. The two men embraced. They were substantial men and I was reminded of the occasion years later seeing the same conductor embraced by Pavarotti during a notable concert in the Roman Forum. That event was watched on TV by millions, but for me the Bombay evening remains the more memorable.

Once again the young players' performance was superb, both in their traditional repertoire and in their accompaniment of Ravi Shankar in his concerto for sitar. During the interval I discussed this work with a group of music critics. Most held that it was not truly a concerto in the western music sense, since it consisted largely of alternating passages of the orchestra's playing alone and the soloist and his tabla man doing likewise. However, all were unstinting in their praise for Ravi Shankar's actual performance and also enthusiastic about the extraordinary dexterity and power of the tabla playing.

While we were discussing details of composition and performance I noticed a disturbance at the side of the platform in the direction of the fireworks man's lorry. A group of shadowy figures seemed to be engaged in some sort of scuffle. The group then split into two and a number of youths emerged into the lighted area beside us. Laughing and shouting they ran across the cricket outfield beyond the rows of chairs. They were pursued by policemen wielding lathis, but the pursuit was half-hearted and the youths clambered into the stands at the back of the audience and were soon lost amongst the crowds there. I assumed they were gate-crashers. Mr Prabhu walked across to investigate. When he returned he looked serious.

"They've kicked through the wiring connecting the fireworks to the concert platform," he reported.

I had forgotten the significance of this arrangement. Mr Prabhu reminded me.

"It was supposed to set off the fireworks at appropriate moments during the 1812 Overture."

"Good Lord! Do you think they broke it deliberately?"

"No. They were just larking about."

"But this is serious. What's going to happen?"

"They've sent a car to bring the electrician to the ground."

"Do you think he'll get here in time?" The second half of the concert was just about to begin.

"I don't think so."

We looked at each other in silence. On many occasions in the past, in the worst of circumstances, when best laid plans seemed on the point of going horrible awry, Mr Prabhu had endeared himself to me by coming up with something reassuring. He did not fail me this time.

"The fireworks man knows western music well. Even without electrical impulses, he'll set the fireworks off all right." He added an aptly-chosen cliche: "He'll play it by ear."

With this we took our seats again, in a lively anticipation tempered only slightly by apprehension.

When a well-loved but often-played piece like Tchaikovsky's 1812 appears in a programme its inclusion is often justified by the consideration that there are bound to be some in the audience who are hearing it for the first time. I think that was certainly true on this occasion. For many of the youngsters at the back the concert may itself have been their first encounter with any kind of western classical music. Not that they had not proved a model audience. Loud in their response to Shashi Kapoor's good-humoured remarks linking the programme items, enthusiastic in their applause at the end of each piece, they had throughout given hushed attention during the playing of the music itself.

So they did now, as the final offering, the 1812, began. In fact, Zubin Mehta took the players so softly through the opening bars of the Russian hymn that I felt the audience straining forward so as not to miss any of the orchestra's sensitive playing. As the music from the middle and lower strings began to swell in the allegro, however, an alarming thing happened. An explosive burst resounded from somewhere just behind the platform - certainly not a cannon burst type of explosion, but undoubtedly of rifle shot volume. The leader jerked his head up to look at the conductor. Zubin Mehta maintained a steady baton. Obviously this veteran was not to be put off his beat by an isolated error of this kind. Almost immediately, however, two further explosions rent the air, this time very authentically representing cannon fire, and at close range. Had the fireworks man's ear for western music deserted him? This was very much too early in the piece for the triumphal cannonade that should accompany its climax. Did I detect a slight increase in tempo at this point, as though the orchestra felt the need to reach the piece's climax before the fireworks man could commit further anticipatory errors? Even as I was pondering this possibility a full salvo of cannon fire was heard. Zubin Mehta had yet to bring the orchestra up to mezzoforte volume and the sound of the music was being entirely swamped. To their credit the young players kept their heads. A young woman violinist whose dapata had become displaced coolly flicked it back over her shoulder and continued bowing rhythmically. The cannon fire now burst out in an almost uninterrupted series of salvos. In terms of volume the Artillery School's authentic weapons could not have surpassed the fireworks man's "bangers". We had yet to reach the passage actually scored for cannon accompaniment when he issued a further challenge, releasing flights of rockets to burst massively, multichromatically and very loudly over the Dinshaw Vachha road end of the ground. The youngsters in the stands, so admirably attentive to the music hitherto, could not now suppress cries of admiration at this pyrotechnic display.

By the time the orchestra finally reached the spectacular musical climax of the piece Zubin Mehta had rallied his players to full fortississimo force. They performed valiantly, the young man with the tubular bell hammer in the percussion meriting a special mention. The cathedral chime effect he produced could be heard, only marginally but nevertheless clearly, above the exploding bangers and rockets. However, in what had developed into something of a battle between orchestra and fireworks man, victory had gone to the latter. His performance had been remarkable in terms of both volume and tempo. Towards the end he was letting off his devices in clusters in almost uninterrupted succession. No mere electrical impulse device could have equalled this.

From a purist point of view, looking at it simply as a musical event, the performance had perhaps been less than perfect. However, considered as a total theatrical experience it had much to be commended. The audience showed its concurrence with this view by unrestrained applause, giving the musicians ovations which had them brought to their feet time and again by the conductor. It was perhaps modesty which inhibited the fireworks man's appearing to share this applause. In any case, he remained in the backstage shadows. He might even have gone home.

Performers in India are always generous with encores. After the unprecedented excitement of the 1812, Zubin Mehta wisely chose as his encore a piece which, while being tuneful and lively, was comparatively undramatic, calculated to calm the audience down before the stadium would have to be cleared.

The orchestra began the Tritsch-Tratsch Polka in a somewhat low-key fashion, handling its two-four time rhythm with delicacy. Gradually the conductor increased volume and tempo. We then realised that the fireworks man had not gone home. He released a batch of rockets he must have held in reserve. Miraculously the fireworks man seemed to be keeping to the musical rhythm. Was he not sending off his devices in two-four time? Perhaps after a temporary lack of control occasioned by the furore of the 1812 his musical ear had recovered its acuteness. In any case, by the time music and fireworks came to an abrupt halt at the end of the polka they had reached a state of near perfect harmony.

The fireworks man, however, had the last word. As Zubin Mehta again brought the orchestra to its feet to acknowledge the applause he set off a huge framework of multi-coloured fireworks which proclaimed in twenty foot high letters: Happy Birthday Maestro.

Mumbai 1987

The Price of Paint

It was an Englishman working for the United Nations who first put me in touch with Ghazi al-Khaldi. Not that he knew Ghazi. He simply passed on to me an invitation he had for the vernissage of an exhibition of the painter's work.

I had arrived in Syria from Libya the week before. Syrian friends in Benghazi had urged me: "Don't judge the Arab world by what you see here." Their own country, I gathered, would be much more sophisticated. First impressions of Damascus were not favourable. The newer part of the city had a drab and neglected air and a high proportion of its population wore khaki. Some of these, I later learnt, were sixth form schoolboys and schoolgirls, required to be on the alert to defend the republic, then on the eve of celebrating its twenty-first anniversary of independence. Others were regular or conscripted soldiers and these carried rifles with bayonets fixed.

They were much in evidence as I made my way towards the broad avenue beside the Barada River where the National Day parade was to be held. In fact, a detachment barred our approach through a narrow passageway leading down to the river. Through their ranks I could just see a group of village people who had infiltrated through an adjoining street. At first, as armed soldiers approached them, they smiled and threw up their hands in conciliatory gestures. The soldiers, implacable, advanced and, when it became apparent that the villagers were not going to give way, reversed their hold on their rifles. Seizing them by the barrels, they set about the villagers with the butt ends, sending them scrambling in a panic towards more troops on the other side of the parade avenue. I lost my desire to see the parade and walked back to the New Omayyad Hotel.

Ghazi's exhibition opened the following day. The invitation card gave the venue as the Modem Art Gallery and an address in King Fouad I street. I double-checked the card on arrival at a narrow door of what appeared to be an office building. However, after ascending several flights of a wooden staircase I came to what was undoubtedly an art gallery, though the building was anything but modem. It was well lighted and the paintings, in oils, though not in an aggressively modem style, were boldly coloured, figurative and entirely free of the constrictions which confine traditional Islamic art to calligraphic and geometrical designs.

The gallery consisted of three interconnected rooms. My eye was immediately drawn to a large painting on the far wall of the farthest of these. Almost completely filling the canvas, three girls formed a compact circle. All three were on the floor, two seated looking down on the third who lay curved in such a way that her head and feet completed the circle. They seemed to be village girls, strongly built and wearing simple gowns. Unlike those in the surrounding canvases, the colours here were subdued, pastel shades. The overall impression was of a quiet solidity, broad application of planes of colour giving the figures a sculpted appearance reminiscent of the figures in the frescoes of Diego Rivera. The catalogue gave the title *The Friends*. I had come only to view, but I had a strong and immediate desire to own the painting. However, the gallery director explained that the painting was already spoken for.

"All the rest are still for sale, but this one, I'm truly sorry, is already sold."

He led me around the walls, talking about the artist, letting me down as gently as possible. I think he sensed how deeply I was disappointed. He left me looking at a number of drawings to attend to other guests. Amongst the drawings, executed with broad strokes in brush and ink, was a pair of studies of a nude model, apparently dashed off in haste in a life class. I was drawn to the urgent vitality of these works and decided to buy them as some consolation for failing to obtain the painting. As I bent to examine the date (1962, two years earlier), I became aware of a small man with dark, penetrating eyes observing me.

"You like these drawings?" he asked.

"Yes, I do. The artist has a very assured touch."

He smiled. "And you like *The Friends*, I think."

"Yes, very much. How did you know?"

"The director told me. I drew this model in Cairo, at art school. *The Friends* are Syrian girls."

"So, you're the artist."

He smiled again, this time more broadly, and offered his hand. As I shook it he placed his other hand on mine, clasping it and looking at me intently. Then he drew me by the hand along the wall of paintings. In front of several he paused and pointed, saying nothing, simply offering an invitation to view. I felt called upon to make some comment on each, doing so hesitantly, ignorant of the terminology used to discuss works of art. I feared the artist would find my comments banal.

He stopped me in front of a large canvas of a female nude reclining on a divan with a red coverlet. I said something about the light from the top left striking the woman's features.

Ghazi nodded. "My wife," he said.

On the card beside it the title in Arabic was also rendered in French and English: *Femme nue couchee* and *Naked.* I had noticed several other infelicities in the English versions of titles in the catalogue.

"I leave you now," said the artist. "Please give me your card. Perhaps I shall have another exhibition."

"Good. Please invite me."

"Not many people understand my paintings."

I felt uneasy, in a false position. Had he assumed from my naive comments that I was knowledgeable about art? As the only Westerner in the gallery perhaps I was expected to have a deeper understanding of the works on display than people brought up in a different cultural tradition. While I wanted to dispel any false impression I might have given, I also wanted to offer some token of friendship, of gratitude for his kindness.

"For your next exhibition, I might be able to help with the English version of the catalogue."

Immediately I regretted saying what might be taken as an unkind criticism of the catalogue in my hand. However, Ghazi again took my hand in both of his and nodded enthusiastically.

"Yes. Please, yes. Very good. Very good."

We parted then and I left the gallery with the director's promise that the drawings of the Cairo model would be sent to me when the exhibition closed. By London standards their price was extremely reasonable.

****

Two weeks later the gallery director phoned me at work. "I have the drawings ready for you. Shall I send them to your office?"

I had moved from the hotel to a flat, just acquired and furnitureless apart from a truckle bed lent me by the owner. The prospect of having something of my own to hang on the wall was very gratifying and I asked him to send the drawings to the flat.

"Would you still like to have the painting of *The Friends*?"

"Of course, but I understood it had been sold."

"Ghazi spoke to the man who bought it. He's a pilot with Syrian Arab Airlines. Ghazi told him you are an Englishman and a guest in our country and that we should let you have it. The pilot agreed. Shall I send it to you?"

So I came to possess a painting which has hung on the walls of the dozen flats or houses we have lived in over the years. Many guests have admired it, though I doubt any have taken the same pleasure from it as I have. A part of that pleasure springs from recalling the happy chance by which it came to me, one of those rare examples of undeserved good fortune.

When the package of drawings and paintings arrived I had a further surprise. In addition to the framed nudes there was an unframed pen and ink sketch of a group of dwellings whose brick and carved wooden facades seemed to suggest rooms cut into a mountain ascending behind them. In contrast to the other drawings, these were finished in some detail. At the bottom, written in both arabic and roman script, was the word *Ma'aloula*. A double mystery here. Why had I acquired this additional, wholly delightful, work of art? and where or what was Ma'aloula? Arab friends at work assured me it was common practice in the city for a purchaser to be presented with a gift to accompany his purchases (and indeed this was shortly afterwards confirmed when a wardrobe I bought arrived with an occasional table inside). Ma'aloula, I was told, was a village in the hills not far from Damascus. Nobody suggested it had any particular significance.

However, when, after some trouble locating Ghazi's studio, I went there to thank him for his kindness in reclaiming *The Friends* for me and for the additional drawing, he told me: "Ma'aloula is a very special place. You must go there. I have a young friend who works in your institute. He will take you there."

The young friend introduced himself as Burahan. He was a student at the university and also had some ill-defined duties at our institute. He was vague about his studies and seemed to be in no hurry to complete his degree, but he did have some interesting information about Ma'aloula. Yes, the people there did live in dwellings cut right into the side of a mountain and had done so since biblical times. Most interesting, however, was the fact that the villagers were the sole surviving people in the world who spoke Aramaic, the language of Christ. I realised that Ghazi was right in insisting that I should go there.

It was some weeks later before our trip could be arranged. By this time my family had arrived to join me in Syria and I had collected my car from the port of Beirut, so it was we who took Burahan to Ma'aloula, rather than the other way round. He told us his girlfriend would join us but, when we called for him, he was accompanied by Ghazi's sister, Nawal, and we concluded that his girlfriend's parents had raised objections to her joining us.

A journey of about an hour took us to the foot of a mountain. Here we had to leave the car and approach the village on foot through a narrow defile, a steep and winding ascent, so narrow that in parts the rocks overhung us, almost blotting out the sky. The day was hot and our children little more than toddlers, so we had to make frequent stops. At one point, as we were resting, we heard voices of people approaching from above and two teenage boys appeared round a bend. They were conversing in low tones. The language was not Arabic.

"Listen carefully," I said to Greta. "This is the language of Christ."

A man appeared following the boys around the bend He was bearded and wearing a maroon turban. I recognised him as an official of one of the United Nations agencies in Damascus, an Indian national.

"It's a long, difficult climb," he told us, "but worth the effort."

We talked for a time and then he continued downhill, saying he had to catch up with his sons. We surmised the boys had been talking Punjabi, though it was a language none of us was familiar with.

We had not heard Aramaic. Nor did we later and this was something of a disappointment, but the rest of our day was not. We eventually emerged into a level space with one modem concrete building. The Syrian national flag flew above it and Burahan identified it as the village school. Nobody was in sight. Above it the mountain continued upwards with the neat facades of rows of dwellings, close packed and ascending in terraced ranks. The highly decorative outer walls and carved wooden balconies were exactly as depicted by Ghazi in his drawing.

A further steep climb brought us to a small Byzantine church on the mountain summit. A Greek Orthodox priest hurried towards us from an adjoining house. He seemed delighted to see us, nodding his tall-hatted head and smiling broadly. He agreed to show us around his church, one door of which, he assured us, dated from the fourth century. He also led us to a nearby cave in which there were on the walls carved symbols of fish, a secret symbol used by Christians when their religion had still been a clandestine, underground movement in these parts. Perched on a ledge beyond the cave we were encouraged to discern the priest's "Sphinx". With some difficulty we identified from the jagged outline of a mountain across the valley a section which might, with a little imagination, be identified as resembling the broken-nosed profile of the statue at Giza. Our vantage point was somewhat precarious and the priest felt constrained to put his arm around Nawal's waist and pull her closely to his side. Finally, our host took us to his house, where his wife served us excellent turkish coffee. He sent us on our way with jars of honey he had made from his own hives.

****

In the following months we lost touch with Ghazi. He was not part of that community of expatriates and young Syrian men we met regularly on summer afternoons at the open-air Andalous swimming pool and again in the evenings in each other's flats. In fact, it was not until the Winter Art Exhibition of 1966 that we saw any further examples of his work. The exhibition was held in the Army Museum. With its graphic displays devoted to the horrors of bloodthirsty conflicts, both ancient and modem (including a section recalling the rout of the army of Syrian citoyens by General Gouraud's French colonial army at Khan Maysalun in 1920), this was an unlikely setting for modern art. However, the hall set aside for the exhibition, with its whitewashed walls, showed off the paintings to good advantage. They were mostly 'modernistic', several clearly influenced by French nineteenth century works. I had no difficulty distinguishing Ghazi's contribution. On a large canvas a nude, strongly-proportioned woman squatted on the ground with chin resting on one hand, calmly confronting a bull pawing at the earth, its head lowered threateningly towards her. She looked more than a match for this creature. Appropriately strong shades of red had been used for the woman. This time I had no difficulty in purchasing the work and in due course it took its place on a wall in our garden flat, facing *The Friends* across the room.

Visitors recognised in the subject of this later work a reference to *Europa and the Bull*, but when I asked Ghazi about this he said he had not heard of the Greek legend. "The woman is the Earth Mother. Nothing can defeat her."

When I asked him why the Army Museum had been chosen for the exhibition, he shrugged his shoulders and said: "There is no good gallery for our art in Damascus. Nobody goes to the Modern Art Gallery any more. Of course, my paintings have nothing to do with war, but what can one do?"

Despite Ghazi's implied aversion to military matters, shared, I suspect, by the young Damascenes who disported themselves at the Andalous pool, rumours of war spread rapidly through the city in the Spring of the following year. General Jadid, whose group had seized power in a *coup d'état*, kept a tight hold on the country, an Israeli spy was convicted and hanged publicly in al-Merjeh Square and sixth form boys and girls who had previously worn khaki on Fridays now went to school in army uniform every day.

Matters came to a head at the beginning of June with the demand by the Egyptian Government that UN peacekeeping troops should be withdrawn from Sharm-el-Sheikh. Since this headland commanded entrance to the Straits of Tiran, through which Israel received its supplies of oil by sea, it seemed unlikely that that country would react other than strongly if the UN agreed to the Egyptian demand. I consulted the political officer at the British Embassy. He was confident that the matter would blow over, as had so many similar crises in recent years, that the UN would hold firm in standing between the Israelis and the Arab nations.

However, in this he was confounded. The UN troops withdrew and the politically aware awaited Israeli action, realising that without oil supplies their war machine would grind to a halt within a week. I managed to obtain tickets for Greta and our two young children to fly from Beirut to London the following Monday. Early that morning, on their way over the Lebanese mountains their taxi driver informed them that war had broken out, translating from Damascus radio: "Arab-Israeli boom-boom." He raised both hands from the wheel to illustrate the action by clashing his fists together. This was June 6th, the start of the Six-Day War of 1967.

Early that Monday morning news spread of a disaster for the Arab cause: the Egyptian airforce had been destroyed, its planes strafed by Israeli aircraft before they were able to take off from their Cairo airbase. In Damascus offices staff sat glued to their radios. Some offices, included my own, virtually closed down. Early in the afternoon there was the sound of aircraft overhead and a series of explosions could be heard across the city. Neighbours in the flats above mine joined me in my semi-basement flat in search of protection. An intrepid French neighbour later reported that he had seen from an upstairs balcony Mirage planes of the Israeli airforce sweeping low over the Syrian airforce base outside the city, making three bombing sorties and a fourth sweep, presumably to inspect the damage they had inflicted. The BBC World Service reported that the Syrian airforce had suffered the same fate as that of their Egyptian allies. My neighbours feared that, denuded of air cover, we had become vulnerable to further attacks.

In the evening I went to our local mini-market to stock up with essential food supplies. As I left the shop and got into my car a boy shouted something incomprehensible to me. After driving a few yards I realised that my headlights were not working. On inspection I discovered that they had been painted navy blue, presumably by the boy outside the shop as a service to help me observe the blackout regulations that I later learnt the Government had imposed. I scraped a small hole in the centre of the paintwork on each headlight and drove home gingerly through the unlighted streets. I realised I should have rewarded the boy with the paintbrush, but did not fancy returning through the darkness.

The following day, Tuesday, was another day of avid radio listening. Our sources were Damascus radio, Kol Israel, the Israeli service from Tel Aviv, and the BBC World Service. In the afternoon Damascus radio made an announcement (shortly afterwards denied by the British government) that the British Royal Airforce had helped the Israelis in their destructive raids over Cairo and Damascus and that, as a result, British personnel were to be expelled from Syria. We were to leave the country within forty-eight hours. I started the difficult task of deciding which essential items I should pack into my car to carry with me over the border into Turkey and which I should leave behind, entrusted to the care of the Swiss Legation.

Amongst the possessions which had to be left (with which I had some apprehension that I would never be reunited), two items I particularly regretted leaving, the paintings by Ghazi Khaldi. Neither the car boot nor the back seat could accommodate such large canvases.

The third day of the war was taken up with planning our evacuation. The British ambassador proposed driving north in his official car with his compatriots following in a motorcade. His Turkish destination struck me as a better prospect than following the Military Attaché's motorcade on the shorter route to Lebanon. While we were involved in plans for leaving, a group of Syrian youths, determined to defend their country, were strenuously digging trenches in the grass partition that separated the dual carriageway of Abu Roumana, the pleasant, tree-lined boulevard that ran through the centre of our residential district of Damascus. I was moved by the way they set about their task, but at the same time it struck me as being pathetic in its inadequacy as a response to the onslaught of what was proving to be a determined and powerful enemy.

In the evening I went to say goodbye to friends. Youssef was watching television at home. The screen showed a detachment of soldiers in troop carriers, clapping their hands and chanting in unison, in what I took to be a triumphal manner. I asked Youssef what the commentary was saying.

"These are Arab troops advancing into Israel," he said.

The impression given was totally at odds with reports on the progress of the war that I had heard earlier from the BBC World Service.

I found Ghazi at work in his studio. The small canvas on an easel in front of him showed a sketchy figure standing before a landscape, also sketched, rather than painted in. One or two similar paintings were on the floor, propped against the wall. There was a spareness about them, quite out of keeping with the bold use of paint I had seen in his earlier works. To emphasise the contrast, one of these works hung alone on the wall. It had been marked nfs at his Modern Art Gallery exhibition four years earlier and depicted a woman standing barefoot alone on a lino floor in a kitchen, sparsely furnished with a chair and table, a bucket on the floor behind her. Her manner of standing, foursquare on the ground, her crossed arms, her head leaning slightly to one side and, above all, the expression on her face, with its strong features and large, soulful eyes, conveyed a deep sadness and resignation to a lot she could not have chosen. The sturdy proportions of this figure again reminded me of the work of Diego Rivera.

When I told Ghazi this, pointing to the earlier work, he smiled and said: "When I was a student, he was my hero." After a pause he added: "I think he is still my hero."

"But why have you changed?" I asked him. "Why aren't you putting on the paint with those sweeping, bold strokes?"

He looked at the palette and the brush in his hand and laid them on a paint-spattered bench beside him before replying: "You know, the price of paint ....." He shrugged his shoulders in a Gallic manner that reminded me of his reaction when asked why he and his fellow artists were displaying their work in the Army Museum. "What can one do?"

I was saddened to leave Ghazi in the diminished state his words conveyed, especially since the following day our deadline ran out and I would have to quit Syria completely along with my compatriots. I had a strong conviction that I would not see Damascus or Ghazi again.

****

My prediction proved wrong, though it was ten years before I was posted back to the Middle East and a further year before I had reason to drive up to Damascus. I was there to attend a conference organised by a British colleague.

On the first day of the conference I asked his Syrian assistant: "Do you know if there's an artist called Ghazi Khaldi still working in Damascus?"

"Mr Khaldi," he said, "oh yes, Mr Khaldi is President of the Syndicate of Syrian Artists. His office is in Fardous Street. It's above the National Gallery of Modern Art."

It seemed that Ghazi had been wonderfully translated and appointed to a post of authority by a Government which liked to keep a tight rein on most human activities, but which had not in earlier days, as far as I was aware, concerned itself with the fine arts.

The conference had a busy schedule, packed into three days, but on the second day I skipped the working lunch and made my way to Fardous Street. Immediately before turning into the street I had to walk three parts of the way round Sa'ahat Youssef al-Azmeh Square. I remembered this as a roundabout with a paved area in the middle. I saw now that boards some nine feet high had been erected around this central area, forming a sort of cyclorama. This cyclorama was vividly painted with scenes showing men in army uniform committing atrocities on cowering civilians, mostly women and children. The soldiers were identified as Israelis by shoulder flashes bearing the star of David. No paintings by war artists on show, for example, at the Imperial War Museum in London can in any way match the starkness of the horror displayed in these scenes. Bayonets figured in most of them and victims' blood flowed copiously. It was impossible to avoid a feeling of revulsion, which was no doubt the emotion that the paintings were intended to arouse.

I had no trouble finding the National Gallery of Modem Art, though it had not existed at the time I lived in the city. I seemed to remember a large bookshop, mostly stocked with works in French, had occupied the building previously. The lower floor was a continuous, brightly-lit space, containing an exhibition of paintings by an artist whose name I did not recognise. A young woman handed me a catalogue with titles of work in Arabic and English. I noticed there were no idiosyncrasies in the English titles.

I asked the young woman: "Does Mr Khaldi have an office here?"

"Yes, he's upstairs. Would you like to go up and see him."

Upstairs consisted of another single continuous space, totally unfurnished save for a chair and a large desk at the far end from the staircase door. Seated at the desk was Ghazi Khaldi, somewhat plumper and balder than when we had last met and dressed as I had never seen him before, in a suit, but unmistakably Ghazi. He looked up as I entered. A look of astonishment was quickly replaced by a broad, beaming smile. He got up and hurried round the desk to greet me, grasping my hand in both of his, as he had done at our first meeting fourteen years earlier.

"My old friend," he said, "you bought my painting, *The*

Friends."

"Yes, and the *Earth Mother*."

"Of course. And I think you have one of my drawings of Ma'aloula."

"Yes and two studies of a model from your student days in Cairo."

"Where have you been all this time. What happened to the paintings?"

"The paintings and the drawings are all hanging on the walls of our flat in Beirut."

I skated rapidly over events since our hurried withdrawal from Syria in 1967, because I was keen to learn something about his own change of fortunes. He seemed reluctant to talk about himself, though I did learn that his son, a little fellow when we parted, was then a student in Moscow studying art.

"Are you still painting," I asked him.

"Oh, yes. Tell me, did you come round Sa'ahat Youssef al-Asmeh Square on the way here? You did? Well, those paintings round the square, they're all mine." He inclined his head to one side and looked at me, smiling.

I must have made some reply, but I remember being almost totally lost for words. In these paintings, which I had seen as crude works of propaganda, I had recognised nothing from Ghazi's hand. Perhaps, if I had not been so strongly repelled, I might have paused long enough to identify some clue to their origin, but I had no wish to go back to test this hypothesis. What saddened me most was that I could see from Ghazi's expression that he was immensely proud of an achievement I found it impossible to admire or even to like.

Of course, I was glad that he had achieved a position of eminence in his country and with it at least a measure of prosperity. Furthermore, being commissioned to paint a large work of public art, displayed in the centre of his country's capital city, indicated a measure of widespread recognition of his work. I remembered that we had once spoken of Diego Rivera, Ghazi's "hero". Possibly Ghazi saw his work as in some way analogous to Rivera's huge frescoes in Mexico City of peasants, oppressed, downtrodden but heroically marching forward to a better future. Undoubtedly Syrian people had suffered bitter hardships and oppression throughout long periods in their history, but it would take more than the paint on plasterboard in Sa'ahat Youssef al-Azmeh Square to win worldwide attention to their cause.

Ghazi urged me most insistently to go home with him, to greet his wife and have lunch. I very much wanted to accept. These leisurely Arab luncheons with many dishes of subtly flavoured food were very much to my liking, but the timetable of the conference was unremitting and I had to hurry away. On parting he handed me a postcard with a reproduction of one of his recent small-scale paintings. It was entitled *An Arab child with his drawings*. For the most part it was very much in Ghazi's old style - the child, a boy of about ten, stands forlornly, his large, soulful eyes, his bearing suggestive of sadness and resignation. Obviously, the painter had lost nothing of his old, sensitive touch. Hanging on a wall behind the boy, however, in the "child's drawings" are horrible reminders of war. In one an armed man holds aloft a sub-machine gun, his features ugly with a pig's snout and eyes and mouth formed by asterisks. An armoured car advances behind him. On the back the postcard says: "With the Compliments of the Youth and Students Delegation of the Syrian Arab Republic."

Ghazi escorted me to the door of his domain, to the street, to say goodbye in the traditionally courteous Arab manner. I congratulated him on his attainments, his official position, his public recognition. I was genuinely pleased for him, for the changes in his life he had effected since our previous goodbye, but I felt that he had paid a price for them.

Damascus 1964 and 1978

Barkis is Willing

When ordered to "proceed on secondment to Hyderabad, Deccan" I can't say I was surprised. Forty years ago the practice of secondment was much more common than it is today. It had something to do with staff development or with bringing mutual benefit to companies and organisations involved or simply with extending aid to an organisation in need of expertise. Nowadays, of course, staff are expected to develop their own skills before offering themselves for short-term contract to employers prepared to buy in those skills, often through head hunters.

The term itself seems to have been borrowed from the French *en second*, meaning either in the second rank or in the second place. I like to think of my secondment in the latter, geographical sense. Certainly Hyderabad was not a place where my organisation had an established base, though it is a city of considerable importance in India and the organisation I joined there of importance to the Government of India, which had established it in interesting circumstances.

Some ten years after India's independence a question was raised in the *Lokh Sabha* (the lower house of parliament) as to what the Minister of Education was going to do about what the questioner perceived to be falling standards in English used throughout the country. The Minister called for the assistance of a British officer whose proffered solution was the establishment of a research and training institution to monitor standards and ensure their maintenance. Surprisingly his report did not suffer the fate of so many documents worldwide of being shelved, but was promptly acted upon. Asked where the institution should be sited he suggested the city nearest to the geographical heart of the country and when asked to become its first director he readily agreed, recruiting three British assistant professors of English to join him to get the place off the ground. It was up and running within the year. When I arrived ten years later these stalwarts had departed, being replaced by Indian experts on their return from postgraduate courses overseas.

I got a warm welcome from these professors and from a Welsh

colleague who had arrived two years before me. One professor only, Dr K from Madras, seemed to hold himself aloof. Discussions in the staff room were animated, revolving around recently formulated theories of language acquisition. Occasionally outside critics alleged that the institution had become too enmeshed in theory, at the expense of fulfilling the practical side of its remit. If there was something in this, it probably stemmed from the seductive teachings of Noam Chomsky, at the time much in vogue at the American and British universities where we had studied.

Apart from our research we concentrated largely upon running courses at the institution for University teachers, but every now and then the call would come in for staff to go off to outside centres and organisations to investigate language problems and propose solutions. I recall that the Government of the southern state of Kerala and the State Bank of India, successor to the venerable Imperial Bank of India, became two of our clients. In answer to such calls I sometimes found myself temporarily seconded, a sort of secondment at second hand from my lengthier secondment.

The University Grants Committee in New Delhi decided to run summer schools for lecturers in English, starting with those at twelve of the country's universities. I was designated Director of Studies for the course at the university at Indore, a town in the previously-named Central Provinces (now Madhya Pradesh) with a population then of half a million. I flew there for a preliminary planning meeting. After a long stopover at Bombay airport I boarded a small Anson aircraft which landed on an airstrip beside which a large group of country people had gathered to witness our arrival. They dispersed as we disembarked and I learnt later that as ours was the only incoming flight of the day it was considered as a noteworthy event by people living nearby. A driver met me and took me directly to Indore University to meet the Vice Chancellor. He greeted me enthusiastically. After ordering me a welcome drink of juice from freshly-crushed sugar cane he told me how important it was for his institution that the standard of English teaching should be raised. He had reserved a room for me in the city's best hotel, where I was to be met by Dr Moses, Dean of the Faculty of Arts, whom he had appointed to be in charge of the staffing and day to day running of the summer school.

At the Oxford Hotel I was met at the door by a gentleman in a white suit who turned out to be not the Dean, but the hotel's proprietor. He hoped I would be very happy at his hotel which, he explained, he had given its name because he himself was "an Oxford man". He was driven away and I did not see him again, either then or during my later, longer stay. Dr Moses threw doubt on the proprietor's association with Oxford, hinting that his claim to be an Oxford man was perhaps no better founded than that of the hero of *The Great Gatsby*.

This I learnt some time later. My first conversation with the Dean, who was awaiting me in the lobby, quickly revealed to me that he did not share his Vice-Chancellor's enthusiasm for the forthcoming summer school. He seemed to resent having the responsibility for it thrust upon him and had obviously made no arrangements apart from allocating a few rooms for our use in his Faculty's building. My main concern was with staffing. No, the Dean did not have any ideas as to where this might come from. He thought the Vice-Chancellor had ordered forty lecturers from constituent colleges to attend. I couldn't see myself keeping them all occupied for six weeks single-handedly. When I pointed this out, Dr Moses reluctantly suggested that he might be able to put me in touch with one possible academic assistant.

"There is one man who may be able to help - Professor Hookens. He's been teaching for some years now and he speaks excellent English."

Even without knowing his cv, given the imminence of the virtually unstaffed course's commencement Professor Hookens seemed like a straw to be grasped. His title was impressive and his name intrigued me.

"Is he an Indian professor?"

"Oh yes, though there may have been someone Dutch in his ancestry. He'll be on vacation now, but I could try to get him to come and see you tomorrow."

The following morning was spent in inspecting premises and

the one or two pieces of equipment (an overhead projector and a tape recorder) set aside for the course. On returning to the hotel to collect my bag for the flight home we found Professor Hookens awaiting us. He was a tall man in his forties, very slim with receding hair and a slight stoop suggestive of academic pursuits. Obviously he was a member of what is known as the Anglo-Indian community, though this includes people of partly Portuguese or Dutch as well as of British descent. Frequently to be found in public services, the railways, police or posts and telegraphs, Anglo-Indians were less likely to be found in academic circles.

Professor Hookens greeted me with a bony handshake and an extensive smile. Already advised by the Dean of the purpose of our meeting, he expressed himself willing to help on the course in whichever way he could. I had time only to outline briefly the teaching requirements as I saw them, running through the language skills which would have to be included. When I came to 'writing skills', Professor Hookens' face lit up.

"That's for me," he said. "I'm a writer myself. I've submitted several articles to the newspapers."

I told him: "If you could take responsibility for showing how our lecturers can help their students develop writing skills, that would be a great contribution, Professor."

"Call me Bill," he said. "I won't let you down."

There was something of the "Barkis is willing" attitude conveyed by his words and body language which sent me back to Hyderabad reassured, though I still had a short-order task of finding two other teachers for our team. Fortunately, in response to urgent requests offers of assistance came promptly. A colleague in London said they knew of an experienced man in Ethiopia who would be glad to spend the summer in India with us and a call from a colleague in Bombay highly recommended a young Parsee woman who, having family in Indore, was prepared to work with us in that city.

The expert from Ethiopia, Charles, arrived early and spent three days with me in Hyderabad helping me draw up a course syllabus. He had long experience in the field in many countries and was truly an expert. An earlier acquaintance with India was when he had served there in World War Two. We tried to make his short stay with us as pleasant as possible, showing him the Saracenic-Gothic architecture of the law courts and the legislative assembly buildings, the Moghul fort impressively crowning Golconda, the brilliant blossom of the flame-of-the-forest trees and the vivid green of the paddy running down the valley from the Banjara Hills towards the city.

This much-travelled man's response was invariably: "It's just the same in Ethiopia."

Desperately seeking to impress, Greta told him: "We had an earthquake here last year."

Charles replied: "We are *expecting* one in Ethiopia."

Greta was not entirely sorry to see him set off with me to Indore. However, despite his air of world-weary indifference to the delights of our surroundings, he proved to be an excellent and conscientious teacher and a stalwart support on the course.

On arrival at the Oxford Hotel in Indore we met up with our other two colleagues and held a planning meeting over dinner in preparation for the course's beginning the next day. The Parsee woman lecturer from Bombay, Miss Freny, was very short, barely five foot, had hair severely combed back from her forehead and wore a simple, cream-coloured sari. I wondered how her slight frame would stand up to the rigours of the heavy teaching load I had divided between the four of us over six weeks of what promised to be an extremely hot summer, but that very evening she gave us evidence of that resilience which would adequately sustain her. During our meal a troublesome wasp flew amongst us, ignoring our attempts to divert it with our napkins.

Suddenly Freny clapped her hand to the side of her neck, declaring: "I've been stung."

We were all concern. Bill Hookens leapt to his feet and ran around to her afflicted side, asking: "Shall I suck the sting out for you."

"Certainly not. Please remain calm." She set an excellent

example of calmness herself, dabbing at the wound with a small handkerchief which she had dipped in a glass of water and continuing her discourse on what she proposed to do about her allotted subject - the development of reading skills. She then left for her relatives' residence and Bill made his way home on his bicycle.

In the morning Charles and I arrived early in a motor rickshaw, or 'phut-phut', to meet them at the Arts Faculty. As soon as the forty course participants had assembled, Dr Moses led a short opening ceremony (garlands for the four of us and a brass lamp lighted) and left the building. Teaching began in earnest and the course seemed to be going well, with full attendance daily. Our only disappointment was in the number of schoolchildren turning up for teaching practice, that part of the course where we demonstrated our skills and participants took it in turns to emulate them, observed by their peers. The UGC had emphasised that this should be a key ingredient of all their summer courses, insisting that classes taught must be of the right size. By this they meant "of a large size", with seventy-plus students, typical of classes in Indian universities. Most of us recognised this as a heavy demand where a subject demanded the development of skills, rather than simply the imparting of knowledge through traditional lectures. Foreign advisers visiting were invariably asked by Indian teachers: "How would you set about teaching large classes?" I recall only one convincing answer, from a woman who said: "I wouldn't."

In an ideal world this was sensible, but in the Indian university world, financed by the UGC, practice teaching had to have large classes. Dr Moses had managed to recruit only seven students, willing boys and girls who had just completed sixth form schooling and looked to start at university in the coming term. If the UGC got to hear of this it would not look good for the Indore team. We urged our seven students to bring their friends, but numbers did not increase.

On the fourth day Charles took me aside and said quietly: "Can we talk about Bill Hookens? The lecturers don't like his classes. Some of them are saying they're not helpful."

Neither of us had sat in on any of Bill's classes, but I thought I'd better do so. At that moment he was addressing the lecturers, speaking without notes, but not eliciting any responses (or 'feedback', in the jargon of the day) from them. His talk was more like a lecture than the participatory process Charles and I favoured, but not a lecture in the formal sense, lacking the clear progression such a term implies. The participants sat in polite silence, but I thought I detected an underlying restlessness.

As I took my place quietly at the back of the class I heard Bill explain: "Winston Churchill was a great writer. Whenever he was short of money he used to go to the States and write articles to sell." He followed this up with several similar observations. Whereas these might constitute excellent motivation for students about to embark on a creative writing course, I could see why the lecturers might not see them as helpful teaching tips.

I went back to Charles and asked him to sit in on one of Bill's classes the following day. He reported back on a talk which had followed the pattern of the one I had heard. We both agreed that Bill seemed unfamiliar with modern teaching methods and it would be advisable to replace him. By great good fortune one of the participants was a Mr Dikshit, older than his fellows, a very experienced lecturer who had contributed perceptively to all our classes. When classes ended for the day I proposed to him that he should switch from participant to teacher. He readily agreed and was thus translated overnight. This choice none of us had any reason to regret.

What I did regret, however, was having to ask Bill Hookens, our willing Barkis, the first to volunteer his services, to stand down. This would require delicate handling. Charles had a suggestion. With the non-appearance, since the opening ceremony, of Dr Moses, practical arrangements for the course were virtually non-existent. Our teaching team were obliged to lug furniture into position for varying purposes - lectures, discussions, teaching practice sessions - and the key-holder for the locked cupboard containing audio-visual aids could not be found.

"Why not," proposed Charles, "put Bill in charge of arrangements for classrooms and so on."

I feared this might be seen as a demotion, but I decided to approach Bill with the proposal that he be appointed the course's 'Director of Administration', a post that needed to be created, even though it would necessitate his giving up his writing skills responsibilities. To my relief Bill readily acceded to this change; in fact he seemed positively to welcome it and I wondered whether he was beginning to exhaust his fund of advice to would-be writers. He took on the duties of his new post enthusiastically. Whatever the class requirement, desks and chairs were ready in the right configuration, placed there under Bill's supervision by two peons who had previously kept themselves well out of sight. Our simple provision of audio-visual equipment also made its appearance and was set up as needed. In addition to this, Bill effected another major improvement.

I had mentioned to him that having only seven students for teaching practice sessions could prove an embarrassment for us if the UGC got to hear of it. His proposal was that students should be given breakfast. I was dubious about this, thinking that students would surely have breakfast at home before setting out for class.

"You will see," said Bill.

And indeed we did see, that he was quite right. How Bill managed to spread the news around town I don't know, but at the beginning of the second week, class sizes began to rise rapidly, students arriving to be greeted by the aroma from large containers of freshly-cooked rice, dal and vegetables carried in by outside caterers. This fare was ladled on to banana leaves at trestle tables where students sat on benches in the hour before our regular sessions began. We had soon reached our requisite complement of seventy students and even had to turn volunteers away owing to lack of space. The aroma persisted throughout the mornings, long after the banana leaves had been thrown away, providing a pleasant, homely atmosphere for our activities.

Bill's administrative improvements provided the setting for a course which I came to see was going well, which was particularly gratifying in view of the hurried, ad hoc manner in which it had been set up. In our scratch team we seemed to complement each other successfully. Mr Dikshit, with his long experience and knowledge of local conditions, immediately won the respect of those who had hitherto been his fellow participants. He enlivened his instruction with a fund of anecdotes of linguistic confusions he had encountered during his teaching career and bursts of laughter were often to be heard from his classes. Miss Freny's mien was more serious, but she also commanded respect. Men older and larger than this diminutive woman sat up and took notice as soon as she entered the classroom and made copious notes as she castigated the prevailing practice of having students read aloud (and expressionlessly) around the class, a practice she labelled "barking at print". Charles and I both benefited from the advantage of coming from distant lands, conferring upon us the status of experts. I was glad to note, however, that my colleague avoided the error of contending that they did things better in Ethiopia, a contention which would have been received in polite silence but would not have gone down well.

The satisfactory improvement in our working conditions was not reflected, for me, in conditions beyond the classrooms. The Oxford Hotel may well have been, as the Vice-Chancellor had described it, "the best hotel in town", but it was distinctly lacking in creature comforts. Bedrooms were bleak, furnished with an iron-frame bed, a large walnut-stained wardrobe and an upright chair. There were no public rooms to relax in, so any meetings had to take place in the dining room. Here simple fare was served thrice daily. Being so far from home I was particularly anxious to avoid falling ill with internal complaints, which in those years I was prone to. For breakfast, therefore, I invariably ordered my egg boiled, which I thought to be a safe option. My cautiousness was a disappointment to our waiter. He regularly rehearsed the full range of egg possibilities - fried, poached, scrambled - but I politely repeated: "Boiled, please." One morning, as soon as I topped my egg I realised it was bad - very bad.

I called the waiter over and told him: "This egg is bad."

He replied: "No. It's a very good egg."

When at my invitation he smelt it, he recoiled, saying reproachfully: "Oh sahib, you should have had it fried."

But it was not the service of the waiter, who was constantly solicitous, but the general ambience of the hotel Charles and I found trying. I ventured into the road, some distance from the town, in search of diversion, but was soon driven back by the fierceness of the heat to my room, which, like the rest of the hotel, had no air conditioning. Foolishly, unlike Charles, I had brought little reading material and the only shop selling books in English in Indore sold only religious (Christian) tracts. We took to remaining in the hotel until eleven-thirty at night, by which time the heat had abated somewhat, and then slowly walking the two miles into town.

Not a lot was happening there at that hour. A few families sat on doorsteps quietly conversing beside their sleeping children. We found one impressive old building whose courtyard we entered unimpeded through an arched gateway. This was the Anna Chattra, an almshouse. A large number of women sat in rows on the ground in silence. From time to time food was brought out from the building for those in the front rows, who ate and departed, making way for those seated behind them. In the narrow streets outside a few late-night traders stood by their barrows, which were lighted by naphtha lamps. Cows wandered between the stalls, attempting to help themselves to the wares, but the stallholders moved them on by the simple expedient of twisting their tails. The flanks of these large-eyed creature gleamed in the naphtha flares and I was moved by the beauty of this and by the cows' gently swaying, unhurried movements. One night I remarked on this and how I could understand the sacred place they held amongst Hindus to an American visitor who had arrived to run a summer school in Chemistry. He was from Texas and did not share my romantic view.

"The only beautiful cows I've ever seen were being herded on a ranch," he said and we understood his interest in them was as potential T-bone steaks.

On the way back to the hotel we regularly stopped to sit on a bench outside a wayside stall and drink Thums-up, the Indian equivalent of coca-cola. For me these simple pleasures were little compensation for the convivial social life I had left behind in the twin cities of Hyderabad and Secunderabad where we regularly entertained each other in large buffet dinner parties at home, ending our meals with envelopes of pan wrapped in thin sheets of beaten silver, prepared, in more traditional households, by the lady of the house in front of her guests in a process involving a variety of tiny silver implements. These were elegant occasions and I did miss them. No doubt circles of friends in Indore enjoyed similar evenings but, during my time there, I didn't really expect an entrée into such circles. (Later a Swiss businessman in Secunderabad who had been many years in India told me I should have let him know of my visit and he would have arranged for me an introduction to the one-time ruling house of Indore, the Holkars, who would certainly have invited me to join them on *shikar* - hunting expeditions. As my only experience with a firearm was on an army firing range, I doubted I would have proved a competent member of their party.)

Occasionally, however, we did entertain a guest, as Bill Hookens came back to the hotel with us after classes and we had a beer together. He regaled us with episodes from his life, the most interesting we found to be those which took place in Liverpool, where he had spent some years. He had worked there as a schoolmaster, but for some reason he had been unable to pursue a teaching career and had obtained a post as a bus conductor with the municipal transport authority. Both in the school and on the buses he had made a determined attempt to follow the mores of his colleagues. While travelling by bus to his school he had been impressed by the friendliness of the conductors, particularly by that of the conductor on his regular route who addressed his passengers as "Love", regardless of their sex. He followed this practice for some time, until an inspector queried his greeting male passengers in this way. Bill explained that he had taken his lead from the conductor on route fourteen.

The inspector retorted: "But he's daft as a brush."

Taking this to heart and amending his ways, Bill nevertheless treasured the inspector's striking simile and had managed to work it into one of the articles he had submitted to a local newspaper. Although he made light of such experiences and even had us laughing together about them, we gradually came to realise that there was in Bill's life an underlying sadness, a sense of potential unfulfilled, of not having found a niche, of being bogged down in an alien world. This may partly have been due to his belonging to the Anglo-Indian community, which had enjoyed certain privileges during the British Raj. Since independence a number of its members had left for Britain or Australia. What he would most have liked to do was to have returned to England and taken up some position suitable to his talents. Failing that, he felt he might do better in the nation's capital, New Delhi.

In private Charles and I considered whether there was any way in which we could help Bill find satisfying employment. We gathered that he found little job satisfaction in his present post as a college lecturer. Our problem was that we had no idea where his strengths lay. We did know that his *inclination* was to become a full-time writer. The articles he told us he had submitted to newspapers may or may not have actually been printed but, in any case, the one rupee or so per column inch which local English-language papers paid contributors would have provided an income somewhat less than the extremely modest salary of a college lecturer, certainly not sufficient to support Bill, his wife and daughter. His wife was English and a return to her home country might have improved his prospects, but then again we knew only that his spells with the local education and transport authorities there had, for reasons unknown, been short lived. Neither of us could think of potentially useful contacts in either Liverpool or New Delhi. We discussed "How can we help Bill?" several times without coming to a conclusion.

We were pleased, however, when he readily accepted our invitation to come with his wife to join us for dinner at the Oxford Hotel. Margaret was rather younger than her husband and, like him, was tall and slim. She dressed in Western clothes. On first meeting she shook hands tentatively and withdrew to stand slightly behind Bill, but when we sat down she gradually relaxed and answered our questions about herself and their family freely. Their three-year-old daughter they had left at home with her ayah. Soon they would need to find a school for her. In Indore, she said, her life had been quite good since she came there two years earlier but when the subject turned to how she had met Bill in Liverpool she talked about the city in such a way that we realised that absent landmarks and familiar activities - the Birkenhead ferry, the Walker Gallery, concert-going at the Philharmonic Hall and taking coffee in Kardomah cafes - were much in her mind.

That evening a trio of Goan musicians played in the dining room, a regular Thursday event. After dinner, in response to Bill's request, they played a number with something approaching a quick-step beat and Bill led Margaret round the dance floor. Further requests gave Charles and me the chance to take Bill's place. Then we drank some beer and again took turns on the floor with the only available partner. There were no other diners. Suddenly the image of the four of us trying to follow strict dance tempo in a large and anything but festive room struck me as funny. I was reminded of M Hulot's gallant and solitary attempt to inject some festivity into the ball at his seaside hotel in *M Hulot's Holiday*. I was Margaret's partner of the moment, but I began laughing so much that I had to leave the floor and sit down. She collapsed in a chair beside me, also laughing uncontrollably and Bill took up the laughter, with even less restraint, slapping the table. Charles alone remained immune, glancing questioningly from one laughing face to another. His bemused expression brought us all to the brink of hysteria. Eventually he allowed himself a slight smile, but this conveyed to us only his unspoken thought: "I don't get it." One more round of beer and our guests left. It was the most convivial, perhaps the only truly convivial, evening of my time in Indore.

If time hung heavily for us in the evenings, its passing was even more oppressively slow on Sundays, when there were no course activities. One Sunday morning I slowly read through a supplement of that day's local newspaper. It was devoted to the life of Subhas Chandra Bose, the anniversary of whose mysterious death, or assumed death, in a vanished aeroplane this was. The article recounted his break with Congress and their non-violent *satyagraha* campaign, his raising of an Indian National Army for an armed revolt against the British Raj, his wartime missions to the Nazi leaders in Berlin and to the Japanese High Command to obtain funds in order to pay and equip this force. It was a lengthy article and I was reading it slowly so as to while away the hours when Bill arrived in a phut-phut and invited me to his house for lunch. Charles was also invited, but he had discovered a Presbyterian church in town and had gone there to worship. I was delighted to give up my newspaper.

Our journey took us some miles out of town to where the main road north came to a junction with a tarmac strip which didn't seem to be heading anywhere. However, a mile along it our taxi turned into the compound of a bungalow standing alone, without visible neighbours. In the front yard a massive pipal tree grew out of the compacted earth. This tree encroached right up to the verandah and front windows of the bungalow and continued to spread itself above it. Beside its trunk was a wooden bench from which Margaret rose to greet us before going into the bungalow for refreshments. She came out with a tray of *nimbu pani* (lime and water) followed by her three-year-old daughter, who was carrying a miniature brush made of twigs. She went to a corner of the compound and began sweeping the dusty surface methodically.

Bill told her: "Come and greet our guest. He has a present for you." I held up a rag doll we had stopped for me to buy from a roadside stall on the way from town, but she continued sweeping with her back turned towards us.

The *nimbu pani* was refreshing, but the air under the pipal tree was stifling. Bill and Margaret talked about contrasting ways of life in Liverpool and Indore. I felt so uncomfortable in the extreme heat that I found even the slight effort required to contribute occasional remarks to the conversation taxing. While we were talking I became aware that the daughter, Anita, had come up behind my canvas chair and was leaning forward to gaze up at me. I turned to smile at her, but she frowned and quickly turned away and set to work with her brush with renewed vigour. Since she was much nearer to us than before, her efforts soon had us covered in a fine layer of dust. Bill told her to desist, but she ignored him.

Her mother said: "Don't interrupt her while she's happily occupied."

The child's attitude suggested grim determination rather than happiness.

What with the dust and the heat, I was not sorry when Margaret called us into the bungalow for lunch. She had prepared an English meal, with beef she had obtained from a Christian butcher. It was a wonderful change from the monotonous fare of the hotel. Anita refused to join us at table and threw herself face down on a rattan settee. When Margaret placed the rag doll I had bought beside her she looked at it fiercely, before seizing it and dashing it down on to the floor. Bill tried pleading with her to come to the table, but her mother said to let her be and she soon fell asleep. Judging by her extremely slight frame she seemed like a girl who ate very little, but it might have been the extreme heat which had robbed her of her appetite on this occasion.

Bill had told me that he lived in government quarters. Looking round the combined sitting and dining room which we had entered directly from the verandah and which had several rooms opening from it, I wondered whether the government had also supplied the furniture. This was almost as comfortless as the pieces in our rooms at the Oxford, consisting of a few rattan chairs, some iron-legged occasional tables with plastic tops, the dining table and six plain wooden dining chairs. Against one wall a small refrigerator chuntered noisily, falling silent from time to time before restarting its laboured, stuttering rhythm.

After lunch we sat in the rattan chairs. Bill insisted I occupied the largest of these, which he described as a 'planter's' chair. He showed me how to extend the arms so that I could I put one leg up on either side on them, assuring me that this is how the British in India relaxed in their clubs. I felt ridiculous spreadeagled in this fashion and feared that a combination of the heat, a feeling of repletion from the meal and the dark shadows in the room cast by the all-enveloping pipal tree would cause me to fall asleep in my recumbent posture. I need not have worried on this score. Anita awoke suddenly and began to scream. When Margaret attempted to comfort her, she relapsed into sobs, standing beside her mother's chair and burying her face in her lap. She agreed to accept the rag doll, holding it in one hand by its ankles, its head resting on the floor.

From time to time she raised her head and shouted at me: *"Nikal jao!"* (Go away), making a pushing gesture with her free hand. I assumed she had learnt Hindi from her ayah as I never heard her parents speak anything but English. Margaret told me that this ayah also cooked for the family, cleaned the house and did the everyday shopping from the fruit and vegetable market. It occurred to me that she and Bill could probably not have afforded these services in Liverpool, but I wondered to what extent they compensated for the facilities available in that city which Margaret had talked about when we had first met. Although she smiled bravely while excusing the behaviour of her daughter, I detected an underlying sadness in her bearing. She had laughed aloud only once, after our dancing at the hotel, but there had been a touch of hysteria in our laughter on that occasion and it now occurred to me that in her case it might have been an indicator of tension brought about by finding herself living in these isolated circumstances so far from her original home.

Concern for my hostess, the antagonism of her daughter, the extreme heat, rather worse indoors than in the yard, gave me a feeling of such discomfort, despite my occupying the bungalow's one easy chair, that I felt compelled to find a reason for taking my leave, without being discourteous. (It was a very early hour for breaking up an Indian lunch party.) I recalled that whenever Bill had left the hotel after having an evening drink with us he had done so with an expressed resolution to go home and mark a set of MA exam papers. If asked the next day he would say that he had yet to make a start with this task. I now asked him when they were due back at the University and how far he had got with them.

"They're due in tomorrow, but I haven't started on them yet."

"Aren't you worried about it?"

"Not really. My brother will help me."

"I didn't know your brother was an academic."

"He isn't. He works for the Posts and Telegraphs."

This was puzzling. I didn't want to enquire into it, but I

thought the imminence of his deadline gave me a pretext for leaving. My resolution was strengthened by renewed cries of *"Nikal jao"* from Anita, who had stopped sobbing and reinforced her command by boldly advancing on me and striking me on my upraised leg with the wooden head of the rag doll as she swung it from its ankles.

Margaret did not try to dissuade me. She had for some time been showing signs of tiredness and the burden of the household, which seemed to lie mainly on her, could not have been a light one. An impediment occurred, though, when I asked Bill if he would call me a taxi. There was no telephone in the house. At intervals taxis did pass along the main road, but these intervals were very irregular in the middle of the afternoon, when the rickshaw wallahs were taking their nap. I remembered seeing many of them curled up on the passenger seats of their phut-phuts as we returned to the University after lunch during the week.

Undeterred, I said I would walk to the junction and take my chances, managing to persuade Bill that he need not accompany me. If Anita was pleased to see me go, she showed no sign of it, stubbornly turning her back when invited to: "Say goodbye to our guest." I set out to walk the mile up the road at a steady pace, slowing down when the effect of the heat hit me.

A solitary thorn tree marked the junction with the main road. I stood beneath it looking alternately in both directions of the main road. Occasionally I also glanced back down the narrow road I had walked up, though I thought it unlikely that help would come from there. It was tedious, standing there and I lifted a rock by the roadside and placed it under the thorn tree to sit on. This tree offered little shade and the sun's heat did not abate as the afternoon wore on. After an hour I saw a vehicle emerging from the side road, but as it drew nearer I saw it was Bill on his bicycle. He seemed unsurprised to see me still there and drew up a stone to sit beside me. I saw no point in his sharing my vigil and persuaded him to go home, assuring him of my confidence (feigned) in a taxi's arriving shortly. It was more than half an hour later that I saw a phut-phut approaching on the main road from the town. When I stopped it and told the driver of my destination he regretted that he could not take me there as he was on his way home. In desperation I offered him what I calculated to be twice the normal fare and he reluctantly turned his vehicle around and took me back to the hotel.

The following Sunday I decided to stay in the hotel all day. In the afternoon I was awakened from a nap by the sound of activity in the corridor. Looking out I saw a familiar figure entering a room at the end of the corridor through a door, next to my own door, which I had never seen opened before. I had assumed that beyond it lay part of the hotel's accommodation not intended for guests. The room now revealed contained well-stuffed armchairs and a gratifyingly cool breeze wafted from it, suggestive of comforts way beyond those of our own rooms, each inadequately cooled by a single, slowly rotating ceiling fan. The newly arrived guest was Dev Anand, a matinee idol of Bollywood films in those days. He was accompanied by several large men, one of them carrying an impressive piece of camera equipment. The door closed behind them, cutting off this vision of a hitherto unimagined domain.

More excitement awaited me downstairs. The hotel garden had been covered by a massive *shamianah*, beneath whose shade a throng of brightly-dressed people of all ages, perhaps two or three hundred strong, circulated between trestle tables full of sweetmeats and soft drinks. The women wore saris predominantly red, many with gold borders, and jangled bangles from their wrists. The men were less resplendent in kurta pyjamas but a small knot of young fellows sported scarlet puggrees round their heads. I realised these were the bridegroom's supporters relaxing at this reception following a wedding. Children were chasing each other around the legs of the standing guests or in and out under the trestle tables. Suddenly the actors in this animated scene froze and stood stock still, as in a tableau, facing the hotel steps. Descending slowly came the matinee idol. With measured tread he passed through the reception, the guests falling back on either side to clear a path for him. He said nothing, but continually turned his head from left to right, smiling benignly. It was like a royal progression. Perhaps a *godlike* progression would be an apter description. Although I had never seen Dev Anand on screen, I knew that this handsome idol must have played gods in Hindi film epics and it was rumoured that many cinemagoers did not distinguish between such screen heroes and the gods themselves. Having regained the hotel entrance, Dev Anand paused at the top of the steps and raised his hand in a goodbye gesture, a sort of blessing for the mortal guests at the wedding, before disappearing inside. By breakfast time the movie star and his retinue had left the hotel, off on location according to the manager. The room, or suite of rooms, he had occupied disappeared as completely as he did.

This turned out to be my last Sunday in Indore. I received a message calling me back to Hyderabad on urgent business and promising to send a stand-in for the last two weeks of the course. Dr Moses turned up to conduct a goodbye ceremony - another garland, several speeches and lots of fond farewells - and said that the two of us would meet again at a round-up conference in New Delhi in the Autumn.

****

Shortly before the two-day conference of summer course directors and directors of studies to review the twelve summer courses, I received a message saying that Dr Moses would not attend, but would be sending Bill Hookens in his stead. I was pleased by this. I thought it might be a final, if slender chance to "do something for Bill", the project Charles and I had discussed fruitlessly several times in Indore. We had come to the conclusion that administration was probably his forte and in New Delhi I decided I would find an opportunity to praise his capability in this field to UGC officials and perhaps to introduce him to colleagues in my parent body's largish office there.

Delegates were accommodated at the India International Centre in the capital and several of us met up there on the eve of the conference. I failed to find Bill, but left a message at reception for him to contact me on his arrival. He didn't and nor did he show up at breakfast. Even when we took our seats at the conference Bill was still missing. However, as the chairman, appointed by the UGC, rose to deliver a formal welcome, Bill hastened into the hall, did a full circle of the horseshoe formation of tables before spotting me and squeezed into his designated chair on my left. The chairman paused as

I and the delegate on the other side of Bill scraped our chairs back and forth to accommodate him.

"I hope now we are all present and ready to get down to business," said the chairman. He looked severely at the Indore representatives.

The session began with opening statements from the twelve directors, outlining their courses' programmes, numbers of participants and so on. The Director from Ahmedabad was up first. He gave an impressive presentation - a successful course, highly qualified teaching team, enthusiastic participating lecturers motivating mustard keen students in teaching practice sessions.

He concluded: "The new methods introduced in the course are even now being implemented in constituent colleges throughout Ahmedabad University."

Then it was our turn. As Bill got to his feet his appearance struck me as odd. I had never seen him formally dressed, but when on duty his attire could be described as "smart casual". Now, however, he looked distinctly dishevelled, his shirt and khaki slacks crumpled and it was obvious he had not shaved that day. He stood out starkly amongst delegates in well pressed safari suits or in white khadi tunics. I had been hoping that time would allow us to have a word about the opening statement. Since he had been there throughout the course's full six weeks he was better able than I to make it. I had just a slight misgiving that Bill might inadvertently reveal that in our first week we had managed to drum up only a very small number of guinea pig students. However, I took reassurance in recalling how during that week I had impressed upon Bill several times that it would not look good for us if the UGC got wind of this breach of their ruling that practice classes should be of "the right size".

Bill began well, with high praise for the efforts of Charles, Miss Freny, Mr Dikshit and myself and the keenness of the course participants, but then went on: "In our first week we had just seven students in our practice classes."

At this point the chairman looked sharply in our direction before writing a note on the pad in front of him. Bill, who was speaking without notes, continued, unperturbed: "So we decided that every student should be given a hearty breakfast."

This caused a ripple of amusement around the horseshoe tables and Bill seemed to be carrying his audience with him as he ended, somewhat abruptly, with a tribute to Dr Moses, the director I remembered as being conspicuous by his absence during most of our course and who regretted, Bill now told us, being unable to be with us today.

The chairman responded only briefly to our presentation, saying: "I cannot emphasise too strongly the UGC requirement that all teaching practice sessions must reflect the actual situation in our university classrooms."

A further ten presentations followed. In most of them there were jocose references to "hearty breakfasts in Indore". I feared our achievements were being overshadowed by recrimination and ridicule. Relief came from an unexpected quarter. Before breaking for coffee the chairman called upon the guest of honour, a distinguished educationist from London, to say a few words.

"I was impressed to hear," he said, "that in one centre a bold experiment was made to introduce micro-teaching."

He was talking about us. It seems that, quite unknown to us in India, the latest thing in educational circles in Europe was to teach *small* groups in order better to examme the learning processes taking place in the individual student's mind.

At lunch break Bill embraced me warmly. After enquiring about Margaret and Anita (both fine, he assured me), I told him I had missed him at the India International Centre, though I had ascertained that he had been booked in there.

"I was lucky," he said. "I managed to get a place to sleep in the Central Station waiting room."

While this was undoubtedly better than sleeping on a railway station platform, as I had seen so many travellers do, it struck me as a strange preference over the comforts of the India International Centre. Bill didn't elaborate and I didn't pursue the matter as it suddenly struck me that his choice had perhaps been made for reasons of economy. Our subsistence allowance was adequate, but Bill may have felt the need to make some savings out of this. In any case it was clear that we would not be at the same venue overnight, but I was glad to see that one of my Delhi colleagues had sent all delegates an invitation for a buffet dinner that evening at his bungalow. When the afternoon session broke up I told Bill I looked forward to seeing him there.

"I hope I'll be able to make it," he said and set off on his own on foot towards the centre of the city.

For some reason he was unable to make it and when we assembled for the second, and final, day of the conference, Bill's chair remained unoccupied. There was no message to say why he was absent and nobody queried why I had become Indore's sole delegate. Some legacy of his presence lingered as I fielded further references to the hearty breakfasts.

Although their introduction had been a master stroke, this was not very much for me to build on in an attempt to further Bill's prospects as a potential administrator in some institution offering more scope for his talents than his present post in Indore. My plan to bring him together with UGC officials or some of my colleagues at meetings outside the formal sessions was thwarted by his abrupt disappearance from the scene. Why this occurred I can only speculate. Possibly his attempt to find a coveted place in the Central Station waiting room for a second night had failed and he had found refuge in an overnight sleeper train travelling south to take him home to Indore.

I never heard from Bill again. When on holiday in the Nilgiri Hills I sent him a picture postcard saying I'd like to hear his news, but he did not reply. I like to think of him and Margaret taking coffee in a Kardomah cafe in Liverpool to celebrate his receiving a hefty cheque from a British journal for one of his articles, but this image is overshadowed by one of the two of them in their isolated bungalow darkened by the encroaching pipal tree, she smiling bravely at their unhappy child and he postponing some irksome college duty.

Hyderabad, Indore, New Delhi 1969

The Kamikaze Pilot

Shortly after I arrived to reopen our centre in Beirut, the early stages of the Lebanese Civil War having come to a precarious stand-off between the warring parties, the office manager, one of three staff fortunate enough to be retained in a caretaker role, told me my predecessor's personal assistant wanted to see me. I had already reengaged all his erstwhile colleagues who had been unable to find alternative employment - an almost impossible quest in the prevailing political climate - although I had little idea how I was going to fill their pay packets. I knew that our London headquarters would not react favourably to my humanitarian gesture, once they got to hear of it. And now another ex-member of staff was at the door, in a supplicatory role, I assumed.

When she was shown into my office I sat up sharply. She was undoubtedly the most smartly turned-out potential PA who ever presented herself for employment. But I had been wrong in thinking she was appearing as a supplicant. Nearly everything she told me suggested the opposite. She explained that she had not come forward to greet me as soon as I had arrived as she knew there would be others in greater need of reemployment than herself. She was fortunate enough to be supported by a husband who had a good post as an airline pilot. Furthermore, she was Lebanese by marriage only, Turkish by birth, and I would probably want to think of the plight of the natives of the country first. Furthermore, her husband bore the name of the family who led one of the two most militant Christian militias, though he was only distantly related to their leader. This might prove an embarrassment for a foreign mission whose neutrality in the simmering conflict was essential.

As she continued through this list of disclaimers to her prospect of reoccupying her former post, the more firmly I became convinced that I should sign her on immediately. Her frankness appealed to me greatly. In the event, she agreed to start the following Monday and we had a wonderful working relationship for almost three years, until she resigned over a baffling (to me) misunderstanding between us.

While not exactly a workaholic, Meyrich insisted on keeping busy and, in consequence, my days became well occupied. On one occasion, after a resumption of the civil war and on a morning when violence across the city prevented me from keeping to my planned schedule for the day, she staggered into my office with a pile of manilla files, which she balanced precariously on the corner of my desk.

"I've been reading the Operations Handbook," she said. "All files have to be weeded every three years. These seem to have been overlooked."

The top file was dated 1943 and contained a handwritten memo from the Deputy Director to the Director of the Centre at that time.

Headed "Thoughts occurring in the small hours of the morning", it read: "It seems to me it would be a good idea if we set up a programme for the teaching of the English language, engaging well-qualified instructors. Not only would this be a useful thing in itself, we could charge for classes and raise funds for our other activities."

This thirty-four year old yellowing scrap of paper was obviously long overdue for destruction, but I cherished it as a document confirming the cyclical nature of history. Weeks earlier, moved by the same thoughts as the long-gone Deputy Director, though occurring in daylight hours, I had taken moves to set up an English teaching programme in the Centre and already two young Cambridge graduates were at work on the ground floor in space converted to classrooms. It was intended that their efforts would not only provide revenue for "our other activities" but also contribute to the staff's pay packets. So the 1943 memo was retained as an historic document, something for the archives, but Meyrich persuaded me to discard a huge pile of material, even though I had found much of it interesting reading.

This no nonsense approach to office procedures was reflected in my PA's outspokenness. I had been accustomed in the Middle East to verbal exchanges that allowed time for skirting around a subject before coming to the nub of it, a nuanced approach that required a careful choice of words throughout.

Meyrich had spent some time in the States, where her father had been the Turkish military attaché, and had perhaps acquired her forthrightness in that country.

She took it upon herself to warn me: "You have to be careful of the mad people."

"Who are they?"

"There's madman number one, madman number two, mad*woman* number one and madwoman number two."

"But in what *sense* are they mad? And how can they affect me?"

"I hope they won't affect you. They demand interviews, but I shall try to keep them at bay. However, they're very insistent and I might eventually have to let them see you."

She would not elaborate further, apparently on the grounds of 'sufficient unto the day ...'

A week later, Meyrich announced: "Good news! Madman number two and madwoman number two have left the country."

It seems these two had joined the exodus of those seeking refuge overseas from the Civil War. This of course left the two awarded the number one slots. I wondered whether they had achieved this status in the same ruthless manner as mafioso labelled public enemy number one in America or whether they had simply been the first of their kind to appear at our Centre. Weeks passed without their reappearing and I felt secure enough to put them out of my mind. It proved to be a false sense of security. I learnt that although they had not been allowed to appear in my presence, this was solely because Meyrich had been holding them at bay.

One morning she told me: "Madwoman number one is in my office again. I don't think I can fob her off any longer. Will you *please* see her."

"Well, yes, but what does she want?"

She put in front of me a piece of paper on which she had written: "Madame J - opera singer."

When she returned to lead Madame J in I was impressed. This

visitor, a woman approaching forty, I estimated, was tall with a large embonpoint but small waisted, formally dressed in a linen suit and pillbox hat in matching lime green. She walked in a stately manner. I rose to greet her and when we were seated she addressed me in a voice that impressed me even more than her appearance. She spoke in fluent, correct English with a slight trace of a French accent, in silvery tones with an underlying timbre suggestive of a deeper resonance she could employ if some operatic role called for it. She told me that she felt the time had come for her to make appearances in Europe. There were only two houses in which she wished to perform - La Scala in Milan and, this is where she needed my assistance, the Royal Opera House in Covent Garden. There were two roles in her repertoire, Amina in *La Sonnambula* and Lucia in *Lucia di Lammermoor*. The latter she intended for Covent Garden.

I was familiar with neither work, but I had a feeling that at some point Lucia was called upon to sing an aria betraying madness. As for La Sonnambula, was not sleepwalking, as in Lady Macbeth's case, for example, also sometimes an indication of a measure of derangement? Until that moment I had dismissed from my mind Meyrich's appellation for Madame J, thinking it must have been a misunderstanding or a term jokingly coined by one of my British predecessors, probably a non-opera-lover. In fact, I had begun to think that it would be a wonderful thing for her country if this Lebanese woman should suddenly take Covent Garden by storm. Hitherto only Farouz was known internationally and her repertoire was popular Arabic song, sometimes with a Western flavour. Madame J's preferred roles - in fact the *only* roles she declared herself willing to perform - now aroused misgivings and I decided I had better introduce a note of caution.

"I'm not sure *Lucia di Lammermoor* is in the Covent Garden repertoire at present."

Madame J was not disconcerted. "It is bound to be. The story is by a Scottish writer." She smiled at me, indulgently.

She spoke as one who had come not as a petitioner but as an artiste who was simply giving me an opportunity to further the cause of high art, of fulfilling the role which she knew to be my function. When I tried to find out something about her background and experience in other operatic parts she dismissed my questions as irrelevant.

"These roles are my forte. I am a dramatic soprano. Also coloratura."

Her air of quiet assurance at this point persuaded me that I should agree to act as intermediary, while not committing myself. I simply wrote to the administrators of Covent Garden that Madame J, a dramatic soprano, also coloratura, wished to sing at their opera house. I received a prompt reply which said that, the next time she was in London, she should present herself at the House's Long Bar to arrange an audition. The letter ended by saying that in response to earlier approaches from my office Madame J had twice been issued such an invitation, but had appeared on neither occasion. We heard nothing more from her during my years in Beirut except that she rang Meyrich to say how grateful she was that I had acted on her behalf. I often wondered whether this was a case where the operatic world had been denied the chance to acclaim an outstanding talent or simply an example of a singer whose confidence in her abilities was illusory. Although I knew of cases where the full, rounded beauty of a singer's voice had emerged only when she had reached a certain maturity, say in her thirties, I knew of no-one who at Madame J's age had made her debut as a fully fledged diva on the world's stage coming, as it were, from nowhere. It may be that her amour-propre had been satisfied by the gesture I had made. Still, I should like to have heard her sing.

Although my encounter with Madame J had left me immersed in unresolved conjectures, a meeting which followed shortly with her male opposite number promised a much more straightforward resolution. Heartened perhaps by the apparent determination of the singer's case, Meyrich, finding the importunity of madman number one no longer resistible, ventured to try my mettle again. This time she gave me a little more background information before ushering the visitor into my office. It appeared that Sheikh S had been denied the award of a degree by a Beirut university, a degree which he insisted he was fully entitled to.

I never discovered how the Sheikh had acquired his honorific title, but he certainly gave the appearance of meriting it. Not that he was dressed in desert robes popularised as appropriate by Hollywood extravaganzas. On the contrary, on our first meeting he wore a pearl-grey suit and sported a rose in his buttonhole. He had long passed the age of the typical recently graduated university student, but, I learnt eventually, his graduation, cruelly denied, should have taken place only two years earlier. However, Sheikh S did not begin by raising this matter. After introducing himself he dwelt instead on the nature of my mission in his country, about which he was well informed.

"You must have a great number of people approaching you for assistance of various kinds."

I nodded.

"Some will want to take part in your Centre activities. Others perhaps to take English courses here. Then again there are those who will wish to visit your wonderful country."

All this was spot on and I readily nodded in agreement. My room had been refurbished and we sat together in easy chairs beside a coffee table. I felt that our interview was going much better than I had expected. At this point Sheikh S reached down into a brief case he had parked beside his chair and produced a brown envelope.

"Naturally I should want to help you in your laudable desire to assist these people. In this envelope there is five thousand pounds sterling. Please do me the honour of accepting it."

He held the envelope out to me and, as I put up my hand in an instinctive refusal, he simply tossed it into my lap. This was not difficult, as we were seated practically knee to knee. I looked at the envelope and felt its weight. It was certainly a bulky one. Did it really contain five thousand pounds? It was a cash sum I never expected to handle. In my uncertainty about my next move I looked up to see that Sheikh S was leaning back in his chair and smiling at me benignly. However, my resolution was firm. This sort of transaction was certainly not on in the field of public service.

I told him: "Your offer is a generous one and much appreciated, but we do in fact have funds budgeted to cover our various activities."

With this I passed the envelope back to him. He looked down at it and then looked up at me with a slightly puzzled expression.

"I'm sure there must be other activities for which this modest contribution would be useful. Yes, I'm confident that you will be able to find a good use for it."

Again he circumvented my raised hand to toss the envelope into my lap. The matter was a delicate one but I realised that the time had come to eschew circumlocution and employ firm words.

"Sheikh S," I said, " It would be quite improper for me to accept your offer. I really must insist that you keep your envelope."

As I leant forward to return it he raised not one but both hands, as though to push me away, but I managed to drop the contentious object between them onto his knees. The situation was becoming farcical. I was reminded of childhood games of pass the parcel and wondered how many more passes there were to come. To my relief my visitor picked up the envelope and, smiling at me ruefully, returned it to his briefcase.

"We must talk about this again. I'm sure that we can come to some arrangement." After a pause he added: "There is one other little matter I wanted to talk to you about, rather a troublesome little matter. I'm sorry to take up your valuable time, but I'm sure this is something you can help me with."

He then outlined to me the case of the missing university degree certificate. It seemed that he had done everything that needed to be done to achieve the award of a BA, had completed all the necessary formalities, but the university authorities had consistently refused to play their part and call him forward at their annual awards ceremony. The university involved was the Arab University of Beirut, a private body founded by a Lebanese philanthropist some years previously. Fortunately I knew the son of the founder, who had taken over his father's responsibilities, a dedicated man who had recruited leading scholars from Cairo as professors and, with our cooperation, a consultant from Liverpool University to advise on science studies. After an exchange of visits we had become firm friends and I knew I would be able to raise Sheikh S's "troublesome little matter" with him and that we'd be able to speak frankly about it. It was, perhaps, merely the result of some minor administrative oversight.

On hearing that I was prepared to take the matter up the Sheikh rose and shook me vigorously by the hand and, after we had exchanged some formal expressions of mutual regard, left the room bearing his briefcase containing the unwelcome envelope with him.

By chance a meeting with my university friend occurred shortly afterwards and I brought up the topic of the degree alleged to have been unjustly withheld. He was obviously well aware of the matter and I suspect that I was not the first to raise it with him. His explanation was that Sheikh S had attended none of the university's courses and had sat none of its examinations and that therefore could not be awarded a degree.

This seemed to me to be quite conclusive and I regretted not having insisted on some form of evidence at my meeting with the Sheikh. However, at our next meeting he dismissed the university's stand as irrelevant, telling me that he *had* documentary evidence of his having amply fulfilled the degree requirements. He produced from his briefcase an envelope which, I was relieved to see, was considerably less bulky than the one produced earlier. From this he drew a single sheet of paper and passed it to me.

It was a letter typed on paper headed with the logo of one of the United Nations agencies and addressed to the Vice-Chancellor of the Beirut Arab University stating that, in a private room in the presence of the undersigned, Sheikh S had completed a written paper which he, the writer, adjudged showed incontrovertible evidence of the Sheikh's deserving to be awarded the degree of the university concerned. When I had finished reading I looked up to see him regarding me with a look of quiet confidence. Here was a dilemma indeed. I knew enough about the workings of my friend's university, its integrity and high standing, to know that the document in my hand would in no way suffice to persuade them that they had acted wrongly. On the other hand, the Sheikh was no doubt sincere in having placed his trust, however naively, in the opinion of his United Nations contact, who, incidentally, seemed to belong to a UN agency which was not, like UNESCO and some others, concerned with educational matters. I tried to find a way of letting him down lightly.

"Although I know something about university regulations in my own country," I told him, "I am not really conversant with such regulations here. I may not, therefore, be the best person to help you. I wonder if there is someone nearer home who may help you clear things up; your UN contact, perhaps."

"Unfortunately he has been posted to the Congo," he said, "and I have lost contact with him. But, in any case, everybody knows that Britain has the best education system in the world and your word will certainly carry more weight than any other."

I did not share his expressed faith in the extent of my influence, but I could think of no way of extricating myself. Fortunately, at this point the alarm buzzer sounded, telling staff that it was time to evacuate the building. Although we were not, in fact, being invaded by an armed militia, this drill to be practised in preparation for such an eventuality had been inaugurated by the Administrative Officer at a most opportune moment for me. Making a great show of taking command of the swift but orderly exodus of staff, students and library members I made my excuses to Sheikh S. He seemed nothing loth to absent himself from our roll calling in the garden but, as he hurried off, he assured me that he would call upon me again in the following week.

When, at our next staff meeting, I mentioned that I feared I had let myself in for a series of meetings with Sheikh S with no conceivable result, one of the young Directors of Study in our Institute of English came up with a suggestion.

"Why not let him take one of our courses. If he passes, we can certainly award him a certificate." He handed me a proof certificate he had just collected from the printers. It was produced on fine quality paper and at the head was our logotype accompanied by what in later years we described as our "mission statement". It was an impressive document, but I doubted it would serve our purposes, for two reasons. Though I had every faith in the excellence of the courses being run downstairs we could not maintain that they reached degree level. Secondly, Sheikh S's English was already near perfect. However, when the Director pointed out that he was about to inaugurate an advanced course, I thought it might be worth trying out his idea.

When I mentioned it to Sheikh S he thoroughly approved the proposal I put to him. I can only think that his declared belief that British education was the best in the world was sincerely held and not simply a form of flattery. In any case he immediately went off to the registrar to enrol. After that, although I often saw him around the building, he never again sought a personal interview.

Meanwhile I received a visit from Abdel-Halim Caracalla, founder, choreographer and leading male dancer in the Caracalla Dance Company, based in the city. He was accompanied by a short man whom he introduced as Mr D. This man had a disconcerting habit of leaning forward on the edge of his chair and nodding his head vigorously, almost in my face, smiling constantly as Mr Caracalla explained the purpose of his visit. The presence of Abdel-Halim's companion surprised me as nothing had been said about it when our appointment was made. Mr Caracalla told me that it was his ambition to have his company perform in a London theatre. I had never seen him and his dancers perform and, remembering my experience with Madame J, the opera singer, wondered whether before agreeing to act as a go-between I should find some way of checking on the company and the seriousness of its leader's intentions. Before I could speak he reassured me.

"Of course, I wouldn't expect you to do anything to help until you've had a chance to see us on stage. I have tickets for you for our opening night next week here in Beirut."

"My wife and I will be delighted to attend."

"Very good. I hope you will like us." He handed me two tickets.

At this point his companion entered the conversation. By his name I knew him to be an Armenian, one of a small community prominent in Beirut life, particularly as jewellers but also in professional fields. I had assumed he was one of Mr Caracalla's associates but he revealed that he had come to see me on a different matter, though allied in that it involved the performing arts. He began by asking if I had seen the group of singers, "from your country", that he had engaged to perform in Beirut the previous year. I had to admit that I had not and that I was unfamiliar with the group, called Boney M, less well-known then than they later became. Mr D seemed surprised at my ignorance. He had mentioned it, I gathered, in order to establish his credentials as an impresario responsible for introducing established overseas artistes into the country. He mentioned several others of these, none from my own country. I had heard of none of them. We had not got off to a good start but Mr D maintained his smiling expression as he revealed plans for his next project.

"I want now to present in Lebanon the Royal Ballet Company from London, in Byblos in September."

I was immediately on my guard. Surely this was far too ambitious an undertaking, even for someone who was proud to have sponsored Boney M. Some note of caution needed to be sounded immediately. "I think you will find," I said, "that the Royal Ballet's touring programme is arranged years in advance."

For the first time Mr D's smile deserted him. In fact, he looked so crestfallen that I sought to soften the blow.

"Of course the Royal Ballet is not the only ballet company in our country. There is, for example, Ballet Rambert."

Mr Caracalla came to my support with: "Ballet Rambert is an excellent company. Years ago I myself trained in London with Dame Marie Rambert, a marvellous woman."

Mr D smiled again, happy to take our word for a suitable alternative and enthusiastically outlined his plans. At Byblos, some thirty miles up the coast north of Beirut, he was having an open air amphitheatre restored with a stage specially constructed for dance performances. The visiting company were to be accommodated at a luxury hotel at Tabarja, on the coast near by. During the day, in between rehearsals the dancers would be given guided tours around the ancient sites of Byblos, a town rich in history since neolithic times with its successive settlement by Phoenicians, Egyptians, Greeks, Romans and Crusaders. His enthusiasm was infectious. I was reminded of the glory days of the annual Baalbek Festival, abandoned with the outbreak of the Civil War, when leading artists, companies and orchestras performed in and around the temples completed by that other Caracalla, the Roman Emperor who, no doubt, had provided my other visitor with the inspiration for his professional name. To reproduce something of that magic, even on a reduced scale, would be an achievement. Though I was dubious of the result I agreed to forward Mr D's invitation to Ballet Rambert, via our Dance and Drama Department in London.

The following Monday evening saw the opening of the Caracalla Dance Company's run of performances at a theatre in Rue Hamra. Greta and I turned up there in good time. In far too good a time as it turned out as the performance could not begin until the Minister for Culture and a number of other officials in high places had turned up. Two hours later motor cycle outriders heralded the Minister's arrival and the performance began with the beating of tambours, playing softly at first but rising to a crescendo as dancers rushed forward from the back of the stage and from the wings on either side. Musicians with ouds and zamrs weaved in and out of the dancers, dressed in Lebanese peasant costume, as they joined hands to circle round the stage, breaking off at intervals to gyrate individually. When the circle finally broke up the dancing became more vigorous, almost a frenzied rhythm and I was not surprised when the whole assembly fell, laughing, to the ground. A single dancer, a young woman, then advanced from backstage and began dancing a slower, more undulating dance in the centre of the circle formed by her exhausted companions. This I later learnt was the company's prima ballerina, protégée of Mr Caracalla, who soon entered to join her. Their dance owed more to the Western ballet tradition than what had gone before, evidence of his training under Madame Rambert. The production was, in fact, a mixture of

Western and Middle Eastern dance forms, telling the story of a village romance, a sort of oriental *Village Romeo and Juliet* or *Cavalleria Rusticana.*

Both Greta and I were tremendously impressed, by the dancing, the music, the setting, in fact by everything about the production and when Mr Caracalla called on me after the short run in the theatre on the Hamra I felt confident enough to tell him that, if we could find a suitable London theatre, I was sure it would be well received there. I proposed putting the matter in the hands of Visiting Arts, a headquarters department charged with fostering overseas performers in Britain. On leaving my office he put to me a question which had me puzzled.

"How is the Kamikaze Pilot's proposal progressing?"

Seeing my bemusement he explained: "I'm sorry, I thought you knew we all called Mr D the Kamikaze Pilot."

He was referring to the Armenian impresario whose plans to put Ballet Rambert on stage in Lebanon I knew, by that time, were going ahead. I did not like the sound of his sobriquet, known apparently to everybody except myself. It suggested some sort of disaster; certainly something I would not want to befall a company who had responded so readily to Mr D's invitation and were prepared to arrive, thirty-eight strong, in three months' time.

"Whyever do you call him the Kamikaze Pilot?"

Mr Caracalla must have sensed my alarm and he endeavoured to reassure me.

"Please don't take it seriously. It's a joke really. Mr D is very enterprising and has many ambitious projects. We admire him for this but, not surprisingly, some of these projects go astray."

"You mean they crash, like Kamikaze pilots' planes."

"No, no. Nobody is injured. Some of his arrangements work very well, but others - they go astray."

I was not reassured and I felt that the uneasy situation I found myself in was in part due to Mr Caracalla himself, who had introduced Mr D to me.

I told him: "I had no idea of all this. I can only think that these projects you're telling me have gone wrong must have done so before I arrived here." I could not forbear adding: "You know, I was happy to listen to Mr D because he came here in some sense under your auspices."

"No, I'm sorry, this is rather a misunderstanding. As I entered your building that day Mr D was outside and came up the stairs with me as I kept my appointment."

It was apparent that the ever-vigilant Meyrich, so efficient in keeping doubtful visitors from my door, had fallen into the same trap as I had and had believed the two visitors entering together had called on common business. On my way home I called in at a local music shop. Yes, they had a record by Boney M and yes, the shop's proprietor believed them to be established performers, though he was a Mozart man himself. They were certainly tuneful songsmiths and one of their numbers I listened to on my newly acquired record album, *Brown Girl in the Ring*, had a rhythm suggestive of dance, though not of ballet.

A page in a Beirut weekly magazine, *Monday Morning*, was devoted to entertainments and had recently carried a featured article on the opening of a new club on the seashore south of Pigeon Rock. In the temporary summer lull in warfare between the various militias in the city, those members of the glitterati who had in pre-Civil War days flocked to the Casino north of the city to enjoy its lavish cabaret and gaming tables and who had not, like many of their wealthy fellow citizens, fled to Paris, New York or London, were delighted with the new club, Summerlands, which was doing good business. *Monday Morning* reported that Mr D was contracting well-known international recording stars to appear there nightly. It was reassuring to read that the Kamikaze Pilot's arrangements were going well at this venue and we crossed our fingers for the Byblos engagement.

In mid-July Mr D announced his biggest coup so far. He had engaged an American singer who, although no longer in her first flush of youth, was known worldwide as appearing in the charts with several numbers, above all with what had become her signature tune, *I Will Survive*. She had agreed to a two week run and her arrival was awaited with lively anticipation. At the airport she gratified her crowd of admirers, mainly youthful but some middle-aged, by seeming to embrace them all with her wide smile and vibrant hand gestures before being guided into a limousine by Mr D and escorted to her room at the Summerlands Club.

Her first night audience, fans who had been successful in obtaining hot tickets, were delighted with her performance, according to the following morning's press, though tiredness had prevented her from according much time to their representatives. Given her long fight, this was not surprising, though summer heat was alleviated by the club's airconditioning, guaranteed to work through their own generator even when power supplies had broken down in most districts. An incidental advantage of air-conditioning was that its regular humming through the night muffled the sound of shellfrre from the East. Although something of a truce obtained between the warring factions, this token shelling continued, though none of the shells from the Christian quarter of Ashrafieh lobbed in our direction reached as far as the seafront region. We had become inured to this regular manifestation and came to regard it as little more than a nuisance, to be ignored. The crackle of small arms fire, also a nightly occurrence, we tended also to ignore since, we consoled ourselves, it often represented only an expression of joy at a wedding, or of sorrow at a funeral. In this way, I believe, citizens adjust themselves to internecine violence in similar situations worldwide, managing to get on with their everday lives. It was noticeable that, even in the most active phases of the conflict, the smallholders brought their fruit and vegetables down from the mountains into the city and the bakers continued to bake bread through the night. Of course the situation might appear less innocuous to a non-citizen, to a temporary resident.

After her second performance at Summerlands the American songstress called Mr D to her room. According to a report in the following week's *Monday Morning*, she asked for a short break in her contract in order to give a single performance, "for one night only", in Cairo, from where her agent had sent her an offer she could not afford to refuse. Mr D agreed on the understanding that she would extend her Summerlands run on her return and he set about placating the club management. The singer set off that lunchtime. She did not return to Beirut, a great disappointment to her fans, some of whom made less than kind comments that they now understood how she had managed for so long to fulfil her expressed determination to "survive". Their disappointment, of course, could in no way have equalled the dismay felt by the intrepid entrepreneur who had once again seen a high-flying undertaking grounded. We ourselves were reminded of the precarious nature of such arrangements and were shortly to undergo a similar experience.

Set against this was some excellent news for Mr Caracalla and his plans to take his dance company to London. The management of Sadlers Wells had agreed to accept them for a fortnight's run. The prospect of appearing in a theatre so strongly associated with world-class ballet was immensely satisfying to their leader. I remembered that a man who had once occupied my present desk, now retired and living in London, had a brother-in-law, Felix Barker, who was chief theatre critic for the *London Evening News*. I wrote to him asking if he could use his influence to get that newspaper to review Caracalla's first night, hoping that a favourable review would bring in good audiences.

Our own plans, less ambitious than Mr D's, to bring performing artists into Lebanon involved two young performers, a pianist and an actor who had devised a one-woman show. Both were to appear at the Gulbenkian Theatre, a modem, almost circular 320-seater theatre gifted to the Beirut University College by the Armenian philanthropist whose name it bore. Excellent acoustics made it suitable alike for piano recitals and intimate theatrical performers. Scheduled to arrive first was Anthony, the pianist. He had performed in Beirut before and, with the aid of a poster campaign and advance notices from a friendly press, we had no difficulty in selling all available tickets. He had the reputation of being a resourceful tourer who always made his own travel arrangements. On this occasion his tour was extensive, taking in performances in many Middle Eastern countries before reaching us.

Due to arrive on a Friday afternoon, having travelled by taxi from Damascus, he was booked in to a hotel near our office and the theatre. However, when I called there in the evening to brief him, he had not arrived. I left a message with the receptionist asking Anthony to phone me at home. There was no contact that night and on checking in the morning we found that he was yet to arrive. This was worrying, as the recital was to take place that evening. Meyrich took it upon herself to contact the hotel at regular intervals throughout the day but by teatime, with no sign of Anthony, we were seriously considering cancelling. Hoping against hope I stationed myself in the hotel lobby while Meyrich sat by the phone in the office, hoping for a last minute word. We had decided that, even if he arrived a mere five minutes before the scheduled hour, eight o'clock, we would ask him if, given a half hour's delay, he could still perform. But at five to eight I had to make my way to the Gulbenkian to apologise to the audience.

This embarrassing duty was made worse by the warm round of applause I received from the audience - many of them had become friends - as I went up on to the platform. After I had explained the situation and given an assurance that money back would be available at our office on the Monday morning I made my way to stand by the exit of the auditorium. As they left each member of the audience pressed my hand, expressing their sorrow at our misfortune, while not mentioning their own, and commenting on the terrible times we were living through. We could not have had a kinder or more generous minded audience.

These commiserations were interrupted by the appearance of a small car being driven into the college forecourt in front of the theatre. It weaved its way through the crowd still milling about and chatting there, no doubt discussing alternative plans for the evening. When it reached the theatre steps, Meyrich leapt out and ran up to me.

"He's here. I've left him at the hotel. He's getting ready."

She was breathless with excitement and effort and looked down on the audience slowly making its way out through the college gates as if preparing to round them up and herd them all back into the theatre. But my heart was no longer in it. I sat her down in the foyer and asked her to tell me what had happened. It transpired that at half-past seven she had received a phone call from a taxi company in the south of the city. They had Anthony delivered to them by one of their drivers and he was wondering how he was going to get to us, as a matter of urgency. They themselves operated only between cities, not across cities. Meyrich had sped there in her own vehicle, by no means an easy journey, collected the pianist and delivered him to the hotel on the understanding that he would freshen up, change into his concert clothes and then be collected again by Meyrich. Meanwhile she had dashed to the theatre in the hope of arriving in time to forestall my announcement. I tried to mitigate her disappointment by praising her efforts, beyond the bounds of duty, in fact in off-duty hours, and asked her for one more favour. She agreed to collect Anthony and bring him to our apartment for a dinner, planned as a post-recital meal, with ourselves and some invited members of the audience.

They and our other guests arrived well before the hour we had planned to have dinner served and Anthony, still in concert clothes, took it upon himself to entertain us at a grand piano we had removed from the centre in order to make room for an additional classroom. He played us pieces by one composer in the style of another, inviting us to identify both. Our guests, experienced concert-goers, entered into the spirit of this, vying with each other to be the first to shout out "Schumann and Schubert" or other correct answers. Much laughter followed every time a correct identification was made. I alone remained unmoved by all this, making mental calculations of our refund commitment.

"Three hundred tickets at thirty-five Lebanese pounds each makes ..."

I could leave out of account the twenty complimentary tickets allocated to our dinner guests, whose delight in Anthony's impromptu performance continued unabated. We really did need the money.

Over dinner Anthony explained how he had so narrowly failed in his attempt to reach the theatre before zero hour. It stemmed from his failure to realise that Lebanon, once the easiest country in the Middle East to enter without formality, merely by presenting oneself at the border with a nominal sum for a visa, had, since the outbreak of the Civil War imposed a visa regime as strict as anyone else's. The visa had to be obtained in advance from the Lebanese consulate in an outside country. Having previously visited Beirut in more easy-going times, Anthony was surprised on arriving at the border with Syria in good time the day before the recital to be refused entry. Once he had grasped the necessity for a visa issued elsewhere he had squeezed into the fourth passenger seat of a service taxi making its way to Damascus, from which city he had set out earlier that day. He wasted some time there searching for a Lebanese consulate; in vain, since none existed there at that time. At the British Embassy he learnt that the nearest possibility was in Amman, Jordan's capital. Another taxi took him there after a long and tedious night time journey, involving delays at the Syrian-Jordanian border. Arriving early Saturday morning he waited for the British Embassy to open to ask directions. A security guard sent him off to an office which he found to be closed and, after waiting outside for some time, he concluded was unlikely to be opened that day. A further taxi ride back to the British Embassy and an interview with the Consul there confirmed this. The Lebanese Consul did not attend his office on Saturdays. Moved by Anthony's desperate plea that he had to give a recital in Beirut that very day the Briton agreed to phone his Lebanese counterpart who agreed to rise and meet Anthony in order to put the necessary stamp in his passport. This vital requirement obtained, Anthony managed to persuade a taxi driver to take off for Damascus without waiting for a full complement of four passengers. With a slightly shorter border delay he changed taxis yet again in Damascus (it was now teatime) and set off towards Beirut, presenting his newly-acquired visa in triumph at the Lebanese border and getting himself delivered, tired but triumphant, to the taxi company's office in South Beirut, at this point only a few, but tricky, miles from his ultimate destination. This is where Meyrich had taken over.

It was an epic journey. Our guests enjoyed its recital immensely. I don't know how many miles over mountain and desert roads it involved; it must have been several hundred.

Certainly Anthony was to be congratulated on his sheer pertinacity. A lesser trouper would have given up after the second or third taxi journey, simply sending a message calling off on the grounds of illness or resorted to some other subterfuge. Amazingly, after these harrowing taxi rides and a night without sleep Anthony seemed to be in lively spirits and remained so until we delivered him to his hotel after midnight. I met him on two occasions in different cities overseas in later years. One both occasions he ribbed me about my having lost faith in him because of this Beirut business, though the reasons I had not engaged him were quite other. He was, and is, a fine pianist.

After this debacle we redoubled our efforts to sell tickets for our next venture, the one-woman show by Marilyn H. We needed to sell double the number, as she was booked for two performances, on a Saturday and a Monday with a weekend's break in between. Staff canvassed every shop on the Rue Hamra to persuade proprietors to display our poster. This was a striking bit of propaganda, based on a publicity photo she had sent us. It showed her face with beautiful large and wide-set eyes gazing out at her public from surrounding blackness. Only her face could be seen. As a result of this, or possibly because the city had been starved of live theatrical performances for some time, sales were brisk and we were soon able to let the press know we had sold out.

Marilyn was due to fly in from Athens on the morning of her first performance and to rest up in our apartment as a house guest until the evening. However, when Mohammed Slim, our driver, returned from the airport he reported in solemn tones that she had not been on the morning flight. His reputation of never failing to get his man, or in this case woman, had obviously upset him and we all had premonitions of a repeat of the Anthony saga of a missing document resulting in fatiguing journeys undertaken in a failed attempt to meet an unrelenting deadline. One ray of hope - her travel arrangements, unlike Anthony's, had been made by our London office.

A final flight from Athens was due at six pm. We determined, hoping against hope that Marilyn would be on it, to get her through customs and immigration as quickly as possible and drive her directly to the theatre, where Greta would organise a holding operation, attempting to retain the audience. The performance was due to begin at seven-thirty.

At the airport Mohammed and I managed to get beyond customs to the arrivals lounge, having been told that the flight was only marginally late. We scanned the passengers filing in from the tarmac. There seemed to be no Europeans amongst them. Mohammed muttered repeatedly that this looked very bad. He was excessively loyal and identified himself one hundred per cent with our organisation's reputation. As the last passengers lined up at customs we turned towards a side exit to drive back to town with our unwelcome news for Greta and the audience she would be entertaining with cartons of wine from our storeroom and the local mini-market. Turning briefly at the exit I saw a lone woman entering the arrivals hall. Unfortunately, as I could see immediately, this was not our performer. She was possibly a European, though large horn-rimmed sunglasses and a beret pulled down partly obscuring her forehead made this difficult to ascertain. She was dressed, unseasonably, in a fawn raincoat reaching almost to her ankles and was sauntering towards a customs bench like a woman who had plenty of time on her hands. I then noticed behind her a porter struggling to balance a huge trunk on a small trolley. Could this be a *theatrical* trunk?

Hastening towards her I asked: "Are you Marilyn?"

She took off her sunglasses and looked at me through beautiful, wide-set eyes.

"How nice of you to come to meet me."

Mohammed bustled forward and helped the porter to manoeuvre the trunk alongside the customs bench, informing the official that he and his colleagues knew us and we were once again escorting a visitor who had come to perform in his city, the underlying message being: "No need for formalities here." Unfortunately the official either did *not* know us or our visitor's unusually large trunk had aroused his curiosity. He indicated that we should put it on his bench. When Mohammed and the porter had managed this difficult operation he ordered Marilyn to unlock it and began to rummage about amongst its contents. The time was ticking on towards seven o'clock. I could understand the custom officer's interest in the opened trunk. It contained an amazingly variegated collection of items of clothing, suitable for both sexes at different points in history, the stock in trade of a quick-change artist putting on a one-woman show. The officer, possibly unfamiliar with this theatrical tradition, pulled out several items and examined them closely as all the other passengers exited from the hall. Looking around to note that his colleagues were also making off he finally threw these garments back in the trunk, closed it and scrawled a chalk mark on the lid.

Free at last to leave the building Mohammed seized the trolley handles from the porter and ran towards our car. Hesitantly, in view of our brief acquaintance, I took Marilyn by an elbow in an attempt to urge her onwards after him. She resisted by stopping to rummage in her handbag for a packet of tissues. I could see she was shaking and I feared she must be in some distress as she took off her dark glasses to wipe her eyes. Tears were there, but they were tears of laughter. She was positively shaking with laughter.

"I'm sorry," she said, "but it was the customs man. I'm glad he didn't get to the bottom of the trunk."

"Why?"

"You'll see tomorrow, when I do my act."

Her reply confirmed what I had suspected as soon as I had seen her sauntering in so leisurely a fashion into the customs hall - she had no idea that she was due on stage that night. It also gave me the opportunity, which I had been looking for desperately, to explain the situation, the waiting audience being kept in good spirits, I hoped, by Greta and the cartons of wine.

"I think you don't realise, you're supposed to be on stage tonight."

"What! In London they told me my first performance was *tomorrow* night."

"A mistake," I told her. "These things happen. But tell me, could you possibly go on stage tonight?"

Marilyn put her tissues away, thrust her glasses resolutely back on her nose and said: "Give me half an hour to set up in the theatre and I'll do it."

I wanted to hug her, there in the car park, but she broke away briskly towards the car crying: "Come on. We'd better get going." and in next to no time Mohammed had her bundled into the back seat and we were speeding between umbrella pines towards the city.

The Gulbenkian Theatre foyer was full of people drinking, laughing and conversing loudly. Nobody seemed at all concerned that the curtain should have gone up an hour earlier. It could have been the wine (I noticed that Greta was just removing the last remaining full bottles from a carton in the corner. A good number of empty bottles were scattered about.) but I remembered that it was not unusual for theatrical events in Beirut to begin well after the time given on the ticket.

Marilyn hurried back stage while I joined Greta in entertaining the audience. Half an hour later we ushered them into the auditorium. The house lights went down and Marilyn, in a satin turquoise gown, her lustrous hair let down to fall about her shoulders, a total transformation from the dowdy figure at the airport, strode on to the stage.

Having taken in every member of her audience in the semi-circle of the auditorium with a sweeping wide-eyed gaze she gave us the sort of smile that makes everybody feel good and told us: "I'm sorry to have kept you waiting." before going straight into her opening number, from a Noel Coward play, sung in a rich contralto voice. From that moment she had us totally absorbed. I was able to sit back and enjoy - something rare I suspect for someone in any way responsible for putting a show before the public - a performance that took us rapidly through an extraordinary variety of acts, ranging from music hall songs to classic choruses, comic monologues to Shakespearean soliloquies, sentimental ballads to hardbitten aphorisms from Dorothy Parker and all enacted in an array of costumes which she got into with bewildering speed from her seemingly inexhaustible store in the trunk in the wings. She gave a new meaning to the concept of "quick change artist." Everything went like finely tuned clockwork to the accompaniment of music from a diminutive cassette player she had placed beside the trunk and which the theatre technician had hooked up to the sound system while she was making up. It never failed to come in on time as she swept back on to the stage in yet another costume - as male or female, young or old. In recommending her my colleague in London had written: "This is the genuine article." His judgement could not have been more fully endorsed by what we were seeing in the Gulbenkian that night. I hope she was as gratified by the audience's reaction as I was. They were right there with her, laughing when advised to "Keep yer 'and on yer 'alfpenny.", wiping away a furtive tear when Christina Rossetti bade them, "... do not grieve", remarkable reactions from people tuning into words in their second or third language.

It did not matter, in the interval, that the wine had run out. We were all on a high, enthusing over what we had seen and anticipating what was yet to come, a lively anticipation, one that was to be fully satisfied and, in one electrifying moment, surpassed.

I do not recall the opening passage of the show's second part - probably a light-weight number judiciously chosen to allow the audience to settle back into their seats, but I do recall, most vividly, what followed. The stage blacked out as Marilyn went into the wings. A moment later a pin spot came on to show her standing stage centre holding between her hands a severed head no nightmare apparition could match for horror. Gasps of dismay ran through the audience. Women clapped hands to mouth and strong men clenched their fists. Blood had drained from the face of the head, leaving a ghastly pallor. The eyes bulged over the cheekbones and the mouth hung open, arrested in a final cry of agony. Long, dark hair was matted with blood at the point where the neck had been jaggedly severed by John the Baptist's bungling butcher. Marilyn held this hideous object aloft for all to see as she recited Oscar Wilde's lines from Salome before inflicting fresh torment on us by kissing its bloodless lower lip lasciviously.

This was the object, I realised, that the customs officer had failed to locate when rummaging through Marilyn's trunk at the airport, a failure that had caused her much amusement. Had she been aware of the realities of the situation in the country amusement would not have been her reaction. Apart from the atrocities committed by all factions in the continuing civil conflict the war had provided opportunities for the settling of old scores and severed body parts, hidden away or hurriedly buried just below ground, were by no means uncommon discoveries. Only the previous month a corpse had been revealed in the boot of a car abandoned for several days at the entrance to our apartment block. The amazingly realistic severed head Marilyn held up for our horripilation would, had the officer come across it, certainly have brought down upon us the full force of the airport security services. For how long we might have been incarcerated before we managed to convince these men, hardened by everday confrontations with violence, that this was no real human body part, simply the creation of the Royal Shakespeare Company's workshop, as Marilyn later informed us, I was unable to calculate. At best we might have been released some hours after the show should have gone on.

These thoughts of dire consequences prevented me from giving full attention to Marilyn's remaining numbers, but I sat through the whole show again on the Monday and saw that the second half was as compelling as the first. On both occasions the audience's applause was so sustained that she found it difficult to leave the stage and on the second night a drama student, while presenting Marilyn with a bouquet, managed to clasp both her hands in his as he delivered an impromptu speech stuffed with fulsome compliments, which had his fellow students in the audience stamping the floor in approbation.

On the intervening Sunday we took Marilyn up into the mountains, to Shemlan, where we had lunch on a hotel terrace looking down over the city. From that height Beirut looked tranquil and we could hear no sound of gunfire. On her return to England she wrote a letter from her Midlands home saying how much she had enjoyed this occasion. We lost touch, but we often thought about Marilyn Heathcock and hoped that she had a good life in the theatre. An actor of great talent and tremendous versatility, she had entered a keenly competitive field with an abundance of able players. Although as a good trouper she made no complaint, we felt that she deserved something better than hauling her trunk around to distant venues for a series of one or two-night stands.

This theatrical success served to salve painful memories of Anthony's unfulfilled engagement. In fact, things seemed at this time to be going well for our endeavours. The first students successfully to complete courses at our Institute of English took part in an awards ceremony in the garden of our centre. I was delighted to see Sheikh S, his madman number one title now discarded, step forward smartly in his pearl grey suit to receive an advanced certificate from the British Ambassador to the muted strains of *Pomp and Circumstance.*

A dramatic reminder of the perils of complacency arrived swiftly. Two weeks before the Ballet Rambert were to appear on stage in Byblos Mr D, the Kamikaze Pilot, called on me in a state of abject despondency to report that: "Criminal elements have blown up the stage." A modern ruin had been created amidst those of ancient times. There was no possibility of salvaging the project. This was a show that definitely would not go on. My first thought, no doubt a cowardly one, was about how deeply we had committed ourselves in putting Mr D in touch with the company. Were there legal implications? How well would our meagre financial resources stand up to a demand for compensation for lost revenue? I was pretty sure we had no insurance against such a contingency. An insurance company would be mad to provide cover in an area subjected to sporadic violence.

In the event we came out of the affair much better than could have been expected. In response to our cable with the tragic news Ballet Rambert sent sincere condolences at what they saw as *our* misfortune, expressing hopes for a better future for Lebanon and telling us that they had managed to fix up a last minute engagement for the period at a festival in Santander, which made us feel much better about the situation.

We had no further dealings with the Kamikaze Pilot during my years in the country though I did learn more about the failed Byblos project. On his return from London Mr Caracalla called in to report on his company's appearances at Sadlers

Wells. He handed me a cutting from the *Evening News* of a glowing revue of their first night by that paper's chief drama critic. This, he believed, had helped to ensure almost full houses throughout their run and Mr Caracalla was immensely elated by their success.

"We neither made money nor lost money. We covered our expenses and I had the great satisfaction of performing in a theatre with a wonderful tradition. I didn't dream of this when I was a young student in London."

I remembered that he had told me that he had been a student of Marie Rambert and, after congratulating him and his company, I asked him if he had heard that in his absence the Kamikaze Pilot had crashed once again, this time bringing down with him the planned tour of the Rambert company.

"I heard about that. It seems Mr D was paying protection money to the wrong people in Byblos. But, you know, I'm not entirely sorry Ballet Rambert did not perform there. Did you see the stage he had erected?" I had not. "It was surrounded with advertisements for UFO jeans. They were his sponsors." After a pause he added: "I don't think Mr D understands the higher arts. Really it would be better if he kept to pop singers - they are his speciality."

From time to time news filtered through that Mr D was indeed sticking to his last and importing pop singers, but the palmy days of big audiences every night at the Casino du Liban had gone with the outbreak of hostilities and it was to be many years before Rafiq Harari with his millions succeeded in rehabilitating his war-torn country. It has not become again what once it purported to be, "the playground of the Middle East", where Western tourists disported themselves on its beaches and oil rich neighbours from the south sought refuge from the heat of their kingdom or emirates in the cool mountain resorts. Nevertheless, with the cessation of war there must have been more scope for light entertainment in many of the old venues and I hope the Kamikaze Pilot survived long enough to benefit from the opportunities this presented for an enterprising impresario.

Beirut 1978

Pukka English

One morning at the end of the monsoon our Director, Dr Mohan, came into the common room with a letter from the National Defence Academy in Dehra Dun. It had been sent on the orders of the Army's C-in-C, Field Marshal Sam Manekshaw, and reported that he had been dissatisfied with the standard of English he had heard spoken by junior officers in the mess there and wanted to know what our institute proposed doing about it. I had seen photographs of this redoubtable warrior in the press. With his upright bearing, hawklike features and waxed moustache he did not look like the kind of man who would brook any deviation from the highest standards. Dr Mohan looked around his assembled staff.

When his eye lighted on my Welsh colleague he said: "David, perhaps you'd better go up to Dehra Dun and investigate the problem at first hand."

He then turned to me and suggested I might like to go to Poona and see whether any such linguistic problem had arisen in the headquarters of Southern Command there. I don't know why he picked on the two expats on his staff. Possibly he thought our view on desirable English would most closely approximate to that of the Field Marshal. I could only guess at what that view might be. Since he was our senior by some years and had perhaps begun his Army career under the command of British officers trained at Sandburst it might be that his standard of excellence was derived from a generation who spoke a form of English going out of fashion. In any case I was quite happy to be going to Poona to do some serious listening.

The city authorities were at that time debating whether to alter the name officially to Pune. I had only passed through the city on the train, but 1 remembered that in my boyhood, in the days of the British Raj, it had featured in a song sung by a comedian in a caddish voice which began, I think: "When I was in Poona in 1894 ..." This gave the place a Blimpish, old fashioned image. Of course, it was unlikely that this reflected present day reality or had any implications for the language now spoken there.

On Sunday Greta drove me to Secunderabad station to put me on the overnight train with the admonition: "Don't forget to eat." - a reference to my having returned from a month's stay in an Indore hotel in the previous year with a loss in weight of nearly a stone. My absence this time was to be for only two weeks.

I always enjoyed train journeys in India, not least because they usually provided good companionship from fellow travellers. This trip to Poona was no exception. I shared a sleeping compartment with a man who had already been travelling for many hours, having set off that morning from Madras en route for Bombay.

Our conversation began in customary fashion by his asking: "May I know your good name, sir?" (I only once heard this courteous approach fail to establish good relationships, when an Englishman who held a copy of the *Times of India* in front of his face as a barrier lowered it momentarily to bark: "Savage." I remember suppressing a fleeting urge to tell him: "If that's your good name, we wouldn't care to know your bad name.") Having exchanged names we then established that I was coming from Hyderabad.

My travelling companion told me: "Then you must be knowing ....." and he reeled off the names of a number of families which indeed I did know. This discovery of mutual acquaintanceships was by no means an uncommon phenomenon. I had been puzzled by this, occurring in such a vast country as India, but a friend told me that although millions travelled by rail, a comparatively small number rode first class and there was a sort of network amongst those whose business required them to do so. Time passed pleasantly with talk of Sunil Gavaskar's batting in the recent test series in England, the Telangana riots and the fiendishness of the cryptic clues of the crosswords in *The Hindu*, which were compiled by one of our mutual Hyderabadi acquaintances, a retired Indian Navy admiral, until the attendant came to make up our beds for the night.

I clambered into the top bunk and slept soundly. When I was wakened by the attendant with a cup of tea the sun was slanting into our carriage and my watch told me we should be nearing my destination. I hurriedly pulled on my trousers, but my companion told me we had only just passed through Kurduwadi Junction. I had some way to go and obviously we were running late. When we finally arrived at Poona station I looked out for my contact. Standing at the end of the platform was a young lieutenant. He had the peak of his cap pulled well down over his eyes in the manner of a British guardsman and held his head back at an unnatural angle to gaze down the length of the platform. As I made my way towards him I noticed that he was exceptionally smartly turned out, buttons and Sam Browne gleaming, and this made me uncomfortably aware of my own dishevelled appearance. I had slept in my bush shirt.

I said to him: "I'm sorry, I'm afraid I'm very late."

Putting his hand inside his service dress jacket he pulled out a hunter watch. This he snapped open to tell me: "The time by my chronometer is precisely eleven ack emma." He said this in the clipped tones that, in my speculating about Sam Manekshaw's voice, I had thought of as one of the accents the Field Marshal might favour, if he had been affected by those of his commanders in his early years. It closely approximated the way of speaking English adopted by David Niven to portray British Army officers in wartime screen epics. I thought: "If all the young officers in Southern Command speak like this there may be no point in my mission." I looked across the line to where a locomotive was getting up steam to draw the up-country train to Secunderabad. A number of passengers were hurrying across the line to board it and I wondered whether I should join them, but the lieutenant took my bag and led me to a jeep waiting outside the station with a driver. He drove us into the cantonment area. The roads here were lined with stones, which were placed at regular intervals and had been whitewashed, following (or preceding?) a practice well known to British squaddies at home. There was an air of good order and military discipline, here and in the imposing archway with the freshly painted crest on its keystone which identified it as the home of the military academy. We drove in and passed the guardroom with a minimum of formality. My escort left me at a bungalow in the extensive, park-like grounds of the academy where the serviceman appointed to be my batman for the next fortnight awaited me.

The daily programme drawn up for me by one of the officer instructors was by no means exacting. I simply sat in on classes in a variety of subjects. Many of these took the form of lectures delivered by serving officers whose manner of speaking closely resembled that of the lieutenant who had met me at the station. Some classes were taught by civilian instructors who tended to speak a form of the language then known as Modified Indian English. The officer cadets were given more chances to contribute in these lessons and I noted that their accents were modelled not on those of their teacher of the moment but on the serving officers'. I soon came to the conclusion that my report to the Field Marshal would not need to be a lengthy one.

The younger serving officers took it upon themselves to make my stay with them at the Academy as entertaining as possible. We lived in a virtually self-sufficient world. In the mess we played snooker and, more frequently, table tennis, in doubles matches together with the officers' wives. The open-air cinema screened a mixed programme of imported and Hindi films. They particularly recommended me to join them to see one of the latter, entitled *Kamoshi* (Silence) and set in an institution for the mentally ill. The medical officer expressed himself contemptuous of this, for professional reasons, but most of us found it a refreshing change from the usual Bollywood extravaganzas, an attempt to portray lives, albeit disturbed lives, in a realistic manner. There were scenes in which the director succeeded in arousing our compassion for the inmates of the institution, though the film as a whole was marred by sequences inviting us to laugh at their wayward behaviour. The score included passages which stayed in my mind for months afterwards and I tried, unsuccessfully, to obtain a recording of it.

I dined in the mess with the unmarried officers. Everything here - crystal, silverware, starched linen - was splendid, except for the food. Our invariable fare consisted of rice, dal and bones. Attached to the bones were exiguous traces of meat. Creme caramel followed and the loyal toast to the President of the Republic was drunk in water, which was puzzling since the armed forces had the privilege of importing foreign liquor duty free and the mess bar was well stocked as a result. One evening at dinner I asked the mess president if he was familiar with Napoleon's words on an army's marching requirements. The major serving as president that evening looked ruefully at his plate.

He smiled and replied: "Yes I'm aware of Napoleon's dictum - 'An army marches on its stomach.'"

I later regretted my words since my remark, although made in jest, might have been construed as casting doubt on the Indian Army's fighting potential. The following year it fought a brilliant campaign against its northern neighbour, a force equipped with more modern armaments than its own, and achieved a quick and comprehensive victory, leading to the foundation of the nation of Bangladesh.

All around the walls of the mess were shields of regiments which had occupied the barracks before the Academy was established there. Most of these were familiar to me as they belonged to British regiments, some of them now disbanded or amalgamated with others. Nothing on the walls celebrated forces more closely associated with the area, those who fought against the Mughals, followers of the great seventeenth century warrior Shivaji or of the Peshwa in the seventeen nineties. Perhaps in a vast nation unifying so many diverse peoples it would be inappropriate to celebrate the victories of Marathas against those whose descendants were now their fellow citizens.

On Saturday mornings the officer cadets and their instructors were addressed in the assembly hall by a guest speaker. A brain surgeon captured our attention by chalking on a board which ran the full width of the hall the digit one followed by a long succession of noughts, ceasing only when he reached the board's far end.

He said: "If I could continue with further noughts this figure would represent the number of brain cells with which you were born." Working from the right he then began erasing noughts in rapid succession, explaining: "This is how you destroy brain cells every time you take a drink of alcohol or smoke a cigarette."

Afterwards, walking with the commanding officer to his

bungalow, I wondered to what extent the surgeon's deliberately chosen sobering words would have an effect on his audience. As we entered a mess waiter approached with a tray of drinks, lime soda and lemonade.

The commanding officer spoke to him sternly. "Take this rubbish away and bring me a whisky soda." Turning to the brain surgeon, who had joined us, he explained: "I have drunk so many whiskies that all my brain cells disappeared many years ago."

This colonel's forbidding air hid a lively sense of humour and he tailored his remarks to his audience.

To me he said: "So you're an English language expert. My brother began to study English but when he came across a newspaper report that 'The sitting member said that if he loses his seat he will not stand again.' he decided to study engineering instead."

He invited me to deliver the next Saturday lecture in the assembly hall, on a topic of my choice. I tentatively suggested 'Cultural Relations Worldwide'. If I'd paused to think I would perhaps have proposed something less high-flown, but the colonel accepted my title with the proviso that I included in my talk an admonition to his cadets to study hard for the Academy examinations they were shortly to sit.

The following day we gathered in the stands of the Poona racecourse to see the ceremony of beating retreat. The swirl of bagpipes heralded the leading ranks coming into view over the rise which led into the home straight before us. The following display by the combined forces of the army's Southern Command was a truly massive affair. Troops marched in lines almost the full width of the course, maintaining perfect precision shoulder to shoulder. The Scottish regalia of the leading contingent was colourful enough, but successive regiments following up outdid them in vivid displays of scarlet or saffron turbans and baldrics, pipe clay webbing and glistening brass accoutrements. Each regiment was led by its own band - pipes and drums, brass bands and more bagpipers. The sheer size of the display made the annual trooping of the colours in Horse Guards Parade seem like a reenactment in miniature or a toytown ceremony. The only equivalent in terms of number was the annual parade which Soviet forces put on in Red Square, but that had a drab and utilitarian quality compared with the exuberance of this display by the Indian Army. I was reminded of a cigarette card series, Uniforms of the Empire, which had been a prized collection of my schooldays. Far outshining the uniforms of soldiers from other continents had been those of the men from the Indian subcontinent.

The music, like the shields in the Academy mess, was familiar. There must be a limit to the extent to which military music, requiring a steady marching rhythm, can be varied. Certainly intricate Indian ragas would not have been suitable for this occasion. Most familiar of all was the piece played by the bands which finally formed up before us, extending almost the full length of the home straight. After what seemed a lengthy period of silence, with muted instruments they played *Abide With Me*, the music floating out in the still evening air over the neighbouring Infantry Lines and Empress Gardens to be answered by the bells of St Mary's Church picking out the melody. The Retreat ended with echo trumpeters placed in upper far corners of the grandstand playing the Last Post. Words like 'memorable' or 'unforgettable' cannot fully convey the extent of the pleasure and privilege I felt at having been allowed to witness this ceremony, a unique experience that I owed ultimately to Sam Manekshaw and to Dr Mohan for having picked me out to follow up in the headquarters of Southern Command the Field Marshal's concerns with the use of English.

The next day I returned to the humdrum task of checking whether these concerns were real or illusory, sitting in on lectures on field engineering and the correct use of explosive devices. At lunchtime my contact told me that one of my colleagues from Hyderabad had arrived to join me in my observations. He did not know the man's name, but he said I should be meeting him at dinner. When we took our places at the long table in the mess that evening, however, he did not appear. As I was leaving the building later I found him sitting in a comer of the mess anteroom with a plate of food and a glass of water on a coffee table in front of him. He turned out to be Dr K, the only one of my Indian colleagues who had failed to greet me on my arrival at the Institute in Hyderabad two years earlier and who had subsequently studiously ignored both me and my Welsh colleague in the common room. Another colleague told us that some years ago he, or it may have been his work, had been slighted by a Briton seconded to the Institute when it was founded. After one or two unreciprocated overtures we decided that his aloofness was something we had to live with and tried to ignore it. Nevertheless it disturbed the otherwise convivial atmosphere in the common room and I found it disconcerting.

On this occasion I was relieved to find that he returned my greeting civilly, perhaps in recognition of a familiar face far from home. I drew up a chair beside him and said that he had been expected to join us at dinner. He replied that he was a vegetarian and did not care to eat at a table where meat was being served. I forbore telling him that the meat served was so exiguous as to be almost indiscernible, appreciating that this could not affect a decision taken on strictly observed principles. We chatted for some time while he ate and I noted that the food on his plate, while strictly speaking 'vegetarian', in no way resembled the delicious vegetarian meals I had enjoyed in a number of South Indian restaurants in Hyderabad. These were subtly flavoured, the result of hours of careful preparation, whereas Dr K was toying with what looked like leaves of vegetables left over from some other, non-vegetarian meal. I only hoped that they had not been cooked in chicken stock. Dr K made no complaint, washing the food down with sips of water. When I rose and invited him to join me at the table tennis table, he said he intended to go to his quarters to write up notes he had made on lessons observed. This was typical of Dr K, who took his scholastic duties seriously. During the week a pattern emerged whereby I joined him in the anteroom after dinner each evening. He turned out to be quite other than the dry-as-dust scholar I had always taken him to be. His conversation was peppered with wry observations on his fellow men and he had enough self-awareness to know how he must appear to others. He came from Madras and his sister had married a film producer there, the home of Tamil language movies. In extravagance of setting, score, and dance routines and in the frequency of the intervention of the gods in the affairs of mortals, these productions lost nothing in comparison with the better known Hindi epics produced in Filmi City (or Bollywood as it later became named). His brother-in-law would arrange private viewings of his films for Dr K prior to their release and quiz him on his reaction.

"What did you think of the plot?"

"Banal."

"And the musical score?"

"Strident. Intolerable."

"The acting?"

"Perfunctory."

"How did you find the dance routines?"

"Interminable. Gross."

"So what is your overall view of the film?"

"Terrible. I don't know how I sat through it."

"Excellent. It's bound to do well at the box office. We don't make films for intellectuals like you."

One evening towards the end of the week Dr K told me that he had contacted Narayanswamy, the poet, who was living in Government quarters not far from Poona, and that he had invited us for dinner. We had got to know Narayanswamy when he had come to our Institute to take an advanced course. Realising that, as an Indian poet writing poetry in English and resident in India, he had little chance of earning a living by his art he had turned to teaching English at tertiary level. After his course he had obtained a post at the prestigious National Defence Academy at Khadakvasla, near Poona.

We took a taxi to his quarters, one of a terrace of small dwellings alongside a field some distance from his academy. He was mightily pleased to see us and we gathered that he did not find his colleagues or the military atmosphere in which he worked congenial. He had prepared an extensive meal with lots of little dishes served on tin thali trays. Narayanswamy kept replenishing our dishes and we ate the delicious food until we could eat no more and had to ask him to desist. I was particularly pleased to see Dr K tucking in so heartily. The food was all vegetarian, but a world away from the insubstantial fare he had to survive on at our Academy. After dinner our host read to us from the proofs of a book of his work then about to be published and he and Dr K reminisced about their boyhood in Tamil Nadu. Time passed quickly and it was nearing midnight when we finally asked Narayanswamy to call us a taxi to take us back to our quarters.

Some further time passed before we heard the Ambassador car chug to a halt outside. The driver spoke to us in Marathi, a language that Dr K was little more familiar with than I was, but he nodded when we named our destination and set off down the unlighted lane. His car was an old one, but well suited to the pot-holed route, having a high clearance. Joining the road he progressed for about a mile before turning into a field and driving diagonally across it. This manoeuvre took us by surprise. We looked at each other but made no comment. At the far side of the field a dim light burned inside a shack made of wood and corrugated iron. Here we halted and the driver told us in English to wait there as he disappeared inside. He soon reappeared, accompanied by a large man, large in height and bulk, who peered at us without speaking and climbed into the front passenger seat.

We bumped across the field again and on to the road, turning, we supposed, in the direction of Poona. Neither of us could be sure of this as we had taken no account of our direction on our way to Narayanswamy's. The two in the front seats conversed in low tones in Marathi. I looked questioningly at Dr K, who simply shrugged his shoulders. I did not know what his thoughts were, but I know mine were distinctly uncomfortable. As a boy I had read about thuggee in India and wondered whether my text book had been wrong in boasting that the British Raj had stamped out this cut-throat practice. It seemed an interminable time before we reached the first lighted avenue on the outskirts of the town, but when we stopped outside the Academy's archway entrance and the driver turned his interior light on I was surprised to find we had been going barely thirty minutes. In my relief I added a weighty tip to the modest fare demanded and at this point the driver's companion spoke to us for the first time, in fluent English.

He said: "I hope you didn't mind my cousin bringing me along with you. He could see you were strangers round here and feared you might be desperadoes."

We were still laughing as we made our way to our quarters through the otherwise silent camp, unable to imagine two less likely highwaymen, he short and rotund, I taller but distinctly undernourished.

Outside his door Dr K asked me: "Were you scared?"

"Scared as hell."

"So was I." He reached up to clap his hands on my shoulders on either side and added: "I'm glad we've had this chance to get to know each other better." and those were exactly my sentiments, though I would have preferred a chance that had not come in such unnerving circumstances.

To celebrate the final evening of my stay with the Army a group of young captains, service instructors, proposed taking me to a night club in Poona, "the hottest spot in town", they assured me. I travelled there riding pillion on a motor scooter with one of them, escorted by his friends, also on motor scooters. They told me that they were in no hurry to be made up to the rank of major as this would necessitate, in keeping with their enhanced status, the expense of purchasing and running a car.

The club was on the outskirts of town with a vestibule and smallish hall with red and gilt decor, small lights on each table around an open area for dancing or performances - a warm and intimate atmosphere. We were seated at a table next to the dance floor. A band on a dais played Western music. Two captains from Goa advised me to join them in ordering sizzler steaks and the three of us enjoyed this succulent dish while our companions ate orthodox, but no less substantial, Hindu fare. We also ordered a number of bottles of Kingfisher beer, produced at a Bangalore brewery and then considered the best in India. My companions ordered up more of these after we had finished our meal. The beer went down well as the atmosphere in the club was somewhat stuffy. Only a few people danced since there were very few women present, none at all in our party as the married officers had left their wives at home.

After some time a drum roll and a flashing spotlight announced the evening's star attraction, Gwendolena - the Sex Bomb. At first sight Gwendolena appeared an unlikely performer for an act whose title suggested something risqué. She was a large woman, formally dressed in a magenta evening gown with matching elbow-length gloves. Her hair was combed back and caught in a bun behind her head. She strode around the perimeter of the dance floor, flashing a friendly smile at each table of diners in turn before breaking into an undulating dance with expressive hand and arm movements, suggestive of early training in the Bharatanatyam tradition. The accompanying music, however, was entirely Western, with a slow tempo. Gwendolena's next move was to tug at the fingers of her left glove, gradually revealing glimpses of forearm. When she reached the stage where the hand part of the glove dangled free she advance on our table and proffered the glove fingers to one of the captains. He pulled the glove free of her arm and rose to offer it to her with a bow. Rewarding him with a smile Gwendolena took the garment and tossed it towards the curtains she had emerged from at the back of the room. A little more dancing around was accompanied by a similar procedure with the right glove and once again the honour of effecting its final removal was accorded to one of our captains. I was reminded of the words of a Hyderabadi neighbour, the wife of an ex-Indian Navy officer, who had told me that all Indian women love men in uniforms. Perhaps this had not been an exaggeration.

The tempo of the music now increased and Gwendolena's next move was to release the band securing the bun at the back of her head to allow a luxuriant growth of hair to cascade down her back as far as the bottom of her spine. Her dance movements became more sinuous, with a great deal of hip shaking and tossing of the head to cause her mane of hair to swish back and forth. She reached behind her and tugged at the zip of her gown to reveal a portion of flesh. This prompted some of the men in the audience to clap their hands together briefly in anticipation, but Gwendolena zipped herself up again and wagged her finger at us. This tantalising manoeuvre was repeated several times before she again approached our party with an invitation to participate in the performance. This time her eye lighted clearly on me. She turned her back and indicated that she required my assistance with the zip. Having assisted my wife during many years of married life I was confident of my ability in this matter, but when I rose to help Gwendolena she made my task difficult by wriggling about and tossing her head from side to side. I did manage to get a firm grip on the top of the zip and began to release it, but at this point she tossed her head again and caused a strand of hair to become entangled in the zip's teeth. As I fiddled with it, delaying the planned action, the band reprised several bars of music in the way that skilled musicians would do for an inexperienced singer who had failed to come in on cue. Gwendolena looked over her shoulder to give me a smile intended to be encouraging. I thought I detected a hint of anxiety in it, but at this point I finally extricated the impeding strand of hair and unzipped the gown completely, leaving Gwendolena free to dance away and step nimbly out of the garment.

I felt I had acquitted myself quite well in the circumstances, but as I sat down one of the captains refilled my beer glass saying: "You'll be needing this."

As I drank Gwendolena continued to dance around the floor in her underwear, which glittered in the spotlight as the two pieces were covered in sequins. Finally she removed the top piece and threw it down to join the garments discarded earlier. She then blew kisses in our direction before disappearing behind the curtains, kicking the garments before her.

One captain remarked: "It's funny she picked on a civilian to help her take her frock off." I thought I detected a note of reproof here. Perhaps professional pride had been affronted.

I replied, smugly: "I think she simply recognised a man of experience."

The man who had supplied the beer said: "It wouldn't have been so bad if you hadn't kept telling her: 'Don't worry, Gwendolena, we can work this out.' "

I saw his point. I suppose I had transformed what should have been a highly charged erotic display into something more domestic. The band began packing up their instruments, but the captains showed no intention of leaving and ordered several more rounds of beer. My glass was continually refilled and I had some difficulty keeping up with my companions.

When we finally left the club I was invited to take the driving saddle of one of the scooters for the journey back to the Academy. This I had no wish to do. Not only was it many years since I had been in charge of such a vehicle; the combined effect of the cool night air after the warmth of the club and that of having consumed more pints of beer than I was accustomed to made me feel decidedly woozy. I admired the stamina of my young companions, who seemed to be suffering no such disablement. Allowed to climb up on to the pillion seat again I held on tight to the man in front as we set off.

At this late hour the roads were deserted, but I was disconcerted to find that we were going along at a smart pace three abreast, ourselves in the middle of the front rank. The riders to either side of us extended an arm each and insisted that I should join hands with them. Behind us the others made loud whooping noises. I had no idea what dangerous practices they might be up to and no desire to look back to find out. At an Aldershot military tattoo I had seen a military police display in which a dozen motor cyclists had stood to form a pyramid on three moving vehicles and I half feared that my companions might suddenly leap up to stand on their saddles or perform some other ill-advised feat of derring-do. Fear and fresh air were having a distinctly sobering effect, but I wondered whether I had been correct in assuming that the alcohol consumed in the club had affected my companions less than me.

Luckily no vehicles came towards us as we sped forward in line but, when we entered a tree-lined avenue nearing home, this formation broke up. My relief was short lived. One captain left the road and began weaving in and out of the trees alongside, the rest of us following in file. The trees had broad bands of white paint around their trunks and the captains seemed to have no trouble taking evasive action as we approached each one. Nevertheless I was very glad when, nearing the Academy gate, the captains returned to the road, their instinct for good order and military discipline taking command. We passed the scrutiny of the guardroom unchallenged and I regained my quarters after a second evening which had proved enjoyable despite offering at its culmination more excitement than I could have wished for.

Next day I overslept, but just managed to reach the station in time to catch the up-country train to Secunderabad. Back at the Institute I conferred with Dr K about what we should report on our short stay with the Army. He said that we should chiefly concern ourselves with the civilian instructors at the Academy on the grounds that they were there permanently, whereas their service instructor colleagues were all on temporary assignments and likely to be posted back to their units at any time. The civilians he regarded as the better teachers, but believed that they could do with some upgrading in modern teaching methods. He would recommend that one or two of them should attend courses at our Institute for this purpose. While I agreed with his proposals, I pointed out that all this would probably be of little interest to the C-in-C, Sam Manekshaw. His concern had been with the use of spoken English. "What did you think of the English we heard the officers and officer cadets speaking?" I asked him.

"I suppose it was what you'd call 'pukka English.' "

"Well, I think I'd call it old-fashioned Received Pronunciation."

"That won't mean anything to the Field Marshal."

In the end we agreed that we would write separate reports. His, on teaching methods, would go to the Academy's Director of Studies, mine to the C-in-C. He soon had his written up, but I laboured over mine. I had in mind not what might be considered the best model of contemporary English, in itself something almost impossible to get a consensus on, but what kind of English Sam Manekshaw would *like* to hear. Would it matter to him that I considered his officers' accents old-fashioned, in a process of being superseded in Britain by more demotic or regional speech patterns, or would he consider this a positive factor. Taking a broader view, I could not see that his men's voices would disadvantage them when meeting fellow professionals from other parts of the English-speaking world, on military missions or joint military manoeuvres, for example. On the contrary, outsiders might well judge their accents more 'correct' or, to use Dr K's term more 'pukka' than their own. The report I finally sent was short, merely saying that I had found the English of the officers in Southern Command satisfactory. There was no response from the C-in-C's office.

****

Almost twenty years later, in Bombay, a retired Indian Army Brigadier rang to invite Greta and me for Sunday lunch in order to meet his cousin. This cousin turned out to be the redoubtable one time Army C-in-C, Sam Manekshaw.

Our host told us: "Please come on time." (An unusual requirement for weekend luncheons in the city.) "The Field Marshal likes to eat at thirteen hundred hours."

Arriving promptly at twelve-thirty we found the old warrior seated in an upright chair, instantly recognisable, his back as straight, his glance as penetrating, his moustache as luxuriant as in the press photos of many years before. His skin, however, had the fine texture of the very old and his handshake was perhaps not as firm as in his days of power. It was a small party and, seated at the dining table, I found myself opposite him.

I took the opportunity to remind him of the animadversions he had once made on the spoken English of the young officers in Dehra Dun and told him how these, conveyed through a chain of command, had eventually resulted in my mission to Poona. The Field Marshal had no recollection of any such incident, but smiled in acknowledgement before occupying himself with his plate of Dhansak curry. It should have come as no surprise that a commander responsible for the deployment of mighty forces at a time when his country was threatened on both its North-West and North-East frontiers should have no recall of something comparatively trivial, but I could not help pondering on the fact that an incident which linked us, however tenuously, and which was so firmly lodged in my own memory should have no place in his.

Pune 1970, Mumbai 1989

Mary and Tom

Shortly after I arrived in Nairobi somebody told me that if I went to the open air market at Westlands on Sunday morning I could buy that day's British newspapers, which would have been flown in from London. In those years before Sunday newspapers became lifestyle magazines they contained lengthy resumés of the preceding week's news, written by correspondents thoroughly grounded in their fields and well argued reviews of literature and the arts. It seemed worth the effort to obtain them and as soon as I parked my car near the market a boy of fourteen or so broke free from a knot of other lads and ran towards me with a pack of papers under his arm. He asked my choice of paper and when I told him *The Observer* produced a copy with a flourish.

The following week this boy again was the first amongst his fellow newspaper sellers to run towards me.

"It's *The Observer*, isn't it sir?"

I was impressed by his memory and by his engaging grin and looked forward to becoming a regular customer. On our third encounter he asked me whether I could find him a job. I asked him whether he had any qualifications and he told me he had "An A in English and a B in maths." I knew that he was talking about his results in the primary school leaving certificate exams. Excellent though these were I couldn't see that of themselves they would ensure him a job in a city with a high level of unemployment. I asked him what his present job was.

"This job-selling papers on Sunday."

It seemed unlikely that the tiny commissions he would earn from this would keep him above the poverty line, even provide enough to subsist on. I suspected that he came from out of town and, sure enough, he told me that he was from Murang'a, a fertile district to the north of the city. It occurred to me that if he had stayed there he would probably be working on the family shamba and that this would at least have provided him with enough to eat, but I could see why a boy who had done well in his exams would be attracted to the city, to the prospect of becoming that one in a thousand for whom the move would provide entry into that wider, and more prosperous, world he had learnt about in school. The fact that the odds were so heavily against him, that his hopes were unlikely to be fulfilled, made me wonder about the value of schooling which had given rise to such hopes while, I conjectured, providing little in the way of developing practical skills.

This line of thought might have led me to conclude that shutting Kenyan children between four classroom walls, following a pattern decreed for British children by the Board School Act of 1870, was a bad alternative to leaving them at home to acquire traditional crafts. In fact, I might have concluded that it would have been better for me to pack my bags and leave the country as I had come there with a specific brief to work on a language teaching programme for government schools, aimed at ensuring that young children then beginning their education would one day emulate the young paper seller and declare: "I got an A in English." But I didn't give up and I'm glad I didn't because, when shortly afterwards I had a chance to visit schools, I was impressed by two things: by the fact that every school, even in the city, had a shamba where children were taught up to date methods of producing crops and by the enthusiasm of the children to learn to speak and read the language. I never saw this enthusiasm, shared by the teachers, surpassed. They not only went at their lessons wholeheartedly, they did so with obvious enjoyment.

Europeans living in the country who were not settlers were mostly engaged in 'projects', educational or developmental in some sense. Amongst the settlers, descendants of farmers who proudly claimed to have "opened up" Kenya in the past seventy years or so, there were those who derided our efforts, saw them as futile and held the view that those they were aimed to help, the African population, lacked the capacity to benefit from European ideas and techniques. They referred to us as 'two year wonders', innocents abroad who, at the end of their brief stay, would leave the country unchanged or at least unimproved We were determined to prove them wrong.

The term 'wonder' worried me. I discovered that in Kiswahili the word *muzungu*, meaning 'a white man' seemed also to denote 'a wonder'. When I met the Kenya colleagues I would be working with for the next three years I felt quite unlike a *wunderkind*, more like a novice who had a lot to learn about the local scene. Foremost amongst these colleagues was Lorna Wandera. She had started the project in partnership with an old friend of mine who, after working twenty-five years in the tropics, had decided to take early retirement and return to his Surrey village home.

Lorna explained that they had settled on an English syllabus for pupils' first three years in school and had nearly completed a pupils' book and a teachers' book for Year One. A colleague, Elizabeth Gatua, was working on readers in fourteen Kenya mother tongue languages. The mother tongue would be the main language of instruction, English the second language. Our task seemed to me a formidable one, to have everything in place within three years, but I felt that Elizabeth's was considerably more taxing. She was young, energetic, slightly built and in sole charge of persuading fourteen teams of writers to produce materials in accordance with a tight schedule. She admitted defeat in only one instance: no member of the Masai tribe would work with her, presumably on the grounds that young Masai were better employed in herding cattle than sitting in school.

Key to the success of the English project was the manager for East Africa of the Oxford University Press, which was to publish any books we produced. Roger was a large, genial and energetic man. He continually harried us to produce materials to be set up by the printer. We in turn urged upon him our requirement that the books should be not only durable and of good quality but available at a price the Ministry of Education could afford. They would be the principal, almost the sole, purchasers and demands on their limited funds, always considerable, had been vastly increased that year by a decision by the President. Jomo Kenyatta, affectionately known as *Mzee* (old man), had established a tradition that in his annual presidential address to mark the anniversary of his country's independence he would announce some plan for the nation's betterment. This year his announcement had been: "Free primary education for all."

This had led to a huge increase in school enrolments.

Throughout the country big boys and girls squeezed themselves into desks designed for their much younger schoolfellows in Standard One. Once these were filled makeshift classroom arrangements were made in school playgrounds. These two million pupils would be the first recipients of our textbooks. As a concession to the Ministry, whose officials had been caught unaware by the President's pronouncement and were struggling manfully to provide for the education-hungry new intake, Roger agreed that the price of the books would be reduced by the amount that would normally be paid to their authors. Lorna and I could have no argument with this arrangement. We were being paid a salary by our respective employers and could hardly expect to receive royalties as well. The satisfaction of being involved in a creative and challenging project would have to be our sole reward.

And it did prove to be rewarding. We were given carte blanche to produce through the characters and incidents in the childrens' books an imagined world, though we decided early on that it should be a world that reflected the everyday experiences of the readers. Since most of these would be living in rural areas the people portrayed would be rural dwellers: children, their families, their schoolmates, their friends, their animals, their shambas. Before my arrival it had been decided that the first children introduced should be a young girl and her younger brother. They would grow year by year as their readers advanced from Standard One to Standard Three. This proposal to concentrate on characters pupils could readily identify with struck me as an excellent idea, but I was unhappy about the names chosen for them - Mary and Tom. Surely, since readers would be almost exclusively African children, they should have African names. My colleagues explained to me that the choice of such names would be problematic. In a nation of many tribes and language groups it was important to avoid names that had distinctive regional significance. The chosen names would be neutral and it was not uncommon for people to have such names as an alternative to one more indigenous. Elizabeth pointed out that though I and her other colleagues always referred to her by that name her 'real' name was Wambui. I was won over and looked forward to our Mary and Tom endearing themselves to the country's schoolchildren, a sort of Kenyan Janet and John.

A third member of our team, though only an occasional one as she was a free-lance illustrator, was Mara Onditi. Mara was from Italy. In her home town she had met and married a Kenyan student who had brought her back to his home near our Nairobi office. She was a most creative artist, sensitive to our aims and requirements and reproducing in her pictures not only all the details in the text but also added details - a quizzical sideways glance from Mary to her brother who had been seated in her classroom by a new teacher's mistake - which gave extra nuances to our stories. Her contributions, for which I suspected she was sadly underpaid, when reproduced in four colour printing, greatly increased our books' attractiveness. Mara, like me new to the African scene, sometimes failed to pass Lorna's scrutiny. Her original cover for the first children's book, *Hallo Children*, showed Mary and Tom running barefoot across a field.

"These children should be wearing shoes," Lorna insisted.

We protested that our journeys through the countryside had convinced us that most children there did not wear shoes. It was even in my mind that barefoot was a more healthy option, but when Laura pointed out that Kenya was a country of aspirations Mara readily took her painting away and fitted each child with a pair of plimsoles.

In a later book, when we had to introduce the words good and bad luck I asked Lorna if there were numbers considered unlucky in Kenya. She told me that she believed thirteen was one such. This was a number I and my fellow Europeans traditionally associated with misfortune, a happy coincidence, I thought, until Lorna added: "Of course, its only the Safari rally drivers who think like that. They never give a car the number thirteen." Since all these drivers were Europeans, with the exception of one Sikh (I remember the Finns always did well.), we had to think again. A number which many of her compatriots really did think to be unlucky was seven.

"But we call it lucky seven," I exclaimed.

"I know, but in that month ladies often fall over and lose the babies they are carrying." This made sense, but reinforced my growing conviction that there were cultural differences that could easily trip up the unwary.

In our second year something which escaped Lorna's watchful eye was picked up by a scrutiny committee we submitted our work in progress to. This committee was headed by a Mr Chinmungeni. He was an enthusiast for our project and our meetings with him and his committee were always pleasantly informal. However, he felt obliged to pick me up on a story I had written about Mary, Tom and friends preparing a soup of grass and water while playing near the river, a soup which had resulted in upset stomachs. The object of the story was to introduce negative injunctions, "Never play with matches." etc. However, "Never drink water from the river." I was told would not do, since rivers were at that time of necessity a common source of drinking water in the countryside.

I tried always to give my stories, however circumscribed by the limited vocabulary available, a rounded nature, with a recognisable beginning, middle and end - children set out to play in the country, hit on the idea of a picnic, eat unwisely, suffer the consequences, are reproved by parents before being comforted and sent to bed - things of this nature. I noticed that Lorna's stories never followed this pattern. They were simply linear, eschewing cause and effect. Something happened, then something else happened, followed by something else until things stopped happening and the story came to an end. I feared that the scrutiny committee might remark on this, but they never did, except to declare themselves delighted with the stories.

Once advance copies of the first year books were in our hands we set out on what was to become an annual round of safaris through the Kenya provinces. Our object was to brief provincial school inspectors on the use of the books. They in turn were to introduce the books to teachers in group meetings throughout their province. Accompanying Lorna and me with our books in English was Elizabeth, with freshly-printed books in the appropriate mother tongue, and an inspector from the Ministry of Education. This young man, Ben Odiambo, was the organising genius behind our briefing arrangements. I suspected he was younger than any of us, though it was difficult to tell because he had a permanently youthful appearance, but this and his quiet-spoken, modest manner, in no way impeded his winning the respect of his older colleagues. His arrangements were impeccable. Transport, accommodation, conference venues and the bringing together into them of the fifty or so local inspectors in each province we took for granted and when Ben took the chair at our meetings we all knew that everything was going to go well. The meetings were not only efficiently run affairs; under Ben's guidance they also became enjoyable occasions. Although we met inspectors in each province only once a year, when we returned in subsequent years they greeted us like old friends. Whoever in the Ministry singled out Ben for wide responsibilities at a young age made a judicious choice and I felt that he was destined to go far in the fledgling Kenyan Civil Service.

These inspectors were resourceful men and women. Each had been provided with a Volkswagen Beetle car and they drove themselves around the schools in their province. These were scattered over wide areas and reaching them often involved driving through difficult terrain, frequently along red laterite roads, a hazardous undertaking during the rainy season. They were the vital link between the educational planners in Nairobi and the country's rural schools. On one memorable occasion they collaborated in an exercise led by the Chief Inspector of Schools himself. In those years Kenya's secondary school pupils sat examinations set by Cambridge University and these were despatched to arrive at a date immediately before the examination date. On this occasion at the critical time the papers had failed to arrive, but it was reported that the ship carrying them was approaching Mombasa harbour. The Chief Inspector, Alex Gitonga, set out by road from Nairobi in a lorry and brought the papers back to that city as soon as they were unloaded in Mombasa, leaving there in the hands of a colleague those intended for distribution throughout Central Coast Province. He had ordered inspectors from all other provinces to converge on Nairobi in their Volkswagens. Once these were loaded up with their assigned batch of papers the inspectors set off to deliver them, groups of Volkswagens streaming out of the city in all directions. It was reported that this operation, planned at short notice with military precision, ensured that school pupils throughout the land were able to sit down to their exams at the appointed hour.

Some time after our first visits to the provinces I heard the Chief Inspector address a group of young Kenyans who were about to leave for the UK on scholarships. I found that in addition to his organisational skills he had a lively appreciation of cultural differences, derived no doubt from his own time as a scholar in our country. The journey there, as he recalled it, had been an interesting one, from a leisurely and vanished past - by flying boat setting down on Lake Nakuru, the Nile, and the Mediterranean off Tunis before reaching Southampton water - but it was what he had to say about life in London that particularly interested me. He warned the young students that on meeting an academic registrar or a hostess on a social occasion they might be asked questions such as: "What have you come here to study?" "What would you like to drink?"

"Have an answer ready," the Chief Inspector advised "They will not tell you what you must study or simply provide you with a drink of their own choosing."

His audience seemed surprised at this but he then posed a question that had them completely flabbergasted.

"You may be sitting in a college refectory and a student comes to sit opposite you with a tray full of food and sits down to eat it without insisting on sharing it with you - can you believe that?"

It was obvious from their gasps of astonishment that they could not. I hope the Chief Inspector's warnings helped those students quickly to adjust to life in our country and that they found the presence of the element of choice compensated to some extent for the absence of the innate obligation to share.

I was reminded of this obligation on our first meeting with provincial inspectors, at Kisumu, on the shores of Lake Victoria. In the evening most of us gathered in our hotel lobby, sitting round in a large circle. In next to no time inspectors were vying with each other at the bar to see who could bring back the largest number of bottles of Tusker beer to distribute around the circle. It seemed to me that these were being emptied at an alarming rate, which I was quite unable to keep pace with. I soon found myself with a half emptied glass in my hand and two full bottles beside me. My companions were in high spirits and we were soon all laughing uncontrollably at jokes which in the light of day would barely raise a smile. One, I recall, concerned the replacement of the battered lorry which used to distribute school supplies around the province with the inspectors' personal Volkswagens and the reaction of an old woman who lived next door to the distribution centre.

"How nice that the old lorry has given birth to such clean little babies."

When a third bottle of Tusker ale appeared beside me I abandoned the struggle to keep up with my drinking companions, made the excuse that I had material to prepare for the following morning's session and, having contributed a trayful of bottles to the party, retreated to my room.

It was a pleasant room, with a view over the lake and the hotel in general was an excellent one. The provision of good hotel accommodation, along with the good companionship, made these safaris particularly pleasant experiences. I recall only one occasion when one of our party from Nairobi found cause to complain. This was in a hotel called the Pig and Whistle, its name no doubt being a whimsical relic of colonial days, standing in rolling grassland with a view of Mount Kenya. We arrived one afternoon to be handed a note at reception from the local senior inspector saying that he had been unable to secure rooms in the main building as these had been taken by health workers attending a conference on family planning there. He had, however, arranged for each of us to have a chalet in the hotel grounds. When we inspected the chalets we found them to be simply furnished, a bit spartan, but, in my view, perfectly adequate. This was not Lorna's view and she settled into her chalet with bad grace.

In the evening I walked across to the main building, where the senior inspector, Mr K, had promised to meet us. I called for Lorna on my way, but she refused to join me saying she would like me to tell Mr K to come to her chalet.

In the garden outside the main building I found Mr K sitting with Ben, drinking beer. When I gave him Lorna's message he asked me what Lorna wanted to see him about. I told him, perhaps disingenuously, that I thought she wanted to say *Jambo* (Greetings) to him. He looked thoughtful at this, a little morose, and continued drinking his beer. From where we were sitting we could see into a meeting room in the hotel where the family planners, nearly all of them women, were holding a working session. Perhaps to lighten his spirits Mr K attempted a pleasantry.

"You see all those family planning women in there. Not one of them has less than five children at home."

I might have laughed, if only out of a sense of solidarity with Mr K, had not Ben responded sharply: "Family planning is an extremely important part of the Government's policy. These women are doing work of national importance."

Chastened, Mr K rose and made his way slowly towards Lorna's bungalow. He was some time there and when he returned he seemed to be in even lower spirits than when he had left. He made no comment, simply applied himself to his glass of ale, but I suspect that Lorna had said something more than *Jambo* to him. Fortunately in the next two days he redeemed himself with useful contributions to our deliberations and we all parted good friends, looking forward to reuniting the following year.

If the Pig and Whistle was something of a disappointment our next hotel more than made up for it. It was on the seashore north of Mombasa, a hotel intended for the international tourist trade with all the facilities which such tourists expect. We had little time to spare for these luxuries, but we did enjoy its excellent restaurant. One evening when Ben and I were dining alone there, Lorna and Elizabeth having gone into town to visit lady friends, I noticed that Ben, usually a lively conversationalist, was continually distracted by something high up and just out of view to my left. When I turned round I realised that he was looking at a television screen. There was no sound, but this didn't much matter as the visual element was self explanatory. It was familiar to me. I recognised the programme that Ben was watching as having been recorded at the Bedford Town Hall, a programme devoted to all-in wrestling. During the 1970s there had been a viewing public in Britain for this kind of wrestling and I had seen some of it broadcast when I was home on leave. I believe the programmes had not stood the test of time, probably because others had come to realize as I had that what they were watching was less a sport than a form of show business and one in which the actors were less than convincing. After they had faded from our screens at home some enterprising salesman must have seen the possibility of selling these programmes to TV stations overseas.

The particular bout that Ben was watching was in the classical mode, filled with spectacular action and lacking, in our showing, only the grunts and groans of the participants and the orgiastic cries of the female spectators. The opponents looked to be grossly ill-matched. I recognised them but had forgotten their adopted titles, which were something like the Dark Avenger and Young Adonis, the former clothed in black ankle-length leotards and mask and several stone heavier than the latter, bare-chested and wearing what appeared to be white long johns. As I joined Ben in viewing the action Young Adonis was lying pressed onto the canvas having one raised ann being twisted and his face continually stamped on. The expression on his squashed face suggested considerable agony. The referee was crouching on the floor peering at Young Adonis's free hand, waiting for the three beats on the canvas which would signify submission. I turned back to my meal so do not know whether this submission came or not but, as I fully expected, the bout was obviously being allowed to continue because Ben was now giving it his undivided attention.

"Who do you think is going to win?"

I intended this ironically, a rhetorical question asked of someone assumed fully to share one's awareness of the nature of the crude farce being enacted. To my surprise Ben raised his brow and looked at me as if I had said something witless, posed a simpleton's question, before replying that the Black Avenger was the obvious winner.

"I don't think so."

Sure enough my contrary view proved correct. Only a minute after I had surprised Ben by it an even more surprised expression on his face prompted me to turn round to see that the inevitable reversal had taken place. Young Adonis had arisen from the canvas and, clutching his opponent by the legs, was repeatedly banging the back of his head and shoulders against the canvas. He then threw him through the ropes and out of the ring where, grappling dazedly to clamber back, he was counted "Out" by the referee. As the victor paraded triumphantly around the ring Ben turned to me, not exactly awestruck but certainly impressed.

"How did you know that was going to happen?"

I hastened to give him an explanation which would absolve me from any claim to prescience, to being the sort of *muzungu* who was also a wonder. I told him about the well-worn conventions of the genre, stemming from David and Goliath legend, from the satisfaction of seeing the apparently down and out, last gasp contestant finally prevail, of gallant little there'll always be an England standing alone to defy the Axis hordes, of how all the moves between the participants were carefully orchestrated in order to avoid causing damage to either man, leaving out only the equation white guy good, black guy bad. This last struck me as being in such bad taste as to make me doubt the wisdom of both my countryman in selling the programme and the Kenya TV executives in buying it. Ben listened carefully, making no comment but nodding in acknowledgement. Obviously I had destroyed his viewing pleasure for that night as he concentrated on his caramel custard and showed no further interest in the small screen. I felt sorry that in having played the wise guy I had done this, but it was entirely in keeping with Ben's nature that having been made aware that the whole thing was a sham he would want no further part in it, even as a spectator far removed in time and space. It was this grounding in the real world which made him such a good administrator.

On our journey back to Nairobi the following day a punctured tyre delayed us in a desolate area near the Voi game reserve. As we huddled by the roadside in the unremitting heat I noticed that the tyres of our car were all almost entirely bald.

Even the spare that the driver was struggling to use as replacement was virtually devoid of tread. Luckily we got home without further incident but I thought that in the next round of safaris, setting off with the books for Standard Two, I might choose to travel in my own car.

When Ben phoned me to propose calling for me on a Sunday the following year so that the four of us should travel together to Kisumu in the Ministry car, I therefore excused myself on the grounds that I proposed visiting a friend in Naivasha on the way and would meet them at the hotel there. I set out in good time, telling myself that if I kept up a steady fifty miles per hour average I would get to Kisumu in six hours, or a little longer if I stopped for lunch. My plan went well and I reached the Tea Hotel at Kericho in such good time that I felt justified in eating there - an excellent buffet meal with lots of good local produce, fresh fruit and vegetables. From there I drove down the hill, a steep descent that landed me in the valley leading to my destination. Here I ran into a tropical storm and the road was soon awash but, conscious of my self-imposed time limit, I kept going at a steady fifty.

This was a mistake. Suddenly I realised that my car was drifting across the road from side to side, unresponsive to my desperate wrenching at the wheel. Aquaplaning helplessly I found myself flying off the nearside of the road, somersaulting and landing in a ditch facing the opposite way to the one in which I had been travelling. When the car came to a halt I was relieved to find that it was resting on its wheels. The engine was still running and the windscreen wipers swung back and forth across a vanished windscreen. Once I had unclutched my white-knuckled fingers from the steering wheel I found that although my lap was full of crystal nuggets from the windscreen I appeared to be uninjured. The silent farewell I had addressed to my wife and children at the moment the car took flight had been premature. The rain stopped as abruptly as it had begun and I was sitting in the ditch in an eerie silence.

The roof above my head had held firm and I was able to open the door and climb out. At the back the roof was squashed down against the rear seats, the boot lid had sprung open and

I was able to retrieve my grip. With it I scrambled up the bank to the deserted road and a lorry driver who came along shortly afterwards gave me a lift the remaining thirty miles into Kisumu. Feeling a desire for a friendly face I asked him to drop me, not at the hotel, but outside a villa on a rise where a British colleague and his wife lived. They were not there and their servant directed me to the Lake Club down the hill where I found Bill sitting at a table by himself in the garden.

"You look as though you could use a drink."

I don't know whether he intended this purely as a conventional greeting or whether he sensed in my appearance something vulnerable, something that cried out for comfort and reassurance. I had not yet got over my surprise at finding myself still alive and Bill's diagnosis of my present need was spot on. When the beer arrived we drank in companionable silence for a while. I was trying to think of a way of explaining my presence. I hadn't told Bill that I was coming to Kisumu and for some reason I was finding it difficult to find the words to explain the stupid behaviour which had led to my arriving at his club on foot. In the event, when I got around to describing the accident he countered with something which put it into perspective.

"That's nothing," he said. "When Margaret and I were driving along in the Land Rover, miles from anywhere, the road collapsed under our nearside wheels and we were thrown down the bank into a river. The river was in spate and we were carried along floating sideways up into the middle. I was just able to open the door above me and drag Margaret out before the vehicle sank. We swam to an island and we were there for two hours before another driver came along the road. I had taken off my shirt and managed to attract his attention by waving it and we had to wait another two hours before the police arrived with a boat to rescue us."

This account of near death by drowning and a prolonged spell marooned on a soggy island made my own experience seem comparatively trivial. I was wondering whether their vehicle was still lying on the river bed when I recalled seeing Bill's official Land Rover, looking dusty but undamaged, parked at the entrance to the club garden as I had entered.

"Did this happen after I saw you in Nairobi last week I asked him?"

"Oh no. This was when we were in Nigeria four years ago."

At this point Margaret joined us. Her grasp of the situation was perhaps more perceptive than her husband's.

"My God! What happened to you?"

When I told her she insisted that I should stay with them at their villa during the conference and asked Bill what they were going to do about my car. He took me to a table where four Asians were playing bridge and introduced me to Pratap Singh, who was in the car recovery business. As soon as they had finished their rubber Pratap drove me into town in search of the young man who was in charge of his company's pick-up truck. At his house, his father told us that John had gone to the cinema. As we arrived there the audience was streaming out, but John was not amongst them. Nor was he part of the crowd leaving the town's other cinema shortly afterwards.

"I know where he is," said Pratap.

We drove to the edge of town and stopped outside a wooden bungalow. Sitting on the verandah which ran the length of the building were several young women in nightdresses. In response to our enquiry one of these laughed and went inside. She returned accompanied by John, who was buttoning up his shirt. From a lock-up garage nearby he collected the pick-up truck and the two of us were soon speeding back along the road to Kericho. John was an unusual Kenyan in that he appeared to be half African and half Asian. He seemed reluctant to talk and when I told him I thought we were near the scene of the crash he merely nodded. Night was falling fast and I feared that I would be unable to identify the spot in the ditch where the car lay as I had failed to note any landmarks when I abandoned it. The surrounding countryside was pretty featureless, but peering through the cab window I spotted the crumpled metal in the ditch. John winched this up efficiently and got the back wheels up onto the back of the truck. The front wheels were still capable of turning and were soon rolling along behind us as we made our return journey.

After a few miles he told me he felt thirsty and turned abruptly up a dirt track. Now it was completely dark and I could see nothing in the truck's headlights except scrubby bushes. Eventually we turned a bend and approached a large, dimly lit building. Inside was one continuous area lit by hurricane lamps hung around the walls, thronged with a mass of people, men and women clinging to each other and dancing energetically.

John forced a way through to the bar for us and ordered two large bottles of beer, which he allowed me to pay for. We drank from the bottle, as did the others at the bar, a less usual practice then than now. Conversation was impossible as a ten-piece band was pumping out rhythmic music at a impressive volume, despite the absence of amplifying equipment. When John started on his second bottle of beer I made gestures towards my watch as I knew Margaret would be preparing dinner. These he ignored. Fortunately he also ignored the efforts of a young woman who was trying to pull him on to the dance floor. I was puzzled as to how so many people had made their way to this venue in what seemed to be the middle of nowhere as outside were parked only a few cars and trucks and in no direction had I been able to detect any signs of habitation. Once John had finished his beer and wiped his mouth on his sleeve with obvious satisfaction we forced our way back to his truck. He manoeuvred it with great skill round the muddy compound and delivered me to Bill's villa.

After a lavish dinner and a good night's sleep in the spare bedroom I awoke to find that, although some bruises had swelled up, the scratches on my arms were healing nicely and I felt perfectly fit and ready for the day's conference. Bill, however, insisted that we should first call on the local insurance agent. This man suggested we take a look at the car, which we found outside Mr Singh's lock-up garage.

"Looks like a write-off to me," he said.

I had to agree and the agent took me back to his office and gave me a claim form which he told me it "won't take a minute" to complete. It took rather longer and I got stuck on the section which required me to illustrate the accident. I thought of drawing a car flying through the air and revolving but finally settled on a simple diagram which showed an arrow on the road pointing one way and another in the adjoining ditch pointing the other way. The agent approved of this and in response to my urgent request agreed to drive me to the hall where I should already have been talking to the province's school inspectors.

I entered from the back of the hall and saw Ben, flanked by Lorna and Elizabeth, seated at the far end, addressing the meeting. As I made my appearance he broke off. The expression on his face certainly signified astonishment, perhaps also horror. I knew my late arrival was a lapse, but this seemed to me an over reaction. The fifty inspectors turned in my direction, left their seats and, forming an orderly queue, came up and shook my hand, each murmuring condolences, *"Upole. Upole."* One, a large man, took my hand in both of his and told me: "We thought you were dead."

Ben called for an early recess and pots of tea. He explained that on their journey the previous day they had spotted the remains of my car in the ditch. Having inspected it they came to the firm conclusion that I must have perished and they had driven straight to the town morgue to inspect the corpse. Since it was not there they concluded that it must be in some other morgue and it was decided that Ben should be the one to break the tragic news to the inspectors. This he was in the process of doing when I had made my untimely appearance.

Once it had been established that I was very much not dead and really in quite good health we were able to get on with the conference. I was moved by the depth of concern shown by the inspectors. We had met only once previously and a year had passed since then. This conference went particularly well. Everybody approved the introduction of Mary and Tom's grandparents and the fact that the grandfather turned out to be a consummate story teller. Lorna had set the verses in the children's main reader to music with tonic sol-fa notation in the teachers' book to show how they should be sung. We had got them recorded on tape by a class of Nairobi schoolchildren and when we played this the inspectors joined in, the women taking the lead in clear, unusually high-pitch voices with the men providing a burden.

For our return to the capital my colleagues called for me in the ministry car at my hosts' villa, where I had enjoyed the best of home comforts. I noted that the car was a replacement, a brand new people carrier with tyres showing no sign of wear. I spent the return journey sitting in the back, quietly chewing over a large slice of humble pie.

Back in Nairobi Lorna and I started earnestly on writing the books for Standard Three. These would need to be substantial works in order to prepare pupils to tackle the books already produced by other authors for the upper primary stage. Lots of new vocabulary for the readers and for Mary and Tom new experiences - school visits to a game park and even a trip to town - and new acquaintanceships. For the main reader we hit on the title *New Friends* and Mara cleverly gave each of these a distinctive appearance, *maridadi* hair style for Helen, Ben long-necked and wide-eyed. One day I was busy typing up a new chapter when an Englishman popped his head round the door. This man had a habit dropping in for a chat from time to time. I got the impression that he was short of work to occupy his time.

"What's this I hear about a curse?" he asked me.

I had no idea what he was talking about, so he decided to tell me. Somebody had told him that some unnamed Africans, offended by my refusal to travel to Kisumu in the ministry car, had put a curse on my car - "not on yourself" - and were now triumphantly claiming that this was why the vehicle was now an almost total wreck.

I found this story intensely offensive. Not only did I not for an instance give credence to the idea of a supernatural cause of the accident, I doubted the provenance of the story, the attribution to Africans unknown of a belief in and recourse to witchcraft. Such stories were not uncommon in Kenya and were circulated in settler circles, amongst those Europeans who farmed in the fertile areas once known as the White Highlands. Typical of these was that in which a farmer's wife discovers a valuable item missing, calls together the African labourers and tells them that the guilty man will be revealed before the night is over. Sure enough, in the morning the culprit, afflicted with a deadly malaise, returns the stolen object. In some versions the accursed man subsequently dies. In others the farmer's wife nurses him back to health and he is utterly changed by the experience.

When I demanded of my informant who these alleged malignant shamans were he replied that he didn't know, that it was simply a story he'd heard, nor could he tell me from whom he had heard it; it was a story that was "going around." This vagueness about sources was entirely typical. I asked the man to ensure that his stupid story went around no further and told him that we had a printer's deadline to meet. He took the hint and left but the noxious atmosphere his presence had created lingered in the room. He was the sort of Englishman who throve on such stories and, despite my request, no doubt he went on relaying it. For all I know it is still going the rounds amongst certain Europeans in Nairobi to this day, thirty years after I left.

My leaving came sooner than I had expected. The books for Standard Three were with the printer and we were arranging to record a new set of accompanying songs when I got a message that I was being transferred to the Middle East and had to prepare to leave as soon as possible. This meant that I should miss that year's round of briefings in the provinces. I told my colleagues this, with regret, but they assured me that they would cope and, wishing me well in my new post, they laid on at short notice a farewell party, complete with Kipsigis singers and dancers.

On the day I was to leave on a night flight, our sea freight having been crated and sent on in advance, Ellen Kitonga, OUP's editor, called on me with copies of the eight Standard Three books, hot off the press. These were my author's copies and we looked through them together and concluded they had turned out well. I had to explain to Ellen that regrettably I could not carry them with me as my suitcases were fully packed and she promised to forward them to me by airmail.

At this time I was travelling a lot and somehow the books failed to reach me. I wrote to a colleague newly posted to Nairobi asking him to approach the OUP office there and ask for one copy of each book for me. I got no reply and let the matter drop, but having formed a sentimental attachment to

Mary and Tom and wanting to have a record of their last reported adventures, I renewed my request to the publishers for the books from time to time via intermediaries in Nairobi. Twelve years passed before one of these, a friendly librarian, replied that he had managed to obtain the eight books and in due course a bulky package arrived. I was delighted to find that over the years since first publication the books had been reprinted twice, thrice or four times almost every year. What this meant in total sales I was unable to judge. Presumably the huge influx of pupils in Standard One stayed on in school through the years, to be joined by their younger siblings, product of a rapidly increasing Kenyan population, and the Ministry of Education had undertaken to supply each child with the main reader for each standard. The initial print run had been a large one and, multiplied some twenty-five times to allow for reprints, by the end of the first twelve years of the books' being in print the number of books sold must have been impressive. No doubt on some OUP computer that number is recorded but I couldn't calculate it.

I read somewhere that sales of a novel by a man called Dan Brown had reached twenty-nine million and his publishers were still counting.. He, of course, had the advantage of world wide sales, whereas our readers were exclusively Kenyans, but while we were not in the same league, Lorna, Mara and I had certainly produced best sellers. No doubt Mr Brown's story is more elaborate than ours but I took much pleasure in rereading our simple tales of the family we had created, of their friends and their adventures at home and in school, at the lake, the game park and the seaside. I hope our readers derived the same sort of pleasure. One thing I sometimes ponder over: once those Kenyan boys and girls had entered Standard Four and started on the much more serious textbooks prescribed there, did they miss Mary and Tom or ever wonder what had happened to those vanished children whose progress they had followed through three years of their lives?

Nairobi 1977

Expats

Removing photograph albums from a cupboard I find that one photograph has become detached and lies alone on the shelf. It is a black and white shot of people picnicking and might have come from any one of the three dozen albums I'm finding a new home for. As it happens, faces I recognise enable me to trace its true home fairly quickly, amongst the albums of the 1960s. In that for 1966, beneath a blank space is the caption *Farewell luncheon for Hulde Neeb at Loui Jabi's farm - October.*

Other pictures of the same occasion on a facing page have captions identifying the picnickers, but I don't need such aide memoire as these people and the setting remain fresh in my mind after more than forty years. Strictly speaking the farm was not Loui's but belonged to his uncle, proprietor of an insurance business. This farm was in the Ghouta, that huge oasis which spreads south from the outskirts of Damascus. Like the gardens of the city it owes its fertility to the streams coming down from mountains to the north, from the Jebel Qassioun. Loui's uncle had obviously acquired or inherited a particularly favoured part of this oasis. The photos reminded me that his plot was full of mature trees and the October sunlight filtering through these gives the scene a peaceful and pastoral air. Given the terrain of most of Loui's country and the political atmosphere prevailing there in those years, this picnic now seems to me to have been an idyllic moment divorced from time and place. Something unreal and transitory pervades the occasion. I remember now that, unlike the rest of the Ghouta, there were no signs of the cultivation of cash crops on this 'farm'. And the photo caption tells us that it was an occasion for farewell.

Something else, that I don't think I was aware of at the time, now strikes me. Although the event is taking place in Syria, the majority of the picnickers, seated on carpets on the grass, are Europeans, not Arabs. Of those I have named in captions, only Loui himself and Adnan Abd-el-Krim, grandson of the warrior who withstood the Spanish army in the Moroccan Rif mountains for many years, were permanently resident in Syria. Hulde was returning from a tour of duty at the Dutch Embassy to her home in Amsterdam. Others belonged to various European missions; John was a young US diplomat. The picnic was unlike the somewhat makeshift al fresco affairs we are accustomed to in Britain. The carpets, of course, were finer and beside a white-clothed trestle table covered with bottles of wine and dishes of food two waiters stand in attendance. They are dressed in white shirts and three-quarter length white trousers with dark-coloured calf length boots. Standing on the edge of the seated group, looking down on the other guests with a quizzical air, is a third Arab young man. He has a shock of spiky hair and, untypically of the casually dressed group, is wearing a suit of some light-coloured material. His first name I remember as Luis, though I never knew his full name. I wonder why he was included in this party. In the rest of the photograph albums of those years he appears only sporadically amongst the thirty or so of us who regularly spent leisure time together. I now recall that before each New Year's Eve he would urge us to join him to celebrate that occasion in a hotel where his father was either manager or proprietor. Our response was invariably a non-committal *In sh'allah* (God willing). In fact, we were intent on celebrating in the apartment of one of the Europeans amongst us. I sometimes felt a bit guilty about this. Luis seemed a thoroughly good-natured person but the truth was that although he was sometimes amongst us, he was not truly one of us.

What it was to be 'one of us' was ill-defined, but we all understood it. One aspect of it was defined for me shortly after my arrival in Damascus by an Italian public health expert, Pino. He called, unexpectedly, on me in my office, ostensibly to compare notes on how our respective 'projects' were progressing. (Many of us expatriates were working on 'projects', bilateral or multilateral schemes to help the Government of Syria in its development plans.) In Pino's own project, he explained, he was handicapped by having inherited records which were "hafazard". His pronunciation of this word had me puzzled and I had to ask him to spell it out before realising that "haphazard" was the word intended. The inconsistencies of English spelling were, of course, responsible for this confusion, but it was a rare lapse for Pino, whose English was extremely fluent and correct, perfected I suspect by a brief spell studying public health in Bristol. In fact, he prided himself on his mastery of the language and was offended when, some time later, an inspecting WHO officer visiting from Geneva, wrote a report suggesting his English left room for improvement. He asked me to write to Geneva correcting this false impression, which I was glad to do, though I have no idea of the effect this might have had.

Pino spoke only briefly about projects before moving on to more personal topics. Was my wife with me? (She had recently joined me.) His own wife was Swedish. We must all meet. He urged me to join the club at the Andalous swimming pool, "a good place to meet". He left me with this prediction: "You will be members of the younger, brighter set."

I was puzzled by this prediction and by the phrase "younger, brighter set", which I presumed he'd picked up in England. It had a dated air, from the 1920s perhaps, suggestive of irresponsible flappers of an age with the century. I was then in my mid-thirties, a married man with two young children. However, Pino appeared to be of my age and had similar family responsibilities. He made it clear that he and his wife belonged, so why not us?

The Andalous swimming pool was in the Ghouta, rather nearer to the city than Loui Jabi's farm, an open air pool surrounded by walls in the Moorish style in keeping with its name. Outside the wall a ring of mature trees provided a further screen from the public, though local people were sometimes to be seen perched in these trees to observe the antics of the club members. The club was officially known as the Diplomatic Pool and subscriptions were paid through the US Embassy, but everybody referred to it simply as 'the Andalous' and only a minority of the members were in fact diplomats. More than half of the members may have been European or from America, though a sizeable minority of those regularly attending the pool were Syrians or nationals of neighbouring Arab countries and not members of the diplomatic corps. The owners were a Syrian family and admitted at their discretion non-members who paid a daily fee. They served drinks and simple meals from a modest, single-storey clubhouse.

The pool was lined with turquoise tiles and its glistening

waters provided a welcome refuge in months when the temperature soared above forty degrees. Paved areas along its length on either side provided tables and chairs under beach umbrellas where people drank, ate and played cards and other games more frequently than they swam. These leisurely pursuits were more popular than swimming, the pool itself being largely used for periodical cooling off. Its turquoise water provided a divide between club members, segregating us into two groups - a strict segregation; we rarely communicated with each other. Gathered on the clubhouse side were the Europeans, Americans and Arabs. On the further side of the pool sat the Soviets and other East Europeans. One defector only crossed from 'their' side to 'ours'. This was Viktor who, in fact, chose to spend all his time amongst us. He told us that he was the correspondent in Syria for *Pravda*, though Western political officers all had him marked down as a member of the KGB.

Viktor was a popular member of 'our side'. He played an excellent hand at bridge and had mastered the game of *beit*, an Arabic version of backgammon which called for counters to be slapped down noisily on a board inlaid with fine woods and mother-of-pearl. We liked his bonhomie and sense of humour. On one occasion he told us he had been the previous evening to the cinema to see *From Russia with Love*. We asked him what he thought of it.

"It was excellent," he said. "I found myself sympathising with poor James Bond suffering from the machinations of those dirty Reds."

His bonhomie, however, did not serve to get him included in those social get togethers our group enjoyed in the city after the pool had closed for the day. Nor, strangely, was Viktor part of the one strenuous activity we indulged in. On a lower level from the pool was a volley ball court. Games there were organised on an ad hoc basis. Whenever half a dozen or so of us felt inclined a game would begin and newcomers would join in as they arrived during the course of the afternoon, until we had our full complement of six a side. Later newcomers would replace drop-outs who went to cool off in the pool. Anybody could play, regardless of sporting ability. The short and rotund cultural attaché at the West German Embassy, Dr W, would make ineffectual lunges at the ball whenever it came in his direction before crying out in dismay as it sailed past him: "Oh, my dears." The Junoesque wife of an American Fullbright professor, making a similar desperate lunge for the ball, burst out of her bikini top. Unabashed and loudly applauded by the French players she went off to the dressing rooms, swinging the wayward garment from a finger. Games were conducted in a variety of languages. For some reason, possibly a carry over from tennis, the score was kept in French. Improper contact with the ball was greeted with Arabic cries of *Haraam* (Forbidden) and line call disputes were usually carried on in English. There were rather a lot of these, since the players themselves called the line, no umpire being considered necessary. These disputes were good natured and part of the casual conduct of our games, played with constantly changing teams of mixed nationalities.

A more serious approach to the sport, however, was evinced by players from the other side of the pool, the Soviets. They usually appeared with two complete teams and waited patiently until we wore ourselves out and went back to cards or backgammon. Taking over the field, they played vigorously and skilfully and in silence, heeding their umpire's rulings punctiliously. On rare occasions, when they could muster only one team, they would challenge us to a match. Despite Gallic flair, British doggedness and Arabic exhortations to greater effort, we invariably ended up the losers. At the end of one season there was a suggestion that there should be a knock-out tournament. The club president, the British Ambassador, seemed dubious about this, but eventually gave his approval with the proviso that no one team should be composed of a single nationality. The Soviets immediately lost interest and the tournament trophy was carried off by a team of Syrian, French and British players with the decisive assistance of an American marine, one of the contingent of guards at the US Embassy, after a closely contested final.

So the season ended on a high note, players and supporters congratulating and embracing each other. Our group, however, did not have to wait until the following season to reunite. The tradition of meeting up every evening in somebody's apartment continued throughout the winter. It was Dennis, a textile specialist from Bradford, who had established the principle that there should be a party every night. Daily, throughout the season at the Andalous, he would go amongst us appointing a host or hostess for the night and letting the rest know that he had done so. It was an equitable system. With twenty or so possible venues (married couples and single people being equally committed) one's own turn as host came round infrequently. Nor was one expected to make elaborate provisions. A sack of ice could be ordered and promptly delivered. Emptied into a zinc bath it served to keep the staple drink of bottled beer cool throughout the night. Bread and cheese sufficed as food.

'Our group' was made up of mixed nationalities, but almost exclusively Arabs, West Europeans and Americans, the card, backgammon and volley ball-playing people from 'our side' of the swimming pool (but excluding Viktor), those Pino had referred to as 'the younger, brighter set', though not noticeably younger, ages ranging from the twenties to the forties. At university vacation times the average age would be lowered temporarily by the arrival of students flying in to join their parents at post. Curiously, in a country with a strong French influence in the wake of the French mandate of the inter-war years, the British formed the largest single nationality group, if only by a small margin. At that time, in the eyes of westernised young Syrians Britain had a reputation as the good time country of Europe. These were the swinging sixties and it was commonly assumed the action centred around swinging London and that anybody from Britain was part of that scene. The aura enclosed all of us Brits, even those who had never set foot in Carnaby Street, worn a befrogged hussar's jacket or a mini skirt, whose knowledge of London was confined to an occasional brief stay at the Travellers Club or, in the case of our friends from the North, to an overnight visit for briefing before setting out for Syria. While not actively playing up the glamorous image this conferred, we saw no need to deny being part of it. The British Ambassador even claimed to own a Beatles' record, though at parties he held to celebrate the Queen's official birthdays he played safe with a repertoire of Elgar and Eric Coates. Anyway, however spurious our links with the swinging scene, I suspect these helped to ensure our inclusion in Damascus's somewhat sedate version of it.

I use the term 'sedate' because, although our parties were thoroughly enjoyable affairs, there was nothing way out about them, little excessive drinking, no drug taking or sexual misdemeanours. We confined ourselves to beer drinking, conversation and dancing. Dennis carried round a tape recorder for the dancing. It contained a single, open-reel tape made up of numbers only slightly out-of-date which people never seemed to tire of, though Dennis was happy to add on any favourites proposed by fellow partygoers.

Musa el-Kher provided a Moroccan-French number, *O Mustafa* (or *Cherie je t'aime*) and Elie Abu-Fadel introduced us to the *Dobke*, a circle dance. Formation dances seemed particularly popular. One called the *Hully-gully* we persevered with long after it had become outdated in the West. The Military Attaché at the British Embassy, a Black Watch colonel, taught Scottish country dances to Sassenachs in his spacious residence. These, too, passed on at second hand, proved to be within the reach of our versatile, multinational group, though performed in a manner the colonel would certainly not have approved of. 'Tonton' Marc, a Belgian freshly transferred from the Congo, insisted we attempt a dance from Africa called the *Watutsi*. Only the volley ball players who had earlier in the day distinguished themselves by spiking the ball close to the net made a good fist at this, because it involved a lot of high leaping. Towards the end of the evening the music would die out and people would lounge about on settees or on the floor, idly chatting.

Looking back on those days I can see little exceptional in our activities or in those of us involved in them. The overriding feeling was one of happiness in each other's company, a sense of security in our being a tightknit community and an unspoken assumption that things would go on for ever, just as they were. This must have been wilful blindness. We were surrounded by intimations of insecurity and transitoriness. The political situation in the country was extremely unstable. Within two years two military dictators were deposed in *coups d'état*. Military presence in the streets showed no sign of relaxing under a third dictator. Successful insurgent leaders simply led their out-of-town garrisons into the city, seized the radio station and declared themselves the country's new rulers. Martial music would be played, interrupted only by announcements that a curfew was in force. This would continue for three days, though exemptions would be announced from time to time for key workers, such as bakers. When the curfew was lifted, people would pour out into the streets amidst a sense of euphoria. Old friends would embrace and urgently invite each other into their homes for coffee or to enjoy cold drinks served by the a'iran seller, poured with unerring accuracy from an ice-packed container on his back into small glasses.

The first *coup* during my time in the city took place during the night and was bloodless but the second event, occurring at midday, cost the lives of several citizens, caught up in crossfire in the broad avenue beside the Barada river. It was rumoured that this was due to a failure in coordination amongst the insurgents, one group primed to attack at eleven a.m. instead of eleven p.m. as their leader intended. This seemed unlikely in an operation which in all other respects went like clockwork.

Rumours, however, abounded in a city where the media, entirely government controlled, never issued denials. Denials, cynics held, would only confirm the truth of the rumours. The leading newspaper, *el-Thawra*, concentrated on attacking enemies within and without the country. Expatriates were lacerated, the mildest term of opprobrium being 'neo-colonialist', applied even to those of us working in good faith to aid the government in its development plans. Although the trial of the alleged spy, Cohen, was taking place *in camera*, snippets of so-called evidence went the rounds. A neighbour told us that the accused posed as a 'fancy pigeon' (which we took to mean 'pigeon fancier') who kept in his *garconierre* a flock of birds used to convey sensitive information to Tel Aviv. More alarming was the story that foreign agents were abducting babies, whose bodies were discovered crammed into refrigerators. It was hard to believe that people would give credence to such stories. A sociology lecturer at the University of Damascus propounded a theory that this kind of rumour was like a stone cast upon the waters. It caused concentric circles to spread out until one met the outer extremity of a similar rumour and returned to confirm its origins.

By unspoken, mutual agreement no discussion of these events or rumours took place within our group. If Viktor were indeed a KGB agent he must have found his attempts at information gathering in our company extremely frustrating. If anything, our partying took on a more carefree air. Jan, a diplomat at the Dutch Embassy, on arrival seemingly a serious and career-minded young man, revealed a flair for mimicry. His party piece was an uncannily exact imitation of a country and western singer's rendition of *Your Cheatin' Heart*. No evening was complete without this. Another new arrival was Irene, a secretary at the West German Embassy. Her image was that of a little girl who had somehow failed to grow up. An American, Nancy, described her as 'simpy', but she must have had something about her as we learnt that she was a defector from the East, having made her way through a heavily guarded frontier. Uniquely, by the end of the evening she would show signs of being the worse for drink, leaning against the furniture and giggling foolishly. It was noted that she was always amongst the last to leave. For some reason this annoyed Jan and on one occasion, when he was the host, he pointedly sang *Goodnight Irene* to her, but to no effect, as she took this as a compliment. Luckily she acquired an admirer, the middle-aged Moroccan exile Adnan Abd-el-Krim, who escorted her home each night. Her boss, Bernhard, the German consul, disapproved of Irene, alleging that the effect of drinking seemed to affect her health only on Thursdays, the day the diplomatic bag arrived from Bonn. Then she would phone in sick and avoid the rush of correspondence this occasioned.

However, it was Bernhard who nudged our group into a somewhat louche direction. He and his wife, Doris, approached Dennis with a request that they should be allowed to step out of turn as party-givers in order to host a party to celebrate the German feast of *Fasching*. The Chargé d'Affaires at the Swiss Legation explained to those of us unfamiliar with this feast: "This is something special. At *Fasching* nobody is married."

The suggestion that this might be an opportunity for some sort of impropriety surprised us, as Bernhard had the reputation of being a diplomat of the old school. He kept a stern eye on the German community in the city. On one occasion, when swimming close to the far side of the Andalous pool, the side of Viktor's compatriots, I overheard a conversation in German. When I told Bernhard of this he seemed annoyed and immediately swam across in order to be able to deny my story.

On return he reported scornfully: "Those people are *peasants*. They are Saxons." It seemed that their accents had betrayed them as coming from East Germany, presumably members of some delegation from the so-called German Democratic Republic.

When a rumour spread that two German men had been arrested by the authorities, Bernhard was concerned, not least because he had been unaware of the presence in the city of persons whose interests he assumed it was his duty to protect. However, on enquiry he discovered that these two were ex-Nazis who, twenty years earlier, had escaped post-war tribunals and fled to the Middle East. There the Syrian Ministry of Foreign Affairs had employed them to check on names of foreigners wishing to enter the country in order to identify those who might be Jewish or even to have some Jewish blood in their ancestry. (These two were no doubt responsible for the non-arrival of the Chicago Symphony Orchestra. An enterprising US official had attempted to arrange a Damascus concert for them after their appearance at the Baalbek Festival, just across the border in Lebanon. A checklist revealed that they would only be allowed to enter Syria minus almost the entire string section, whose members contravened the ban-all-Jews decree.) These ex-Nazis seemed now to have fallen foul of their Syrian masters. We never knew their fate. Bernhard said no more about the case and we felt inhibited from enquiring further.

Anticipation of the *Fasching* party ran high, especially when Doris announced that fancy dress would be *de rigeur*. Several guests opted for costumes that had served for previous parties, for a shipwreck party, for example, at the same time taking account of the Swiss Chargé's suggestion of high jinks to dress down somewhat from the earlier mode. Carlos and Rosemarie repeated their success as vicar and tart. Barely thirty years old, Carlos was already number two at the Spanish Embassy, destined to go far in his country's diplomatic service. Both tall and dark, he and Rosemarie were clearly the most handsome couple in our midst. They had two beautiful little children, doll-like with eyes even blacker than their mother's. As a tart, Rosemarie was hardly convincing. Her fine, patrician features shone clearly through the heavy maquillage she had applied. Carlos, however, might well have passed for a shameless vicar. In my photo album for 1967 he appears in formal black jacket and dog collar, but trouserless, dancing with his bent right leg raised high, his socks sustained by old-fashioned suspenders, a nice touch. His broad smile reflects the essence of a party that is going with a swing.

For all this, I can recall only one incident that went beyond the normal relaxed atmosphere of our parties. The evening was well under way when the Swiss Chargé suddenly burst out of the kitchen dressed only in his underpants, in the front of which he had lodged a large block of ice. This was the gentleman who had assured us that at *Fasching* "no-one is married." In his own case he was clearly wrong.

In thunderous tones his wife cried out in English: "My husband, what are you doing! Put on your trousers."

Sobered, he returned meekly to the kitchen. Bernhard and especially Doris clearly did not approve. The incident seemed to put a damper on the party and shortly afterwards we broke up.

It may have been the lack of total success of the *Fasching* party, to which we had looked forward with such high expectations, that dented for some that sense of assurance which had held us together for so long. There were plenty of indicators of our vulnerability, indicators that applied to all of us, Syrian citizens and foreigners alike. For a start, there was an increasing awareness of the presence of the *deuxieme bureau*. This was not the official designation of the Syrian secret service, but it was the one everybody knew it by. Letters from abroad began arriving after lengthy delays and with signs of having been tampered with. Nancy received one from an old high school friend written entirely in Arabic, a language she knew her friend to be unfamiliar with, as she herself was. When she asked Jacques to translate it she discovered that it contained the sort of news any typical American college student might send - "We're having a hell of a good time on campus this semester."

Jacques explained: "This is an Arabic version of your friend's letter made by a translator for his boss, a censor who does not understand English. It seems to have been found harmless, but an official has mistakenly put back into the envelope the translation instead of the original."

A US Fullbright professor and his wife phoned the Posts and Telegraphs Department to complain that a call they had made to Talahassie, Florida had not lasted the fifteen minutes for which they were billed. An official called back to say: "We have checked your call. It did, in fact, last fifteen minutes. Would you like to hear it?"

Attempts were made to circumvent the censor. Souheil's wife, a Lithuanian, persuaded her father to write to her in the language of their homeland, even though their first language was German. She assumed no translator would be found in the *Bureau* competent in that language. No such subterfuge was possible in our own case. Greta's mother's letters began to arrive irregularly, with clear indications of their envelopes having been opened and resealed. We puzzled over what could interest the censor in an elderly woman's account of everyday interchanges with neighbours and friends at church until we realised that the name of her church was Zion Hall, a one-time mission to seamen. Mention of Zion clearly would not do.

In a tactfully worded note we advised mother: "When telling us of your church visits, do not bother to mention the *name* of the church."

Her next letter told us: "I went to the usual place on Sunday and showed them your photographs. They were very interested."

The fact that the photographs were snapshots of her very young grandchildren, sent as a record of how well these toddlers were progressing, was not made clear to the censor, who continued to keep us all under observation.

Whereas interference from the censor was regarded as a mere inconvenience, or even a cause of wry amusement, another indicator of the fragility of our group was more disturbing: we were beginning to lose numbers. Not through volition but through carelessness, foolishness of simply malign fate members of our group fell away, some to disappear completely. For Prem, recently graduated from Oxford to take up a career appointment with the United Nations, exile was self-imposed. On the transfer from Syria of the head of his mission, the wife of his replacement, formerly a senior Austrian diplomat, sent Prem a formal invitation to dinner. For some reason on the night in question Prem became involved with a group of young Lebanese visitors and entirely forgot the invitation. He called on us in a state of agitation, begging our advice.

Greta told him: "Get hold of the largest bunch of flowers you can obtain, put on your best suit and arrive on your boss's doorstep tonight at the time appointed for last night. This will be seen as a genuine error and you may even be able to laugh it off."

He went away to ponder this advice, but we later learnt that he had instead handed in his resignation from the UN service, abandoning what promised to be a brilliant career. Shortly afterwards he flew back to his home town, New Delhi, and took up a career in journalism.

Jurgen, on the other hand, had no wish to leave Syria, but most of us felt that, like Prem, he brought his exile (or, in his case *deportation*) upon himself. An information officer at the German Embassy, he had decided to interest himself in the way of life of the Druse community. These people, living in the Jebel Druse, were regarded with some suspicion by many of their fellow citizens, as a secretive people, possibly even disloyal. Colleagues advised Jurgen to interest himself elsewhere in the country, but when a German TV company proposed a visit Jurgen insisted that they should film the Druse and that he should accompany them to their Jebel. This proved too much for the Syrian authorities and, despite his diplomatic immunity, he was ordered to leave the country within forty eight hours. He went out in some style. We were all invited to a buffet lunch at his bachelor penthouse apartment which ended with his Palestinian servant appearing with a tray of champagne. Raising his glass in farewell, he urged us all to stay on to enjoy the remaining bottles before running down the stairs to the official car which would take him to the Lebanese border in time to meet his deadline.

A young couple, he British, she American, enjoyed no such diplomatic immunity. A US diplomat from Damascus met them by chance in Beirut, where they had come in search of work, any sort of work. He recruited them on the spot to teach at the hard-pressed Damascus Community School, where his children were enrolled. They had barely had time to become familiar with our group at the Andalous when the Syrian authorities ordered them to leave the country immediately. They had time only to get a message to us to visit their apartment and share out the few pieces of household goods they had managed to accumulate during their short stay. We assumed their deportation was the result of guilt by association, with 'neo-colonialists'.

Sorry as we were to lose these and other friends in similar circumstances, the fate of Abd-el-Hadi affected us much more deeply. On two occasions, at times of tension in the city, he disappeared for a month, reappearing to tell us that the authorities had held him in gaol. He told us he had been charged with no offence and was convinced that he had committed none even though, on his release, he was told to avoid reoffending. He came to believe that the reason for his arrests dated from his time as a student in Britain. During the Suez crisis ten years earlier he, along with many students both British and foreign, had taken part in a demonstration against the British government's actions. The Arab students involved came to be thought of as 'Nasserites'. At the time this was a non-controversial term in the Middle East, where the Egyptian President was universally regarded as the leader of the Arab world. In time, however, and particularly after the break-up of the short-lived Egyptian-Syrian union in 1961, 'Nasserite' became a term of opprobrium, attaching itself to Abd-el-Hadi and his fellow Trafalgar Square demonstrators. Like the Community School teachers he had become guilty by association, but unlike them he had no country other than

Syria to go to. A third time he disappeared. We assumed he was incarcerated, but he did not reemerge and after some time his name dropped from our conversation. We did not feel good about this.

Pino called on me with a gift for my thirty-fifth birthday, a copy of *The Glory that was Greece*. (Reading it gave me a strong desire to visit Knossos, to see the restorations to the palace carried out by Arthur Evans, but it was not until after my retirement many years later that I was able to fulfil this wish.) Pino told me that he was thinking of leaving Syria. I gather he had become frustrated by his inability to get into order the 'haphazard' records he had inherited in his public health office. He was looking at the possibility of a UN agency post in some neighbouring country as he had become enamoured of the Middle East. He was reading Lawrence's *Seven Pillars of Wisdom* and shared none of the reservations about its accuracy of some of its British critics. We knew we should be sorry to see him and Ingrid go as they had become firm friends.

I remember he said to me: "So now you're thirty-five. I reached that age last year; it's the middle of life. From now on our lives will be a down hill journey." I hoped he was jesting. At least his departure from Syria would be of his own choosing.

As a UN official, Pino would have no difficulty in leaving, but this was not the case for all of us. Exit visas became increasingly difficult to obtain, subject to more complicated and lengthier bureaucratic procedures. Those of us expats working on development programmes were allotted distinctive, non-diplomatic licence plates for our cars, subjected to varying, arbitrarily imposed time limits. In most cases their validity lasted a mere three months and, since they were issued in arrears and only after long delays, we found ourselves driving on expired licences. While this seemed of no interest to the traffic police, it did debar us from leaving the country in our cars, even if we had obtained exit visas. The delights of the Holy Land to the south and the pleasures of the playboy world to the west in Lebanon in those years before its long drawn out civil war, became largely alien to us. The situation for our Syrian friends was generally worse. Occasionally one of them would manage to make a break for Europe, returning with news and evidence of the great world outside our narrow circle Musa el-Kher brought us a tape of music from a review he had seen staged by a South African company in London. In one number a whining Afrikaans child pleads with his father: "Oh Daddy, won't you take us to the drive-in. (It's only eight hours in the Chevrolet.)" This struck us as both funny and forlorn, coming from a land where most of its citizens suffered from the afflictions of apartheid. Confined though we were, our situation was incomparably better than theirs and though rumours of imminent war with our well-armed neighbour beyond Mount Hermon abounded, our partying went on, unhampered by the authorities. In fact, new members arrived from abroad to join our circle and replace those we had lost.

Dennis reported that he had recruited the newly-arrived daughter of the Haitian ambassador. Her appearance was awaited with lively anticipation as somebody had spread the word that she was acquainted with, if not possessed of, the power of voodoo. Late one evening she certainly made a promising entrance as we were dancing the Watutsi. She was a slim girl, with a mass of untamed hair and threw herself into the dance vigorously, improvising wildly. However, when we tackled her on the subject of voodoo she was obviously taken aback and denied all knowledge of its rituals, or even of its existence. She was a product of Cheltenham Ladies College and more acquainted with the fine arts than the magic arts. She was good company and fitted effortlessly into the group.

Stefan arrived from the then Republic of Yugoslavia and became our sole representative from Eastern Europe, perhaps fittingly as his President was at that time set on steering a line somewhat independent of his Comintern neighbours'. He had come to give specialist advice in a medical research centre. Victim of a regrettable breakdown in understanding between two governments, his own and his host's, over who was responsible for his pay, allowances and the provision of accommodation, he found himself almost entirely without means. Insisting in taking his turn as host, he invited us to his apartment furnished with boxes serving as chairs and tables.

"I am going to serve you a drink from my own country," he announced. "We call it slivovitz. I have made it myself."

We sipped the colourless liquid cautiously. It made a change from beer and certainly packed a punch. Asked how he made it, Stefan explained: "It contains alcohol from our laboratory. In it I put fruits, but I don't know their name in English." We eventually ascertained that these were prunes. Some of us acquired a taste for it, but after a few glasses felt vaguely unwell and our party broke up earlier than usual.

Unlike Stefan, the Syrian bachelors in our group, perhaps because they lived with parents who would not approve, did not entertain at home. They more than made up for this by taking us to the Caves du Roi, one of the very few restaurants serving French cuisine that remained in Damascus, though there were many excellent eating places for Lebanese food on terraces alongside the Barada river. For some reason a man dressed as a Roman centurion stood guard outside this restaurant, but inside the atmosphere and the menu were authentically French. Here we dined on fare incomparably more varied and well prepared than our habitual bread and cheese.

We formed a larger group than usually booked in at the Caves du Roi and were no doubt valued customers, but it seemed to me that the proprietor was exceptionally accommodating to us. He was happy to play Dennis's tape for us and to clear a space for dancing. I recall one evening when Marwan was our host that a charade was enacted in which our party became a supposed engagement celebration for two of our American friends, John and Nancy. Seated side by side, they played along with this, exchanging languorous glances, the very image of a besotted betrothed couple. In our hearts we all knew that such a betrothal was far less than probable, that something unspoken in a class system less well-defined than ours in Europe or in the Arab world, but nevertheless compelling, would keep them apart. John was at the US Embassy, reputed to be a high-flyer who would go far in the diplomatic world. At home in several languages, he liked to chat up the daughters of the Italian Ambassador in their own tongue, having served his apprenticeship in Rome. Nancy's connection to the Embassy was through her father, a Marine sergeant in the security detachment there. She was what her compatriots described as a 'hometown' girl, from Texas, pretty, frequently laughing while throwing back her mane of auburn hair. John's good looks were more classical, an aquiline nose, high forehead; a blonde-haired, young Adonis type.

To an outsider our charade must have been convincing. Our sole fellow diners that evening were young Lebanese, a small, animated group seated at a table to one side of the restaurant. (They were reversing the normal trend; young people seeking a good time aspired to go westward from Syria *into* Lebanon, not in the opposite direction.) These young people sent the proprietor across to our table with a bottle of champagne to toast the 'happy couple'. Later, Dennis's tape, to which we were dancing between numerous courses, reached its Scottish section, an eightsome reel. As we were less than adroitly finding our way through its intricate movements, we were surprised to discover that one of the young Lebanese women had entered enthusiastically into the mêlée. Accommodating a ninth dancer in a reel intended for eight proved difficult and a measure of chaos ensued, though nobody had the heart to reject someone from whom we had unjustifiably received a gift for a supposedly special occasion.

This evening at the Caves du Roi, though nearly so, was not the last meeting of our group I ever attended, but it stands out in my mind because of the sumptuousness of the food, the geniality of our surroundings and the high spirits, higher than usual, I think, of our friends. There was also the element of playacting. Perhaps there had been a trace of this in all our meetings over the previous three years and it is only the fact that our little world was about to fall apart, that the real world was about to intrude so starkly, that makes me especially conscious of the artificiality of that evening.

As a prelude to the end an aerial combat over the skies of Damascus one Sunday ended with a plane crashing in flames to the east of the city and sent people scurrying to the shops to stock up with emergency supplies of food. The Government announced that one of a marauding band of Israeli aircraft had been downed by its own fighters. A French engineer who found his way to the site of the destroyed plane returned to report that it carried Russian markings and was almost certainly part of the Syrian airforce. He disappeared suddenly, believed to have been deported by the authorities. Although this was a small-scale engagement it was taken to presage a wider conflict in the area.

It also presaged the appearance in Damascus of a young Englishman who immediately acquired the title of 'the great white whale'. Arriving at the Andalous he stripped off to reveal a body so immense, so well covered that not a trace of bone or muscle was discernible, a body startlingly white, with the glow, though certainly not the texture, of marble. This body he plunged into the pool, causing a large displacement of water and alarming the smaller children swimming nearby. Wallowing in the pool or shaking drops from his immense frame beside it, he was obviously overwhelmed with delight to be amongst us. Even the most northern European of us, however prone to sunburn and peeling skin, appeared bronze beside him. He entered readily into our games of bridge and backgammon, but not of volley ball and made no secret of the fact that he had been sent to Damascus on a special mission from Whitehall. This aroused the interest of Viktor, but their acquaintanceship was short lived, as the great white whale made only that one, spectacular appearance at the Andalous. We learnt later that the British Ambassador had ordered him confined to the embassy, charged with the task of destroying sensitive documents as a precaution against their having to withdraw from the country at short notice.

This precaution soon proved to be judicious. Days later, two days after the outbreak of the Six Day War between Israel and its Arab neighbours, British and US personnel were given by the Syrian Government forty-eight hours notice to leave the country following an unsubstantiated report that the Western powers' airforces had aided the enemy. So we left, ourselves, Dennis and Pat, John, Nancy and others perceived officially as the enemy, leaving the group behind us, not knowing whether their cohesion and good fellowship would survive. We were sad to leave as, despite restrictions and occasional harassment, we had formed a love for the country and the people we had come to know through work or play. They had been generous and hospitable hosts to strangers who had tried, though perhaps not always successfully, to behave well as guests.

In a final gesture of hospitality, our group, including those of us about to leave, were invited to lunch at his home by Jacques. This took place some days before we received our official order to depart. Possibly Jacques, a lawyer, had some premonition of this, though he was not employed by the government. If so, it was a particularly warm gesture, consorting with those about to be disgraced in public.

Jacques' residence was, untypically in an area of apartment blocks, a house, an attractive, modest building dating from the 1930s at the lower end of the boulevard that gave the district its name, Abu Roumana. On arrival we were greeted by Jacques and his sister, a sweet-natured, unmarried woman who joined in our activities only occasionally. His elderly father was also there. After a typical Arab meal, starting with a great number of mezze dishes and ending with sweetmeats, a quietly enjoyable, leisurely affair, Jacques' father took me by the hand and led me into a room to the rear. This small room was furnished in traditional Middle Eastern style and we sat upon an ottoman, an appropriate item of furniture in view of what followed.

Jacque's father told me that before the First World War he been in the service of the Ottoman Empire, posted in Beirut as Legal Secretary to the Turkish Governor there. Six Arab insurgents had been arrested and the Governor favoured the extreme penalty, whereas his secretary's instinct was for clemency. His story gave a fascinating glimpse into the intricacies of Ottoman court life and judicial processes in those distant days before Turkey's enemies breathed fire into the revolt of the Arabs, only to become in turn the enemies of these long-subjected people. Before he could finish his story, the party in the adjoining room broke up and I had to leave with the other guests, missing the story's conclusion, much to my regret.

The next few days passed in a flurry of activity - making difficult decisions about essential possessions to be stuffed into cars, a round of farewells, discussions on the best route to extricate ourselves from the country, accompanied by reports that the great white whale was working overtime in the embassy destroying documents. The Andalous pool was closed and no further meetings of our group took place. We finally left in a column of private cars, our departure rendered no less ignominious by the Ambassador's decision to fly the British diplomatic standard on his official Bentley at the head of the column. At the Turkish border there was a long delay caused by the Syrian authority's refusal to allow those of us without diplomatic status to proceed on the grounds that our cars carried number plates that were the property of the Ministry of Transport and that, in any case, none of us had an exit visa. Here the Ambassador displayed the qualities that had raised him to his position in the Foreign service, refusing to abandon us and calmly advising us to sit tight until our forty-eight hours notice of expulsion expired. Sure enough, at that hour we were allowed to cross the border into Turkey. There we were well received. Preoccupation with an uncertain future and the need to reorientate our lives pushed the memory of the previous three years into the background, though we sometimes thought of those days and wondered about the fate of members of our group. Although we came to belong to other circles, in other countries, none of these had the relaxed and closeknit quality of the group of friends at the Andalous and the passing of the years ensured that we were never again members of a 'younger, brighter set'.

****

It was eleven years before Greta and I again had the opportunity of visiting Damascus. Although it was not the main purpose of our visit, we determined to try to find news of old friends. Jacques' house was our obvious starting place. Of all our group's permanent residents, his was the only home we had ever met in. Apart from this, Jacques was the focal point of all our Syrian friends, the still centre around which many of our meetings revolved. He was invariably good humoured and could not be imagined having a bad word for anybody. How he conducted himself in court none of us knew.

After our abrupt departure we had kept no contact with friends in the city, initially through not wanting to embarrass them with letters the censor would surely intercept and later through sheer inanition, so we arrived on Jacques' doorstep at lunchtime uncertain of our reception or whether he would still be living in the house. But sure enough, there he was, answering the doorbell himself. Strangely, he did not seem oversurprised to see us. Smiling in his old, slightly one-sided manner, he embraced us and drew us into the house.

We asked after his own health (obviously good) and that of his sister (also good. She was out of the house, working in an office downtown). I couldn't think how to ask about his father. The old man appeared to have been in his mid-eighties when we had last met and I doubted he was still with us, so I simply asked: "And your father?"

"He's very well," said Jacques. "He will want to see you."

He led us into the room to the rear. His father was seated on the ottoman there, exactly where I had left him eleven years before, looking only slightly older. He greeted us in gracious Arab fashion, his arm across his heart and motioned us to sit either side of him. Then, holding a hand of each of us he said: "This Turkish governor in Beirut ....."

Beginning precisely where he had left off, he recounted the story, dating from 1916, of the Governor, his Legal Secretary (himself) and the six Arab insurgents. This time he was able to reach the conclusion, which was a triumphal one. Despite the Governor's determination to impose a capital sentence, Jacque's father was able to convince him that under prevailing Ottoman law he had no powers to impose one. The arguments he used accorded with his own overriding conviction that this was an occasion for clemency. It was heartening to hear of the prevalence of law in an area where the response to opposition had become one of violence leading to escalating violence and where the ancient appeals for clemency were overwhelmed by the desire for revenge.

When the story ended the old man retired for a nap and Jacques led us into the dining room, where the table had been laid up for the three of us. After a brief résumé of our lives in the years since we had last met and talk about changes in the country, which, with the aid of funds from oil-rich friendly Arab nations, had made much material progress, we got on to the subject of mutual old friends.

We ourselves did not have much to offer. We knew that Prem

on his return to India had gone into journalism, working his way up to editorship of an English-language national daily. This was a position of some importance, though his paper was not the leading one of its kind and, in any case, the vast majority of Indian readers took vernacular-language newspapers. From his editor's chair he might well be looking back to a career as an international civil servant, the envy of all UN personnel on short-term contracts in Damascus, abandoned because of a minor breach of etiquette. Dennis and Pat had returned with their tape of dance music to their home in Bradford. They had been the youngest married couple amongst us, very much in love on their first experience of life as expats, but their marriage had not survived the bitterness occasioned by a casual affair entered upon in Damascus.

Jacques' information was much more extensive. He began by telling us that our group had not survived the Six Day War and the sudden departure of the British and Americans, but went on to give us details of an impressive number of those now dispersed members of it. We should not have been surprised by this as, if there was anyone of us the rest would want to keep contact with, Jacques was the obvious choice. For the most part, what he had to tell us was no less disheartening than our own brief report.

Jurgen on arrival in the Congo as his country's information officer had somehow got across the authorities in the same way in which he had antagonised the Government of Syria. Two such misfortunes in succession had proved unacceptable to the German Foreign Office and Jurgen was no longer in its service. The career of the American, John, seemingly assured of success in the diplomatic corps, the young 'high-flyer', had crashed on his return to the States, where he had become irreclaimably addicted to drugs.

The ideal marriage represented by Carlos and Rosemarie with their two beautiful children had proved no more enduring than that of Pat and Dennis. At that time they were divorced and engaged in disputing their childrens' custody. Saddening though this news was, worse was to follow. Pino, instrumental in introducing us to the group, whom I remembered forecasting a downward trajectory in our lives following our thirty-fifth birthdays, had fulfilled his ambition of getting a UN post in a neighbouring country. On returning to Ankara, driving by night, with his wife and children from a visit to old friends in Damascus his car met in head-on collision a Turkish lorry, the driver of which was thought to have fallen asleep. Pino, Ingrid and their middle child were killed outright. Their daughter and baby boy survived, to be brought up by grandparents, she in Stockholm, he in Rome.

The sole success story he had concerned Jan, the Dutch diplomat who had amazed us with the authenticity of his rendering of *Your Cheatin' Heart*. Jacques understood that he now occupied an imposing desk in his country's foreign ministry, in command of awesome responsibilities. (Years later I was able to confirm this report. When I asked the Dutch Consul-General in Bombay, returning to Holland on home leave and for debriefing at his ministry, to convey a friendly message to Jan, he told me: "Dr S doesn't talk to the likes of mere Consuls-General.")

Of 'Tonton' Marc, a confirmed bachelor who had acquired his nickname because all the smaller children at the Andalous gravitated towards him, of the impecunious Yugoslav Stefan and of all our other expats Jacques had no news except that they had left Syria. He had, however, kept track of many of our Syrian friends.

Abd-el-Hadi, the alleged Nasserite, had not reappeared and several others had gone into exile, extricating themselves with difficulty from their homeland for a new life in neighbouring Lebanon. Adnan E was now practising medicine in the Barbir Hospital in Beirut. Ghassan, an assistant professor at Damascus University, had taken up lecturing twice a week in the same prosperous and easy-going city and it was feared that he, too, might settle there permanently as part of Syria's brain drain. Ghassan had once arranged for all of us to see his University production of *Much Ado About Nothing*, an excellent production marred only by the decision of the student playing Dogberry to give the constable an accent he believed to be cockney, rendering his lines unintelligible to everybody in the audience.

Planned and conscious decision making had led to the exodus, much regretted by the Syrian authorities, of such specialists, but the departure of Loui, our generous host at picnics in the Ghouta, was hurried and the result of distressing circumstances. On the nationalisation of his uncle's insurance company the government had allowed him to continue in his managerial position. A section of the company's workers took exception to this, imprisoned Loui in a cellar for several days and subjected him to beatings. On his release he, too, not surprisingly sought refuge across the border.

It was a route we were to take later that day and we had to break off this lengthy catching up with the past, which we had very much looked forward to, but which had not proved a comfortable process. What we had learnt from Jacques would make it difficult for us to look back on our years with the group in the same way, as a time fenced off from the outside world in a zone of security protected by good fellowship and mutual regard. Those who believe in the fates might say that a greater awareness of external reality would have made us less susceptible to the heavy hand of Nemesis, but I believe the misfortunes of so many of us were simply the result of time and circumstances in a politically unstable world.

As we were leaving Jacques' house I suddenly recalled someone we had overlooked. "What happened to Luis?" I asked. "We never went to his New Year's Eve parties, did we?"

Jacques looked uncomfortable and paused some time before replying: "We are very ashamed about Luis. We discovered that in all those years he was being used by the *deuxieme bureau* to keep an eye on us."

This made us feel bad for Jacques. We attached no blame to him. In all our meetings neither he nor anyone else had introduced the topic of politics and the reports Luis was able to give to his masters must have been as disappointing to them as those submitted by Viktor were to the KGB. Undoubtedly Luis's actions were a betrayal, but it seemed to me that if we had given him something to report, that if we as expats had maligned or in some way sought to harm our host country, that would have been a greater betrayal. We tried to reassure Jacques by reminding him of the innocent nature of our time together. He had, characteristically, been frank with us and we knew what it had cost him to tell us of the behaviour of his fellow countryman. He could have said nothing about the sorry business.

So we left after a reunion somewhat overshadowed by Jacques' revelation. From time to time Western expats like ourselves must often have returned on nostalgic journeys to countries where they had been happy and, given the passing of time and changed circumstances, come away chastened. They have the consolation of knowing that, armed with the correct documents, they can come and go as they please, whereas many citizens of the countries where we have worked, constrained by bureaucratic restrictions or even detained by arbitrary law, can leave only at great risk, suffering severance from family and loved ones. Expats enjoy some sort of immunity, whether diplomatic or otherwise. The worst that could happen to them is that they might be asked or forced to go before the expiry of their allotted time.

Damascus 1964 - 1967

Abu Salem

Shortly before joining a group for a journey through Libya our travel agent told us: “There will be a Libyan policeman travelling with you. This is required by government regulations.”

On the flight to Tripoli we discussed this. None of us fancied being accompanied everywhere by a minder. Our purpose was to visit archaeological sites, Greek and Roman with, perhaps, some traces of Carthaginian, led by a university specialist from Cardiff with the assistance of a local courier. The addition of a police escort, probably a ‘heavy’, a silent type who while purporting not to speak our language would be listening out for any indiscrete comments in order to report us to his masters, seemed unlikely to add to our enjoyment or scholarly aspirations. Our agent had also informed us that our fortnight’s visit was conditional on our observing total abstinence and some of our party had been fortifying themselves against this deprivation by making good use of the airline’s free drinks service.

So we passed through Tripoli airport’s agreeably uncomplicated immigration procedure in a state of euphoria. Greta and I were first through into the customs area. There a slim young man with a ready smile, recognising our luggage labels, sprang forward and introduced himself.

“I’m Abdullah. Please follow me.”

He took our cases and led us to a bench where a customs officer was allowing a passenger to close a case he had been examining.

“These people are with me,” he explained and in next to no time had us outside and was loading our cases into a coach.

Here Peter, our university professor guide, introduced both himself and our courier, el Khamis, who was helping Abdullah with the cases. When we were all aboard and heading towards our seaside hotel it struck me that Abdullah, sitting beside el Khamis in the front seat and chatting animatedly, neither our guide nor our courier and obviously not an airport porter, must be our policeman. So it turned out to be and we could not have had a more amiable or attentive travelling companion throughout our stay in his country. On lengthy, and sometimes hot and dusty, journeys he was constantly leaping off our coach to obtain bottles of mineral water and packets of biscuits for us and, together with el Khamis, even managed to brew up our tea while we were travelling. All this he accomplished in an unvaryingly friendly and good-natured manner. He quickly established himself as a firm favourite with all of us.

It was a great joy to be back in Libya after almost forty years. The country was just opening up to tourists after many years of partial isolation Its attractions featured in several British travel company's brochures and when we found one that promised return air travel between Tripoli and Benghazi we signed on immediately. Rival companies proposed making such journeys by road, a road we had no wish to traverse again having done so, starting from Benghazi, in our own car many years earlier. It had been a trying thousand kilometre journey in the heat of summer, not least for our eleven month old son, and beset by difficulties - a burst radiator hose which, repaired with Greta's swimming cap, had enabled us to complete the final two hundred kilometres only at a snail's pace. A sudden wind from the south had piled sand across the road at one point and we had visions of being cut off in days, before the great oil strikes, when lorries passed at infrequent intervals. Our overnight stay in the township of Sirte, a half way point, had failed to afford much comfort. One of the half dozen scattered buildings there was a single storey hotel whose name I forget, but it was an impressive one, possibly the Grand Imperial Palace. In its dark interior we had difficulty finding a member of staff. Eventually a man appeared from a recess and led us through corridors to a small room at the rear of the building. In the corner was a wash basin.

"There is water," the man said and turned on the tap to allow a small amount of the precious liquid to escape before turning it off again. After he left we were unable to obtain any more water, nor could we find the man again to report the problem. Sirte's one consolation we discovered to be a tiny restaurant where an elderly Italian woman cooked us delicious pasta. Why this woman remained there twenty years after the British Eighth Army had driven her compatriots from the area we were unable to discover as the Signora was taciturn and affected not to understand our halting Italian.

I remember the road followed the seashore for much of its length and on setting out early in the morning the sea to the right and the sand dunes to our left had made a pleasing contrast. At points where the road veered away from the shore we became aware of mirages, but the novelty soon wore off and the abiding memory is of tedium and discomfort. A quick flight between the country's two major cities offered a much more inviting prospect.

Getting to Libya on this occasion had proved less problematic than forty years earlier. The travel agent had obtained our visas whereas previously I had presented myself personally at the Libyan consulate in London. On hearing my explanation that I had been recruited to serve his government on a two year contract as a lecturer in English at the University of Libya's Benghazi campus an official had told me that he regretted he could not grant me a visa. From a phone booth outside I had contacted the organisation that had recruited me. They told me to wait fifteen minutes before returning to ask for a Mrs Smith. This woman simply took my passport into a rear office and brought it back to me with the visa entered.

A week later we flew into Tripoli on a Belgian aircraft from Geneva. There we were met by the senior official in the country of the organisation that had recruited me and his wife, an English couple who seemed to us elderly, but were probably in their fifties. They took us to the airport tearoom and when we declined his offer of a drink, having been well fed on the plane, he remarked: "Probably wise." While he briefed me about the University in Benghazi a fly landed on his forehead. He slowly raised a hand in that direction but reached the spot only long after the fly had departed. He was wearing a linen suit and sweating profusely and indeed it was hot. His air of resignation, even perhaps of dejection, led me to wonder whether this country might have a debilitating effect, even on comparative youngsters such as ourselves. It was kind of them to come out to the airport, especially since it had obviously cost them some effort. An hour later we were flying on to Benghazi and Greta told me about the briefing she had received from the official's wife.

"When you arrive they will take you to the apartment of the previous professor and you will cry and want to go home. But don't worry; whitewash can do wonders."

Our first acquaintance with Tripoli had been confined to that hour or so at the airport and our only other visit, when passing through two years later on our way to Tunis and a boat to Europe, had lasted only a few days so we were now looking forward to a longer stay, in the city and in the province of Tripolitania, before revisiting more familiar sites in Cyrenaica.

At our hotel, an imposing building recently constructed, Peter briefed our group on the coming days. We could stay one night only in our present hotel as it was to be taken over for an official conference on the morrow.

In fact, one night stays would be the norm for our tour as such conferences made bookings uncertain. Our courier, el Khamis, would however ensure that we never found ourselves without a bed for the night. (This proved to be true. El Khamis's resourcefulness was exceptional.) A morning in the city would be followed by two days in the hinterland, in the jebel, where we would visit not classical archaeological remains but sites of more indigenous historic interest. This was something the Ministry of Tourism was keen to promote, Peter explained. He seemed to imply that this would prove to be an unwelcome divergence from his and our purposes, but in the event most of our group found what we saw in the jebel to be of great interest.

In the city museum next morning we were approached by a group of young women. They were wearing hijabs covering their hair but their faces were unveiled and their dresses or skirts and sweaters and high-heeled shoes were entirely in Western European style. They were keen to talk in English and to know where we had come from. We should have expected some changes in the country over forty years but the appearance and behaviour of these women represented a truly dramatic change. In earlier days no Libyan woman would appear in public unless entirely enveloped in a *burka*, an all-enveloping ankle-length garment, with head scarf pulled across the face and parted only to allow from time to time a one-eyed view of the surrounding world. Certainly no woman would approach and engage in conversation a stranger, either compatriot or European. These young women were students at the Tripoli university campus. Recalling that no more than four percent of the students were women in my teaching days I asked them about the present situation.

"Over half of us are women," one replied and added with a laugh, "Our President believes in women."

We shook hands on parting, a contact unthinkable once and, when visiting a nearby bookshop to buy postcards, spotted a book which seemed to confirm what the student had told us. It was in English and entitled *Is Gaddafi a Feminist?* On the final page the author answers with a simple "Yes."

Reflecting on these fashionably dressed, laughing young women I recalled an encounter in a Benghazi street forty years earlier with four women swathed in black (untypically in Cyrenaica in those years when *burkas* were customarily of vertically striped turquoise, purple and white, an attractive combination). The women blocked my path. I was taken aback by this unwonted behaviour in a country where the male was invariably given way to. As I stood back to gaze at them I realized that inside their *burkas* the women were shaking with laughter.

"You don't recognize us, do you, sir? We are your students."

Indeed they were, members of my second year seminar group who, once safely on University premises, had removed their outdoor garments to appear in modest dresses. I recall that in our seminars they had sometimes laughed as freely and it had been good to know that beneath the *burka* a sense of fun prevailed. It had been some time after my arrival that I had met up with these students or, indeed, any students at all, as in my anxiety to take up my new post I had arrived in Beghazi far too early for the start of the academic year there.

This allowed a settling in period, which, judging by the advice of our contact in Tripoli, might well involve the application of whitewash to the walls of an apartment which without it would reduce its occupants to tears. It was to be some weeks before we were called upon to deal with this. On arrival in Benghazi we were met by the Professor of English, a distinguished literary scholar, one-time a fellow at a Cambridge college, who took us to a modern hotel in the centre of town. He left us there with a suggestion that we might at some time like to call in at the British Council centre nearby to find out "what goes on around here." At the centre we met the wife of a British army sergeant whose regiment was in barracks outside the town. She was in charge during the absence on UK leave of the director. My two established colleagues at the University, she told us, were also on UK leave and I should have to await their return for briefing about the English Department as the professor was a new appointment and knew no more than I did. She was good on protocol and advised me to call at the office of the British Consul General to "sign the book" and at the residence of the First Secretary, where I should leave a card, putting the services of the centre's car and driver at our disposal for these purposes. These tasks completed, the driver returned us to our hotel. The result of our compliance with protocol was that the First Secretary in due course called on us and left his card (though we never met) and the following summer the Consul General invited us to the Queen's birthday party which he hosted.

Left to our own devices we explored the town on foot. This did not take long as it consisted principally of two main streets, once Via Roma and Via Milano, now Sharia Omar al Mukhtar and Sharia el Istiklal. These two met at an L-junction and enclosed within the L was a network of narrower streets, entered through archways. These, we were later told, constituted in the days of the Italian occupation the Arab quarter, to which the indigenous people had to return at nightfall in accordance with the imperial authority's decree. Sharia Omar al Mukhtar led to the municipal square and thence into the souk. From Sharia el Istiklal roads lined with flowering jacaranda trees led down to the corniche where, overlooking the sea, stood what had once been the town's smartest hotel, the Berenice. In its basement was a nightclub where belly dancing and other cabaret acts were performed. This had been unkindly dubbed by Europeans who frequented it the 'Snake Pit'. Also on the Corniche were the University's two Benghazi faculties, of Arts, recently-constructed, and of Commerce, housed in an imposing building in a Moorish-Italianate style, one time headquarters of Marshal Graziani, the Italian Governor, and later the palace of Libya's ruling monarch, King Idris.

I decided that I had better call on the authorities in the Arts Faculty, to which I had been assigned. Its corridors seemed deserted but in an office at the back of the building I found a young administrator who led me upstairs to the office of the 'Director', (or Vice-Chancellor). Using the administrator as an interpreter the Director, a Syrian, expressed great pleasure in meeting me and, over cups of Turkish coffee, we exchanged sentiments of mutual regard. I tried to make it clear that I was there to serve and that the sooner I could take up my duties the more pleased I should be. The Director simply nodded at this and I went on to broach the question of accommodation, which I understood it was the University's responsibility to provide. After an exchange in Arabic our interpreter told me that the Director had said that this was a matter for the administration and that I would be informed about it in due course. After a further exchange of pleasantries there was nothing for me to do but to return to our hotel.

After a week of virtual inactivity in the hotel I was becoming concerned about our financial situation, especially about our ability to meet the hotel bill whenever it might be presented. I had deposited a small amount in the British Bank of the Middle East on arrival. When I went there to draw some of it out I was agreeably surprised to find that the University had deposited a month's salary there for me. While this was a relief, it did not lessen our desire to get ourselves into some sort of family accommodation or, in my case, to begin doing some useful work to justify the University's contribution to our finances.

With the return from England of the two colleagues who together with Professor Blackstone and me made up our English teaching team, I felt confident some progress would be made on both counts. These two were old hands, which was reflected in their being dubbed 'Ancient Egyptians'. This was in consequence of their having served for over twenty years in the education service of Egypt. After the deposition of King Farouk they, along with many other British civil servants, had been expelled from the country. Unable to acclimatise themselves to life in Britain they had taken up various posts in the Mediterranean before finding their way along the North African coast to Benghazi when the University had opened there a few years previously. Unfortunately for the harmony of our English Department the two men, both confirmed bachelors, disliked each other intensely. Seldom seen in each other's company, I never heard them exchange a word. James was scholarly. No conversation with him lasted long without his introducing the subject of the Copts, whose language and texts were his scholarly interest. Fred, in contrast, had no pretension to learned interests, not even in English Literature which he had undertaken to teach. However, by virtue of his practical nature he had been appointed Assistant Professor and it was to him I turned for advice. He immediately set about assigning duties, beginning with his newly appointed Professor's timetable.

Professor Blackstone declared himself very amenable in this regard. He did not mind, he declared, which hours he taught providing they were between ten a.m. and twelve noon and between Tuesday and Thursday. Aside from these six hours he would devote himself to research. This Cambridge scholar whose book *The English Blake* had established him as the leading authority on the works of the visionary poet and engraver had, since his wartime recruitment by the British Council as a visiting professor in Buenos Aires, war service considered appropriate for a man virtually blind in one eye, taken a liking to expatriate life and had never returned to Cambridge.

Fred explained that as the junior member of the team I would be expected to teach students in their first year, before they opted to specialise in a single subject and would therefore have less contact with those showing a special interest in English.

"Don't worry; James will be teaching there alongside you," he said. He smiled at this, seemingly with a measure of self satisfaction.

I had no objection to this arrangement but I told Fred of Greta and my concern about moving into university accommodation. On this he advised me again not to worry as he would be calling on the Director the following day and would seek an opportunity to raise the matter. However, when he reported back on his meeting he told us that although it had been a lengthy one, during which many cups of coffee had been drunk, he had not found an opportunity for discussing our problem. While this was a salutary lesson on the avoidance of unseemly haste in conducting affairs in Libya it left us feeling distinctly unsettled.

We should not have worried. The following afternoon we were awakened from siesta by a persistent hammering on the door of our hotel room. The young administrator that I had met in the University was there, accompanied by two colleagues. They seemed to be in a state of high excitement.

"We have come to show you your house," they said.

We dressed hurriedly and they led us to a five storey building standing at the intersection of the town's two main streets, close to the harbourside and together we climbed up the stone stairs (there was no lift) to the top floor. The whole of this floor was occupied by a single flat, seven rooms leading off a corridor to one side with a kitchen on the other. The kitchen faced a stairwell and an adjoining building, but the other rooms had splendid views in two directions, over the harbour one way and the sea the other. While this was not a house, it was certainly a spacious flat, presumably the one we had been advised in Tripoli would give rise to tears. Undoubtedly its walls could do with a lick of whitewash and we had noted that the building's outer walls were pockmarked by shell fire, not surprisingly since Benghazi had the misfortune of being liberated by a succession of European armies during World War Two on several occasions, but we were both wholly taken by the flat and could not wait to move in.

This we did the following day and felt immediately at home. Some difficulty arose over the furnishings, no more than a three-piece suite in rexine, a table, a few kitchen chairs and a bed. When we requested additions we were told that as we were a family of only two persons some of the existing items should be returned to the university store. We managed to hold on to what we had and at breakfast one morning we saw the ship carrying our sea freight sail into harbour and that very day we were reunited with our personal possessions. On a floor on the landing off the stairs immediately below our flat we discovered a large, almost empty room which seemed also to be ours and there, with the aid of some carpentry tools from the souk, I was able to knock up additional furniture - armchairs, a coffee table, a record cabinet - using the wood from the crates we had unpacked. The souk also provided us with some rough blankets in alternating shades - white, black and brown - of undyed sheep's wool and these served as carpets.

In this Robinson Crusoe way we attained domestic content beyond what we had left behind in our cramped London flat. With the birth of our first child, a boy, in a nearby missionary hospital the following summer, an occasion for limitless congratulations from our Arab colleagues and neighbours, we felt ourselves to be very much a Benghazi family. Even the discovery that the roof above us was not entirely proof against the occasional heavy downpour of winter rain worked to our advantage as neighbours in flats below hastened to our assistance as soon as the rain had ceased, carrying plastic buckets. Together we baled out on the flat roof, tipping bucketloads of water into the street five floors below. The task completed we sat down to an impromptu al fresco meal to which everybody contributed. With summer came drought and I was then obliged to use my bucket to carry water from the University up the five flights of stairs. Greta and I had to make the same ascent with our son, each grasping a handle of his carry cot as he swung between us.

In the midst of this domestic activity I was getting to grips with my university commitments, though my first encounter with the students proved morc problematic than moving into the flat. Sitting on the roof one Saturday morning I spotted a crowd of young men milling around the university entrance, some four hundred yards up Sharia el Istiklal. I hurried there and found that I was right in thinking that this marked the beginning of the semester. Breaking through a cluster of students around the notice board in the entrance hall I picked out my name on a timetable, listed under the first period of that day. I deciphered this much but was unsure about the room I should be teaching in, not having fully mastered the symbols for numbers which were not the same as those we are accustomed to call Arabic numbers. Fortunately James turned up and led me along the corridor, explaining that we were between us about to teach the first year students.

"I'll be in the room next door," he said and ushered me into a lecture room with serried ranks of benches rising before me. "Good luck," he added and closed the door behind me.

The hall was sparsely populated with twenty young men in small groups conversing animatedly and four young women sitting quietly in the centre of the front row. These four were the only ones who took any notice of my entry, opening up notebooks and poising pens above them.

After I had shouted "Good morning" twice the young men sat down and looked in my direction. I was unsure of how to proceed after this initial success as our teaching team was waiting on our professor's decision as to the contents of the English course. All we knew, via Assistant Professor Fred, was that they would not be the same as in the previous year. I decided to give a discourse on the English language, its origins, subsequent accretions, dialect varieties, curious inconsistencies between its spelling and pronunciation and how it had reached its apogee through literature. It was difficult to maintain a persistent thread as my words were constantly interrupted by students bursting into the hall through a door behind the topmost bench in front of me. Having entered, these newcomers gazed about them until they discovered familiar faces before bounding down the steps to embrace fellow students, old school chums or people from their own neighbourhood, presumably. Hugging each other they exchanged salaams and praised God loudly for having reunited them in such boisterous good health.

After half an hour the numbers had swelled alarmingly. I feared that by some mistake I had attracted the whole of the first year intake and that James would be keeping a solitary vigil next door. When I decided to check on this I found that I was unable to exit into the corridor, as in closing the door behind me James seemed to have locked me in. I scribbled a note on a scrap of paper and asked a student to take it to the room next door. He made his way out through the back door and returned with the note and some friends he had picked up outside. Beneath my words of mild desperation: "How many students have you? I seem to have about seventy." James had added: "So have I. Carry on."

I obeyed James's instruction, despite further ebullient interruptions until, after fifty minutes, I had run out of steam and my stock of impromptu remarks about the English language.

"Have any of you any questions you would like to ask?" I demanded.

The young men broke off their exchanges of greetings and looked at me in astonishment but, to my relief, one of the women in the front row tentatively raised a hand. I was impressed by these students. All four of them had assiduously taken notes throughout my disjointed lecture and I felt sure I could rely upon an intelligent question which would give me an opportunity to use up the remaining ten minutes of the period.

"'Please sir, is this the Faculty of Commerce?"

This question disconcerted me, though not to the extent that my reply disconcerted the young women. Informed that they were in the Faculty of Arts, the women gave cries of dismay, hastily gathered up their notebooks and ran up the steps to the rear exit, loudly applauded by their male fellow students. I saw no point of continuing in the hubbub that followed and made my way up the steps and out of the hall with as much dignity as I could muster. I never had the pleasure of lecturing to those attentive young women again. I hope they were able to find some use for their notes, though I fear they had little relevance to the everyday world of commerce.

The following week James and I demanded some direction from Professor Blackstone. He decided that our classes should be devoted to 'English composition', but could give us no guidance how this was to be achieved with groups of eighty students. However, we took it upon ourselves to conduct this weekly activity as sensibly as possibly and I never again had anything but polite, if slightly bored, attention from these students. However, there were a dozen or so who were specialising in English in each of years two to four and it is difficult to imagine any students more diligent, courteous, friendly or good natured than these.

Apart from these classes I had also to teach a group of Algerian exiles that the Government of Libya had taken under its wing. These also were devoted students but an air of dejection hung about them. They were presumably dissidents wanted by the French authorities in their own country, possibly members of the Algerian resistance, the FLN. In my second year at the university their cause proved triumphant and their leader, Ben Bella, newly released from a prison in France, undertook a triumphal tour of Arab cities to thank their citizens for their support in the long struggle against the French colonial power. In due course he arrived in Benghazi and the University decided to award him an honorary degree.

For this occasion a welcoming party of faculty members was lined up along one side of an archway leading into the university courtyard, facing a line of students selected, I assumed, as being relied upon for decorous behaviour. The Algerian leader appeared flanked by well-built men and slowly made his way down the faculty members' line, shaking hands Before he reached me the students' enthusiasm prompted them to abandon decorum and surge forward to embrace their hero. Alarmed, his escorts seized him by his elbows and, lifting him slightly above the ground, hustled him through the archway and the courtyard into a back door of the main Arts Faculty. My fellow lecturers hurried in his wake and I decided to follow suit. When I emerged into the open courtyard I found that a storm had started, a torrential downpour. This did nothing to quell the enthusiasm of the students, those considered less likely to behave with restraint, who had massed there.

These were jumping up and down and shouting: "Death to America. Death to Britain." (For some reason France was exempt from their execration.)

As I forced my way between them those in my path broke off to greet me with the words: "Good morning sir. How are you today?"

I was getting very wet and was anxious to pass indoors but when I reached the closed door through which Ben Bella had disappeared and hammered on it, it was opened only briefly by one of the Algerian leader's escorts who promptly shut it again in my face. Somebody inside must have explained that I was "one of us" because the door was reopened and I was dragged inside and allowed to witness the ceremony of the honorary degree award in the faculty hall.

A few days later I met the Algerian exiled students making their way through the streets on a dismal winter evening. They invariably went around in a group of their own and I never saw them with our other students, who were somewhat younger, nor did they join in any student extra-curricular activities, picnics and so on. They had a melancholy air about them and although they greeted me with affection I sensed an underlying puzzled resentment.

"You don't teach us now, sir."

This was because a new member of staff, even more junior than me, had been assigned to teach their class. When I explained that this change was purely an administrative matter they nodded understandingly but I left them looking forlorn, standing in a knot on the street corner.

To my surprise they did not return to their homeland once it became independent and their leader was installed as president there. However, when I heard two years later that Ben Bella had been deposed and placed under house arrest I wondered whether there were factional differences which made their return problematic.

In these years I struggled unsuccessfully to master Arabic. One of my early attempts involved my attending a lecture by a young colleague in the Department of Sociology, a Libyan recently returned from post-graduate studies in the States, one of a series of public lectures given by staff of the University. His subject was 'The Economy of Libya'. Next morning he sought me out in the staff room. Thanking me for attending, he asked me how well I had understood his lecture and, when I admitted having understood very little, he kindly outlined its thesis.

Reports of the first finds of oil in the Libyan desert were just coming in and the concessions granted to Western oil companies carrying out the exploration included the right to a percentage on the marketing of all the oil which would eventually be produced. Dr Fuad believed that the King's ministers, who were inexperienced and relied upon the advice of British and Egyptian officials, had granted these concessions at a rate insufficiently favourable to Libya, which, he maintained, should negotiate a larger share of the revenue, particularly in view of the needs of its increasing population. Some eight years later, when the King was deposed, these oil companies were expelled, with the singular exception of the company founded and headed by the determined and adaptable Mr Bunker Hunt.

More immediately understandable was a lecture given, in English, at the British Council Centre by Richard Goodchild, the British head of the Cyrenaican Department of Antiquities. He spoke about excavations he was directing in cities the Greeks had founded in the Jebel Akhdar (Green Mountain) area - at Cyrene, Apollonia, Tolmeitha and Teucheira. His talk and the accompanying slides gave us a desire to visit these legendary places immediately and, as soon as we acquired a car, we were able to spend many wonderful hours there. Professor Goodchild had brought with him a young Libyan assistant to project his slides and introduced him to us after the lecture. He told us it was his ambition to arrange a scholarship for him at the Institute of Archaeology in London. The country had just celebrated its tenth year of independence and I wondered whether this young man and others such as Dr Fuad would play a prominent role in its future. However, none of us foresaw the emergence of Muammar Gaddafi, then a student at the University's Tripoli campus but soon to enter the Military Academy.

On our return to Libya so many years later there were sites to be visited in Tripolitania before our party would fly on to Benghazi, giving us the opportunity of revisiting the ruined Cyrenaican cities which had given us so much pleasure forty years earlier. The most notable of the sites in the former province is, of course, the splendid Roman city of Leptis Magna, by good fortune preserved beneath the sand until it was discovered in the twentieth century.. We had stopped off for an hour there during our drive to Tripoli, had wanted to stay longer but had motored on, being uncertain about how long Greta's swimming cap would survive as a makeshift radiator hose and anxious to get our baby son into a comfortable hotel.

Now we were to have a whole day on this extensive site, with the advantage of being taken around by our very erudite guide. The day began well with Peter pointing out features we might not have spotted on our own - an inscription on the arch of Septimus Severus, the local boy made good, and a bas relief of a flying phallus - but in mid-morning a hot wind from the South, which the Italians called the *ghibli*, sprang up and our party was soon covered by a fine layer of sand. Most of us were elderly, the youngest being a GP from Manchester who had come along to support her mother, an American widow who had come to Tripoli in 1950 as a secretary with the US State Department in the hope of finding a husband. In this she was successful, marrying a Welsh doctor and spending the rest of her life in Wales. She was one of three whose acquaintance with Libya pre-dated our own as there were also in our party two men who had completed their National Service in Tripoli, also in the fifties. However, although that made five of us who had spent some years in the country, none of us was more immune to the fierce attack of the *ghibli* than our fellow travellers and we joined them, in a miserable huddle sheltering below a wall of the Nymphaeum.

Some of us were suffering from prickly heat. All of us were uncomfortable with the apparent exception of Dr Barbara from Manchester who urged us to get to our feet and shepherded us in the direction of the tea room with our backs to the storm. There we took refuge beneath ceiling fans whose slow rotation offered little relief but some travellers passed round wet wipes they had had the foresight to obtain from Boots the chemist before leaving UK. EI Khamis, who had remained seated in our coach, appeared and, sensing our disconsolate state, once again showed his resourcefulness. He had successfully scouted out decent eating houses in unlikely places in the Jebel and made sure we were never without supplies of bottled drinking water. Now he made a quick phone call and established that a new hotel on the point of completion, situated on the seashore very near to Leptis Magna, was prepared to receive us and make us comfortable.

This hotel was planned to accommodate its guests in chalets strung out along a winding path leading from the single storey reception and restaurant building. Still battling against the storm we reached our assigned chalet and stripped off to get under the shower to rid ourselves of sand lodged in our hair or clinging to our bodies. Outside we could hear cases being trundled up and down along the path by guests less fortunate them ourselves, having been assigned chalets with non-functioning air-conditioning or faulty plumbing. Eventually all were settled. We had been told that through French windows at the rear we had access to the beach and a stretch of sea safe for swimming. Looking out in that direction we could see nothing but swirling sand, so we settled on the beds for a long siesta.

When we awoke the storm had stopped and we had a clear view of the sea, azure and unruffled. We made our way to the restaurant, where most of our group had already forgathered. Two young men were in charge and they proposed a simple meal, a very early dinner, which they went off to prepare themselves. They returned with dishes of couscous which we all voted to be delicious and when a woman who had been the leading advocate of tanking up with alcohol on the inward flight in preparation for abstinence discovered in a cold cabinet beside the kitchen door bottles of a liquid which looked, smelled and tasted like beer our spirits were totally restored.

This meal was so good that one of our party, a priest who had renounced holy orders, averred that it must have been produced by Tunisians, citizens of a country known to have inherited French culinary skills. He insisted on addressing our two young hosts in French, though it was obvious to the rest of us that their first foreign language was English. Our questions revealed that they came from Khums, a small town two miles along the coast. This localisation of the hospitality business was one of a number of changes that struck us forcibly as in much earlier days restaurants and hotels had been run by Greeks or, occasionally, by members of the Italian community who had stayed on after Libyan independence.

The next day we were due to fly to Benghazi at noon. Greta and I looked forward to this with lively anticipation. On arrival we were to have a free afternoon, which would give us the opportunity of walking again through the streets which had once delighted us so much, in the hope of finding familiar landmarks, though we were aware that much must have changed and even admitted the possibility that *everything* might have changed beyond recognition.

After a brief visit to see the mosaic floor of a recently unearthed Roman villa we set off in what we thought was the direction of Tripoli airport, but we were surprised when our coach parked alongside the seashore in a sheltered bay. El Khamis explained that our flight had been delayed. A few people were swimming but none of us decided to join them, as it would have been troublesome to unpack our costumes from suitcases stacked in the belly of the coach. When we left the bay we once again diverted from the airport road to stop at a hotel perched on a small hill. There we took light refreshments on a terrace overlooking a lawn where a film sequence was being shot. An actor in a dark suit was escorted to a table where he was interviewed by two burly men in shirt sleeves His replies appeared to be unsatisfactory, causing one of the interviewers to bang on the table and gesture for the dark-suited man, who looked totally bemused by the whole procedure, to be led away. We were unable to understand the dialogue but speculated on a possible title for the film. The suggestion that received most general acceptance was that we were witnessing the shooting of an Arabic version of Kafka's *The Trial*. For the actor playing the interviewee it was certainly a trial in the more general sense as the director demanded a great number of retakes, between each of which his sweating brow had to be mopped and his make-up restored.

While this was diverting entertainment for us we were aware that the scheduled hour for our flight had long since passed. El Khamis kept in touch by mobile phone with a colleague at the airport but it was seven in the evening when, after several more diversions, we finally arrived there. This did not, however, herald our immediate boarding of our plane, which was yet to arrive. We gathered that, owing to a long lasting world-wide boycott on trade in machine parts imposed by most of the outside world on Libya, the national airline had been reduced to a single aircraft, the one that plied the route between Tripoli and Benghazi, which was often subject to lengthy delays at either end owing to the need for maintenance or repairs.

We settled down to a wait which el Khamis explained might be a long one. He and Abdullah sat guard over our baggage as near as possible to the entrance to the departure lounge. One of our party opened a book on the probable hour of our arrival in Benghazi. Each of us deposited a Libyan pound in a kitty which would go to the one who most nearly forecast this.

Some cynics opted for very late hours, eleven, even midnight. The woman who had discovered the near beer outbid these with a forecast of three a.m. We hoped against hope she would be proved way out, but it was nearly midnight before we were allowed into the departure lounge. Even here we were forced to settle down to a further wait. The lounge was already crowded when we were joined by a group of athletic-looking young men. Abdullah explained that these were members of the national football squad. There seemed to be almost enough of them to make up three teams.

An hour later Abdullah made furtive gestures to our party that we should go downstairs and wait outside a locked wrought iron gate. We did this as unobtrusively as possible, leaving the footballers and other potential travellers drinking coffee upstairs. There was lively speculation that the flight was overbooked and that it was only by this furtive approach to the final barrier that we stood a chance of getting aboard. Through the gate we could see only a corridor that turned sharply to the right after a few yards. For what seemed like a very long time, but was perhaps no more than an hour, our group kept a solitary watch, standing pressed up against the gate. Then one of our number, declaring that his legs were "not clever", sat down on the bottom step of the staircase we had descended. Soon several of us followed suit but one of those with her nose still pressed to the bars of the gate called out that she thought she could see passengers being led away from us down the corridor. Surely these must be arrivals from Benghazi and our plane must finally have arrived from there. We rallied to the gate and were rewarded shortly afterwards by the approach of a uniformed official from the far side who prepared to unlock it.

At this point a commotion on the staircase behind us gave warning of the headlong approach of a phalanx of footballers who burst through our ranks as the gate opened. We old-timers offered stout resistance, beating at them with our hand luggage, but we were no match for these extremely fit young men and they soon passed ahead of us through the open gate and disappeared round the bend in the corridor. We retrieved our scattered belongings and were just about to follow when we saw them reappear, escorted by a number of stern-faced officials, some of them with weapons on their hips. Once these footballers were ejected their escort ushered us courteously forward and we were the first to board the aircraft, followed by all the other passengers who had crowded the departure lounge, with the exception of the footballers. Only when we were all comfortably seated were these athletes allowed to make their way sheepishly to the rear of the plane. Fortunately for them there proved to be just the right number of seats for all of us and our vigil at the gate had been a wasted expenditure of energy, decidedly ebbing at two o'clock in the morning. Mixed with our sense of triumph was an acknowledgement that we had witnessed a small, but to us significant, expression of Libya's determination to show a welcoming face to the foreign tourist.

We were all relieved finally to get to our Benghazi hotel and the woman who had forecast a three a.m. arrival triumphantly accepted the kitty as she was almost spot on. This hotel proved to be the most comfortable we stayed at throughout our tour and had a welcoming staff, most of them, in contrast to those of other hotels, women. It was on the coast, some way from town, which we viewed as a distant prospect in the morning without being able to identify any familiar features. Nor did we recognise the parts of the town we were driven through by a series of flyovers and ring roads to emerge onto the coast road which would take us to Cyrene.

El Khamis had told our coach driver that two of us had once lived in Benghazi and he, as a native of that place, was greatly interested. When we stopped for coffee we showed him pages of photographs we had removed from our album. He identified the block of flats we had lived in and promised to drive past the site on our return to the city the following day. He was even more interested in a photo which showed us standing with some students and asked for their names. I could remember only some of their first names - Moussa, Chtewi-Chtewi, Abdul-Wahid - and this was not much help in tracing in their youthful features lineaments of men who would by now be grandfathers. In any case, most students had come from outside Benghazi. Abdul-Wahid I recalled was a small town boy from Derna. He had become the butt of his fellow students' jokes. On one occasion, when they had gathered in our flat for afternoon tea, they had asked me about reproductions of works of art we had hung on the walls. Abdul-Walid had surprised us all by declaring that he had once been a painter We pressed him for more details - what medium did he use? oils? water colours?

"Distemper."

We gathered he had been a painter and decorator rather than a practitioner of fine arts. Perhaps he had returned to his own delightful town with its villas and flowering shrubs, once a resort and leave centre for Italian army officers. The driver urged me to recall names and eventually we hit on a mutual acquaintance, Mohammed Sadawiya, one-time Dean of the Faculty of Arts, a genial man who, unlike some of his colleagues, was always ready to respond to invitations to Western parties or receptions where alcohol was freely consumed in those more easy-going days. Alas, he had died some years earlier as had Said Shatshat, an electrician who had impressed us by handling live wires when repairing electrical connections in our flat.

Cyrene was an eye-opener. This city, from which Simon had made his way to Jerusalem and there helped Christ carry his cross up the Via Dolorosa, we remembered as being littered with fallen pillars, scattered over a wide area. These had to a large extent now been reerected and clearly delineated the temples, baths, agora and gymnasium, work carried out by visiting teams of archaeologists from Europe and America who had left plaques to commemorate their achievements. Rivalling Leptis Magna in its vast extent it has the added attraction of being set amongst pine groves and we remembered once, when we had visited the site in the month of February, during the University's half year break, the ground between the ruins had been strewn with carpets of tiny red and yellow flowers.

The Jebel Akhdar deserves its appellation "green" as it is indeed a fertile region and we had been impressed to see that land largely untended and marked only by the scattered remains of Italian farmhouses was now intensely cultivated with fruit and vegetables. After a night in El Beida we were driven back through this area the following day after a brief visit to Apollonia. We were to stop off at Tolmeitha. Greta and I were particularly looking forward to this. Although it lacks the grandeur of Cyrene and the legendary associations of Apollonia with its partly submerged ruins, Tolmeitha is compact, readily comprehensible as the port it once was and slopes dramatically down to the sea at one point. Furthermore, it was familiar to us as it was in reasonable reach of Benghazi by car and we had often driven there on Sundays to picnic amidst its deserted ruins. In fact we were carrying with us a photo taken on one such occasion, showing us balancing our nine month old son on the still standing lower portion of a broken pillar, in the hope that we might be able to identify the spot.

On arrival at Tolmeitha, Peter told us that he would not be accompanying us around the site as the curator of the place insisted on doing so himself. There was some tut-tutting at this, but when the curator appeared and started to lead us around we soon realised that here was a man who not only was thoroughly acquainted with his brief but also had the ability to explain every aspect of it in fluent terms. He had introduced himself as Abu Salem and was elderly, spare-framed but sprightly. In fact he was so nimble that some of us had difficulty in keeping up with him. We were determined to do so, however, in order not to miss any of his learned commentary. Unlikely many guides whose uninterrupted flow indicates that they have simply memorised their words, Abu Salem was not thrown by questions and was prepared to answer them convincingly. It was obvious that he not only knew the site intimately but that he had an affection for it.

At one point he led us down through a small hole beneath the Gymnasium into a network of high vaulted chambers which, he explained, had originally been cisterns designed to provide the city with enough water to withstand a siege. On our earlier visits we had no idea that these cisterns existed. On emerging we managed to catch up with our guide and show him our photograph. Glancing at it without stopping he told us he knew exactly where this had been taken and that he would in due course show us the spot. This proved to be the Odeon and sure enough there was the stepped seating on which the proud parents had stood, but the broken piece of pillar on which their son had sat had, Abu Salem told us, been pushed over by vandals.

In fact, unlike at Cyrene, there were very few standing pillars. The most restored part of the site was the Amphitheatre, sloping down towards the sea on the Western side of the site. Here it was easy to imagine how things must have been in classical times. Abu Salem proudly told us that he had managed to recruit groups of local labourers who, at times of year when little agriculturally was required, had over a number of years worked with him to restore the theatre to its ancient glory.

When we finally paused for refreshments he came over to talk to Greta and me.

“So you were here before.”

“Yes, several times, but many years ago.” I tried a long shot. “Do you remember Professor Goodchild?”

Abu Salem’s face lit up. “But of course. He was a wonderful man. He sent me to London to study.”

It then occurred to me that in the distant past we might have met. Was this Abu Salem the young man I had met in the British Council Centre in Benghazi, the young man who had been brought along to assist in his professor’s slide lecture?

"I remember Professor Goodchild lecturing in the British Council Centre in 1961," I said.

We looked at each other for some time, slowly nodding our heads like a pair of puppets. Was there really a shock of recognition? Did I really recognise in this elderly, balding man the deferential archaeological student and did he see in my lined face, white bearded, a trace of the aspiring university lecturer of those years? I cannot say for sure. I could not even recall his name which, in any case, he had changed in order to celebrate the birth of his son. I doubt he was any more certain than I was but on both sides there must have been a determination to reclaim the past in some way because we both said, almost simultaneously: "Yes, we have met before."

Abu Salem's story was one of early expectations thwarted by adversity and ill fortune. On returning from London he had been put in charge of the Tolmeitha site under the supervision of Richard Goodchild and had taken sole responsibility when Goodchild retired to England. Shortly afterwards, with Lieutenant Gaddafi's successful coup and his subsequent installation as head of state, funds for archaeological work had been frozen and later renewed only at a much reduced rate. Abu Salem seemed to bear no resentment, pointing out that the state had many priorities - the creation of the Man Made River, of educational and medical services. What he could do with his limited resources, the employment of occasional labour, the taking of photographs to make postcards for sale to tourists, he did. Now, with the opening up of the country to tourists after many years of isolation from the international community, he foresaw a more hopeful future. There was talk of extra funding for Tolmeitha in the coming year. He, alas, was nearing retirement and would perhaps no longer be in service to reap the benefits. Perhaps more young people would be trained up to succeed him.

As I thought about Abu Salem's life I could not help contrasting our fortunes, how most of his working life had been thwarted by circumstance, whereas mine, although I had not stuck with my intended career in academe, had been attended by opportunities for interesting and rewarding work. I asked him about his son, whose name now formed part of his own name.

Here was further cause for sorrow. As a young man Salem had been killed in a road accident. I thought of our own son, photographed as a baby in the Odeon, now living comfortably with his wife and children in Cambridge.

Abu Salem came with us in our coach as far as the little town near the site, where he pointed out the modest house which Richard Goodchild had once occupied. We left him standing at the roadside waving farewell. Obviously he was expecting no more visitors that day. We hoped that tourists would follow in our footsteps in droves but, with Benghazi having no link by air to the outside world, we knew that this was unlikely.

On the road back to Benghazi el Khamis gave us some surprising news. The next day we would not be flying to Tripoli, as planned. It had been decided that relying on the national airline's single aircraft was too risky. Our Benghazi driver, along with his mate, would take us by coach along the road which we had once traversed and vowed never to traverse again, having chosen this particular tour in order to avoid having to do so. This came as unwelcome news to Greta and me, not only the prospect of the journey but also because it ruled out our being able to spend the final morning of our stay in Cyrenaica in a nostalgic walk through the city. The drive, forecast to take fourteen hours, would require an early morning start. We determined, however, to go into the centre of Benghazi that evening, once we had been returned to our hotel.

Our return was delayed by Peter's insisting on our making an unscheduled stop to look at a curiously carved rock at the entrance to a cave near Tocra so it was well after sundown before we were able to take a taxi from the hotel across the salt lake into the city. We asked the driver to set us down at a hotel marked on a recently published map that had not been there in our day, calculating that this was approximate to our old block of flats. Sure enough we had only to cross the street to reach it, still standing, now with it pockmarked walls patched up and painted a sombre shade of chocolate brown instead of the greyish white we remembered. Across the high entrance, once freely open at all hours, a barred gate had been installed. This was locked, but we were able to peer through its bars at the first flight of stairs which we had carried our son up in his carry cot so many times.

When our taxi had dropped us off we had had some difficulty in crossing the street until a driver in a stream of vehicles had stopped for us and courteously ushered us across, by no means an unusual example, we had found, of Libyan drivers' demonstration of consideration towards pedestrians but rare in our experience in other countries around the Mediterranean. However, in the brief moments we had spent contemplating the entrance to the Berenice building the traffic behind us had simply vanished, leaving us in darkness and in silence. We made our way down Sharia Omar al Mukhtar past the adjoining Berenice Cinema, which showed no sign of having been open to the public for some time. Briefly, when we had lived next door, the manager had tried a bold experiment - special performances for women only every Thursday afternoon. These proved very popular and we would watch large groups of women in their brightly coloured *burkas* passing into the foyer. After three weeks of sold out performances Benghazi's menfolk, presumably alert to the pernicious ideas wives and daughters might imbibe from these Hollywood imports, called a halt and women were no more seen at the Berenice. It was hard to imagine that their daughters and granddaughters with whom we had been able to converse freely in casual encounters on our present tour would succumb to such restrictions.

The other buildings in the street, banks, shops and coffee houses also showed no sign of life as we walked, totally alone, the length of the street to the municipal square. As we were standing in the middle of this, looking at the Moorish style old Town Hall and remembering the difficulty we had in locating in its labyrinthine interior the office where we were required to register the birth of our son, there was a startling sign that the city was not wholly deserted. From a narrow side street a boy of sixteen or so burst into the square at full speed on a skateboard. With merciful adroitness he stopped just short of crashing into us full tilt. He looked almost as alarmed at our presence as we were at his. Then he remounted his skateboard, said "I'm very sorry." in English and skated off up another side street. Silence returned to the square and accompanied us as we retraced our steps and set off along Sharia el Istiklal - silence and solitude.

It seemed as if what had once been a compact city bustling with life until well into the night had become a ghost town. Our guide book, a recent publication, referred to this area as the "old town", though very little had been there before the Italian colonisers had built it up in the 1920s and 1930s. This implied that there must be a "new town" or, at least, suburban districts and it must have been to these that the traffic we had seen earlier was flowing, probably via the flyovers and roundabouts we had used on leaving the city three days earlier. I recalled that at one time there had been a settlement of modern villas called the Garden Suburb. There oilmen, most noticeably Texans in their ten-gallon hats and cowboy boots, had returned from their desert explorations to join their families one week in every four.

Along Sharia el Istiklal we were saddened to see the Rex cinema shuttered up. In its restaurant upstairs its immensely fat Greek proprietor had once sat behind a small table, which he was never seen to leave. There he ate and there he handled the takings. It was rumoured that he had eaten so many of his own excellent Chateaubriand steaks that he was unable to extricate his expanded girth from the confines of the table. Further along, the Horriya cinema, painted in stripes of vivid colours resembling those of a knickerbocker glory ice cream sundae had disappeared entirely. There were no tables laid out in the long arcade where waiters used to serve coffee, tea and fizzy drinks to customers who clapped their hands sharply to gain their attention. Both university buildings were shut up. This we were prepared for as we had learnt from a Sunday supplement that a new out of town campus with state of the art buildings had been created.

We walked down to the Corniche. There was no sign of life in the building which had once housed the British Consul General and his garden, in which he had hosted parties to celebrate the Queen's birthday, was overgrown. The Cathedral we had been told had been converted into a mosque. It looked much the same, with its distinctive double-domed roof. In a novel written by the man who had lived in our flat in the city before our arrival and his transfer to Istanbul he had referred to the "twin bosomed cathedral". Set in and around Benghazi the novel had been avidly read by Gwyn Williams's fellow expatriates hoping, or fearing, to identify themselves with characters portrayed in it. Sales elsewhere were disappointing though it began, scandalously enough for the 1950s, with a scene of a couple making love at dawn in a Salvation Army hostel.

When we reached the Berenice Hotel, once the city's grandest and most fashionable, we saw the first signs of life since narrowly escaping injury by skateboard half an hour earlier. We peered into the foyer and saw a few people sitting around low tables, but there was nothing like the animation which had enlivened the restaurant and night club in former times. Across the road, where gharry drivers had once reined in their brightly caparisoned horses, three taxi drivers sat on a wall beside their vehicles quietly conversing. It was time to go back to our modern out of town hotel and prepare for our early morning departure. There we met members of our group finishing after-dinner coffee. They asked us how we had found things in our brief foray into town. When we told them that we had seen several buildings which, surprisingly after forty years, looked much the same, one of the women remarked that she felt glad for us that we had been able to satisfy our feelings of nostalgia. We couldn't finds the words to explain that this did not quite represent how we felt about our experience.

The following day's drive turned out not to be the ordeal we had anticipated. EI Khamis and Abdullah kept us supplied with tea, biscuits and bottled water, we made several comfort stops and we enjoyed the company of our fellow travellers. During our two weeks together we had become a tight-knit group, united by a common interest in classical remains, rendering mutual assistance over sometimes difficult terrain and keeping our spirits up despite the absence of alcohol. The journey had offered many revelations of developments inevitable in a country whose population had increased fivefold in forty years. Agedabia, which we remembered as little more than a filling station and rest stop for lorry drivers,was now a flourishing township and Sirte, where we had stayed in the wretched waterless hotel, had become a sizable town with streets of neat villas running from the main road towards the sea. Abdullah told us that this town was near the birthplace of the country's leader and that he had a particular interest in its well being.

At the border of Cyrenaica and Tripolitania we stopped and el Khamis led us to see a bizarre sight. Behind a filling station, lying half buried in the sand, lay broken pieces of what had once been a massive statue. As we peered at it we gradually discerned the features of Mussolini, the jutting jaw and Roman nose. "Nothing beside remains." but il Duce, unlike Ozymandias, had inspired no Shelley to commemorate his hubristic fall. Once this statue had stood as a crowning piece of a triumphal arch erected by Italian colonisers to celebrate their imperial triumphs and we could imagine with what joyful vigour one-time subjects had set about the image with pickaxes.

One day only remained for sightseeing, spent at Sabratha, once one of the three great Roman cities which gave Tripolitania its name. At the airport the following day we found that our flight to London was to leave on time. Here we said goodbye to el Khamis and Abdullah. The former's name, translating as 'Thursday', had intrigued me and he had explained that his parents had settled on it because he had been born on that day. Peter persuaded me to make a farewell speech in Arabic before handing over the proceeds of a whip-round to him and to the two drivers. I had wanted to make a reference to Chesterton's *The Man who was Thursday*, contrasting that villain's deviousness with el Khamis's open-natured reliability, but my Arabic was by no means equal to this and I had to fall back on those conventional blessings and expressions of good will in which the language abounds. Of course I included Abdullah in my remarks. We were saddened when Peter warned us that no part of our collection could go his way in view of his being a member of the Libyan police force, a fact that all of us had entirely forgotten. He joined el Khamis in escorting us as far as allowable through the airport, to the point where he had originally greeted us, smiling now as amiably as then, before going home to his young wife and new-born baby for a brief respite before joining the next tour of foreigners he was entrusted to keep a benevolent eye on.

On the flight home I reflected on a journey which had brought us full circle back to the point where we had started our expatriate life. We had had opportunities to revisit other countries and cities where I had once been posted, but never after the passing of so many years. We had seen remarkable developments in a nation which seemed to have managed rapid population growth with a measure of prosperity for all. On a personal level, the familiar sights that remained had been grounds for joyful recognition, for memories only occasionally tinged with sadness. I speculated on what might have happened if I had renewed my two year contract and stayed on in Libya. Unlike Abu Salem I would have worked in a well funded field, since education had been a government priority. I might have moved to the University's new desert campus, under the leadership of Dr Fuad, the young sociology lecturer who had so clearly seen the importance of oil revenue to his country and who had become the University's director. Probably I would not have stayed on long enough to emulate my old colleague, Assistant Professor Fred Koerner, one of the 'Ancient Egyptians', who had died in harness. Reports of his funeral suggested an impressive affair. He lay in his coffin on the back of an open lorry with the entire faculty and student body of the University processing behind him along Sharia el Istiklat. In front marched the band of the municipal police force playing, in slow time, *Yes, we have no bananas*, a detail Fred would have appreciated.

One abiding memory is of Abu Salem standing at the roadside in front of his mentor's former home, his hand raised in a gesture of hail and farewell. I have a photo taken by Greta of him standing with me, arms linked, in the Odeon of his beloved Tolmeitha site. In the album it has its place beside a photo he in turn took of us, holding an imagined baby on a vanished broken pillar.

Libya 1961 and 2001